THE POLITICS
OF
WOMEN'S BODIES

THE POLITICS
OF
WOMEN'S BODIES

Sexuality, Appearance, and Behavior

THIRD EDITION

Rose Weitz
Arizona State University

New York   Oxford
OXFORD UNIVERSITY PRESS
2010

Oxford University Press, Inc., publishes works that further
Oxford University's objective of excellence in research, scholarship, and education.

Oxford   New York
Auckland   Cape Town   Dar es Salaam   Hong Kong   Karachi
Kuala Lumpur   Madrid   Melbourne   Mexico City   Nairobi
New Delhi   Shanghai   Taipei   Toronto

With offices in
Argentina   Austria   Brazil   Chile   Czech Republic   France   Greece
Guatemala   Hungary   Italy   Japan   Poland   Portugal   Singapore
South Korea   Switzerland   Thailand   Turkey   Ukraine   Vietnam

Published by Oxford University Press, Inc.
198 Madison Avenue, New York, New York 10016

www.oup.com

Oxford is a registered trademark of Oxford University Press

Library of Congress Cataloging-in-Publication Data
The politics of women's bodies : sexuality, appearance, and behavior /
[edited by] Rose Weitz. — 3rd ed.
   p.   cm.
Includes bibliographical references.
ISBN 978-0-19-539063-6 (pbk. : alk. paper)
1. Women—Psychology.   2. Women—Physiology.   3. Women—Social conditions.
4. Human body—Social aspects.   5. Human body—Political aspects.   I. Weitz,
Rose, 1952–
HQ1206.P56 2010
305.42—dc22
                                                                    2009029408

Printing number: 9   8   7   6   5   4   3   2   1

Printed in the United States of America
on acid-free paper

Contents

Preface   *x*

PART I THE SOCIAL CONSTRUCTION OF WOMEN'S BODIES   *1*

1   A History of Women's Bodies   *3*
    Rose Weitz

This article delineates how ideas about the female body have changed—or not—over time, as well as the very real impact those ideas have had on women's lives.

2   Believing Is Seeing: Biology as Ideology   *13*
    Judith Lorber

Lorber argues that binary sex differences are a social construction: They appear to be natural and real only because our cultural practices *make* them real.

3   Becoming a Gendered Body: Practices of Preschools   *27*
    Karin A. Martin

Martin explores how preschools teach young children to "perform gender" and to develop embodied selves that are "properly" gendered.

4   Women and Medicalization: A New Perspective   *49*
    Catherine Kohler Riessman

This article examines why women sometimes have supported the medicalization of their bodies, and how medicalization has both benefited and harmed women.

5 Affronting Reason*   *67*
   Cheryl Chase

Chase describes the medicalization of intersex—and the price she, personally, paid for it. Medicalization, she argues, has served more to reinforce cultural ideas about sex and gender than to help intersex children.

6 Foucault, Femininity, and the Modernization of Patriarchal Power   *76*
   Sandra Lee Bartky

Bartky describes how women internalize social expectations regarding female appearance and behavior and then adopt "disciplinary practices" to meet those expectations thereby reinforcing their subordination to men.

PART II THE POLITICS OF SEXUALITY   *99*

7 Menarche and the (Hetero)sexualization of the Female Body   *101*
   Janet Lee

This article explores how girls' experiences with menstruation affect their sense of self and body, and how those experiences can serve as sites of resistance.

8 Daring to Desire: Culture and the Bodies of Adolescent Girls   *120*
   Deborah L. Tolman

Tolman describes how teenage girls think about sexual desire and explores how their ideas are shaped by both the promise of sexual pleasure and the threat of sexual danger.

9 "Get Your Freak On": Sex, Babies, and Images of Black Femininity*   *143*
   Patricia Hill Collins

This article explores contemporary images of African-American women, discusses how these images reinforce racism, and shows how African-American women use these images to assert control over their bodies and lives.

10   Brain, Brow, and Booty: Latina Iconicity in U.S. Popular
     Culture*   *155*
       Isabel Molina Guzmán and Angharad N. Valdivia

       The authors analyze the gendered and racialized media
       portrayals of Jennifer Lopez, Salma Hayek, and Frida
       Kahlo.

11   "So Full of Myself as a Chick": Goth Women, Sexual
     Independence, and Gender Egalitarianism*   *163*
       Amy C. Wilkins

       Wilkins shows how Goth women are exempted from
       dominant cultural norms for sexuality and appearance;
       their postfeminist assumptions, however, camouflage
       gender and sexual inequality within Goth
       culture.

PART III   THE POLITICS OF APPEARANCE   *177*

12   Breasted Experience: The Look and the Feeling   *179*
       Iris Marion Young

       This article explores women's relationships with their
       breasts; women sometimes view their breasts as objects to
       be used and sometimes act as subjects whose breasts are
       part of their essential selves.

13   Designing Women: Cultural Hegemony and the Exercise
     of Power among Women Who Have Undergone Elective
     Mammoplasty*   *192*
       Patricia Gagné and Deanna McGaughey

       The authors show how women actively choose cosmetic
       surgery (exercising free will) but do so in the context of
       hegemonic cultural norms that make it difficult for them to
       consider other choices.

14   Women and Their Hair: Seeking Power Through
     Resistance and Accommodation   *214*
       Rose Weitz

       Weitz uses women's experiences with their hair to illustrate
       how resistance and accommodation are interwoven in
       women's everyday bodily experiences.

15   Branded with Infamy: Inscriptions of Poverty and Class in
         the United States*   *232*
         Vivyan C. Adair

This article describes how poverty and its stigma are
physically marked on the bodies of poor women and how
that stigma both supports public policies that discipline
poor women's bodies and encourages poor women to
discipline their own bodies.

16   Letting Ourselves Go: Making Room for the Fat Body in
         Feminist Scholarship*   *245*
         Cecilia Hartley

Hartley dissects cultural norms that stigmatize fat women,
explores how those norms affect all women, and suggests
that fatness can be a form of feminist resistance.

17   Rip Tide: Swimming Through Life with Rheumatoid
         Arthritis*   *255*
         Andrea Avery

Avery describes her embodied experiences living as a young
woman with rheumatoid arthritis; she explores how she has
developed a positive embodied self that acknowledges her
illness but does not let it define her.

18   Reclaiming the Female Body: Women Body Modifiers and
         Feminist Debates*   *268*
         Victoria Pitts

This article analyzes both how women use body
modification to take control of their bodies and the
benefits and limitations of this embodied
resistance.

PART IV   THE POLITICS OF BEHAVIOR   *283*

19   From the "Muscle Moll" to the "Butch" Ballplayer:
         Mannishness, Lesbianism, and Homophobia in U.S.
         Women's Sport   *285*
         Susan K. Cahn

Cahn traces the modern history of women in sports and
shows how gendered and racial stereotypes led women
athletes to become stigmatized, first as heterosexually
"loose" and later as presumed lesbians.

20　"Holding Back": Negotiating a Glass Ceiling on Women's
　　　Muscular Strength　　*301*
　　　　Shari L. Dworkin

Dworkin describes how women who work out in gyms are
discouraged from building muscle, thus reinforcing sex
differences and the idea that women *cannot* build muscle.

21　Compulsive Heterosexuality: Masculinity and
　　　Dominance*　　*318*
　　　　C. J. Pascoe

This article describes how male high school students
demonstrate their heterosexuality and their dominance
over girls' bodies—sometimes violently—in order to claim
masculine power and identity for themselves.

22　Till Death Us Do Part　　*329*
　　　　Margo Wilson and Martin Daly

The idea of women's bodies as men's property, the authors
argue, underpins wife battering and murder around the world.

23　Backlash and Continuity: The Political Trajectory of Fetal
　　　Rights*　　*344*
　　　　Rachel Roth

Roth describes how the battle over reproductive rights has
led to the recent push for "fetal rights"—an idea she
believes has served more to punish women for
nontraditional behavior than to protect their children.

* New to this edition

Preface

Since the start of the modern feminist movement, many writers and scholars have examined how the female body and ideas about the female body affect women's lives. They have produced a large and diverse literature, spread across many academic disciplines and using many theoretical approaches, on topics ranging from the nature of lesbianism, to the sources of eating disorders, to the consequences of violence against women. Taken together, this literature forms the nucleus of a new field, the politics of women's bodies. At the time the first edition of this book was published, however, no monograph or anthology had brought this literature together and demonstrated its coherence. Thus, this book aimed to cast a new light on this growing field and bring it the attention it deserved. The current edition continues in this tradition.

Three themes unite the readings in this anthology: How ideas about women's bodies are socially constructed, how these social constructions can be used to control women's lives, and how women can resist these forces.

The social construction of women's bodies refers to the process through which cultural ideas (including scientific ideas) about women's bodies develop and become accepted. As this anthology demonstrates, this is a political process, which reflects, reinforces, or challenges the distribution of power between men and women.

Like all other political processes, the social construction of women's bodies develops through battles between groups with competing political interests and with differential access to power and resources. For example, doctors have presented their ideas about the existence, nature, and consequences of "premenstrual syndrome" (PMS) as objective medical truths. Yet those ideas reflect both a particular context—in which women are increasingly willing to speak up about their anger and dissatisfaction—and a particular set of cultural rather than scientific ideas regarding the frailty and dangerousness of the female body. Doctors' ability to convince the public to accept these ideas has depended both on their economic and social power and on the support they have received from women who believe they have PMS and want validation for and treatment of their symptoms.

The social construction of women's bodies often serves as a powerful tool in the social control of women's lives by fostering material changes in women's lives and bodies. Again, we can use PMS as an example. The existence of this diagnostic category gives employers an excuse not to hire or promote women—regardless of whether they have PMS—on the grounds that women's menstrual cycles make them physically and emotionally unreliable. Similarly, when a woman acts or speaks in ways that others find threatening, those others may dismiss her actions or remarks as symptoms of PMS—regardless of whether the woman herself believes she experiences such a syndrome and even regardless of whether she is at that moment premenstrual. Finally, this social construction of PMS encourages medical practices (including the use of sedatives, hormones, and hysterectomies) that materially change and control women's bodies, while encouraging women to police their own behaviors more closely during their premenstrual days.

As Michel Foucault has so vividly described, a powerful array of disciplinary practices—both internalized and external—are used to produce "docile bodies" that willingly accede to their own social control. Yet women are not always passive victims of these disciplinary practices. Rather, they may collaborate in or resist their creation and maintenance. For example, many women fought for the social construction of PMS because they believed it would provide medical legitimation for behaviors and emotions that were otherwise socially unacceptable. Conversely, many other women have fought against this social construction. Similarly, some women resist pressures to conform to social norms of female appearance by refusing to get breast implants following mastectomies, while other women live a lesbian life despite the social construction of lesbianism as deviant and the social control of lesbians through stigma, discrimination, and physical violence. Consequently, this volume also examines the possibilities for and limits on women's resistance.

Unfortunately, given the burgeoning nature of the field, no one volume—or at least no volume of reasonable size and price—can do justice to the full range of topics that touch on the politics of women's bodies. Consequently, despite the growing and important literature on how men's bodies are also gendered, political, and socially constructed, this edition continues to focus solely on women's bodies. Similarly, rather than barely touch on international issues by adding a few articles based in other countries, I chose instead to focus only on women's lives within the United States. For better or worse, the United States disproportionately affects other countries due to its broad cultural, economic, and political impact, and so ideas about women's bodies in this country are particularly important.

Changes to this Edition

This edition of *The Politics of Women's Bodies* retains the basic structure of the previous edition. However, 11 of the 23 articles are new to this edition. Important new topics include intersexuality, fatness, cultural images of the Latina body, how poverty is marked on the female body, and reclaiming the body through tattoos and other bodily modification.

To increase accessibility, beginning with this edition I have included brief introductions for each article. These introductions are designed to help readers put the articles in context and understand their general perspectives.

Overview of volume

Part I of this volume looks at the social construction of women's bodies. The first article (which I wrote specifically for this anthology) provides a context for the rest of the anthology by providing a broad overview of the history of social ideas about women's bodies and demonstrating how changes in these ideas can either challenge or reinforce women's position in society. The other articles draw on both poststructuralist and traditional social scientific theoretical traditions to provide a framework for questioning our most basic ideas about the female body, examining the political process through which those ideas develop, and exploring how and why women accept or resist those ideas.

The remainder of this volume looks in more detail at how the politics of women's bodies affects women's lives. I have somewhat arbitrarily divided these readings into three parts: the politics of sexuality, appearance, and bodily behavior. (Obviously, these three parts overlap, as, for example, to present a culturally acceptable appearance, women must engage in certain behaviors, with certain consequences for how their sexuality is perceived by others.)

Part II, on the politics of sexuality, addresses how women are socialized toward a Euro-American, heterosexual norm that emphasizes male pleasure and female restraint. Two articles discuss cultural attitudes toward the sexuality of African-American and Latina women as well as the price these women pay for those attitudes. The other articles examine how norms of heterosexual romance are taught and the social consequences suffered by those who resist these norms.

Part III explores the politics of appearance. It looks at the myriad ways that women are taught to adopt cultural norms regarding female appearance and at the dilemmas faced by those who cannot meet those norms. This part also explores the ways in which appearance norms restrict women's lives and raises questions regarding the possibilities for, and limits, on resistance to these norms.

Part IV opens with two articles on women and athletics. The first explores the impact of homophobia on women athletes and the second explores how women athletes learn to "hold back" when lifting weights in gyms. The remaining readings look at reproductive rights and violence against women and explore how political interests have attempted to define women's bodies and bodily behaviors in ways that reduce women's life options and power.

The readings included in this volume were selected to cover a wide range of topics related to women and the body. All the readings are intellectually stimulating but written in a fashion accessible to any literate audience. The articles present theoretical concepts as well as data, but avoid the sort of convoluted "academese" and complex statistical techniques that nonacademic readers might find difficult to comprehend.

My other goal in choosing readings was to find readings relevant to a diverse population of women, while reflecting diverse academic perspectives. Readings were selected with attention to issues of diversity with regard to class, ethnicity, age, and sexual orientation. Three of the authors included in this volume write primarily for the popular press. The rest come from psychology, history, literature, communications, political science, philosophy, and sociology. Two classic articles were first published in the 1980s, 9 were published in the 1990s, and 12 were published after 2000.

To increase accessibility, I have shortened most of the articles, deleting some of the more tangential issues. (Deleted text is marked with ellipses.) This editing also allowed me to cover many topics while restricting the book's size and, consequently, price. I also have edited the readings to regularize spelling and style, to further increase accessibility. Finally, and as noted earlier, I have also included brief introductions for each article.

Acknowledgments

My ideas for this anthology came together during many years of teaching courses at Arizona State University on women's health, women's sexuality, feminist theory, the sociology of women, and women and the body. The Women's Studies Program at the university provided fertile ground for exploring these ideas. I especially benefited from many conversations with Georganne Scheiner and Mary Logan Rothschild. My ideas were developed further in discussions with Myra Dinnerstein of the University of Arizona, who has been a valued collaborator and confidante, and who first suggested the idea of bringing together readings on women and the body. I would also like to thank Judith Lorber, Beth Rushing, and Wendy Simonds, who, in addition to Georganne, Mary, and Myra, read parts of the manuscript and helped me to improve it. Members of the electronic bulletin board of Sociologists for Women in Society tolerated many questions from me and provided many useful suggestions. My research assistants, Tanya Nieri, Bethany Gizzi, and Kathleen Nagle Barnett, cheerfully tracked down obscure references, reviewed the literature, and copy-edited readings. Many others, including the anonymous reviewers of previous editions of this book, provided invaluable assistance by recommending topics and readings for this anthology. I am grateful to have this opportunity to thank the reviewers of this edition:

- Orit Avishai-Bentovim (University of California—Berkeley)
- Susan Cayleff (San Diego State University)

- Denise Donnelly (Georgia State University)
- Jacqueline Ellis (New Jersey City University)
- Rita Jones (University of Northern Colorado)
- Sharon M. Meagher (The University of Scranton)
- Tonja Olive (The Colorado College).

Without their assistance, this would be a far weaker book. Finally, I would like to thank my husband, Mark Pry, for his love and sense of humor, and for keeping our household running (despite the demands of his own work) while I worked on this project.

THE POLITICS
OF
WOMEN'S BODIES

I

THE SOCIAL CONSTRUCTION OF WOMEN'S BODIES

The articles in this section provide the historical and theoretical underpinnings for analyzing social ideas about women's bodies. The central theme of this section is the social construction of women's bodies. "Social construction" refers to the process through which ideas become culturally accepted. As we will see, this is an intensely political process, reflecting different groups' competing vested interests and differential access to power. This section will also explore how these socially constructed ideas are reinforced both through the actions of teachers, doctors, and others in positions of power, as well as by each of us, as we come to internalize these ideas and to police our own bodies and actions.

The first article in this section, by Rose Weitz, explores how across Western history, ideas about women's bodies embedded in law, culture, and medicine have both reflected and affected women's position in society. The second article, "Believing Is Seeing: Biology as Ideology," by Judith Lorber, looks at how the everyday structure of our society reinforces the idea that there are two and only two sexes and reinforces the differences between those two sexes. Karin Martin provides an example of how this process occurs among very young children in her article "Becoming a Gendered Body: Practices of Preschools."

In the next article, "Women and Medicalization: A New Perspective," Catherine Kohler. Riessman examines how, why, and with what consequences both women and doctors have sometimes pressed to define women's bodies as ill (a process known as medicalization). Then Cheryl Chase, in "Affronting Reason," provides a very personal example of the consequences of medicalization for those whose bodies do not neatly fit "standard" sex cateories. Finally, in "Foucault, Femininity, and the Modernization of Patriarchal Power," Sandra Lee Bartky explores how society trains women to discipline themselves to fit cultural ideas about proper female appearance and behavior.

1

A History of Women's Bodies

ROSE WEITZ

"A History of Women's Bodies," by Rose Weitz (the editor of this anthology), provides an outline history of the politics of women's bodies. This article delineates how ideas about the female body have changed over time, as well as the very real impact those ideas have had on women's lives. As we will see, three ideas about women's bodies recur consistently in western history. First, societies typically have regarded women's bodies as mentally and physically inferior to men's. Second, societies have considered women's bodies to be men's property. Finally, societies have assumed that women's bodies inherently turn them into sexual seductresses who threaten men's bodies and souls.

At the same time, as Weitz describes, throughout Western history these general ideas about women's bodies have been applied in very different ways to women of different social classes and ethnic, racial, or religious groups. So, for example, whereas U.S. law in the 1820s treated white women more or less like property (refusing them the right to vote, assigning their earnings to their husbands, and so on), enslaved black women were literally regarded as property to be bought and sold. Similarly, whereas cultural belief in the physical and mental frailty of middle-class white women made it impossible for most to seek higher education, cultural belief in the animal-like physical strength of poor women allowed factory owners to expose their women workers to dangerous conditions without any moral qualms or risk of legal sanction.

Finally, this brief history illustrates how whenever women have fought to change ideas about their bodies and to improve their situations, others have fought to keep them in their places. This battle continues to this day.

3

Women's Bodies, Women's Lives

Throughout history, ideas about the nature of women's bodies have played a dramatic role in either challenging or reinforcing power relationships between men and women. As such, we can regard these ideas as political tools and can regard the battle over these ideas as a political struggle. This article presents a brief history of women's bodies, looking at how ideas about the female body have changed over time in western law and biological theory.

Beginning with the earliest recorded western legal system, the Babylonian Code of Hammurabi, and continuing nearly to the present day, western law typically has defined women's bodies as men's property. In ancient societies, women who were not slaves belonged to their fathers before marriage and to their husbands thereafter. For this reason, Babylonian law, for example, treated rape as a form of property damage, requiring a rapist to pay a fine to the husband or father of the raped woman, but nothing to the woman herself. Similarly, marriages in ancient societies typically were contracted between prospective husbands and prospective fathers-in-law, with the potential bride playing little if any role.

Women's legal status as property reflected the belief that women's bodies were inherently different from men's in ways that made women both defective and dangerous. These ideas come through clearly in the writings of Aristotle, whose ideas about women's bodies would form the basis for "scientific" discussion of this topic from the fourth century B.C. through the eighteenth century (Martin 1987; Tuana 1993). Aristotle's biological theories centered around the concept of heat. According to Aristotle, only embryos that had sufficient heat could develop into fully human form. The rest became female. In other words, woman was, in Aristotle's words, a "misbegotten man" and a "monstrosity"—less than fully formed and literally half-baked. Based on this premise, Galen, a highly influential Greek doctor, would later declare that women's reproductive organs were virtually identical to men's, but were located internally because female embryos lacked the heat needed for those organs to develop fully and externally. This view would remain common among doctors until well into the eighteenth century.

Lack of heat, classical scholars argued, also produced a plethora of other deficiencies in women, including a smaller stature, frailer constitution, less developed brain, and emotional and moral weaknesses that could endanger any men who came under their spell. These ideas later would resonate with ideas about women embedded in Christian interpretations of Mary and Eve. Christian theologians argued that Eve had caused the fall from divine grace and the expulsion from the Garden of Eden by succumbing when the snake tempted her with the forbidden fruit. This "original sin" had occurred, these theologians argued, because women's nature made them inherently more susceptible to sexual desire and other passions of the flesh, blinding them to reason and morality and making them a constant danger to men's souls. Mary, meanwhile, had avoided this fate only by remaining virginal. Such ideas later would play a large role in fueling the witchcraft hysteria in early modern Europe and colonial America. Women formed the vast majority of the tens of thousands executed as witches during these centuries because both Protestants and Catholics assumed that women were less intelligent than men, more driven by sexual passions, and hence more susceptible to the Devil's blandishments (Barstow 1994).

By the beginnings of the modern era, women's legal and social position had changed little. When the famous English legal theorist, Sir William Blackstone, published his encyclopedic codification of English law in 1769, non-slave women's legal status still remained closer to that of property than to that of non-slave men. According to Blackstone, "By marriage, the husband and wife are one person in the law; that is, the very being and legal existence of the woman is suspended during the marriage, or at least is incorporated into that of her husband under whose wing, protection and cover she performs everything" (1904, 432). In other words, upon marriage a woman experienced "civil death," losing any rights as a citizen, including the right to own or bestow property, make contracts or sue for legal redress, hold custody over minor children, or keep any wages she earned. Moreover, as her "protector," a husband had a legal right to beat her if he believed it necessary, as well as a right to her sexual services. These principles would form the basis of marital law in the United States from its founding.

Meanwhile, both in colonial America and in the United States for its first 89 years, slave women *were* property. Moreover, both the law and contemporary scientific writings often described African-American women (and men) as animals, rather than humans. Consequently, neither slave women nor slave men held any of these rights of citizenship. By the same token, African-American women slaves were completely subject to their white masters. Rape was common, both as a form of "entertainment" for white men and as a way of breeding more slaves, since the children of slave mothers were automatically slaves, regardless of their fathers' race. Nor did African-American women's special vulnerability to rape end when slavery ended.

Both before and after the Civil War, the rape of African-American women was explained, if not justified, by an ideology that defined African-Americans, including African-American women, as animalistically hypersexual, and thus blamed them for their own rapes (Gilman 1985; Giddings 1995). For example, an article published by a white southern woman on March 17, 1904 in the popular periodical, the *Independent*, declared:

> Degeneracy is apt to show most in the weaker individuals of any race; so Negro women evidence more nearly the popular idea of total depravity than the men do. They are so nearly lacking in virtue that the color of a Negro woman's skin is generally taken (and quite correctly) as a guarantee of her immorality.... I sometimes read of a virtuous Negro woman, hear of them, but the idea is absolutely inconceivable to me...

These ideas about sexuality, combined with ideas about the inherent inferiority of African Americans, are vividly reflected in the 1861 Georgia penal code. That code left it up to the court whether to fine or imprison men who raped African-American women, recommended two to twenty years imprisonment for white men convicted of raping white women, and mandated the death penalty for African-American men convicted of raping white women (Roberts 1990, 60). Moreover, African-American men typically were lynched before being brought to trial if suspected of raping a white woman, while white men were rarely convicted for raping white women and probably never convicted for raping African-American women.

For both free and slave women in the United States, the legal definition of women's bodies as men's property experienced its first serious challenges during the nineteenth century. In 1839, Mississippi passed the first Married Women's Property Act. Designed primarily to protect family farms and property from creditors rather than to expand the rights of women (Speth 1982), the law gave married women the right to retain property they owned before marriage and any wages they earned outside the home. By the end of the nineteenth century, similar laws had passed in all the states.

Also during the nineteenth century, both white and African-American women won the right to vote in Wyoming, Utah, Colorado, and Idaho, and a national suffrage campaign took root. Meanwhile, beginning with Oberlin College in 1833, a growing number of colleges began accepting women students, including free African-American women, with more than 5,000 women graduating in 1900 alone (Flexner 1974, 232). At the same time, the industrial revolution prompted growing numbers of women to seek paid employment. By 1900, the U.S. census would list more than 5 million women gainfully employed outside the home (Flexner 1974, 250). This did not reflect any significant changes in the lives of African-American women— who had worked as much as men when slaves and who often worked full-time post-slavery (Jones 1985)—but was a major change for white women.

Each of these changes challenged the balance of power between men and women in American society. In response to these challenges, a counterreaction quickly developed. This counterreaction combined new "scientific" ideas with older definitions of women's bodies as ill or fragile to argue that white middle-class women were unable to sustain the responsibilities of political power or the burdens of education or employment.

Ideas about middle-class women's frailty drew heavily on the writings of Charles Darwin, who had published his groundbreaking *On the Origin of the Species* in 1872 (Tuana 1993). As part of his theory of evolution, Darwin argued that males compete for sexual access to females, with only the fittest succeeding and reproducing. As a result, males continually evolve toward greater "perfection." Females, on the other hand, need not compete for males, and therefore are not subject to the same process of natural selection. Consequently, in any species, males will be more evolved than females. In addition, Darwin argued, females must expend so much energy on reproduction that they retain little energy for either physical or mental development. As a result, women remain subject to their emotions and passions: nurturing, altruistic, and child-like, but with little sense of either justice or morality.

These ideas meshed well with Victorian ideas about middle-class white women's sexuality, which depicted women as the objects of male desire, emphasized romance and downplayed female sexual desire, and reinforced a sexual double standard. Middle-class women were expected to have passionate and even romantic attachments to other women, but these attachments were assumed to be emotional, rather than physical. Most women who had "romantic friendships" with other women were married to men, and only those few who adopted male clothing or behavior were considered lesbians (Faderman 1981). Lesbianism only became more broadly identified and stigmatized in the early twentieth century, when women's entry into higher education and the workforce enabled some women to survive economically without marrying, and lesbianism therefore became more of a threat to male power.

With women's increasing entry into education and employment, ideas about the physical and emotional frailty of women—with their strong echoes of both Christian and Aristotelian disdain for women and their bodies—were adopted by nineteenth century doctors as justification for keeping women uneducated and unemployed. So, for example:

> The president of the Oregon State Medical Society, F. W. Van Dyke, in 1905, claimed that hard study killed sexual desire in women, took away their beauty, and brought on hysteria, neurasthenia [a mental disorder], dyspepsia [indigestion], astigmatism [a visual disorder], and dysmenorrhea [painful menstruation]. Educated women, he added, could not bear children with ease because study arrested the development of the pelvis at the same time it increased the size of the child's brain, and therefore its head. The result was extensive suffering in childbirth by educated women. (Bullough and Voght 1984, 32)

Belief in the frailty of middle-class women's bodies similarly fostered the epidemic rise during the late nineteenth century in gynecological surgery (Barker-Benfield 1976; Longo 1984). Many doctors routinely performed surgery to remove healthy ovaries, uteruses, and clitorises, from women who experienced an extremely wide range of physical and mental symptoms—including symptoms such as rebelliousness or malaise which reflected women's constrained social circumstances more than their physical health. These operations were not only unnecessary but dangerous, with mortality rates up to 33 percent (Longo 1984).

Paradoxically, at the same time that scientific "experts" emphasized the frailty of middle-class white women, they emphasized the robustness of poorer women, both white and non-white. As Jacqueline Jones (1985, 15) explains:

> Slaveholders had little use for sentimental platitudes about the delicacy of the female constitution.... There were enough women like Susan Mabry of Virginia, who could pick 400 or 500 pounds of cotton a day (150 to 200 pounds was considered respectable for an average worker) to remove from a master's mind all doubts about the ability of a strong, healthy woman field worker. As a result, he conveniently discarded his time-honored Anglo-Saxon notions about the type of work best suited for women.

Similar attitudes applied toward working-class white women. Thus, Dr. Lucien Warner, a popular medical authority, could in 1874 explain how middle-class women were made frail by their affluence, while "the African negress, who toils beside her husband in the fields of the south, and Bridget [the Irish maid], who washes, and scrubs and toils in our homes at the north, enjoy for the most part good health, with comparative immunity from uterine disease" (cited in Ehrenreich and English 1973, 12–13).

At any rate, despite the warnings of medical experts, women continued to enter both higher education and the paid workforce. However, although education clearly benefited women, entering the workforce endangered the life and health of many women due to hazardous working conditions.

Although male workers could hope to improve their working conditions through union agitation, this tactic was far less useful for women, who more often worked in non-unionized jobs, were denied union membership, or were uninterested in joining unions. As a result, some feminists began lobbying for protective labor laws that would set maximum working hours for women, mandate rest periods, and so on (Erickson, 1982). In 1908, the U.S. Supreme Court first upheld such a law in *Muller v. Oregon*. Unfortunately, it soon became clear that protective labor laws hurt women more than they helped, by bolstering the idea that women workers were inherently weaker than men.

Twelve years after the *Muller* decision, in 1920, most female U.S. citizens finally won the right to vote in national elections. (Most Asian-born and Native American women, however, were ineligible for citizenship, and most African-American women—like African-American men—were kept from voting through both legal and illegal means.) Unfortunately, suffrage largely marked the close of decades of feminist activism rather than the start of any broader reforms in women's legal, social, or economic position.

By the 1960s, little had changed in women's status. For example, although the fourteenth amendment (passed in 1868) guaranteed equal protection under the law for all U.S. citizens, not until 1971, in *Reed v. Reed*, would the Supreme Court rule that differential treatment based on sex was illegal. Similarly, based still on Blackstone's interpretation of women's legal position and the concept of women as men's property, until the 1970s courts routinely refused to prosecute wife batterers unless they killed their wives, and not until 1984 did any court convict a man for raping a woman to whom he was married and with whom he still legally resided.

Recognition of these and other inequities led to the emergence of a new feminist movement beginning in the second half of the 1960s (Evans 1979). In its earliest days, this movement adopted the rhetoric of liberalism and the civil rights movement, arguing that women and men were morally and intellectually equal and that women's bodies were essentially similar to men's bodies. The (unsuccessful) attempts to pass the Equal Rights Amendment, which stated that "equality of rights under the law shall not be denied or abridged by the United States or any state on account of sex," reflected this strain of thinking about gender.

The goal of these liberal feminists was to achieve equality with men within existing social structures—for example, to get men to do a fair share of child care. Soon, however, some feminists began questioning whether achieving equality within existing social structures would really help women, or whether women would be served better by radically restructuring society to create more humane social arrangements—for example, establishing communal living arrangements in which child care could be more broadly shared. Along with this questioning of social arrangements came questions about the reality not only of sex differences but also of the categories "male" and "female."

In contrast, a more recent strand of feminist thought, known as "cultural feminism," has reemphasized the idea of inherent differences between men and women. Unlike those who made this argument in the past, however, cultural feminists argue that women and their bodies are *superior* to men's. From this perspective, women's ability to create human life has made women (especially mothers) innately more pacifistic, loving, moral, creative, and life-affirming than men (e.g., Daly 1978). For the same reason, some feminists, such as Susan Griffin (1978), now argue that women also have an inherently deeper connection than men to nature and to ecological concerns. (Ironically, many in the anti-abortion movement and on the far right use rhetoric similar to that of cultural feminists to argue that women belong at home.)

Despite the differences among feminists in ideology and tactics, all share the goal of challenging accepted ideas about women's bodies and social position. Not surprisingly, as the modern feminist movement has grown, a backlash has developed that has attempted to reinforce more traditional ideas (Faludi 1991). This backlash has taken many forms, including (*1*) increasing pressure on women to control the shape of their bodies, (*2*) attempts to define premenstrual and postmenopausal women as ill, and (*3*) the rise of the anti-abortion and "fetal rights" movements.

Throughout history, women have experienced social pressures to maintain acceptable appearances. However, as Susan Faludi (1991), Naomi Wolf

(1991), and many others have demonstrated, the backlash against modern feminism seems to have increased these pressures substantially. For example, since 1978, a steady 70% of *Playboy* centerfolds have been significantly underweight, while the average weight of Miss America winners has decreased sharply, even though average height has increased (Rubinstein and Caballero 2000; Katzmarzyk and Davis 2001).

Current appearance norms call for women to be not only painfully thin, but muscular and buxom—qualities that only can occur together if women spend vast amounts of time on exercise, money on cosmetic surgery, and emotional energy on diet (Seid 1989).

The backlash against feminism also has affected women's lives by stimulating calls for the medical control of premenstrual women. Although first defined in the 1930s, the idea of a "premenstrual syndrome" (PMS) did not garner much attention either inside or outside medical circles until the 1970s. Since then, innumerable popular and medical articles have argued that to function at work or school, women with PMS (or the more serious PMDD—premenstrual dysphoric disorder) need medical treatment to control their anger and discipline their behaviors. Similarly, many doctors now believe that menopausal women need drugs to maintain their sexual attractiveness and to control their behavior and emotions.

Finally, the backlash against feminism has restricted women's lives through facilitating the rise of the anti-abortion and "fetal rights" movements. Prior to the twentieth century, abortion was generally considered both legally and socially acceptable, although dangerous. By the mid-twentieth century, abortion had become a safe medical procedure, but legal only when deemed medically necessary. Doctors were deeply divided, however, regarding when it was necessary, with some performing abortions only to preserve women's lives and others doing so to preserve women's social, psychological, or economic well-being (Luker 1984). To protect themselves legally, beginning in the 1960s, those doctors who favored more lenient indications for abortion, along with women who considered abortion a right, lobbied heavily for broader legal access to abortion. This lobbying culminated in 1973 when the U.S. Supreme Court ruled, in *Roe v. Wade*, that abortion was legal in most circumstances. However, subsequent legislative actions and Court decisions (including the 1976 Hyde Amendment and the Supreme Court's 1992 decision in *Planned Parenthood v. Casey*) have reduced legal access to abortion substantially, especially for poor and young women.

Embedded in the legal battles over abortion is a set of beliefs about the nature of women and of the fetus (Luker 1984). On the one side stand those who argue that unless women have an absolute right to control their own bodies, including the right to abortion, they will never attain fully equal status in society. On the other side stand those who argue that the fetus is fully human and that women's rights to control their bodies must be subjugated to the fetus's right to life.

This latter belief also underlays the broader social and legal pressure for "fetal rights." For example, pregnant women around the country—almost all of them non-white and poor—have been arrested for abusing alcohol or illegal drugs while pregnant, on the grounds that they had no right to expose their fetuses to harmful substances. Others—again, mostly poor and non-white—have been forced to have cesarean sections against their will. In these cases, the courts have ruled that the fetus's interests are more important than women's right to determine what will happen to their bodies—in this case, the right to refuse invasive, hazardous surgery—and that doctors know better than mothers what is in a fetus's best interests. Still other women have been refused jobs by employers who have argued that hazardous work conditions might endanger a pregnant worker's fetus; these employers have ignored evidence that the same conditions would also damage men's sperm and thus any resulting fetuses.

Conclusions

Throughout history, ideas about women's bodies have centrally affected the strictures within which women live their lives. Only by looking at the embodied experiences of women, as well as at how those experiences are socially constructed, can we fully understand women's lives, women's position in society, and the possibilities for resistance against that position.

References

Barker-Benfield, G. J. 1976. *The Horrors of the Half-known Life: Male Attitudes Towards Women and Sexuality in 19th Century America*. New York: Harper.

Barstow, Anne Llewellyn. 1994. *Witchcraze: A New History of the European Witch Hunts*. San Francisco: Pandora.

Blackstone, Sir William. 1904. *Commentaries on the Laws of England in Four Books*. Volume I, edited by George Sharswood. Philadelphia: Lippincott.

Bullough, Vern, and Martha Voght. 1984. Women, Menstruation, and Nineteenth Century Medicine. In *Women and Health in America: Historical Readings*, edited by Judith Walzer Leavitt. Madison: University of Wisconsin Press.

Daly, Mary. 1978. *Gyn/Ecology: The Metaethics of Radical Feminism*. Boston: Beacon.

Darwin, Charles. 1872. *On the Origin of the Species*. Akron, OH: Werner.

Ehrenreich, Barbara, and Deirdre English. 1973. *Complaints and Disorders: The Sexual Politics of Sickness*. Old Westbury, NY: Feminist Press.

Erickson, Nancy S. 1982. Historical Background of "Protective" Labor Legislation: Muller v. Oregon. In *Women and the Law: A Social Historical Perspective*. Volume II, edited by D. Kelly Weisberg. Cambridge, MA: Schenkman.

Evans, Sara M. 1979. *Personal Politics: The Roots of Women's Liberation in the Civil Rights Movement and the New Left*. New York: Vintage Books.

Faderman, Lillian. 1981. *Surpassing the Love of Men: Romantic Friendship and Love Between Women from the Renaissance to the Present*. New York: Morrow.

Faludi, Susan. 1991. *Backlash: The Undeclared War Against American Women*. New York: Crown.

Flexner, Eleanor. 1974. *Century of Struggle: The Women's Rights Movement in the United States.* New York: Atheneum.

Giddings, Paula. 1995. The last taboo. In *Words of Fire: An Anthology of African-American Feminist Thought,* edited by Beverly Guy-Sheftall. New York: New Press.

Gilman, Sander. 1985. Black bodies, white bodies: Toward an iconography of female sexuality in late nineteenth century art, medicine, and literature. In *"Race," Writing and Difference,* edited by Henry Louis Gates. Chicago: University of Chicago Press.

Griffin, Susan. 1978. *Woman and Nature: The Roaring Inside Her.* New York: Harper.

Jones, Jacqueline. 1985. *Labor of Love, Labor of Sorrow: Black Women, Work, and the Family from Slavery to the Present.* New York: Basic.

Katzmarzyk, P. T., and C. Davis. 2001. Thinness and body shape of *Playboy* centerfolds from 1978 to 1998. *International Journal of Obesity* 25:590–92.

Longo, Lawrence D. 1984. The Rise and Fall of Battey's Operation: A Fashion in Surgery. In *Woman and Health in America,* Judith Walzer Leavitt. Madison: University of Wisconsin Press.

Luker, Kristin. 1984. *Abortion and the Politics of Motherhood.* Berkeley: University of California Press.

Martin, Emily. 1987. *The Woman in the Body.* Boston: Beacon.

Roberts, Dorothy E. 1990. The future of reproductive choice for poor women and women of color. *Women's Rights Law Reporter* 12(2):59–67.

Rubinstein, Sharon, and Benjamin Caballero. 2000. Is Miss America an undernourished role model? *JAMA* 283:1569.

Seid, Roberta Pollack. 1989. *Never Too Thin: Why Women Are at War with Their Bodies.* New York: Prentice Hall.

Speth, Linda E. 1982. The married women's property acts, 1839–1865: Reform, reaction, or revolution? In *Women and the Law: A Social Historical Perspective.* Volume II, edited by D. Kelly Weisberg. Cambridge, MA: Schenkman.

Tuana, Nancy. 1993. *The Less Noble Sex: Scientific, Religious, and Philosophical Conceptions of Woman's Nature.* Bloomington: Indiana University Press.

Wolf, Naomi. 1991. *The Beauty Myth: How Images of Beauty Are Used Against Women.* New York: W. Morrow.

2

Believing Is Seeing

Biology as Ideology

JUDITH LORBER

Judith Lorber's article, "Believing Is Seeing: Biology as Ideology," attacks head on our assumptions about men's and women's nature. Like other scholars, she uses the term sex *to refer to the* biological *categories of male and female (to which we are assigned based on our chromosomal structure, genitalia, hormones, and the like) and uses the term* gender *to refer to the* social *categories of masculine and feminine and to social expectations regarding masculinity and femininity. Most if not all feminist scholars agree that gender is a social construction (that is, our ideas about what is properly masculine and feminine are products of culture, not biology). Lorber goes one step further and argues that sex, too, is a social construction.*

First, Lorber argues, there is no definition of the word female *that could include everyone we label as female. Some individuals whom we label female have a uterus, others don't. Some have XX chromosomes, others don't. And so on. Thus our definition of femaleness glides over evidence that this sex category is based on social expectations, not on clear biological evidence. Similarly, Lorber argues, we can treat sex as a binary concept (i.e., a concept that has only two possible categories, male and female)—only by ignoring (or hiding) the evidence regarding intermediate sexes. This is what sociologists call a self-fulfilling prophesy, something we believe to be true and then, through our actions, make into the truth. In this case, because we expect all humans to be either male or female, we then as a society do everything necessary (including surgery) to make sure everyone appears to be either male or female. Similarly, Lorber argues, our assumptions about the biological differences between men and women have led us to construct a world that heightens (or even creates) those differences. For*

Originally published in *Gender & Society* 7(4): 568–581. Copyright 1993 by Sage Publications. Reprinted by permission of Sage Publication.

example, male gymnasts are judged primarily by their performance in routines that rely on physical strength, whereas female gymnasts are judged primarily on their agility and gracefulness. Consequently, we most often encourage strong men to become gymnasts and then train them to become stronger, whereas we most often encourage exceptionally petite young girls to become gymnasts and then encourage them to keep their weight down. Subsequently, we praise male gymnasts for their power, ignoring their grace, and praise female gymnasts for their grace, ignoring their physical strength. Each of these steps is based on cultural assumptions about biological differences between males and females, each increases those biological differences, and each makes those differences seem natural.

Finally, Lorber argues, in a society in which (1) men and women are assumed to be innately different and (2) men overall have more power than women, it should not surprise us that the human-built environment is designed to fit male bodies. For example, the fact that tables in corporate conference rooms are permanently fixed at a height too tall for most women reflects and reinforces male power, even while it disadvantages both most women and shorter men.

Until the eighteenth century, Western philosophers and scientists thought that there was one sex and that women's internal genitalia were the inverse of men's external genitalia: the womb and vagina were the penis and scrotum turned inside out (Laqueur 1990). Current Western thinking sees women and men as so different physically as to sometimes seem two species. The bodies, which have been mapped inside and out for hundreds of years, have not changed. What has changed are the justifications for gender inequality. When the social position of all human beings was believed to be set by natural law or was considered God-given, biology was irrelevant; women and men of different classes all had their assigned places. When scientists began to question the divine basis of social order and replaced faith with empirical knowledge, what they saw was that women were very different from men in that they had wombs and menstruated. Such anatomical differences destined them for an entirely different social life from men.

In actuality, the basic bodily material is the same for females and males, and except for procreative hormones and organs, female and male human beings have similar bodies (Naftolin and Butz 1981). Furthermore, as has been known since the middle of the nineteenth century, male and female genitalia develop from the same fetal tissue, and so infants can be born with ambiguous genitalia (Money and Ehrhardt 1972). When they are, biology is used quite arbitrarily in sex assignment. Suzanne Kessler (1990) interviewed six medical specialists in pediatric intersexuality and found that whether an infant with XY chromosomes and anomalous genitalia was categorized as a boy or a girl depended on the size of the penis—if a penis was very small, the child was categorized as a girl, and sex-change surgery was used to make an artificial vagina. In the late nineteenth century, the presence or absence of ovaries was the determining criterion of gender assignment for hermaphrodites because a woman who could not procreate was not a complete woman (Kessler 1990, 20).

Yet in Western societies, we see two discrete sexes and two distinguishable genders because our society is built on two classes of people, "women" and "men." Once the gender category is given, the attributes of the person are also gendered: Whatever a "woman" is has to be "female", whatever a "man" is has to be "male." Analyzing the social processes that construct the categories we call "female and male," "women and men," and "homosexual and heterosexual" uncovers the ideology and power differentials congealed in these categories (Foucault 1978). This article will use two familiar areas of social life—sports and technological competence—to show how myriad physiological differences are transformed into similar-appearing, gendered social bodies. My perspective goes beyond accepted feminist views that gender is a cultural overlay that modifies physiological sex differences. That perspective assumes either that there are two fairly similar sexes distorted by social practices into two genders with purposefully different characteristics or that there are two sexes whose essential differences are rendered unequal by social practices. I am arguing that bodies differ in many ways physiologically, but they are completely transformed by social practices to fit into the salient categories of a society, the most pervasive of which are "female" and "male" and "women" and "men."

Neither sex nor gender are pure categories. Combinations of incongruous genes, genitalia, and hormonal input are ignored in sex categorization, just as combinations of incongruous physiology, identity, sexuality, appearance, and behavior are ignored in the social construction of gender statuses. Menstruation, lactation, and gestation do not demarcate women from men. Only some women are pregnant and then only some of the time; some women do not have a uterus or ovaries. Some women have stopped menstruating temporarily, others have reached menopause, and some have had hysterectomies. Some women breast-feed some of the time, but some men lactate (Jaggar 1983, 165 fn). Menstruation, lactation, and gestation are individual experiences of womanhood (Levesque-Lopman 1988), but not determinants of the social category "woman," or even "female." Similarly, "men are not always sperm-producers, and in fact, not all sperm producers are men. A male-to-female transsexual, prior to surgery, can be socially a woman, though still potentially (or actually) capable of spermatogenesis" (Kessler and McKenna [1978] 1985, 2).

When gender assignment is contested in sports, where the categories of competitors are rigidly divided into women and men, chromosomes are now used to determine in which category the athlete is to compete. However, an anomaly common enough to be found in several women at every major international sports competition are XY chromosomes that have not produced male anatomy or physiology because of a genetic defect. Because these women are women in every way significant for sports competition, the prestigious International Amateur Athletic Federation has urged that sex be determined by simple genital inspection (Kolata 1992). Transsexuals would pass this test, but it took a lawsuit for Renée Richards, a male-to-female transsexual, to be able to play tournament tennis as a woman, despite his male sex chromosomes (Richards 1983). Oddly, neither basis for gender categorization—chromosomes nor genitalia—has anything to do with sports prowess (Birrell and Cole 1990).

In the Olympics, in cases of chromosomal ambiguity, women must undergo "a battery of gynecological and physical exams to see if she is 'female enough' to compete. Men are not tested" (Carlson 1991, 26). The purpose is not to categorize women and men accurately, but to make sure men don't enter women's competitions, where, it is felt, they will have the advantage of size and strength. This practice sounds fair only because it is assumed that all men are similar in size and strength and different from all women. Yet in Olympics boxing and wrestling matches, men are matched within weight classes. Some women might similarly successfully compete with some men in many sports. Women did not run in marathons until about twenty years ago. In twenty years of marathon competition, women have reduced their finish times by more than one-and-one-half hours; they are expected to run as fast as men in that race by 1998 and might catch up with men's running times in races of other lengths within the next 50 years because they are increasing their fastest speeds more rapidly than are men (Fausto-Sterling 1985, 213–18).

The reliance on only two sex and gender categories in the biological and social sciences is as epistemologically spurious as the reliance on chromosomal or genital tests to group athletes. Most research designs do not investigate whether physical skills or physical abilities are really more or less common in women and men (Epstein 1988). They start out with two social categories ("women," "men"), assume they are biologically different ("female," "male"), look for similarities among them and differences between them, and attribute what they have found for the social categories to sex differences (Gelman et al. 1986). These designs rarely question the categorization of their subjects into two and only two groups, even though they often find more significant within-group differences than between-group differences (Hyde 1990). The social construction perspective on sex and gender suggests that instead of starting with the two presumed dichotomies in each category—female, male; woman, man—it might be more useful in gender studies to group patterns of behavior and only then look for identifying markers of the people likely to enact such behaviors.

What Sports Illustrate

Competitive sports have become, for boys and men, as players and as spectators, a way of constructing a masculine identity, a legitimated outlet for violence and aggression, and an avenue for upward mobility (Dunning 1986; Kemper 1990, 167–206; Messner 1992). For men in Western societies, physical competence is an important marker of masculinity (Fine 1987; Glassner 1992; Majors 1990). In professional and collegiate sports, physiological differences are invoked to justify women's secondary status, despite the clear evidence that gender status overrides physiological capabilities. Assumptions about women's physiology have influenced rules of competition; subsequent sports performances then validate how women and men are treated in sports competitions.

Gymnastic equipment is geared to slim, wiry, prepubescent girls and not to mature women; conversely, men's gymnastic equipment is tailored for muscular, mature men, not slim, wiry prepubescent boys. Boys could compete with girls, but are not allowed to; women gymnasts are left out entirely. Girl gymnasts are just that—little girls who will be disqualified as soon as they grow up (Vecsey 1990). Men gymnasts have men's status. In women's basketball, the size of the ball and rules for handling the ball change the style of play to "a slower, less intense, and less exciting modification of the 'regular' or men's game" (Watson 1987, 441). In the 1992 Winter Olympics, men figure skaters were required to complete three triple jumps in their required program; women figure skaters were forbidden to do more than one. These rules penalized artistic men skaters and athletic women skaters (Janofsky 1992). For the most part, Western sports are built on physically trained men's bodies:

> Speed, size, and strength seem to be the essence of sports. Women *are* naturally inferior at "sports" so conceived.
>
> But if women had been the historically dominant sex, our concept of sport would no doubt have evolved differently. Competitions emphasizing flexibility, balance, strength, timing, and small size might dominate Sunday afternoon television and offer salaries in six figures. (English 1982, 266, emphasis in original)

Organized sports are big businesses and, thus, who has access and at what level is a distributive or equity issue. The overall status of women and men athletes is an economic, political, and ideological issue that has less to do with individual physiological capabilities than with their cultural and social meaning and who defines and profits from them (Messner and Sabo 1990; Slatton and Birrell 1984). Twenty years after the passage of Title IX of the U.S. Civil Rights Act, which forbade gender inequality in any school receiving federal funds, the goal for collegiate sports in the next five years is 60 percent men, 40 percent women in sports participation, scholarships, and funding (Moran 1992).

How access and distribution of rewards (prestigious and financial) are justified is an ideological, even moral, issue (Birrell 1988, 473–76; Hargreaves 1982). One way is that men athletes are glorified and women athletes ignored in the mass media. Messner and his colleagues found that in 1989, in TV sports news in the United States, men's sports got 92 percent of the coverage and women's sports 5 percent, with the rest mixed or gender-neutral (Messner, Duncan, and Jensen 1993). In 1990, in four of the top-selling newspapers in the United States, stories on men's sports out-numbered those on women's sports 23 to 1. Messner and his colleagues also found an implicit hierarchy in naming, with women athletes most likely to be called by first names, followed by Black men athletes, and only white men athletes routinely referred to by their last names. Similarly, women's colle-giate sports teams are named or marked in ways that symbolically feminize and trivialize them—the men's team is called Tigers, the women's Kittens (Eitzen and Baca Zinn 1989).

Assumptions about men's and women's bodies and their capacities are crafted in ways that make unequal access and distribution of rewards accept-able (Hudson 1978; Messner 1988). Media images of modern men athletes glorify their strength and power, even their violence (Hargreaves 1986). Media images of modern women athletes tend to focus on feminine beauty and grace (so they are not really athletes) or on their thin, small, wiry androgenous bodies (so they are not really women). In coverage of the Olympics,

> loving and detailed attention is paid to pixie-like gymnasts; special and extended coverage is given to graceful and dazzling figure skaters; the cam-era painstakingly records the fluid movements of swimmers and divers. And then, in a blinding flash of fragmented images, viewers see a few minutes of volleyball, basketball, speed skating, track and field, and alpine skiing, as television gives its nod to the mere existence of these events. (Boutilier and SanGiovanni 1983, 190)

Extraordinary feats by women athletes who were presented as mature adults might force sports organizers and audiences to rethink their stereotypes of women's capabilities, the way elves, mermaids, and ice queens do not. Sports, therefore, construct men's bodies to be powerful: women's bodies to be sexual. As Connell (1987, 85) says,

> The meanings in the bodily sense of masculinity concern, above all else, the superiority of men to women, and the exaltation of hegemonic masculinity over other groups of men which is essential for the domination of women.

In the late 1970s, as women entered more and more athletic competi-tions, supposedly good scientific studies showed that women who exercised intensely would cease menstruating because they would not have enough body fat to sustain ovulation (Brozan 1978). When one set of researchers did a yearlong study that compared 66 women—21 who were training for a marathon, 22 who ran more than an hour a week, and 23 who did less than an hour of aerobic exercise a week—they discovered that only 20 percent of the women in any of these groups had "normal" menstrual cycles every month (Prior et al. 1990). The dangers of intensive training for women's fertility therefore were exaggerated as women began to compete successfully in arenas formerly closed to them.

Given the association of sports with masculinity in the United States, women athletes have to manage a contradictory status. One study of women college basketball players found that although they "did athlete" on the court—"pushing, shoving, fouling, hard running, fast breaks, defense, obscenities and sweat" (Watson 1987, 441), they "did woman" off the court, using the locker room as their staging area:

> While it typically took fifteen minutes to prepare for the game, it took approximately fifteen minutes after the game to shower and remove the sweat of an athlete, and it took another thirty minutes to dress, apply make-up and style hair. It did not seem to matter whether the players were going out into the public or getting on a van for a long ride home. Average dressing time and rituals did not change. (Watson 1987, 443)

Another way women manage these status dilemmas is to redefine the activity or its result as feminine or womanly (Mangan and Park 1987). Thus women bodybuilders claim that "flex appeal is sex appeal" (Duff and Hong 1984, 378).

Such a redefinition of women's physicality affirms the ideological subtext of sports that physical strength is men's prerogative and justifies men's physical and sexual domination of women (Hargreaves 1986, Messner 1992, 164–72; Olson 1990; Theberge 1987; Willis 1982). When women demonstrate physical strength, they are labeled unfeminine:

> It's threatening to one's takeability, one's rapeability, one's femininity, to be strong and physically self-possessed. To be able to resist rape, not to communicate rapeability with one's body, to hold one's body for uses and meanings other than that can transform what *being a woman means*. (MacKinnon 1987, 122, emphasis in original)

Resistance to that transformation, ironically, was evident in the policies of American women physical education professionals throughout most of the twentieth century. They minimized exertion, maximized a feminine appearance and manner, and left organized sports competition to men (Birrell 1988, 461–62; Mangan and Park 1987).

Dirty Little Secrets

As sports construct gendered bodies, technology constructs gendered skills. Meta-analysis of studies of gender differences in spatial and mathematical ability have found that men have a large advantage in ability to mentally rotate an image, a moderate advantage in a visual perception of horizontality and verticality and in mathematical performance, and a small advantage in ability to pick a figure out of a field (Hyde 1990). It could be argued that these advantages explain why, within the short space of time that computers have become ubiquitous in offices, schools, and homes, work on them and with them has become gendered: Men create, program, and market computers, make war and produce science and art with them; women microwire them in computer factories and enter data in computerized offices; boys play games, socialize, and commit crimes with computers; girls are rarely seen in computer clubs, camps, and classrooms. But women were hired as computer programmers in the 1940s because

> the work seemed to resemble simple clerical tasks. In fact, however, programming demanded complex skills in abstract logic, mathematics, electrical circuitry, and machinery, all of which...women used to perform in their work. Once programming was recognized as "intellectually demanding," it became attractive to men. (Donato 1990, 170)

A woman mathematician and pioneer in data processing, Grace M. Hopper, was famous for her work on programming language (Perry and Greber 1990, 86). By the 1960s, programming was split into more and less skilled specialties, and the entry of women into the computer field in the 1970s and 1980s was confined to the lower-paid specialties. At each stage, employers invoked women's and men's purportedly natural capabilities for the jobs for which they were hired (Cockburn 1983, 1985; Donato 1990; Hartmann 1987; Hartmann et al. 1986; Kramer and Lehman 1990; Wright et al. 1987; Zimmerman 1983).

It is the taken-for-grantedness of such everyday gendered behavior that gives credence to the belief that the widespread differences in what women and men do must come from biology. To take one ordinarily unremarked scenario: In modern societies, if a man and woman who are a couple are in a car together, he is much more likely to take the wheel than she is, even if she is the more competent driver. Molly Haskell calls this taken-for-granted phenomenon "the dirty little secret of marriage: the husband-lousy-driver syndrome" (1989, 26). Men drive cars whether they are good drivers or not because men and machines are a "natural" combination (Scharff 1991). But the ability to drive gives one mobility; it is a form of social power.

In the early days of the automobile, feminists co-opted the symbolism of mobility as emancipation: "Donning goggles and dusters, wielding tire irons and tool kits, taking the wheel, they announced their intention to move beyond the bounds of women's place" (Scharff 1991, 68). Driving enabled them to campaign for women's suffrage in parts of the United States not served by public transportation, and they effectively used motorcades and speaking from cars as campaign tactics (Scharff 1991, 67–88). Sandra Gilbert also notes that during World War I, women's ability to drive was physically, mentally, and even sensually liberating:

For nurses and ambulance drivers, women doctors and women messengers, the phenomenon of modern battle was very different from that experienced by entrenched combatants. Finally given a chance to take the wheel, these post-Victorian girls need motorcars along foreign roads like adventurers exploring new lands, while their brothers dug deeper into the mud of France.... Retrieving the wounded and the dead from deadly positions, these once-decorous daughters had at last been allowed to prove their valor, and they swooped over the wastelands of the war with the energetic love of Wagnerian Valkyries, their mobility alone transporting countless immobilized heroes to safe havens. (1983, 438–39)

Not incidentally, women in the United States and England got the vote for their war efforts in World War I.

Social Bodies and the Bathroom Problem

People of the same racial ethnic group and social class are roughly the same size and shape—but there are many varieties of bodies. People have different genitalia, different secondary sex characteristics, different contributions to procreation, different orgasmic experiences, different patterns of illness and aging. Each of us experiences our bodies differently, and these experiences change as we grow, age, sicken, and die. The bodies of pregnant and nonpregnant women, short and tall people, those with intact and functioning limbs, and those whose bodies are physically challenged are all different. But the salient categories of a society group these attributes in ways that ride roughshod over individual experiences and more meaningful clusters of people.

I am not saying that physical differences between male and female bodies don't exist, but that these differences are socially meaningless until social practices transform them into social facts. West Point Military Academy's curriculum is designed to produce leaders, and physical competence is used as a significant measure of leadership ability (Yoder 1989). When women were accepted as West Point cadets, it became clear that the tests of physical competence, such as rapidly scaling an eight-foot wall, had been constructed for male physiques—pulling oneself up and over using upper-body strength. Rather than devise tests of physical competence for women, West Point provided boosters that mostly women used—but that lost them test points in the case of the wall, a platform. Finally, the women themselves figured out how to use their bodies successfully. Janice Yoder describes this situation:

I was observing this obstacle one day, when a woman approached the wall in the old prescribed way, got her fingertips grip, and did an unusual thing: she walked her dangling legs up the wall until she was in a position where both her hands and feet were atop the wall. She then simply pulled up her sagging bottom and went over. She solved the problem by capitalizing on one of women's physical assets: lower-body strength. (1989, 530)

In short, if West Point is going to measure leadership capability by physical strength, women's pelvises will do just as well as men's shoulders.

The social transformation of female and male physiology into a condition of inequality is well illustrated by the bathroom problem. Most buildings that have gender-segregated bathrooms have an equal number for women and for men. Where there are crowds, there are always long lines in front of women's bathrooms but rarely in front of men's bathrooms. The cultural, physiological, and demographic combinations of clothing, frequency of urination, menstruation, and child care add up to generally greater bathroom use by women than men. Thus, although an equal number of bathrooms seems fair, equity would mean more women's bathrooms or allowing women to use men's bathrooms for a certain amount of time (Molotch 1988).

The bathroom problem is the outcome of the way gendered bodies are differentially evaluated in Western cultures: Men's social bodies are the measure of what is "human." Gray's *Anatomy*, in use for 100 years, well into the twentieth century, presented the human body as male. The female body was shown only where it differed from the male (Laqueur 1990, 166–67). Denise Riley says that if we envisage women's bodies, men's bodies, and human bodies "as a triangle of identifications, then it is rarely an equilateral triangle in which both sexes are pitched at matching distances from the apex of the human" (1988, 197). Catharine MacKinnon also contends that in Western society, universal "humanness" is male because

> virtually every quality that distinguishes men from women is already affirmatively compensated in this society. Men's physiology defines most sports, their needs define auto and health insurance coverage, their socially defined biographies define workplace expectations and successful career pattens, their perspectives and concerns define quality in scholarship, their experiences and obsessions define merit, their objectification of life defines art, their military service defines citizenship, their presence defines family, their inability to get along with each other—their wars and rulerships—define history, their image defines god, and their genitals define sex. For each of their differences from women, what amounts to an affirmative action plan is in effect, otherwise known as the structure and values of American society. (1987, 36)

The Paradox of Human Nature

Gendered people do not emerge from physiology or hormones but from the exigencies of the social order, mostly, from the need for a reliable division of the work of food production and the social (not physical) reproduction of new members. The moral imperatives of religion and cultural representations reinforce the boundary lines among genders and ensure that what is demanded, what is permitted, and what is tabooed for the people in each gender is well-known and followed by most. Political power, control of scarce resources, and, if necessary, violence uphold the gendered social order in the face of resistance and rebellion. Most people, however, voluntarily go along with their society's prescriptions for those of their gender status because the norms and expectations get built into their sense of worth and identity as a certain kind of human being and because they believe their society's way is the natural way. These beliefs emerge from the imagery that pervades the way we think, the way we see and hear and speak, the way we fantasize, and the way we feel. There is no core or bedrock human nature below these endlessly looping processes of the social production of sex and gender, self and other, identity and psyche, each of which is a "complex cultural construction" (Butler 1990, 36). The paradox of "human nature" is that it is always a manifestation of cultural meanings, social relationships, and power politics—"not biology, but culture, becomes destiny" (Butler 1990, 8).

Feminist inquiry has long questioned the conventional categories of social science, but much of the current work in feminist sociology has not gone beyond adding the universal category "women" to the universal category "men." Our current debates over the global assumptions of only two categories and the insistence that they must be nuanced to include race and class are steps in the direction I would like to see feminist research go, but race and class are also global categories (Collins 1990; Spelman 1988). Deconstructing sex, sexuality, and gender reveals many possible categories embedded in the social experiences and social practices of what Dorothy Smith calls the "everyday/everynight world" (1990, 31–57). These emergent categories group some people together for comparison with other people without prior assumptions about who is like whom. Categories can be broken up and people regrouped differently into new categories for comparison. This process of discovering categories from similarities and differences in people's behavior or responses can be more meaningful for feminist research than discovering similarities and differences between "females" and "males" or "women" and "men" because the social construction of the conventional sex and gender categories already assumes differences between them and similarities among them. When we rely only on the conventional categories of sex and gender, we end up finding what we looked for—we see what we believe, whether it is that "females" and "males" are essentially different or that "women" and "men" are essentially the same.

References

Birrell, Susan J. 1988. Discourses on the gender/sport relationship: From women in sport to gender relations. In *Exercise and Sport Science Reviews*, Vol. 16, edited by Kent Pandolf. New York: Macmillan.

Birrell, Susan J., and Sheryl L. Cole. 1990. Double fault: Renée Richards and the construction and naturalization of difference. *Sociology of Sport Journal* 7:1–21.

Boutilier, Mary A., and Lucinda SanGiovanni. 1983. *The Sporting Woman*. Champaign, IL: Human Kinetics.

Brozan, Nadine. 1978. Training linked to disruption of female reproductive cycle. *New York Times*, 17 April.

Butler, Judith. 1990. *Gender Trouble: Feminism and the Subversion of Identity*. New York and London: Routledge & Kegan Paul.

Carlson, Alison. 1991. When is a woman not a woman? *Women's Sport and Fitness*, March:24–29.

Cockburn, Cynthia. 1983. *Brothers: Male Dominance and Technological Change*. London: Pluto.

———— 1985. *Machinery of Dominance: Women, Men and Technical Know-how*. London: Pluto.

Collins, Patricia Hill. 1990. *Black Feminist Thought: Knowledge, Consciousness, and the Politics of Empowerment*. Boston: Unwin Hyman.

Connell, R. W. 1987. *Gender and Power*. Stanford, CA: Stanford University Press.

Donato, Katharine M. 1990. Programming for change? The growing demand for women systems analysts. In *Job Queues, Gender Queues: Explaining Women's Inroads into Male Occupations*, edited by Barbara F. Reskin and Patricia A. Roos. Philadelphia: Temple University Press.

Duff, Robert W., and Lawrence K. Hong. 1984. Self-images of women bodybuilders. *Sociology of Sport Journal* 2:374–80.

Dunning, Eric. 1986. Sport as a male preserve: Notes on the social sources of masculine identity and its transformations. *Theory, Culture and Society* 3:79–90.

Eitzen, D. Stanley, and Maxine Baca Zinn. 1989. The deathleticization of women: The naming and gender marking of collegiate sport teams. *Sociology of Sport Journal* 6:362–70.

English, Jane. 1982. Sex equality in sports. In *Femininity, Masculinity, and Androgyny*, edited by Mary Vetterling-Braggin. Boston: Littlefield, Adams.

Epstein, Cynthia Fuchs. 1988. *Deceptive Distinctions: Sex, Gender and the Social Order*. New Haven, CT: Yale University Press.

Fausto-Sterling, Anne. 1985. *Myths of Gender: Biological Theories about Women and Men*. New York: Basic Books.

Fine, Gary Alan. 1987. *With the Boys: Little League Baseball and Preadolescent Culture*. Chicago: University of Chicago Press.

Foucault, Michel. 1978. *The History of Sexuality: An Introduction*, translated by Robert Hurley. New York: Pantheon.

Gelman, Susan A., Pamela Collman, and Eleanor E. Maccoby. 1986. Inferring properties from categories versus inferring categories from properties: The case of gender. *Child Development* 57:396–404.

Gilbert, Sandra M. 1983. Soldier's heart: Literary men, literary women, and the Great War. *Signs: Journal of Women in Culture and Society* 8:422–50.

Glassner, Barry. 1992. Men and muscles. In *Men's Lives*, edited by Michael S. Kimmel and Michael A. Messner. New York: Macmillan.

Hargreaves, Jennifer A., ed. 1982. *Sport, Culture, and Ideology*. London: Routledge & Kegan Paul.

————. 1986. Where's the virtue? Where's the grace? A discussion of the social production of gender relations in and through sport. *Theory, Culture, and Society* 3:109–21.

Hartmann, Heidi I., ed. 1987. *Computer Chips and Paper Clips: Technology and Women's Employment*. Vol. 2. Washington, DC: National Academy Press.

Hartmann, Heidi I., Robert E. Kraut, and Louise A. Tilly, eds. 1986. *Computer Chips and Paper Clips: Technology and Women's employment*. Vol. 1. Washington, DC: National Academy Press.

Haskell, Molly. 1989. Hers: He drives me crazy. *New York Times Magazine*, 24 September, 26, 28.

Hudson, Jackie. 1978. Physical parameters used for female exclusion from law enforcement and athletics. In *Women and Sport: From Myth to Reality*, edited by Carole A Oglesby. Philadelphia: Lea and Febiger.

Hyde, Janet Shibley. 1990. Meta-analysis and the psychology of gender differences. *Signs: Journal of Women in Culture and Society* 16:55–73.

Jaggar, Alison M. 1983. *Feminist Politics and Human Nature*. Totowa, NJ: Rowman & Allanheld.

Janofsky, Michael. 1992. Yamaguchi has the delicate and golden touch. *New York Times*, 22 February.

Kemper, Theodore D. 1990. *Social Structure and Testosterone: Explorations of the Socio-biosocial Chain*. New Brunswick, NJ: Rutgers University Press.

Kessler, Suzanne J. 1990. The medical construction of gender: Case management of intersexed infants. *Signs: Journal of Women in Culture and Society* 16:3–26.

Kessler, Suzanne J., and Wendy McKenna. [1978] 1985. *Gender: An Ethnomethodological Approach*. Chicago: University of Chicago Press.

Kolata, Gina. 1992. Track federation urges end to gene test for femaleness. *New York Times*, 12 February.

Kramer, Pamela E., and Sheila Lehman. 1990. Mismeasuring women: A critique of research on computer ability and avoidance. *Signs: Journal of Women in Culture and Society* 16:158–72.

Laqueur, Thomas. 1990. *Making Sex: Body and Gender from the Greeks to Freud*. Cambridge, MA: Harvard University Press.

Levesque-Lopman, Louise. 1988. *Claiming Reality: Phenomenology and Women's Experience*. Totowa, NJ: Rowman & Littlefield.

MacKinnon, Catherine. 1987. *Feminisms Unmodified*. Cambridge, MA: Harvard University Press.

Majors, Richard. 1990. Cool pose: Black masculinity in sports. In *Sport, Men and the Gender Order: Critical Feminist Perspectives*, edited by Michael A. Messner and Donald F. Sabo. Champaign, IL: Human Kinetics.

Mangan, J. A., and Roberta J. Park. 1987. *From Fair Sex to Feminism: Sport and the Socialization of Women in the Industrial and Post-industrial Eras*. London: Frank Cass.

Messner, Michael A. 1988. Sports and male domination: The female athlete as contested ideological terrain. *Sociology of Sport Journal* 5:197–211.

———. 1992. *Power at Play: Sports and the Problem of Masculinity*. Boston: Beacon Press.

Messner, Michael A., Margaret Carlisle Duncan, and Kerry Jensen. 1993. Separating the men from the girls: The gendered language of television sports. *Gender & Society* 7:121–37.

Messner, Michael A., and Donald F. Sabo, eds., 1990. *Sport, Men, and the Gender Order: Critical Feminist Perspectives*. Champaign, IL: Human Kinetics.

Molotch, Harvey. 1988. The restroom and equal opportunity. *Sociological Forum* 3:128–32.

Money, John, and Anke A. Ehrhardt. 1972. *Man & Woman, Boy & Girl*. Baltimore, MD: Johns Hopkins University Press.

Moran, Malcolm. 1992. Title IX: A 20-year search for equity. *New York Times*, sports section, 21, 22, 23 June.

Naftolin, F., and E. Butz, eds. 1981. Sexual dimorphism. *Science* 211:1263–1324.

Olson, Wendy. 1990. Beyond Title IX: Toward an agenda for women and sports in the 1990s. *Yale Journal of Law and Feminism* 3:105–51.

Perry, Ruth, and Lisa Greber. 1990. Women and computers: An introduction. *Signs: Journal of Women in Culture and Society* 16:74–101.

Prior, Jerilynn C., Yvette M. Yigna, Martin T. Shechter, and Arthur E. Burgess. 1990. Spinal bone loss and ovulatory disturbances. *New England Journal of Medicine* 323:1221–27.

Richards, Renée, with Jack Ames. 1983. *Second Serve*. New York: Stein and Day.

Riley, Denise. 1988. *Am I That name? Feminism and the Category of Women in History*. Minneapolis: University of Minnesota Press.

Scharff, Virginia. 1991. *Taking the Wheel: Women and the Coming of the Motor Age*. New York: Free Press.

Slatton, Bonnie, and Susan Birrel. 1984. The politics of women's sport. *Arena Review* 8 (July):entire issue.

Smith, Dorothy E. 1990. *The Conceptual Practices of Power: A Feminist Sociology of Knowledge*. Toronto: University of Toronto Press.

Spelman, Elizabeth. 1988. *Inessential Woman: Problems of Exclusion in Feminist Thought*. Boston: Beacon Press.

Theberge, Nancy. 1987. Sport and women's empowerment. *Women Studies International Forum* 10:387–93.

Vecsey, George. 1990. Cathy Rigby, unlike Peter, did grow up. *New York Times*, sports section, 19 December.

Watson, Tracey. 1987. Women athletes and athletic women: The dilemmas and contradictions of managing incongruent identities. *Sociological Inquiry* 57:431–46.

Willis, Paul. 1982. Women in sport in ideology. In *Sport, Culture, and Ideology*, edited by Jennifer A. Hargreaves. London: Routledge & Kegan Paul.

Wright, Barbara Drygulski, et al., eds. 1987. *Women, Work, and Technology: Transformations*. Ann Arbor: University of Michigan Press.

Yoder, Janice D. 1989. Women at West Point: Lessons for token women in male-dominated occupations. In *Women: A Feminist Perspective*, edited by Jo Freeman, 4th ed. Palo Alto, CA: Mayfield.

Zimmerman, Jan, ed. 1983. *The Technological Woman: Interfacing with Tomorrow*. New York: Praeger.

3

Becoming a Gendered Body

Practices of Preschools

KARIN A. MARTIN

The previous article laid the theoretical groundwork for understanding how both sex and gender categories are socially constructed. In this article, Karin A. Martin uses her in-depth observations of preschools to illustrate how this process works in practice. Challenging our typical image of preschools as places where children freely play and explore, Martin illustrates how instead preschools serve as places where children learn bodily discipline. As she shows, preschool teachers use subtle (and not so subtle) rewards and punishments to teach girls to dress up, sit quietly, restrain their voices, and otherwise act "feminine," while encouraging boys to reject femininity and to act "masculine."

Through these actions, Martin argues, children from very young ages learn to "do gender" or to "perform gender"—two terms used more or less interchangeably by scholars to refer to the (somewhat) conscious actions individuals take to mark their selves and their bodies as "properly" masculine or feminine. For example, women "do gender" whenever they put on lipstick and men "do gender" whenever they refrain from crying during sad movies. Similarly, Martin notes, in part through preschool training, gender becomes embodied in both girls and boys. By this she means that our gender comes to seem as much part of our bodies and our very selves as does our skin or our feelings about chocolate. By molding children at such young ages to conform to gender norms, Martin argues, preschools help to convince the rest of us that the differences between girls and boys, men and women, are natural, rather than socially constructed.

Social science research about bodies often focuses on women's bodies, particularly the parts of women's bodies that are most explicitly different from men's—their reproductive capacities and sexuality (E. Martin 1987; K. Martin 1996; but see Connell 1987, 1995). Men and women in the United States also hold and move their bodies differently (Birdwhistell 1970; Henley 1977; Young 1990); these differences are sometimes related to sexuality (Haug 1987) and sometimes not. On the whole, men and women sit, stand, gesture, walk, and throw differently. Generally, women's bodies are confined, their movements restricted. For example, women take smaller steps than men, sit in closed positions (arms and legs crossed across the body), take up less physical space than men, do not step, twist, or throw from the shoulder when throwing a ball, and are generally tentative when using their bodies (Birdwhistell 1970; Henley 1977; Young 1990). Some of these differences, particularly differences in motor skills (e.g., jumping, running, throwing) are seen in early childhood (Thomas and French 1985). Of course, within gender, we may find individual differences, differences based on race, class, and sexuality, and differences based on size and shape of body. Yet, on average, men and women move differently.

Such differences may seem trivial in the large scheme of gender inequality. However, theoretical work by social scientists and feminists suggests that these differences may be consequential. Bodies are (unfinished) resources (Shilling 1993, 103) that must be "trained, manipulated, cajoled, coaxed, organized and in general disciplined" (Turner 1992, 15). We use our bodies to construct our means of living, to take care of each other, to pleasure each other. According to Turner, "...social life depends upon the successful presenting, monitoring and interpreting of bodies" (p. 15). Similarly, according to Foucault (1979), controlled and disciplined bodies do more than regulate the individual body. A disciplined body creates a context for social relations. Gendered (along with "raced" and "classed") bodies create particular contexts for social relations as they signal, manage, and negotiate information about power and status. Gender relations depend on the successful gender presentation, monitoring, and interpretation of bodies (West and Zimmerman 1987). Bodies that clearly delineate gender status facilitate the maintenance of the gender hierarchy.

Our bodies are also one *site* of gender. Much postmodern feminist work (Butler 1990, 1993) suggests that gender is a performance. Microsociological work (West and Zimmerman 1987) suggest that gender is something that is "done." These two concepts, "gender performance" and "doing gender," are similar—both suggest that managed, adorned, fashioned, properly comported and moving bodies establish gender and gender relations.

Other feminist theorists (Connell 1987, 1995; Young 1990) argue that gender rests not only on the surface of the body, in performance and doing, but becomes *embodied*—becomes deeply part of whom we are physically and psychologically. According to Connell, gender becomes embedded in body postures, musculature, and tensions in our bodies.

> The social definition of men as holders of power is translated not only into mental body-images and fantasies, but into muscle tensions, posture, the feel and texture of the body. This is one of the main ways in which the power of men becomes naturalized.... (Connell 1987, 85)

Connell (1995) suggests that masculine gender is partly a feel to one's body and that bodies are often a source of power for men. Young (1990), however, argues that bodies serve the opposite purpose for women—women's bodies are often sources of anxiety and tentativeness. She suggests that women's lack of confidence and agency are embodied and stem from an inability to move confidently in space, to take up space, to use one's body to its fullest extent. Young (1990) suggests "that the general lack of confidence that we [women] frequently have about our cognitive or leadership abilities is traceable in part to an original doubt of our body's capacity" (p. 156). Thus, these theorists suggest that gender differences in minute bodily behaviors like gesture, stance, posture, step, and throwing are significant to our understanding of gendered selves and gender inequality. This feminist theory, however, focuses on adult bodies.

Theories of the body need gendering, and feminist theories of gendered bodies need "childrening" or accounts of development. How do adult gendered bodies become gendered, if they are not naturally so? Scholars run the risk of continuing to view gendered bodies as natural if they ignore the processes that produce gendered adult bodies. Gendering of the body in childhood is the foundation on which further gendering of the body occurs throughout the life course. The gendering of children's bodies makes gender differences feel and appear natural, which allows for such bodily differences to emerge throughout the life course.

I suggest that the hidden school curriculum of disciplining the body is gendered and contributes to the embodiment of gender in childhood, making gendered bodies appear and feel natural. Sociologists of education have demonstrated that schools have hidden curriculums (Giroux and Purpel 1983; Jackson 1968). Hidden curriculums are covert lessons that schools teach, and they are often a means of social control. These curriculums include teaching about work differentially by class (Anyon 1980; Bowles and Gintis 1976; Carnoy and Levin 1985), political socialization (Wasburn 1986), and training in obedience and docility (Giroux and Purpel 1983). More recently, some theorists and researchers have examined the curriculum that disciplines the body (Carere 1987; Foucault 1979; McLaren 1986). This curriculum demands the practice of bodily control in congruence with the goals of the school as an institution. It reworks the students from the outside in on the presumption that to shape the body is to shape the mind (Carere 1987). In such a curriculum teachers constantly monitor kids' bodily movements, comportment, and practices. Kids begin their day running wildly about the school grounds. Then this hidden curriculum funnels the kids into line, through the hallways, quietly into a classroom, sitting upright at their desks, focused at the front of the room, "ready to learn" (Carere 1987; McLaren 1986). According to Carere (1987), this curriculum of disciplining the body serves the curriculums that seek to shape the mind and renders children physically ready for cognitive learning.

I suggest that this hidden curriculum that controls children's bodily practices serves also to turn kids who are similar in bodily comportment, movement, and practice into girls and boys, children whose bodily practices are different. Schools are not the only producers of these differences. While the process ordinarily begins in the family, the schools' hidden curriculum further facilitates and encourages the construction of bodily differences between the genders and makes these physical differences appear and feel natural. Finally, this curriculum may be more or less hidden depending on the particular preschool and particular teachers. Some schools and teachers may see teaching children to behave like "young ladies" and "young gentlemen" as an explicit part of their curriculums.

Data and Method

The data for this study come from extensive and detailed semistructured field observations of five preschool classrooms of three to five-year-olds in a midwestern city. Four of the classrooms were part of a preschool (Preschool A) located close to the campus of a large university. A few of the kids were children of faculty members, more were children of staff and administrators, and many were not associated with the university. Many of the kids who attended Preschool A attended part-time. Although teachers at this school paid some attention to issues of race and gender equity, issues of diversity were not as large a part of the curriculum as they are at some preschools (Jordan and Cowan 1995; Van Ausdale and Feagin 1996). The fifth classroom was located at Preschool B, a preschool run by a Catholic church in the same city as Preschool A. The kids who attended Preschool B were children of young working professionals, many of whom lived in the vicinity of the preschool. These children attended preschool "full-time"—five days a week for most of the day....

A total 112 children and fourteen different teachers (five head teachers and nine aides) were observed in these classrooms. All teachers were female....

A research assistant and I observed in these classrooms about three times a week for eight months. Our observations were as unobtrusive as possible, and we interacted little with the kids.... We observed girls and boys for equal amounts of time, and we heeded Thorne's (1993) caution about the "big man bias" in field research and were careful not to observe only the most active, outgoing, "popular" kids. . . .

Results

Children's bodies are disciplined by schools. Children are physically active, and institutions like schools impose disciplinary controls that regulate children's bodies and prepare children for the larger social world. While this disciplinary control produces docile bodies (Foucault 1979), it also produces gendered bodies. As these disciplinary practices operate in different contexts, some bodies become more docile than others. I examine how the following practices contribute to a gendering of children's bodies in preschool: the effects of dressing-up or bodily adornment, the gendered nature of formal and relaxed behaviors, how the different restrictions on girls' and boys' voices limit their physicality, how teachers instruct girls' and boys' bodies, and the gendering of physical interactions between children and teachers and among the children themselves.

Bodily Adornment: Dressing Up

Perhaps the most explicit way that children's bodies become gendered is through their clothes and other bodily adornments. Here I discuss how parents gender their children through their clothes, how children's dress-up play experiments with making bodies feminine and masculine, and how this play, when it is gender normative, shapes girls' and boys' bodies differently, constraining girls' physicality.

DRESSING UP (I). The clothes that parents send kids to preschool in shape children's experiences of their bodies in gendered ways. Clothes, particularly their color, signify a child's gender; gender in preschool is in fact color-coded. On average, about 61 percent of the girls wore pink clothing each day. Boys were more likely to wear primary colors, black, florescent green, and orange. Boys never wore pink.

> The teacher is asking each kid during circle (the part of the day that includes formal instruction by the teacher while the children sit in a circle) what their favorite color is. Adam says black. Bill says "every color that's not pink." (Five-year-olds)

Fourteen percent of three-year-old girls wore dresses each day compared to 32 percent of five-year-old girls. Wearing a dress limited girls' physicality in preschool. However, it is not only the dress itself, but knowledge about how to behave in a dress that is restrictive. Many girls already knew that some behaviors were not allowed in a dress. This knowledge probably comes from the families who dress their girls in dresses.

Vicki, wearing leggings and a dress-like shirt, is leaning over the desk to look into a "tunnel" that some other kids have built. As she leans, her dress/shirt rides up exposing her back. Jennifer (another child) walks by Vicki and as she does she pulls Vicki's shirt back over her bare skin and gives it a pat to keep it in place. It looks very much like something one's mother might do. (Five-year-olds)

Four girls are sitting at a table—Cathy, Kim, Danielle, and Jesse. They are cutting play money out of paper. Cathy and Danielle have on overalls and Kim and Jesse have on dresses. Cathy puts her feet up on the table and crosses her legs at the ankle; she leans back in her chair and continues cutting her money. Danielle imitates her. They look at each other and laugh. They put their shoulders back, posturing, having fun with this new way of sitting. Kim and Jesse continue to cut and laugh with them, but do not put their feet up. (Five-year-olds)

Dresses are restrictive in other ways as well. They often are worn with tights that are experienced as uncomfortable and constraining. I observed girls constantly pulling at and rearranging their tights, trying to untwist them or pull them up. Because of their discomfort, girls spent much time attuned to and arranging their clothing and/or their bodies.

Dresses also can be lifted up, an embarrassing thing for five-year-olds if done purposely by another child. We witnessed this on only one occasion—a boy pulled up the hem of a girl's skirt. The girl protested and the teacher told him to stop and that was the end of it. Teachers, however, lifted up girls' dresses frequently—to see if a child was dressed warmly enough, while reading a book about dresses, to see if a child was wet. Usually this was done without asking the child and was more management of the child rather than an interaction with her. Teachers were much more likely to manage girls and their clothing this way—rearranging their clothes, tucking in their shirts, fixing a ponytail gone astray. Such management often puts girls' bodies under the control of another and calls girls' attentions to their appearances and bodily adornments.

DRESSING UP (2). Kids like to *play* dress-up in preschool, and all the classrooms had a dress-up corner with a variety of clothes, shoes, pocketbooks, scarves, and hats for dressing up. Classrooms tended to have more women's clothes than men's, but there were some of both, as well as some gender-neutral clothes—capes, hats, and vests that were not clearly for men or women—and some items that were clearly costumes, such as masks of cats and dogs and clip-on tails. Girls tended to play dress-up more than boys—over one-half of dressing up was done by girls. Gender differences in the amount of time spent playing dress-up seemed to increase from age three to age five. We only observed the five-year-old boys dressing up or using clothes or costumes in their play three times, whereas three-year-old boys dressed up almost weekly. Five-year-old boys also did not dress up elaborately, but used one piece of clothing to animate their play. Once Phil wore large, men's winter ski gloves when he played monster. Holding up his now large, chiseled looking hands, he stomped around the classroom making monster sounds. On another occasion Brian, a child new to the classroom who attended only two days a week, walked around by himself for a long time carrying a silver pocketbook and hovering first at the edges of girls' play and then at the edges of boys' play. On the third occasion, Sam used ballet slippers to animate his play in circle.

When kids dressed up, they played at being a variety of things from kitty cats and puppies to monsters and superheroes to "fancy ladies." Some of this play was not explicitly gendered. For example, one day in November I observed three girls wearing "turkey hats" they had made. They spent a long time gobbling at each other and playing at being turkeys, but there was nothing explicitly gendered about their play. However, this kind of adornment was not the most frequent type. Children often seemed to experiment with both genders when they played dress-up. The three-year-olds tended to be more experimental in their gender dress-up than the five-year-olds, perhaps because teachers encouraged it more at this age.

> Everett and Juan are playing dress-up. Both have on "dresses" made out of material that is wrapped around them like a toga or sarong. Everett has a pocketbook and a camera over his shoulder and Juan has a pair of play binoculars on a strap over his. Everett has a scarf around his head and cape on. Juan has on big, green sunglasses. Pam (teacher) tells them, "You guys look great! Go look in the mirror." They shuffle over to the full-length mirror and look at themselves and grin, and make adjustments to their costumes. (Three-year-olds)

The five-year-old children tended to dress-up more gender normatively. Girls in particular played at being adult women.

> Frances is playing dress-up. She is walking in red shoes and carrying a pocketbook. She and two other girls, Jen and Rachel, spend between five and ten minutes looking at and talking about the guinea pigs. Then they go back to dress-up. Frances and Rachel practice walking in adult women's shoes. Their body movements are not a perfect imitation of an adult woman's walk in high heels, yet it does look like an attempt to imitate such a walk. Jen and Rachel go back to the guinea pigs, and Frances, now by herself, is turning a sheer, frilly lavender shirt around and around and around trying to figure out how to put it on. She gets it on and looks at herself in the mirror. She adds a sheer pink and lavender scarf and pink shoes. Looks in the mirror again. She walks, twisting her body—shoulders, hips, shoulders, hips—not quite a (stereotypic) feminine walk, but close. Walking in big shoes makes her take little bitty steps, like walking in heels. She shuffles in the too big shoes out into the middle of the classroom and stops by a teacher. Laura (a teacher) says, "don't you look fancy, all pink and purple." Frances smiles up at her and walks off, not twisting so much this time. She goes back to the

mirror and adds a red scarf. She looks in the mirror and is holding her arms across her chest to hold the scarf on (she can't tie it) and she is holding it with her chin too. She shuffles to block area where Jen is and then takes the clothes off and puts them back in dress-up area. (Five-year-olds)

I observed not only the children who dressed up, but the reaction of those around them to their dress. This aspect proved to be one of the most interesting parts of kids' dress-up play. Children interpreted each others' bodily adornments as gendered, even when other interpretations were plausible. For instance, one day just before Halloween, Kim dressed up and was "scary" because she was dressed as a woman:

Kim has worn a denim skirt and tights to school today. Now she is trying to pull on a ballerina costume–pink and ruffly—over her clothes. She has a hard time getting it on. It's tight and wrinkled up and twisted when she gets it on. Her own clothes are bunched up under it. Then she puts on a mask—a woman's face. The mask material itself is a clear plastic so that skin shows through, but is sculpted to have a very Anglo nose and high cheek bones. It also has thin eyebrows, blue eye shadow, blush, and lipstick painted on it. The mask is bigger than Kim's face and head. Kim looks at herself in the mirror and spends the rest of the play time with this costume on. Intermittently she picks up a plastic pumpkin since it is Halloween season and carries that around too. Kim walks around the classroom for a long time and then runs through the block area wearing this costume. Jason yells, "Ugh! There's a woman!" He and the other boys playing blocks shriek and scatter about the block area. Kim runs back to the dress-up area as they yell. Then throughout the afternoon she walks and skips through the center of the classroom, and every time she comes near the block boys one of them yells, "Ugh, there's the woman again!" The teacher even picks up on this and says to Kim twice, "Woman, slow down." (Five-year-olds)

The boys' shrieks indicated that Kim was scary, and this scariness is linked in their comments about her being a woman. It seems equally plausible that they could have interpreted her scary dress as a "trick-or-treater," given that it was close to Halloween and she was carrying a plastic pumpkin that kids collect candy in, or that they might have labeled her a dancer or ballerina because she was wearing a tutu. Rather, her scary dress-up was coded for her by others as "woman."

Other types of responses to girls dressing up also seemed to gender their bodies and to constrain them. For example, on two occasions I saw a teacher tie the arms of girls' dress-up shirts together so that the girls could not move their arms. They did this in fun, of course, and untied them as soon as the girls wanted them to, but I never witnessed this constraining of boys' bodies in play.

Thus, how parents gender children's bodies through dressing them and the ways children experiment with bodily adornments by dressing up make girls' and boys' bodies different and seem different to those around them. Adorning a body often genders it explicitly—signifies that it is a feminine or masculine body. Adornments also make girls' movements smaller, leading girls to take up less space with their bodies and disallowing some types of movements.

Formal and Relaxed Behaviors

Describing adults, Goffman (1959) defines front stage and backstage behavior:

> The backstage language consists of reciprocal first-naming, co-operative decision making, profanity, open sexual remarks, elaborate gripping, smoking, rough informal dress, "sloppy" sitting and standing posture, use of dialect or substandard speech, mumbling and shouting, playful aggressivity and "kidding," inconsiderateness for the other in minor but potentially symbolic acts, minor physical self-involvements such as humming, whistling, chewing, nibbling, belching, and flatulence. The front stage behavior language can be taken as the absence (and in some sense the opposite) of this. (p. 128)

Thus, one might not expect much front stage or formal behavior in preschool, and often, especially during parents' drop-off and pick-up time, this was the case. But a given region of social life may sometimes be a backstage and sometimes a front stage. I identified several behaviors that were expected by the teachers, required by the institution, or that would be required in many institutional settings, as formal behavior. Raising one's hand, sitting "on your bottom" (not on your knees, not squatting, not lying down, not standing) during circle, covering one's nose and mouth when coughing or sneezing, or sitting upright in a chair are all formal behaviors of preschools, schools, and to some extent the larger social world. Crawling on the floor, yelling, lying down during teachers' presentations, and running through the classroom are examples of relaxed behaviors that are not allowed in preschool, schools, work settings, and many institutions of the larger social world (Henley 1977). Not all behaviors fell into one of these classifications. When kids were actively engaged in playing at the water table, for example, much of their behavior was not clearly formal or relaxed. I coded as formal and relaxed behaviors those behaviors that would be seen as such if done by adults (or children in many cases) in other social institutions for which children are being prepared.

In the classrooms in this study, boys were allowed and encouraged to pursue relaxed behaviors in a variety of ways that girls were not. Girls were more likely to be encouraged to pursue more formal behaviors. Eighty-two percent of all formal behaviors observed in these classrooms were done by girls, and only 18 percent by boys. However, 80 percent of the behaviors coded as relaxed were boys' behaviors.

These observations do not tell us *why* boys do more relaxed behaviors and girls do more formal behaviors. Certainly many parents and others would argue that boys are more predisposed to sloppy postures, crawling on the floor, and so on. However, my observations suggest that teachers help construct this gender difference in bodily behaviors. Teachers were more likely to reprimand girls for relaxed bodily movements and comportment. Sadker and Sadker (1994) found a similar result with respect to hand-raising for answering teachers' questions—if hand raising is considered a formal behavior and calling out a relaxed behavior, they find that boys are more likely to call out without raising their hands and demand attention:

> Sometimes what they [boys] say has little or nothing to do with the teacher's questions. Whether male comments are insightful or irrelevant, teachers respond to them. However, when girls call out, there is a fascinating occurrence: Suddenly the teacher remembers the rule about raising your hand before you talk. (Sadker and Sadker 1994, 43)

This gendered dynamic of hand-raising exists even in preschool, although our field notes do not provide enough systematic recording of hand-raising to fully assess it. However, such a dynamic applies to many bodily movements and comportment:

> The kids are sitting with their legs folded in a circle listening to Jane (the teacher) talk about dinosaurs. ("Circle" is the most formal part of their preschool education each day and is like sitting in class.) Sam has the ballet slippers on his hands and is clapping them together really loudly. He stops and does a half-somersault backward out of the circle and stays that way with his legs in the air. Jane says nothing and continues talking about dinosaurs. Sue, who is sitting next to Sam, pushes his leg out of her way. Sam sits up and is now busy trying to put the ballet shoes on over his sneakers, and he is looking at the other kids and laughing, trying to get a reaction. He is clearly not paying attention to Jane's dinosaur story and is distracting the other kids. Sam takes the shoes and claps them together again. Jane leans over and tells him to give her the shoes. Sam does, and then lies down all stretched out on the floor, arms over his head, legs apart. Adam is also lying down now, and Keith is on Sara's (the teacher's aide) lap. Rachel takes her sweater off and folds it up. The other children are focused on the teacher. After about five minutes, Jane tells Sam "I'm going to ask you to sit up." (She doesn't say anything to Adam.) But he doesn't move. Jane ignores Sam and Adam and continues with the lesson. Rachel now lies down on her back. After about ten seconds Jane says, "Sit up, Rachel." Rachel sits up and listens to what kind of painting the class will do today. (Five-year-olds)

Sam's behavior had to be more disruptive, extensive, and informal than Rachel's for the teacher to instruct him and his bodily movements to be quieter and for him to comport his body properly for circle. Note that the boys who were relaxed but not disruptive were not instructed to sit properly.

It was also common for a teacher to tell a boy to stop some bodily behavior and for the boy to ignore the request and the teacher not to enforce her instructions, although she frequently repeated them.

The gendering of body movements, comportment, and acquisitions of space also happens in more subtle ways. For example, often when there was "free" time, boys spent much more time in child-structured activities than did girls. In one classroom of five-year-olds, boys' "free" time was usually spent building with blocks, climbing on blocks, or crawling on the blocks or on the floor as they worked to build with the blocks whereas girls spent much of their free time sitting at tables cutting things out of paper, drawing, sorting small pieces of blocks into categories, reading stories, and so on. Compared to boys, girls rarely crawled on the floor (except when they played kitty cats). Girls and boys did share some activities. For example, painting and reading were frequently shared, and the three-year-olds often played at fishing from a play bridge together. Following is a list from my field notes of the most common activities boys and girls did during the child-structured activity periods of the day during two randomly picked weeks of observing:

Boys: played blocks (floor), played at the water table (standing and splashing), played superhero (running around and in play house), played with the car garage (floor), painted at the easel (standing).

Girls: played dolls (sitting in chairs and walking around), played dress-up (standing), coloring (sitting at tables), read stories (sitting on the couch), cut out pictures (sitting at tables).

Children sorted themselves into these activities and also were sorted (or not unsorted) by teachers. For example, teachers rarely told the three boys that always played with the blocks that they had to choose a different activity that day. Teachers also encouraged girls to sit at tables by suggesting table activities for them—in a sense giving them less "free" time or structuring their time more.

> It's the end of circle, and Susan (teacher) tells the kids that today they can paint their dinosaur eggs if they want to. There is a table set up with paints and brushes for those who want to do that. The kids listen and then scatter to their usual activities. Several boys are playing blocks, two boys are at the water table. Several girls are looking at the hamsters in their cage and talking about them, two girls are sitting and stringing plastic beads. Susan says across the classroom, "I need some painters, Joy, Amy, Kendall?" The girls leave the hamster cage and go to the painting table. Susan pulls out a chair so Joy can sit down. She tells them about the painting project. (Five-year-olds)

These girls spent much of the afternoon enjoying themselves painting their eggs. Simon and Jack joined them temporarily, but then went back to activities that were not teacher-structured.

Events like these that happen on a regular basis over an extended period of early childhood serve to gender children's bodies—boys come to take up more room with their bodies, to sit in more open positions, and to feel freer to do what they wish with their bodies, even in relatively formal settings. Henley (1977) finds that among adults men generally are more relaxed than women in their demeanor and women tend to have tenser postures. The looseness of body-focused functions (e.g., belching) is also more open to men than to women. In other words, men are more likely to engage in relaxed demeanors, postures, and behaviors. These data suggest that this gendering of bodies into more formal and more relaxed movements, postures, and comportment is (at least partially) constructed in early childhood by institutions like preschools.

Controlling Voice

Speaking (or yelling as is often the case with kids) is a bodily experience that involves mouth, throat, chest, diaphragm, and facial expression. Thorne (1993) writes that an elementary school teacher once told her that kids "reminded her of bumblebees, an apt image of swarms, speed, and constant motion" (p. 15). Missing from this metaphor is the buzz of the bumblebees, as a constant hum of voices comes from children's play and activities. Kids' play that is giggly, loud, or whispery makes it clear that voice is part of their bodily experiences.

Voice is an aspect of bodily experience that teachers and schools are interested in disciplining. Quiet appears to be required for learning in classrooms. Teaching appropriate levels of voice, noise, and sound disciplines children's bodies and prepares them "from the inside" to learn the school's curriculums and to participate in other social institutions.

The disciplining of children's voices is gendered. I found that girls were told to be quiet or to repeat a request in a quieter, "nicer" voice about three times more often than were boys. This finding is particularly interesting because boys' play was frequently much noisier. However, when boys were noisy, they were also often doing other behaviors the teacher did not allow, and perhaps the teachers focused less on voice because they were more concerned with stopping behaviors like throwing or running.

Additionally, when boys were told to "quiet down" they were told in large groups, rarely as individuals. When they were being loud and were told to be quiet, boys were often in the process of enacting what Jordan and Cowan (1995) call warrior narratives:

> A group of three boys is playing with wooden doll figures. The dolls are jumping off block towers, crashing into each other. Kevin declares loudly, "I'm the grown up." Keith replies, "I'm the police." They knock the figures into each other and push each other away. Phil grabs a figure from Keith. Keith picks up two more and bats one with the other toward Phil. Now all three boys are crashing the figures into each other, making them dive

off towers. They're having high fun. Two more boys join the group. There are now five boys playing with the wooden dolls and the blocks. They're breaking block buildings; things are crashing; they're grabbing each other's figures and yelling loudly. Some are yelling "fire, fire" as their figures jump off the block tower. The room is very noisy. (Five-year-olds)

Girls as individuals and in groups were frequently told to lower their voices. Later that same afternoon:

> During snack time the teacher asks the kids to tell her what they like best in the snack mix. Hillary says, "Marshmallows!" loudly, vigorously, and with a swing of her arm. The teacher turns to her and says, "I'm going to ask you to say that quietly," and Hillary repeats it in a softer voice. (Five-year-olds)

These two observations represent a prominent pattern in the data. The boys playing with the wooden figures were allowed to express their fun and enthusiasm loudly whereas Hillary could not loudly express her love of marshmallows. Girls' voices are disciplined to be softer and in many ways less physical—toning down their voices tones down their physicality. Hillary emphasized "marshmallows" with a large swinging gesture of her arm the first time she answered the teacher's question, but after the teacher asked her to say it quietly she made no gestures when answering. Incidents like these that are repeated often in different contexts restrict girls' physicality.

It could be argued that context rather than gender explains the difference in how much noise is allowed in these situations. Teachers may expect more formal behavior from children sitting at the snack table than they do during semistructured activities. However, even during free play girls were frequently told to quiet down:

> Nancy, Susan, and Amy are jumping in little jumps, from the balls of their feet, almost like skipping rope without the rope. Their mouths are open and they're making a humming sound, looking at each other and giggling. Two of them keep sticking their tongues out. They seem to be having great fun. The teacher's aide sitting on the floor in front of them turns around and says, "Shhh, find something else to play. Why don't you play Simon Says?" All three girls stop initially. Then Amy jumps a few more times, but without making the noise. (Five-year-olds)

By limiting the girls' voices, the teacher also limits the girls' jumping and their fun. The girls learn that their bodies are supposed to be quiet, small, and physically constrained. Although the girls did not take the teacher's suggestion to play Simon Says (a game where bodies can be moved only quietly at the order of another), they turn to play that explores quietness yet tries to maintain some of the fun they were having:

> Nancy, Susan, and Amy begin sorting a pile of little-bitty pieces of puzzles, soft blocks, Legos, and so on into categories to "help" the teacher who

> told them to be quiet and to clean up. The three of them and the teacher are standing around a single small desk sorting these pieces. (Meanwhile several boys are playing blocks and their play is spread all over the middle of the room.) The teacher turns her attention to some other children. The girls continue sorting and then begin giggling to each other. As they do, they cover their mouths. This becomes a game as one imitates the other. Susan says something nonsensical that is supposed to be funny, and then she "hee-hees" while covering her mouth and looks at Nancy, to whom she has said it, who covers her mouth and "hee-hees" back. They begin putting their hands/fingers cupped over their mouths and whispering in each others' ears and then giggling quietly. They are intermittently sorting the pieces and playing the whispering game. (Five-year-olds)

Thus, the girls took the instruction to be quiet and turned it into a game. This new game made their behaviors smaller, using hands and mouths rather than legs, feet, and whole bodies. Whispering became their fun, instead of jumping and humming. Besides requiring quiet, this whispering game also was gendered in another way: The girls' behavior seemed to mimic sterotypical female gossiping. They whispered in twos and looked at the third girl as they did it and then changed roles. Perhaps the instruction to be quiet, combined with the female role of "helping," led the girls to one of their understandings of female quietness—gossip—a type of feminine quietness that is perhaps most fun.

Finally, by limiting voice teachers limit one of girls' mechanisms for resisting others' mistreatment of them. Frequently, when a girl had a dispute with another child, teachers would ask the girl to quiet down and solve the problem nicely. Teachers also asked boys to solve problems by talking, but they usually did so only with intense disputes and the instruction to talk things out never carried the instruction to talk *quietly*.

> Keith is persistently threatening to knock over the building that Amy built. He is running around her with a "flying" toy horse that comes dangerously close to her building each time. She finally says, "Stop it!" in a loud voice. The teacher comes over and asks, "How do we say that, Amy?" Amy looks at Keith and says more softly, "Stop trying to knock it over." The teacher tells Keith to find some place else to play. (Five-year-olds)

> Cheryl and Julie are playing at the sand table. Cheryl says to the teacher loudly, "Julie took mine away!" The teacher tells her to say it more quietly. Cheryl repeats it less loudly. The teacher tells her, "Say it a little quieter." Cheryl says it quieter, and the teacher says to Julie, "Please don't take that away from her." (Three-year-olds)

We know that women are reluctant to use their voices to protect themselves from a variety of dangers. The above observations suggest that the denial of women's voices begins at least as early as preschool, and that restricting voice, usually restricts movement as well.

Finally, there were occasions when the quietness requirement did not restrict girls' bodies. One class of three-year-olds included two Asian girls, Diane and Sue, who did not speak English. Teachers tended to talk about them and over them but rarely to them. Although these girls said little to other children and were generally quiet, they were what I term body instigators. They got attention and played with other children in more bodily ways than most girls. For example, Sue developed a game with another girl that was a sort of musical chairs. They'd race from one chair to another to see who could sit down first. Sue initiated this game by trying to squeeze into a chair with the other girl. Also, for example,

> Diane starts peeking into the play cardboard house that is full of boys and one girl. She looks like she wants to go in, but the door is blocked and the house is crowded. She then goes around to the side of the house and stands with her back to it and starts bumping it with her butt. Because the house is cardboard, it buckles and moves as she does it. The teacher tells her, "Stop—no." Diane stops and then starts doing it again but more lightly. All the boys come out of the house and ask her what she's doing. Matt gets right in her face and the teacher tells him, "Tell her no." He does, but all the other boys have moved on to other activities, so she and Matt go in the house together. (Three-year-olds)

Thus, Diane and Sue's lack of voice in this English-speaking classroom led to greater physicality. There may be other ways that context (e.g., in one's neighborhood instead of school) and race, ethnicity, and class shape gender and voice that cannot be determined from these data (Goodwin 1990).

Bodily Instructions

Teachers give a lot of instructions to kids about what to do with their bodies. Of the explicit bodily instructions recorded 65 percent were directed to boys, 26 percent to girls, and the remaining 9 percent were directed to mixed groups. These numbers suggest that boys' bodies are being disciplined more than girls. However, there is more to this story—the types of instructions that teachers give and children's responses to them are also gendered.

First, boys obeyed teachers' bodily instructions about one-half of the time (48 percent), while girls obeyed about 80 percent of the time. Boys may receive more instructions from teachers because they are less likely to follow instructions and thus are told repeatedly. Frequently I witnessed a teacher telling a boy or group of boys to stop doing something—usually running or throwing things—and the teacher repeated these instructions several times in the course of the session before (if ever) taking further action. Teachers usually did not have to repeat instructions to girls—girls either stopped on their own with the first instruction, or because the teacher forced them to stop right then. Serbin (1983) finds that boys receive a higher proportion of teachers' "...loud reprimands, audible to the entire group. Such patterns of response, intended as punishment, have been repeatedly demonstrated to reinforce aggression and other forms of disruptive behavior" (p. 29).

Second, teachers' instructions directed to boys' bodies were less substantive than those directed to girls. That is, teachers' instructions to boys were usually to stop doing something, to end a bodily behavior with little suggestion for other behaviors they might do. Teachers rarely told boys to change a bodily behavior. A list of teachers' instructions to boys includes: stop throwing, stop jumping, stop clapping, stop splashing, no pushing, don't cry, blocks are not for bopping, don't run, don't climb on that. Fifty-seven percent of the instructions that teachers gave boys about their physical behaviors were of this undirected type, compared with 15 percent of their instructions to girls. In other words, teachers' instructions to girls generally were more substantive and more directive, telling girls to do a bodily behavior rather than to stop one. Teachers' instructions to girls suggested that they alter their behaviors. A list of instructions to girls includes: talk to her, don't yell, sit here, pick that up, be careful, be gentle, give it to me, put it down there. Girls may have received fewer bodily instructions than did boys, but they received more directive ones. This gender difference leaves boys a larger range of possibilities of what they might choose to do with their bodies once they have stopped a behavior, whereas girls were directed toward a defined set of options.

Physical Interaction between Teachers and Children

Teachers also physically directed kids. For example, teachers often held kids to make them stop running, tapped them to make them turn around and pay attention, or turned their faces toward them so that they would listen to verbal instructions. One-fourth of all physical contacts between teachers and children was to control children's physicality in some way, and 94 percent of such contacts were directed at boys.

Physical interaction between teachers and children was coded into three categories: positive, negative, or neutral. Physical interaction was coded as positive if it was comforting, helpful, playful, or gentle. It was coded as negative if it was disciplining, assertive (not gentle), restraining, or clearly unwanted by the child (e.g., the child pulled away). Physical interaction was coded as neutral if it seemed to have little content (e.g., shoulders touching during circle, legs touching while a teacher gave a group of kids directions for a project). About one-half of the time, when teachers touched boys or girls, it was positive. For example, the teacher and child might have bodily contact as she tied a shoe, wiped away tears, or tickled a child, or if a child took the teacher's hand or got on her lap. For girls, the remaining physical interactions included 15 percent that were disciplining or instructing the body and about one-third that were neutral (e.g., leaning over the teacher's arm while looking at a book). For boys, these figures were reversed: Only 4 percent of their physical interactions with teachers were neutral in content, and 35 percent were negative and usually included explicit disciplining and instructing of the body.

This disciplining of boys' bodies took a particular form. Teachers usually attempted to restrain or remove boys who had "gone too far" in their play or who had done something that could harm another child:

> Irving goes up to Jack, who is playing dress-up, and puts his arms up, makes a monster face and says, "Aaarhhh!" Jack looks startled. Irving runs and jumps in front of Jack again and says "Aaarrhh!" again. Marie (teacher) comes from behind Irving and holds him by the shoulders and arms from behind. She bends over him and says, "Calm down." He pulls forward, and eventually she lets him go. He runs up to Jack again and growls. Marie says, "He doesn't want you to do that." (Three-year-olds)

As Serbin (1983) suggests, frequent loud reprimands of boys may increase their disruptive behavior; more frequent physical disciplining interactions between teachers and boys may do so as well. Because boys more frequently than girls experienced interactions in which their bodies were physically restrained or disciplined by an adult who had more power and was angry, they may be more likely than girls to associate physical interaction with struggle and anger, and thus may be more likely to be aggressive or disruptive.

Physical Interaction among Children

Thorne (1993) demonstrates that children participate in the construction of gender differences among themselves. The preschool brings together large groups of children who engage in interactions in which they cooperate with the hidden curriculum and discipline each others' bodies in gendered ways, but they also engage in interactions in which they resist this curriculum.

Girls and boys teach their same-sex peers about their bodies and physicality. Children in these observations were much more likely to imitate the physical behavior of a same-sex peer than a cross-sex peer. Children also encourage others to imitate them. Some gendered physicality develops in this way. For example, I observed one boy encouraging other boys to "take up more space" in the same way he was.

> James (one of the most active boys in the class) is walking all over the blocks that Joe, George, and Paul have built into a road. Then he starts spinning around with his arms stretched out on either side of him. He has a plastic toy cow in one hand and is yelling, "Moo." He spins through half of the classroom, other children ducking under his arms or walking around him when he comes near them. Suddenly he drops the cow and still spinning, starts shouting, "I'm a tomato! I'm a tomato!" The three boys who were playing blocks look at him and laugh. James says, "I'm a tomato!" again, and Joe says, "There's the tomato." Joe, George, and Paul continue working on their block road. James then picks up a block and lobs it in their direction and then keeps spinning throughout this half of the classroom saying he's a

tomato. Joe and George look up when the block lands near them and then they get up and imitate James. Now three boys are spinning throughout much of the room, shouting that they are tomatoes. The other children in the class are trying to go about their play without getting hit by a tomato. (Five-year-olds)

The within-gender physicality of three-year-old girls and boys was more similar than it was among the five-year-olds. Among the three-year-old girls there was more rough and tumble play, more physical fighting and arguing among girls than there was among the five-year-old girls.

During clean up, Emily and Sara argue over putting away some rope. They both pull on the ends of the rope until the teacher comes over and separates them. Emily walks around the classroom then, not cleaning anything up. She sings to herself, does a twirl, and gets in line for snack. Sara is behind her in line. Emily pushes Sara. Sara yells, "Aaahh," and hits Emily and pushes her. The teacher takes both of them out of line and talks to them about getting along and being nice to each other. (Three-year-olds)

Shelly and Ann have masks on. One is a kitty and one is a doggy. They're crawling around on the floor, and they begin play wrestling—kitties and doggies fight. The teacher says to them, "Are you ok?" They stop, lift up their masks, and look worried. The teacher says, "Oh, are you wrestling? It's ok, I just wanted to make sure everyone was ok." The girls nod; they're ok. Then, they put their masks back on and crawl on the floor some more. They do not resume wrestling. (Three-year-olds)

From lessons like these, girls have learned by age five that their play with each other should not be "too rough." The physical engagement of girls with each other at age five had little rough-and-tumble play:

Two girls are playing with the dishes and sitting at a table. Keisha touches Alice under the chin, tickles her almost, then makes her eat something pretend, then touches the corners of her mouth, telling her to smile. (Five-year-olds)

I do not mean to suggest that girls' physical engagement with each other is the opposite of boys' or that all of boys' physical contacts were rough and tumble. Boys, especially in pairs, hugged, gently guided, or helped each other climb or jump. But often, especially in groups of three or more and especially among the five-year-olds, boys' physical engagement was highly active, "rough," and frequent. Boys experienced these contacts as great fun and not as hostile or negative in any way. . . .

The physical engagement of boys and girls *with each other* differed from same-sex physical engagement. Because girls' and boys' play is semi-segregated, collisions (literal and figurative) in play happen at the borders of these gender-segregated groups (Maccoby 1988; Thorne 1993). As

Thorne (1993) demonstrates, not all borderwork is negative—40 percent of the physical interactions observed between girls and boys were positive or neutral.

> Ned runs over to Veronica, hipchecks her and says "can I be your friend?" and she says "yes." Ned walks away and kicks the blocks again three to four times. (Five-year-olds)

However, cross-gender interactions were more likely to be negative than same-sex interactions. In fact, physical interactions among children were twice as likely to be a negative interaction if they were between a girl and boy than if they were among same-gender peers. Approximately 30 percent of the interactions among girls and among boys were negative (hostile, angry, controlling, hurtful), whereas 60 percent of mixed-gender physical interactions were negative. Sixty percent of 113 boy-girl physical interactions were initiated by boys, 39 percent were initiated by girls, and only 1 percent of these interactions were mutually initiated.

At the borders of semi-segregated play there are physical interactions about turf and toy ownership:

> Sylvia throws play money on the floor from her play pocketbook. Jon grabs it up. She wrestles him for it and pries it from his hands. In doing this she forces him onto the floor so that he's hunched forward on his knees. She gets behind him and sandwiches him on the floor as she grabs his hands and gets the money loose. Then, two minutes later, she's giving money to kids, and she gives Jon some, but apparently not enough. He gets right close to her face, inches away and loudly tells her that he wants more. He scrunches up his face, puts his arms straight down by his sides and makes fists. She steps back; he steps up close again to her face. She turns away. (Five-year-olds)

Negative interactions occur when there are "invasions" or interruptions of play among children of one gender by children of another:

> Courtney is sitting on the floor with the girls who are playing "kitties." The girls have on their dress-up clothes and dress-up shoes. Phil puts on big winter gloves and then jumps in the middle of the girls on the floor. He lands on their shoes. Courtney pushes him away and then pulls her legs and clothes and stuff closer to her. She takes up less space and is sitting in a tight ball on the floor. Phil yells, "No! Aaarrhh." Julie says, "It's not nice to yell." (Five-year-olds)

As Thorne (1993) suggests, kids create, shape, and police the borders of gender. I suggest that they do so physically. In this way, they not only sustain gender segregation, but also maintain a sense that girls and boys are physically different, that their bodies are capable of doing certain kinds of things. This sense of physical differences may make all gender differences feel and appear natural.

Conclusion

Children also sometimes resist their bodies being gendered. For example, three-year-old boys dressed up in women's clothes sometimes. Five-year-old girls played with a relaxed comportment that is normatively (hegemonically) masculine when they sat with their feet up on the desk and their chairs tipped backward. In one classroom when boys were at the height of their loud activity—running and throwing toys and blocks—girls took the opportunity to be loud too as the teachers were paying less attention to them and trying to get the boys to settle down. In individual interactions as well, girls were likely to be loud and physically assertive if a boy was being unusually so:

> José is making a plastic toy horse fly around the room, and the boys playing with the blocks are quite loud and rambunctious. José flies the toy horse right in front of Jessica's face and then zooms around her and straight toward her again. Jessica holds up her hand and waves it at him yelling, "Aaaarrrh." José flies the horse in another direction. (Five-year-olds)

These instances of resistance suggest that gendered physicalities are not natural, nor are they easily and straightforwardly acquired. This research demonstrates the many ways that practices in institutions like preschools facilitate children's acquisition of gendered physicalities.

Men and women and girls and boys fill social space with their bodies in different ways. Our everyday movements, postures, and gestures are gendered. These bodily differences enhance the seeming naturalness of sexual and reproductive differences, that then construct inequality between men and women (Butler 1990). As MacKinnon (1987) notes, "Differences are inequality's post hoc excuse..." (p. 8). In other words, these differences create a context for social relations in which differences confirm inequalities of power.

This research suggests one way that bodies are gendered and physical differences are constructed through social institutions and their practices. Because this gendering occurs at an early age, the seeming naturalness of such differences is further underscored. In preschool, bodies become gendered in ways that are so subtle and taken-for-granted that they come to feel and appear natural. Preschool, however, is presumably just the tip of the iceberg in the gendering of children's bodies. Families, formal schooling, and other institutions (like churches, hospitals, and workplaces) gender children's physicality as well.

Many feminist sociologists (West and Zimmerman 1987) and other feminist scholars (Butler 1990, 1993) have examined how the seeming naturalness of gender differences underlies gender inequality. They have also theorized that there are no meaningful natural differences (Butler 1990, 1993). However, how gender differences come to feel and appear natural in the first place has been a missing piece of the puzzle.

Sociological theories of the body that describe the regulation, disciplining, and managing that social institutions do to bodies have neglected the gendered nature of these processes (Foucault 1979; Shilling 1993; Turner 1984). These data suggest that a significant part of disciplining the body consists of gendering it, even in subtle, micro, everyday ways that make gender appear natural. It is in this sense that the preschool as an institution genders children's bodies. Feminist theories about the body (Bordo 1993; Connell 1995; Young 1990), on the other hand, tend to focus on the adult gendered body and fail to consider how the body becomes gendered. This neglect may accentuate gender differences and make them seem natural. This research provides but one account of how bodies become gendered. Other accounts of how the bodies of children and adults are gendered (and raced, classed, and sexualized) are needed in various social contexts across the life course.

References

Anyon, Jean. 1980. Social class and the hidden curriculum of work. *Journal of Education* 162:67–92.

Birdwhistell, Ray. 1970. *Kinesics and Contexts*. Philadelphia: University of Pennsylvania Press.

Bordo, Susan. 1993. *Unbearable Weight*. Berkeley: University of California Press.

Bowles, Samuel, and Herbert Gintis. 1976. *Schooling in Capitalist America*. New York: Basic Books.

Butler, Judith. 1990. *Gender Trouble*. New York: Routledge.

———. 1993. *Bodies That Matter*. New York: Routledge.

Carere, Sharon. 1987. Lifeworld of restricted behavior. *Sociological Studies of Child Development* 2:105–38.

Carnoy, Martin, and Henry Levin. 1985. *Schooling and Work in the Democratic State*. Stanford, CA: Stanford University Press.

Connell, R. W. 1987. *Gender and Power*. Stanford, CA: Stanford University Press.

———. 1995. *Masculinities*. Berkeley: University of California Press.

Foucault, Michel. 1979. *Discipline and Punish: The Birth of the Prison*. New York: Vintage Books.

Giroux, Henry, and David Purpel. 1983. *The Hidden Curriculum and Moral Education*. Berkeley, CA: McCutchan.

Goffman, Erving. 1959. *The Presentation of Self in Everyday Life*. Garden City, NY: Doubleday.

Goodwin, Marjorie Harness. 1990. *He-Said-She-Said: Talk as Social Organization among Black Children*. Bloomington: Indiana University Press.

Haug, Frigga. 1987. *Female Sexualization: A Collective Work of Memory*. London: Verso.

Henley, Nancy. 1977. *Body Politics*. New York: Simon and Schuster.

Jackson, Philip W. 1968. *Life in Classrooms*. New York: Holt, Rinehart and Winston.

Jordan, Ellen, and Angela Cowan. 1995. Warrior narratives in the kindergarten classroom: Renegotiating the social contract. *Gender and Society* 9:727–43.

Maccoby, Eleanor. 1988. Gender as a social category. *Developmental Psychology* 24:755–65.

MacKinnon, Catharine. 1987. *Feminism Unmodified*. Cambridge, MA: Harvard University Press.

Martin, Emily. 1987. *The Woman in the Body*. Boston: Beacon Press.

Martin, Karin. 1996. *Puberty, Sexuality, and the Self: Boys and Girls at Adolescence*. New York: Routledge.

McLaren, Peter. 1986. *Schooling as a Ritual Performance: Towards a Political Economy of Educational Symbols and Gestures*. London: Routledge and Kegan Paul.

Sadker, Myra, and David Sadker. 1994. *Failing at Fairness: How America's Schools Cheat Girls*. New York: Charles Scribner and Sons.

Serbin, Lisa. 1983. The hidden curriculum: Academic consequences of teacher expectations. In *Sex Differentiation and Schooling*, edited by M. Marland. London: Heinemann Educational Books.

Shilling, Chris. 1993. *The Body and Social Theory*. London: Sage.

Thorne, Barrie. 1993. *Gender Play: Girls and Boys in School*. New Brunswick, NJ: Rutgers University Press.

Thomas, Jerry, and Karen French. 1985. Gender differences across age in motor performance: A meta-analysis. *Psychological Bulletin* 98:260–82.

Turner, Bryan S. 1984. *The Body and Society: Explorations in Social Theory*. New York: Basil Blackwell.

———. 1992. *Regulating Bodies: Essays in Medical Sociology*. London: Routledge.

Van Ausdale, Debra, and Joe R. Feagin. 1996. Using racial and ethnic concepts: The critical case of very young children. *American Sociological Review* 61:779–93.

Wasburn, Philo C. 1986. The political role of the American school. *Theory and Research in Social Education* 14:51–65.

West, Candace, and Don Zimmerman. 1987. Doing gender. *Gender and Society* 1:127–51.

Young, Iris. 1990. *Throwing Like a Girl*. Bloomington: Indiana University Press.

4

Women and Medicalization

A New Perspective

CATHERINE KOHLER RIESSMAN

Earlier in this section, Judith Lorber described the social construction of sex and gender. In much the same way, Catherine K. Riessman describes the social construction of illness in her article "Women and Medicalization: A New Perspective."

Medicalization, Riessman explains, refers to the process through which human experiences and conditions become defined as medical problems requiring medical intervention. For example, pharmaceutical companies now advertise that individuals who are shy or who have "restless legs" need to seek medical diagnosis and treatment. As this suggests, medicalization is always a political process—that is, a process in which one group uses its power to press its views on another group.

In this article, Riessman examines the medicalization of women's lives and bodies. But whereas earlier scholars focused on how doctors fought to medicalize women's bodies and how women lost power and freedom as a result, Riessman uses the history of childbirth, abortion, and contraception to explore why women sometimes fought for medicalization and how women benefited (or hoped to benefit) from it. Finally, she provides cogent reasons to believe that women's bodies continue to be medicalized more often than men's bodies. Since this article was written, however, the power of the pharmaceutical industry and of the cosmetic surgery industry has resulted in substantial medicalization of men's bodies (Viagra for impotence, Rogaine for hair loss, pectoral implants, liposuction for everyone), calling this conclusion somewhat into question.

Originally published as "Women and Medicalization: A New Perspective," by Catherine K. Riessman, *Social Policy* (Summer, 1993): pp. 3–18. Reprinted by permission of *Social Policy*.

Illness expands by means of two hypotheses. The first is that
every form of social deviation can be considered an illness.
Thus, if criminal behavior can be considered an illness, then
criminals are not to be condemned or punished but to be
understood (as a doctor understands), treated, cured. The
second is that every illness can be considered psychologically.
Illness is interpreted as, basically, a psychological event, and
people are encouraged to believe that they get sick because
they (unconsciously) want to, and that they can cure
themselves by the mobilization of will; that they can choose
not to die of the disease. These two hypotheses are
complementary. As the first seems to relieve guilt, the second
reinstates it. Psychological theories of illness are a powerful
means of placing the blame on the ill. Patients who are
instructed that they have, unwittingly, caused their disease
are also made to feel that they have deserved it.

Susan Sontag, 1979

It is widely acknowledged that illness has become a cultural metaphor for
a vast array of human problems. The medical model is used from birth to
death in the social construction of reality. Historically, as a larger number
of critical events and human problems have come under the "clinical gaze"
(Foucault 1973), our experience of them has been transformed. For women
in particular, this process has had far-reaching consequences.

Feminist health writers have emphasized that women have been the
main targets in the expansion of medicine. These scholars have analyzed
how previous religious justifications for patriarchy were transformed into
scientific ones (Ehrenreich and English 1979). They have described how
women's traditional skills for managing birth and caring for the sick were
expropriated by psychomedical experts at the end of the nineteenth century
(Ehrenreich and English 1973). Feminist writers have described the multiple
ways in which women's health in the contemporary period is being jeop-
ardized by a male controlled, technology-dominated medical-care system
(Dreifus 1978; Frankfort 1972; Ruzek 1978; Seaman 1972). These critics have been important voices in changing women's consciousness about
their health. They have identified the sexual politics embedded in conceptions of sickness and beliefs about appropriate care. In addition, they
have provided the analytic basis for a social movement that has as its primary goal the reclaiming of knowledge about and control over women's
bodies.

However, in their analyses, feminists have not always emphasized the
ways in which women have simultaneously gained and lost with the medicalization of their life problems. Nor have the scholars always noted the
fact that women actively participated in the construction of the new medical

definitions, nor discussed the reasons that led to their participation. Women were not simply passive victims of medical ascendancy. To cast them solely in a passive role is to perpetuate the very kinds of assumptions about women that feminists have been trying to challenge.

This paper will extend the feminist critique by emphasizing some neglected dimensions of medicalization and women's lives. I will argue that both physicians and women have contributed to the redefining of women's experience into medical categories. More precisely, I will suggest that physicians seek to medicalize experience because of their specific beliefs and economic interests. These ideological and material motives are related to the development of the profession and the specific market conditions it faces in any given period. Women collaborate in the medicalization process because of their own needs and motives, which in turn grow out of the class-specific nature of their subordination. In addition, other groups bring economic interests to which both physicians and women are responsive. Thus a consensus develops that a particular human problem will be understood in clinical terms. This consensus is tenuous because it is fraught with contradictions for women, since, as stated before, they stand both to gain and lose from this redefinition.

I will explore this thesis by examining . . . childbirth [and] reproductive control. . . .

The Medicalization Framework

The term medicalization refers to two interrelated processes. First, certain behaviors or conditions are given medical meaning—that is, defined in terms of health and illness. Second, medical practice becomes a vehicle for eliminating or controlling problematic experiences that are defined as deviant, for the purpose of securing adherence to social norms. Medicalization can occur on various levels: conceptually, when a medical vocabulary is used to define a problem; institutionally, when physicians legitimate a program or a problem; or on the level of doctor-patient interaction, when actual diagnosis and treatment of a problem occurs (Conrad and Schneider 1980).

Historically, there has been an expansion of the spheres of deviance that have come under medical social control (Ehrenreich and Ehrenreich 1978; Freidson 1970; Zola 1972). Various human conditions such as alcoholism, opiate addiction, and homosexuality—which at one time were categorized as "bad"—have more recently been classified as "sick" (Conrad and Schneider 1980). Currently, more and more of human experience is coming under medical scrutiny, resulting in what Illich (1976) has called "the medicalization of life." For example, it is now considered appropriate to consult physicians about sexuality, fertility, childhood behavior, and old-age memory problems. It is important to note that the medical profession's jurisdiction over these and other human conditions extends considerably beyond its demonstrated capacity to "cure" them (Freidson 1970).

There is disagreement about what causes medicalization. Some have assumed that the expansion of medical jurisdiction is the outcome of "medical imperialism"—an effort on the part of the profession to increase its power (Illich 1976). Others have argued that an increasingly complex technical and bureaucratic society has led to a reluctant reliance on scientific experts (Zola 1972, 1975). Other scholars have stressed the ways in which the medical establishment, in its thrust to professionalize, organized to create and then control markets (Larson 1977). In order for the occupational strategy of this emerging professional class to succeed, it was necessary to control the meaning of things, including interpretations of symptoms and beliefs about health care. Stated differently, professional dominance could be achieved only if people could be convinced of the medical nature of their problems and the appropriateness of medical treatment for them. Thus physicians, as part of an occupational strategy, created conditions under which their advice seemed appropriate (Starr 1982).

In spite of the disagreement about what motivates medicalization, there is a consensus that it has mixed effects. Greater humanitarianism, tolerance, and other benefits associated with "progress" may be more likely with medical definitions than with criminal ones. Yet medical labeling also has negative social consequences. Far from reducing stigma, the label of illness may create deviance. For example, the career of a psychiatric patient begins with a diagnosis of schizophrenia. As a result, family and friends perceive and interpret the patient's behavior in light of the illness, even after the acute symptoms subside (Mills 1962). Another consequence of medicalization is that the shroud of medical language mystifies human problems, and thus removes them from public debate (Conrad and Schneider 1980). A deskilling of the populace takes place when experts manage human experiences. The application of medical definitions makes it more likely that medical remedies will be applied, thereby increasing the risk of iatrogenic disease. In addition, both the meaning and interpretation of an experience is transformed when it is seen as a disease or syndrome (Freidson 1970). For example, the meaning of murder is significantly altered when the label of "sociopathic personality" is used to account for the behavior. In this way, moral issues tend not be faced and may not even be raised (Zola 1975). Finally and most important, awareness of the social causes of disease is diminished with medicalization. As Stark and Flitcraft (1982) state:

> Medicine attracts public resources out of proportion to its capacity for health enhancement, because it often categorizes problems fundamentally social in origin as biological or personal deficits, and in so doing smothers the impulse for social change which could offer the only serious resolution.

Medicalization is a particularly critical concept because it emphasizes the fact that medicine is a social enterprise, not merely a scientific one. A biological basis is neither necessary nor sufficient for an experience to be defined in terms of illness. Rather, illness is constructed through human action—that is, illness is not inherent in any behavior or condition, but conferred by others. Thus, medical diagnosis becomes an interpretive process through which illnesses are constructed (Mishler 1981)....

Finally, the medicalization framework emphasizes that the power of physicians to define illness and monopolize the provision of treatment is the outcome of a political process. It highlights the ways in which medicine's constructions of reality are related to the structure of power at any given historical period. The political dimension inherent in medicalization is underscored when we note that structurally dependent populations—children, old people, racial minorities, and women—are subject disproportionately to medical labeling. For example, children's behavior is medicalized under the rubric of juvenile delinquency and hyperkinesis (Conrad and Schneider 1980). Old people's mental functioning is labeled organic brain syndrome or senility. Racial minorities, when they come in contact with psychiatrists, are more likely than whites to be given more severe diagnoses for comparable symptoms and to receive more coercive forms of medical social control, such as psychiatric hospitalization (Gross et al. 1969). Women, as I will argue, are more likely than men to have problematic experiences defined and treated medically. In each of these examples, it is important to note that the particular group's economic and social powerlessness legitimates its "protection" by medical authorities. Of course, physicians act on behalf of the larger society, thus further reinforcing existing power relations.

Although medicalization theory has emphasized power, it has tended to minimize the significance of class. Historically, as I will suggest, the medicalization of certain problems was rooted in specific class interests. Physicians and women from the dominant class joined together—albeit out of very different motives—to redefine certain human events into medical categories. Women from other class groups at times embraced and at other times resisted these class-based definitions of experience.

In sum, the medicalization framework provides useful analytic categories for examining the medicalization of women's problems as a function of (1) the interests and beliefs of physicians; (2) the class-specific needs of women; and (3) the "fit" between these, resulting in a consensus that redefines a human experience as a medical problem. As stated before, I will use this framework to explore childbirth [and] reproductive control.... Clearly, because of space considerations, it is impossible to discuss each example in depth. Instead, I hope to provide a fresh look at each problem and lay out the issues as I perceive them at this point.

Childbirth

Today, pregnancy and birth are considered medical events. This was not always the case. Moreover, there is nothing inherent in either condition that necessitates routine medical scrutiny. In fact, birth is an uncomplicated process in roughly 90 percent of cases (Wertz and Wertz 1979). In order to understand the medicalization of childbirth, it must be analyzed as the outcome of a complex sociopolitical process in which both physicians and women participated.

In mid-nineteenth-century America, virtually anyone could be a doctor. As a result, there was an oversupply of healers—a series of competing sects with varying levels of training. These included "regular" college-trained physicians, physicians trained by apprenticeship, homeopaths, botanic physicians, male accoucheurs, midwives, and other healers (Drachman 1979). The "regular" physicians—white, upper-class males—struggled to achieve professional dominance as boundaries between professional and lay control shifted. It is important to emphasize that this group sought control over the healing enterprise at a time when they were not more effective than their competitors in curing disease. As Larson (1977) has noted, the diffusion of knowledge about scientific discoveries in microbiology that revolutionized medical care occurred only after medicine successfully gained control over the healing market. Thus, in the absence of superior skill, it was necessary to convert public perceptions. In order to gain "cultural authority" (Starr 1982) over definitions of health and disease and over the provision of health services, "regular" doctors had to transform general human skills into their exclusive craft. Social historians of medicine have documented the political activities that succeeded in guaranteeing a closed shop for "regular" doctors in late nineteenth- and early twentieth-century America (Reverby and Rosner 1979; Walsh 1977).

A central arena for the struggle over professional dominance was childbirth. In colonial America, this event was handled predominantly by female midwives who, assisted by a network of female relatives and friends, provided emotional support and practical assistance to the pregnant woman both during the actual birth and in the weeks that followed. Over a period of more than a century, "social childbirth" was replaced (Wertz and Wertz 1979). The site of care shifted from the home to the hospital. The personnel who gave care changed from female midwives to male physicians. The techniques changed from noninterventionist approaches to approaches relying on technology and drugs. As a consequence, the meaning of childbirth for women was transformed from a human experience to a medical-technical problem.

A crucial historical juncture in the medicalization of childbirth occurred in the second decade of the twentieth century. In 1910, about 50 percent of all reported births were attended by midwives. The medical profession and the laity generally believed that the midwife—essentially a domestic worker— was an adequate birth attendant. Nature was thought to control the process of birth. As a result, there was little to be done in case of difficulty. The teaching of obstetrics in medical schools was minimal, and direct experience with birth by medical students was rare (Kobrin 1966).

Beginning around 1910, a contest began between the emerging specialty of obstetrics, the general practitioner, and the midwife. Although seemingly about issues of science and efficacy, this struggle was also about class and race. Obstetricians were from the dominant class, whereas midwives were mostly immigrant and Black women. Struggling to differentiate themselves from general practitioners, obstetricians fought to upgrade the image of their field. They searched for a respectable science to legitimate their work. They argued that normal pregnancy and parturition were an exception rather than the rule. Because they believed that birth was a pathological process, obstetricians often used surgical interventions as well as instruments, such as high forceps previous to sufficient dilation. These approaches, used routinely and often unnecessarily, frequently had deleterious effects on both mother and child. Over a period of several decades, obstetricians were successful in persuading both their physician colleagues and the general public of the "fallacy of normal pregnancy," and therefore of the need for a "science" of obstetrical practice. Their political activities, coupled with changing demographic trends, resulted in the demise of midwifery (Kobrin 1966).

It is important to note that the medical management of childbirth did not result in greater safety for women, at least in the short run. The evidence suggests that both maternal and infant mortality rates actually rose during the period between 1915 and 1930 when midwives' attendance at birth abruptly declined (Wertz and Wertz 1979). In the long run, there has been a steady decline in death rates, which has coincided with modern childbirth practice. However, it is not clear how much of this decline is due to improved environmental circumstances and nutrition and how much to medical care.

In light of these facts, what motivated women to go along with the medicalization of childbirth? Because childbirth is an event that occurs without complications in most cases, it is tempting to emphasize the many losses that accompanied its medicalization. In modern birth, the woman is removed from familiar surroundings, from kin and social support, and subjected to a series of technical procedures—many of which are dehumanizing and others of which carry significant health risks (Rothman 1982; Shaw 1974). A woman's experience of birth is alienated because the social relations and instrumentation of the medical setting remove her control over the experience (Young 1984). Because of these negative consequences of modern birth, there is a tendency to romanticize the midwife and pretechnological childbirth and fail to consider the contradictory nature of the process.

Women participated in the medicalization of childbirth for a complex set of reasons. First, nineteenth-century women wanted freedom from the pain, exhaustion, and lingering incapacity of childbirth. Pregnancy every other year was the norm for married women, and this took a significant toll on the reproductive organs. Contraception was not a viable alternative, for reasons I will discuss shortly. For working-class women, the problems of maternity were intensified by harsh working and housing conditions. The letters of early twentieth-century working class women vividly portray the exhaustion of motherhood (Davies 1978). Albeit for different reasons, women from different class groups experienced birth as a terrifying ordeal (Dye 1980).

In the early decades of the twentieth century, relief from the pain of childbirth was promised with "twilight sleep," a combination of morphine and scopolamine, which European physicians had begun to use. Historical analysis of the twilight sleep movement in the United States reveals that it was women who demanded it, frequently pitting themselves against the medical profession who both resented lay interference and feared the dangers of the drug (Leavitt 1980). These women—middle- and upper-class reformers with a progressive ideology—wanted to alter the oppressive circumstances of women's lives. Thus, the demand for anesthesia in childbirth was part of a larger social movement. Pregnancy was no longer seen as a condition to be endured with fatalism and passivity (Smith-Rosenberg and Rosenberg 1973). As Miller (1979) argues, people believed that civilization had increased the subjective experience of pain in childbirth, and that anesthesia would once again make childbirth natural. The upper class experienced greater pain than working-class women, who were thought to be more like primitive peoples. People believed that upper-class women had been particularly warped by civilization. (The corset also may have distorted their internal organs.) In other words, pain had accompanied the progress of civilization. If freed from painful and exhausting labor, women could (the reformers felt) more fully participate in democratic society (Miller 1979).

Second, because of declining fertility in upper- and middle-class women at the end of the nineteenth century, the meaning of birth was particularly significant to them. Because childbirth was a less frequent event, concern about fetal death was greater. In addition, women were fearful because it was common to have known someone who had died in childbirth (Dye 1980). Thus, well-to-do women wanted to be attended by doctors not only because they were of higher social status compared to midwives but also because they possessed the instruments and surgical techniques that might be beneficial in cases of prolonged labor, toxemia, fetal distress, and other abnormal conditions. Of course, physicians used these fears to gain control over the entire market, including routine births.

Thus, the demise of midwifery and the resultant medicalization of childbirth were consequences of forces within the women's community as well as from outside it. Furthermore, it was a class-specific process. Well-to-do women wanted to reduce the control that biology had over their lives. They wanted freedom from pain. Because of their refinement, medical ideology of the period insisted that well-do-do women were more delicate and hence, were more likely to experience pain and complications. By contrast, working-class women were believed to be inherently stronger (Cott 1972). Perhaps as a way of resisting these ideological assumptions, well-to-do women wanted control over the birthing process—the right to decide what kind of labor and delivery they would have. The contradiction was that the method these women demanded—going to sleep—put them out of control (Leavitt 1980).

Obstetricians also wanted control. They believed that birth was a pathological process and that "scientific birth" would result in greater safety for affluent women especially. In addition it was in the interest of physicians to capture the childbirth market, because this event provided a gateway to the family, and hence the entire healing market (Wertz and Wertz 1979). Physicians were particularly anxious to attend the births of well-to-do women, because the social status of these women lent legitimacy and respectability to the shift from midwifery to obstetrics (Drachman 1979). In order to control childbirth, physicians needed drugs and technology to appear indispensable (Miller 1979). Therefore, they went along with twilight sleep, at least for a time. The irony for women was that this approach to the pain of childbirth served to distance women from their bodies and redefine birth as an event requiring hospitalization and physician attendance (Leavitt 1980).

Currently, the medicalization of childbirth is taking new forms. First, there is the strikingly high rate of cesarean deliveries [Ed: about 30% in the United States as of 2008, more than twice the rate recommended by the World Health Organization]. Although some of these are necessary for maternal health as well as infant survival, evidence suggests that many caesareans are unnecessary (O'Driscoll and Foley 1983). In view of medicalization, it is important to point out that the potential need for a cesarean places childbirth squarely and exclusively in the hands of the physician. Vaginal delivery, by contrast, can be the province of nonphysician experts, such as nurse-midwives.

Second, there is a trend to make the birth experience more humane, for both mother and baby. Hospitals are developing "birthing rooms" and other alternatives to the usual delivery room atmosphere of steel tables, stirrups, and bright lights. After birth, maternal-infant contact is permitted so as to foster "bonding." Pediatricians believe that a critical period exists for the development of an optimal relationship between mother and newborn (Klaus and Kennell 1976). Thus, pediatricians are joining obstetricians in medicalizing the childbirth experience. By defining what should be (and therefore what is) deviant, pediatricians create social norms for parenting.

The contradiction is that the recent changes in the hospital environment of birth have both helped and hurt women. Birthing rooms and early contact between mother and newborn are a welcome change from previous oppressive obstetrical and pediatric practices (which poor women still face because these reforms are more characteristic of elite hospitals than of public ones). Yet the contemporary feminist critique of childbirth practice has been cut short by these reforms. As in many reform movements, larger issues are silenced. Challenges to the medical domination of pregnancy and demands for genuine demedicalization have been co-opted by an exclusive focus on the birth environment. Even when "natural" childbirth occurs in birthing rooms, birth is still defined medically, is still under the control of physicians, and still occurs in hospitals (Rothman 1981).

Moreover, the social meaning of parenting changes when scientific rationales such as "bonding" and "attachment" are used to justify mothers being near their babies after giving birth (Arney 1980). In addition, sex roles are reinforced when it is mothers and not fathers who need to be "bonded" to their infants.

Reproductive Freedom

Abortion

Today, abortion is treated as a medical event. Yet in previous historical periods, it was defined in nonmedical terms. Physicians brought specific professional and class interests to the abortion issue in the nineteenth century. To realize their interests, they needed to alter public beliefs about the meaning of unwanted pregnancy. Well-to-do women formed an alliance with doctors in this redefinition process because of their own needs.

As Mohr (1978) documents, abortion before quickening (the perception of fetal movement) was widely practiced in the mid-nineteenth century and was not seen as morally or legally wrong. Information on potions, purgatives, and quasisurgical techniques was available in home medical manuals. As autoabortive instruments came on the market, women became skillful in performing their own abortions, and they shared information with one another. In addition, midwives, herbal healers, and other "irregular" doctors established lucrative practices in the treatment of "obstructed menses." It is estimated that by 1878 one in five pregnancies was intentionally aborted. The growing frequency of abortion was particularly evident in the middle and upper classes (Mohr 1978).

"Regular" physicians were central figures in redefining abortion as a social problem. The practice of abortion was leading to a declining birth rate, especially among the middle and upper classes who feared that this could lead to "race suicide" (Smith-Rosenberg and Rosenberg 1973). One physician warned that abortion was being used "to avoid the labor of caring for and rearing children" (Silver as quoted in Mohr 1978). In other words, women were shirking the responsibilities of their seemingly biologically determined role.

Mohr (1978) argues that physicians led the moral crusade against abortion not so much out of these antifeminist feelings, but primarily in order to restrict the practice of medicine. They wanted to get rid of competitors ("irregulars" and "doctresses") and gain a monopoly over the practice of medicine. By altering public opinion and persuading legislators, they succeeded in establishing their code of ethics (which specifically excluded abortion) as the basis for professional practice. These actions limited the scope of medicine's competitors, especially women doctors whose practices were devoted to the care of female complaints. By the late 1870s, anti-abortion statutes were on the books. Professional dominance was further strengthened in the 1880s when physicians became more organized. They used the scientific paradigm to force more and more folk practitioners from the field.

It is interesting to note the social relations at work in the nineteenth-century abortion struggle. First, the "regulars"—upper- and middle-class men—had natural allies in the state legislators, who were also men from prosperous families. Second, patriarchal class interests in general and nativism in particular provided the racist and sexist ideology for the anti-abortion movement. Physicians, legislators, and other well-to-do men wanted their women to reproduce the species, or, more specifically, the dominant class of the species. These groups, fearing the increasing numbers of the foreign-born, were concerned that the upper classes would be outbred. Finally, the conflict between the "regular" doctors and their competitors was not only about issues of science and professional control but also about the issues of class and patriarchy. The "irregular" doctors were, in general, not from families of the dominant class. In addition, these practitioners were more likely to be female. Thus social characteristics provided the rationale for exclusion, further reinforcing patriarchal class relations.

Women's participation in the anti-abortion crusade of the 1870s also was class-specific. Feminists of the period—well-to-do women—came out against abortion, arguing instead for voluntary motherhood. These early feminists recommended periodic or permanent abstinence as methods of birth control because they did not approve of contraceptive devices (Gordon 1976).

It is obvious that women lost significant freedoms when abortion was defined as a medical procedure and ruled illegal. Yet, from the perspective of the sexual politics of late nineteenth-century America, it is significant that women favored abstinence over abortion. Abstinence was a more radical response to the power relations in the patriarchal family than a pro-abortion stance would have been.

Well-to-do women of the late nineteenth century had a level of hostility toward sex, both because it brought unwanted and dangerous pregnancy and because it was a legally prescribed wifely duty. Even more important, Gordon (1976) argues that these women resented the particular kind of sexual encounter that was characteristic of American Victorian society: intercourse dominated by the husband's needs and neglecting what might bring pleasure to a woman. Men's style of lovemaking repelled women. They felt that men were oversexed and violent. Furthermore, because men visited prostitutes, marital sex for women not infrequently resulted in venereal disease. Under these conditions, a woman's right to refuse was central to her independence and personal integrity.

In sum, the termination of an unwanted pregnancy underwent a series of changing definitions: it went from a human problem to a topic of medical concern to a crime. With the 1973 Supreme Court decision [in *Roe v. Wade*], it was remedicalized, but this time with the support of the medical profession. Physicians no longer needed this issue to advance their sovereignty.

Contraception

In the twentieth century, well-to-do women joined physicians again in the medicalization of reproduction with the issue of contraception. These women struggled to define a "new sense of womanhood" that did not require sexual passivity, maternity, domesticity, and the absence of ambition. In order to achieve these goals feminists overcame their scruples against artificial contraception. Importantly, women ultimately won the battle of reproductive freedom. Technology to limit family size was developed in response to the social demand for it (Gordon 1976).

But as women gained from this newly won independence, they also lost. Birth control technology is not without problems, both in its female centricity and its risk. Furthermore, as Gordon argues, the professionalism and medicalization of birth control stripped it of its political content. As a result of its definition as a health issue, contraception became somewhat separate from the larger social movement that gave rise to the demand for birth control in the first place. Finally, the battle over medicalization was lost again when birth control methods went in the direction of high technology. The pill, the IUD, and injectable contraceptives are forever in the hands of medicine, because access to these drugs and devices is legally controlled. In contrast, the low-technology barrier methods—the condom, cervical cap, or diaphragm—require little medical intervention or control.

These historical examples underscore the fact that women's experience was a site for the initial medicalization effort. Medicine "staked claims" for childbirth, abortion, and birth control and secured them as "medical turf" by altering public beliefs and persuading the state of the legitimacy of their claim (cf. Conrad and Schneider 1980.) Physicians used science as the rationale for professional dominance. As I have suggested, women's participation in the redefinition of each experience was the result of complex historical and class specific motives, and they not only gained but lost with the medicalization of each area. . . .

The Fit Between Women's Interests and Physicians' Interests

These examples illustrate a general point about medical social control: there are times when the interests of women from the middle and upper classes are served by the therapeutic professions, whose political and economic interests are in turn served by transforming these women's complaints into illnesses. In other words, both historically and currently, there has tended to be a "fit" between medicine's interest in expanding its jurisdiction and the need of women to have their experience acknowledged. I have emphasized that this "fit" has been tension-filled and fraught with contradictions for women, who have both gained and lost with each intrusion medicine has made into their lives.

While necessary, the particular interests of women and physicians do not alone explain the expansion of the clinical domain. Other communities also influence what occurs in the doctor's office. In the context of a capitalist economy and a technologically dominated medical-care system, large profits accompany each redefinition of human experience into medical terms, since more drugs, tests, procedures, equipment, and insurance coverage are needed. [Certainly] specific medical industries have played a direct role in influencing both physicians' and women's perceptions of reproductive control [and other health care issues.] Yet it is important to emphasize that corporations, in their effort to maximize profits, work *through* both physicians and women.

Implicit in my analysis is the assumption that women's experience has been medicalized more than men's. Yet it could be argued instead that medicine has encroached into men's lives in a different but equal fashion. For example, medicine has focused on childhood hyperactivity and the adult addictions—problems more common in males than females (Conrad and Schneider 1980). Occupational medicine has tended to focus on male jobs. In particular, "stress management" programs are targeting male executives. However, while not to diminish these examples, I believe that women's lives have undergone a more total transformation as a result of medical scrutiny. Medicalization has resulted in the construction of medical meanings of *normal* functions in women—experiences the typical woman goes through, such as menstruation, reproduction, childbirth, and menopause. By contrast, routine experiences that are uniquely male remain largely unstudied by medical science and, consequently, are rarely treated by physicians as potentially pathological. For example, male hormonal cycles and the male climacteric remain largely unresearched. Less is known about the male reproductive system than about that of the female. Male contraceptive technology lags far behind what is available for women. Baldness in men has not yet been defined as a medical condition needing treatment, even though an industry exists to remedy the problem of hair loss. Men's psychological lives have not been subjected to psychiatric scrutiny nearly to the degree that women's emotions have been studied. As a result, male violence, need for power, and overrationality are not defined as pathological conditions. Perhaps only impotence has been subject to the same degree of medical scrutiny as women's problems.

Why has women's experience been such a central focus for medicalization? In addition to the complex motives that women bring to each particular health issue, physicians focus on women as a primary market for expansion for a number of reasons. First, there is a good match between women's biology and medicine's biomedical orientation. External markers of biological processes exist in women (menstruation, birth, lactation, and so forth), whereas they are more hidden in men. Given modern medicine's biomedical orientation, these external signs make women easy targets for medical encroachment. A different medical paradigm (one that viewed health as the consequence of harmony between the person and the environment, for example) might have had less basis for focusing on women.

Second, women's social roles make them readily available to medical scrutiny. Women are more likely to come in contact with medical providers because they care for children and are the "kin keepers" of the family

(Rossi 1980). In concrete terms, women are more likely to accompany sick children and aged relatives to the doctor.

Third, women have greater exposure to medical labeling because of their pattern of dealing with their own symptoms, as well as medicine's response to that pattern. Women make more visits to physicians than men, although it is not clear whether this is due to the medicalization of their biological functions, "real" illness, behavior when ill, or cultural expectations (Nathanson 1975). When they visit the doctor for any serious illness, they are more likely than men to be checked for reproductive implications of the illness. They are more subject to regular checks of their reproductive systems, in the form of yearly pap smears or gynecological exams. Importantly, whenever they visit the doctor there is evidence that they receive more total and extensive services—in the form of lab tests, procedures, drug prescriptions, and return appointments—than do men with the same complaints and sociodemographic risk factors (Verbrugge and Steiner 1981). Thus, a cycle of greater medical scrutiny of women's experiences is begun with each visit to the doctor.

Finally, women's structural subordination to men has made them particularly vulnerable to the expansion of the clinical domain. In general, male physicians treat female patients. Social relations in the doctor's office replicate patriarchal relations in the larger culture, and this all proceeds under the guise of science. (Patriarchal control is most evident when physicians socialize young women regarding appropriate sexual behavior, perhaps withholding contraceptive advice, or lecturing them about the dangers of promiscuity). For all these reasons, it is not surprising that women are more subject to medical definitions of their experience than men are. In these ways, dominant social interests and patriarchal institutions are reinforced.

As a result, women are especially appropriate markets for the expansion of medicine. They are suitable biologically, socially, and psychologically. The message that women are expected to be dependent on male physicians to manage their lives is reinforced by the pharmaceutical industry in drug advertisements and by the media in general. Yet it is far too simple to portray the encroachment of medicines as a conspiracy—by male doctors and the "medical industrial complex"—to subordinate women further. Although some have argued that medicine is the scientific equivalent of earlier customs like marriage laws and kinship rituals that controlled women by controlling their sexuality, such an analysis is incomplete. As I have stressed, medicalization is more than what doctors do, although it may be through doctors that the interests of other groups are often realized. Nor does a conspiracy theory explain why, for the most part, women from certain class groups have been willing collaborators in the medicalization process. Rather than dismissing these women as "duped," I have suggested some of the complex motives that have caused certain classes of women to participate with physicians in the redefinition of particular experiences.

In addition, a conspiracy theory does not explain why medicalization has been more virulent in some historical periods and in some medical specialties than in others. For example, gynecologists initially trivialized menopausal discomfort, only to reclaim it later for treatment [as premenstrual syndrome]. At the same time that gynecologists were unwilling to acknowledge the legitimacy of women's complaints, the developing specialty of psychiatry moved in with the psychogenic account. I have argued that these shifts and inter-professional rivalries over turf are explained by internal issues facing each specialty at particular points in history. Thus, an analysis of the market conditions faced by physicians in general, and certain specialties in particular, is necessary to explain the varying response of medicine to women's problems.

Further research is needed to capture more fully the historical aspect of these shifts in medical perception. Such an analysis needs to focus in depth on specific events in women's experience and trace their medicalization in historical and class context: the issues brought in turn by groups of women, by the particular medical specialties, by the pharmaceutical industry, and by the "fit" between these that resulted in a redefinition. A conspiracy theory fails to capture the nuances of this complex process.

Conclusion

The medicalization of human problems is a contradictory reality for women. It is part of the problem and of the solution. It has grown out of and in turn has created a series of paradoxes. As women have tried to free themselves from the control that biological processes have had over their lives, they simultaneously have strengthened the control of a biomedical view of their experience. As women visit doctors and get symptom relief, the social causes of their problems are ignored. As doctors acknowledge women's experience and treat their problems medically, problems are stripped of their political content and popular movements are taken over. Because of these contradictions, women in different class positions have sought and resisted medical control.

I have argued that the transformation of such human experiences as childbirth, reproduction, premenstrual problems, weight, and psychological distress into medical events has been the outcome of a reciprocal process involving both physicians and women. Medicine, as it developed as a profession, was repeatedly redefined. The interest of physicians in expanding jurisdiction into new areas coincided with the interest of certain class groups in having their experience in those areas understood in new terms. In other words, physicians created demand in order to generate new markets for their services. They also responded to a market that a class of women created. . . .

As Conrad and Schneider note, the potential for medicalization increases as science discovers the subtle physiological correlates of human behavior. A wealth of knowledge is developing about women's physiology. As more becomes known, the issue will be how to acknowledge the complex biochemical components that are related to menstruation, pregnancy, weight, and the like without allowing these conditions to be distorted by scientific understanding. The issue will be to gain understanding of our biology, without submitting to control in the guise of medical "expertise." The answer is not to "suffer our fate" and return exclusively to self-care, as Illich recommends, thereby turning our backs on discoveries and treatments that may ease pain and suffering. To "demedicalize" is not to deny the biological components of experience but rather to alter the ownership, production, and use of scientific knowledge....

In sum, women's health is faced by a series of challenges. We need to expose the "truth claims" (Bittner 1968) of medical entrepreneurs who will seek to turn new areas of experience into medical events, and instead introduce a healthy skepticism about professional claims. We need to develop alternatives to the masculinist biomedical view and place women's health problems in the larger context of their lives. Specifically, it is not at all clear what form pregnancy, menstruation, weight, sexuality, aging, or other problems would take in a society "that allowed women to normally and routinely express anger, drive, and ambition, a society in which women felt more empowered" (Harrison 1982). We need to reconceptualize our whole way of thinking about biology and explore how "natural" phenomena are, in fact, an outgrowth of the social circumstances of women's lives (Hubbard 1981).

In the meantime, because we will continue to need health care, the challenge will be to alter the terms under which care is provided. In the short term, we need to work for specific reforms and gain what we can while, at the same time, acknowledging the limitation of reform. As I have argued, reform is not what we want in the long run. For certain problems in our lives, real demedicalization is necessary; experiences such as routine childbirth, menopause, or weight in excess of cultural norms should not be defined in medical terms, and medical-technical treatments should not be seen as appropriate solutions to these problems. For other conditions where medicine may be of assistance, the challenge will be to differentiate the beneficial treatments from those that are harmful and useless. The real challenge is to use existing medical knowledge selectively and to extend knowledge with new paradigms so as to improve the quality of our lives.

References

Arney, William R. 1980. Maternal-infant bonding: The politics of failing in love with your child. *Feminist Studies* 6:547–570.

Bittner, Egon. 1968. The structure of psychiatric influence. *Mental Hygiene* 52: 423–30.

Conrad, Peter, and Joseph W. Schneider. 1980. *Deviance and Medicalization: From Badness to Sickness.* St. Louis: C. V. Mosby.

Cott, Nancy F., ed. 1972. *Root of Bitterness: Documents of the Social History of American Women.* New York: E. P. Dutton.

Davies, Marjorie L. 1978. *Maternity: Letters from Working Women*. New York: Norton.

Drachman, V. G. 1979. The Loomis Trial: Social mores and obstetrics in the mid-nineteenth century. In *Health Care in America: Essays in Social History*, edited by Susan E. Reverby and David Rosner. Philadelphia: Temple University Press.

Dreifus, Claudia, ed. 1978. *Seizing Our Bodies: The Politics of Women's Health*. New York: Vintage.

Dye, Nancy S. 1980. History of childbirth in America. *Signs* 97:97–108.

Ehrenreich, Barbara, and John Ehrenreich. 1978. Medicine and social control. In *The Cultural Crisis of Modern Medicine*, edited by J. Ehrenreich. New York: Monthly Review Press.

Ehrenreich, Barbara, and Deidre English. 1973. *Complaints and Disorders: The Sexual Politics of Sickness*. Old Westbury, NY: Feminist Press.

———. 1979. *For Her Own Good: 150 Years of the Experts' Advice to Women*. Garden City, NY: Anchor.

Foucault, Michel. 1973. *The Birth of the Clinic: An Archeology of Medical Perception*. New York: Pantheon.

Frankfort, Ellen. 1972. *Vaginal Politics*. New York: Quadrangle Books.

Freidson, Eliot. 1970. *Profession of Medicine*. New York: Dodd, Mead.

Gordon, Linda. 1976. *Woman's Body, Woman's Right: A Social History of Birth Control in America*. New York: Penguin.

Gross, H. S., M. R. Herbert, G. L. Knatterud, and L. Donner. 1969. The effect of race and sex on the variation of diagnosis and disposition in a psychiatric emergency room. *Journal of Nervous and Mental Disease* 148:638–43.

Harrison, Michelle. 1982. *Self-Help for Premenstrual Syndrome*. Cambridge: Matrix Press.

Hubbard, R. 1981. *The Politics of Women's Biology*. Lecture given at Hampshire College.

Illich, Ivan. 1976. *Medical Nemesis: The Expropriation of Health*. New York: Pantheon.

Klaus, Marshall H., and John H. Kennell. 1976. *Maternal-Infant Bonding: The Impact of Early Separation or Loss on Family Development*. St. Louis: C. V. Mosby.

Kobrin, Francis E. 1966. The American midwife controversy: A crisis of professionalization. *Bulletin of the History of Medicine* 40:350–63.

Larson, Magali S. 1977. *The Rise of Professionalism: A Sociological Analysis*. Berkeley: University of California Press.

Leavitt, Judith W. 1980. Birthing and anesthesia: The debate over twilight sleep. *Signs* 6:147–64.

Miller, L. G. 1979. Pain, parturition, and the profession: Twilight sleep in America. In *Health Care in America: Essays in Social History*, edited by Susan E. Reverby and David Rosner. Philadelphia: Temple University Press.

Mills, E. 1962. *Living with Mental Illness: A Study of East London*. London: Routledge and Kegan Paul.

Mishler, Elliot G. 1981. The social construction of illness. In *Social Context of Health, Illness, and Patient Care*, edited by Elliot G. Mishler, Lorna R. AmaraSingham, Stuart T. Hauser, Samuel D. Osherson, Nancy E. Waxler, and Ramsay Liem. Cambridge: Cambridge University Press.

Mohr, John C. 1978. *Abortion in America: The Origins and Evolution of National Policy, 1800–1900*. New York: Oxford University Press.

Nathanson, Constance. 1975. Illness and the feminine role: A theoretical review. *Social Science and Medicine* 9:57–62.

O'Driscoll, K., and M. Foley. 1983. Correlation of decrease in perinatal mortality and increase in caesarean section rates. *Obstetrics and Gynecology* 61:1–5.

Reverby, Susan E., and David Rosner, eds. 1979. *Health Care in America: Essays in Social History*. Philadelphia: Temple University Press.

Rossi, Alice. 1980. Life span theories and women's lives. *Signs* 6:4–32.

Rothman, Barbara Katz. 1981. Awake and aware, or false consciousness: The cooptation of childbirth reform in America. In *Childbirth: Alternative to Medical Control*, edited by Sherry Romalis. Austin: University of Texas Press.

———. 1982. *In Labor: Women and Power in the Birthplace*. New York: Norton.

Ruzek, Sheryl B. 1978. *The Women's Health Movement: Feminist Alternatives to Medical Control*. New York: Praeger.

Seaman, B. 1972. *Free and Female*. New York: Coward, McCann, and Geoghegan.

Shaw, Nancy S. 1974. *Forced Labor: Maternity Care in the United States*. New York: Pergamon Press.

Smith-Rosenberg, Carroll, and Charles Rosenberg. 1973. The female animal: Medical and biological views of woman and her role in nineteenth-century America. *Journal of American History* 60:332–55.

Sontag, Susan. 1979. *Illness as Metaphor*. New York: Vintage.

Stark, Evan, and Anne Flitcraft. 1982. Medical therapy as repression: The case of battered women. *Health and Medicine* 1:29–32.

Starr, Paul. 1982. *The Social Transformation of American Medicine*. New York: Basic Books.

Verbrugge, Lois M., and R. P. Steiner. 1981. Physician treatment of men and women patients: Sex bias or appropriate care? *Medical Care* 19:609–32.

Walsh, Mary R. 1977. *Doctors Wanted: No Women Need Apply*. New Haven, CT: Yale University Press.

Wertz, Richard W., and Dorothy C. Wertz. 1979. *Lying In: A History of Childbirth in America*. New York: Free Press.

Young, Iris M. 1984. Pregnant embodiment: Subjectivity and alienation. *Journal of Medicine and Philosophy* 9:45–62.

Zola, Irving K. 1972. Medicine as an institution of social control. *Sociological Review* 20:487–504.

———. 1975. In the name of health and illness: On some socio-political consequences of medical influence. *Social Science and Medicine* 9:83–87.

5

Affronting Reason

CHERYL CHASE

The previous article provided an excellent overview of the process of medicaliza-
tion. In this article, Cheryl Chase focuses on the medicalization of intersex—and
the price she, personally, paid for it. As Chase notes, intersexuality—the condi-
tion of having characteristics of both sexes—is not uncommon. (In fact, although
she writes that it occurs in one in 2,000 births, a comprehensive review pub-
lished in 2000 concluded that it occurs in one to two of every 100 births).[1] Yet
intersexuality has been rendered nearly invisible by surgical interventions on
infants and hormonal treatments later in life that wedge intersex individuals
more neatly into the binary sex categories—male and female—that our culture
teaches us to expect.

More stunning, as Chase describes, these surgeries have become almost uni-
versal for intersex babies even though no research has ever proven that they work
(i.e., that they result in adults who are satisfied with their assigned sex, enjoy
a happy and healthy romantic and sexual life, and enjoy average levels of self-
esteem and mental health). Rather, it is clear that these surgeries typically reduce
individuals' chances of sexual pleasure dramatically and may increase depres-
sion and a sense of stigma. Thus, Chase argues, current treatment of intersex
(increasingly referred to as Disorders of Sexual Development, or DSD) reflects
and reinforces cultural ideas about sex and gender more than it helps intersex
children.

"It seems that your parents weren't sure for a time whether you were a girl
or a boy," Dr. Christen explained, as she handed me three fuzzy photostatted
pages. I was 21 years old, and had asked her to help me obtain records of a
hospitalization which occurred when I was a year and a half old, too young

for me to recall. I was desperate to obtain the complete records, to determine who had surgically removed my clitoris, and why. I wanted to know against whom my rage should be directed.

"Diagnosis: true hermaphrodite. Operation: clitorectomy." The hospital record showed Charlie admitted, age 18 months. His typewritten name had been crudely crossed out and "Cheryl" scribbled over it.

Though I recall clearly the scene of Dr. Christen handing me the records, dismissing me from her office, I can recall nothing of my emotional reaction. How is it possible that I could be a *hermaphrodite?* The hermaphrodite is a mythological creature. I am a woman, a lesbian woman, though I lack a clitoris and inner labia. What did my genitals look like before the surgery? Was I born with a penis?

Fifteen years of emotional numbness passed before I was able to seek out the answers to these and many other questions. Then, four years ago, extreme emotional turmoil and suicidal despair arrived suddenly, threatening to crush me. "It's not possible," I thought. "This cannot be anyone's story, much less mine. I don't want it." Yet it *is* mine. I mark that time as the beginning of my coming out as a political intersexual, an "avowed intersexual," to borrow the epithet which until recently adhered to homosexuals who refused to stay invisible.

The story of my childhood is a lie. I know now that after the clitorectomy my parents followed the physicians' advice, and discarded every scrap of evidence that Charlie had ever existed. They replaced all of the blue baby clothing with pink and discarded photos and birthday cards. When I look at grandparents, aunts, uncles, I am aware that they must know that one day Charlie ceased to exist in my family, and Cheryl was there in his place.

The medical establishment uses the terms *hermaphrodite* and *intersexual* to refer to us. The word hermaphrodite, with its strong mythological associations, reinforces the notion that hermaphroditism is a fantasy, not your neighbor, your friend, your teacher, or—especially—your baby. And, because it falsely implies that one individual possesses two sets of genitals, it allows my clitoris to be labeled as a penis, and the clitorectomy performed on me to be justified as "reconstructive surgery." For these reasons I prefer the term *intersexual.* . . .

At the beginning of my process of coming out as intersexual, I chose to examine again the three pages of medical records that I had set aside for fifteen years. The word "hermaphrodite" was horribly wounding and drove me to the brink of suicide. I thought back to my earlier process of coming out as lesbian. The way out of this pain was to reclaim the stigmatized label, to manufacture a positive acceptance of it. This second coming out was far more painful and difficult. As a teenager recognizing my attraction to women, I visited the library, stealthily examined Del Martin and Phyllis Lyon's *Lesbian/Woman*, Radclyffe Hall's *The Well of Loneliness*. I learned that other lesbians existed, that they somehow managed to live and to love women. Somehow I would find them. There was a community where my lesbianism would be understood, would be welcome. No such help was available to reclaim my intersexuality. The only images I found were absolutely pathologized case histories in medical texts and journals, closeups of genitals being poked, prodded, measured, sliced, and sutured—full body shots with the eyes blacked out.

For many months, I struggled to reclaim the label "hermaphrodite." I knew that I had been horribly mutilated by the clitorectomy, deprived of the experience of sexuality that most people, male or female, take for granted. What would my life be had I been allowed to keep my genitals intact? "No," I thought. "I don't wish to have a penis between my legs, for my body to look like a man's body. I could never relate sexually to a woman as if I were a man."

"Never mind, just don't think about it," was the advice of the few people to whom I spoke, including two female therapists: "You look like a woman."

There is a powerful resistance to thinking about intersex. Because they look at me and make a female attribution, most people find it impossible to imagine that my experience and my history are not female. The resistance to thinking about what my sexual experience might be is even more profound. Most people, including the two therapists mentioned above, are paralyzed by the general prohibition on explicit sex talk. But sex radicals and activists are little better. They assume that I am having "vaginal orgasms" or even "full body orgasms." If I persist in asserting my sexual dysfunction, many patronize me. "I am completely confident that you will learn how to orgasm," one man told me, then continued his explanation of how male circumcision was just as damaging as clitorectomy, my experience to the contrary.

What is most infuriating is to read, nearly every day in popular media, denunciations of African female genital mutilation as barbaric abuses of human rights, which fail to mention that intersexed children's clitorises are removed every day in the U.S. Such writers occasionally note that clitorectomy has been practiced in the U.S., but always hurry to assure the reader that the practice ended by the 1930s. Letters to these authors receive no reply. Letters to editors pointing out the inaccuracy are not published.

In 1996, Congress passed H.R. 3610, prohibiting "the removal or infibulation (or both) of the whole or part of the clitoris, the labia minor, or the labia major." However, the next paragraph specifically excludes from prohibition these operations if they are performed by a licensed medical practitioner who deems them necessary. As early as 1993, Brown University Professor of Medical Science Anne Fausto-Sterling had joined intersexuals to ask Congresswoman Pat Schroeder, in drafting the prohibition, not to neglect genital surgery performed on intersexed infants. Ms. Schroeder's office made no reply. Newspaper accounts in 1996 lauded the bill's passage as an end to clitorectomy in the U.S.

It took months for me to obtain the rest of my medical records. I learned that I had been born, not with a penis, but with intersexed genitals: a typical vagina and outer labia, female urethra, and a very large clitoris. Mind you, "large" and "small," as applied to intersexed genitals, are judgments which exist only in the mind of the beholder. From my birth until the surgery, while I was Charlie, my parents and doctors considered my penis to be monstrously small, and with the urethra in the "wrong" position.

My parents were so shamed and traumatized by the appearance of my genitals that they allowed no one to see them: no baby-sitters, no possibility of tired parents being spelled for diaper-changing by a helpful grandmother or aunt. Then, at the very moment the intersex specialist physicians pro-nounced that my "true sex" was female, my clitoris was suddenly monstrously large. All this occurred without any change in the objective size or appearance of the appendage between my legs.

Being intersexed is humanly possible, but (in our culture) is socially unthinkable. In modern industrial cultures, when a child is born the experts present, whether midwives or physicians, assign a sex based on the appear-ance of the infant's genitals. They are required—both legally and by social custom—to assign the child as either male or female. Were parents to tell inquiring friends and relatives that their newborn's sex was "hermaphrodite," they would be greeted with sheer disbelief. Should the parents persist in labeling their child "hermaphrodite" rather than "male or female with a congenital deformity requiring surgical repair," their very sanity would be questioned.

Thus, intersexed children are always assigned to either male or female sex. In making these problematic sex assignments, specialist physicians are generally consulted. The assignment may not be made for several days, and it is sometimes changed, as was done with me. In fact, there are documented cases in which the sex assignment has been changed, without soliciting the opinion of, or even *informing* the child, as many as three times. [See Money 1991, 239].

Most people take for granted, even assume as "scientific fact," that there are two, and only two, sexes. In reality, however, about one in two thousand infants is born with an anatomy that refuses to conform to our preconcep-tions of "male" and "female." Few outside the medical profession are even aware of our existence. I now know that hundreds of thousands of peo-ple in the U.S. alone share my experience, and we are organizing ourselves through the Intersex Society of North America.[2] My ability to embrace the term *hermaphrodite*, however halting and uncertain at first, has grown in depth, conviction, and pride as I have met other intersexuals, sharing our stories, our lives, and our anger.

Struggling to understand why society so utterly denies the phenomenon of intersexuality, I read widely in such diverse fields as philosophy, history, psychology, and ethnography. I was excited to discover that in recent years a number of scholars in these fields have begun to examine the ways in which sex and gender are socially constructed. These and related works constitute a recognition that the paradigms of previous investigators have caused them to overlook information about non-reproductive sexual conduct, practices, and categories. Data which were at odds with their culturally-determined heterosexist, dimorphic point of view were ignored because they could not be accounted for.

Americans are apt to express disbelief when confronted with evidence of intersexuality. Modern Western culture is the first to rely upon technology to enforce gender dichotomy. Since the 1950s or so, surgical and hormonal means have been used to erase the evidence from intersexed infants' bodies. Medical literature speaks with one voice on the necessity of this practice, even as it concedes that surgical intervention may damage sexual function. Silence has been considered evidence of patient satisfaction.

> For over 40 years, some form of clitorectomy or clitoroplasty has been used to treat little girls with adrenogenital syndrome (one of dozens of reasons why an infant may be born intersexed). The only indication for performing this surgery has been to improve the body image of these children so that they feel "more normal...." Not one has complained of loss of sensation even when the entire clitoris was removed.... The clitoris is clearly not necessary for orgasm. (Edgerton 1993, 956).[3]

What are genitals for? It is my position that *my* genitals are for *my* pleasure. In a sex-repressive culture with a heavy investment in the fiction of sexual dichotomy, infant genitals are for discriminating male from female infants. It is very difficult to get parents, or even physicians, to consider the infant as a future adult, sexual being. Medical intersex specialists, however, pride themselves on being able to do just that.

For intersex specialists, male genitals are for active penetration and pleasure, while female genitals are for passive penetration and reproduction: Men have sex, women have babies. Asked by a journalist why standard practice assigns 90% of intersexed infants as females (and surgically enforces the assignment by trimming or removing the clitoris), one prominent surgical specialist reasoned, "you can make a hole, but you can't build a pole" (Hendricks 1993, 15).

Notice how John Gearhart, a noted specialist in genital surgery for intersex children, evades questioning about orgasmic function following presentation of his paper on additional surgeries for repair of vaginas surgically constructed in intersexed infants. (Dr. Frank, in attendance at the presentation, shares a professional interest in such surgery; the discussion was published in the *Journal of Urology* along with the paper.)

> *Dr. Frank:* How do you define successful intercourse? How many of these girls actually have an orgasm, for example? How many of these had a clitorectomy, how many a clitoroplasty, and did it make any difference to orgasm?

> *Dr. Gearhart:* Interviews with the families were performed by a female pediatric surgeon who is kind and caring, and who I think got the maximum information from these patients. Adequate intercourse was defined as successful vaginal penetration.... (Bailez et al. 1992, 684)

Gearhart has since condemned outspoken intersexed adults as "zealots" (Angier 1996), and minimized reports by former patients of damaged sexual function after clitoral surgery because "some women who have never had surgery are anorgasmic" (Chase 1996, 1140).

Intersex specialists often stress the importance of a heterosexual outcome for the intersexed children consigned to their care. For instance, Slijper et al. state, "parents will feel reassured when they know that their daughter can develop heterosexually just like other children" (Slijper et al. 1994, 15). Dr. Y, a prominent surgeon in the field of intersexuality, agreed to be interviewed by Ellen Lee only under condition of anonymity. He asserts that the ultimate measure of success for sex assignment of intersexed children is the "effectiveness of intercourse" they achieve as adults (Lee 1994, 60). Intersexuals assigned female who choose women as sexual partners, and those assigned male who choose men as sexual partners, must then represent failures of treatment in the eyes of our parents and of intersex specialists. Indeed, my mother's reaction upon learning that I was sexual with women was to reveal to my siblings, but not to me, my hermaphroditism and history of sex change and to regret that she had allowed physicians to assign me female, rather than male.

My mother and father took me into their room one day, to share a secret with me. I was ten years old, still utterly ignorant about sexual matters. "When you were a baby, you were sick," they explained. "Your clitoris was too big, it was *enlarged*." The way they spoke the word *enlarged*, it was clear that it was being given some special, out of the ordinary, meaning. "You had to go into the hospital, and it was removed."

"What is a 'clitoris'?" I asked.

"A clitoris is a part of a girl that would have been a penis if she had been a boy. Yours was *enlarged*, so it had to be removed. Now everything is fine. But don't ever tell this to anyone else."

Who am I? I look at my body. It *looks* female. Yet I have always harbored a secret doubt. I remember myself as a withdrawn, depressed adolescent, trying to steal a glance of a woman's genitals. Do hers look like mine? I had never seen a naked woman up close. I had no idea that my genitals were missing parts. In fact, one cannot discern the difference between my genitals and those of any other woman without parting the outer labia. I do recall learning, from a book, about the phenomenon of masturbation. Try as I might, I could not locate a focus of pleasurable sensation in my genitals, couldn't accomplish the trick that I had read about. I wasn't able to associate this failure with the secret about the *enlarged* clitoris that had been removed. I simply couldn't take in that such an irreversible harm had been done to me, and by adults who were responsible for my well-being. I often woke from a nightmare in which my life was in danger, my gender in question, and my genitals were somehow horribly deformed, spilling out of me like visceral organs. It wasn't until I became a young adult that I was able to make the connection between the removal of my clitoris and my feeble sexual response, my inability to experience orgasm.

Who am I? I now assert both my femininity and my intersexuality, my "not female"-ness. This is not a paradox; the fact that my gender has been problematized is the source of my intersexual identity. Most people have never struggled with their gender, are at a loss to answer the question, "How do you know you are a woman (a man)?"

I have been unable to experience myself as totally female. Although my body passes for female, women's clothing does not fit me. The shoulders are too narrow, the sleeves too short. Most women's gloves won't go on my hands, nor women's shoes on my feet. For most women, that wouldn't be more than an inconvenience. But when the clothing doesn't fit, I am reminded of my history.

Of course, men's clothing doesn't fit either. The straight lines leave no room for my large breasts or broad hips. Still, I experience something about the way that I work and move in the world as relatively masculine. And when a man expresses an intimate attraction to me, I often suspect that he may be wrestling with a conflicted homosexual orientation, attracted to a masculine part of me, but my feminine appearance renders his attraction safely heterosexual.

As a woman, I am less than whole. I have a secret past. I lack important parts of my genitals and sexual response. When a lover puts her hand to my genitals for the first time, the lack is immediately obvious to her. Finally, I simply do not feel myself a woman (even less a man). But the hermaphrodite identity was too monstrous, too Other, too freakish, for me to easily embrace. A medical anomaly, patched up as best the surgeons could manage. I had an article from a medical journal that stated that only twelve "true hermaphrodites" (the label applied to me by my medical records) had *ever* been recorded (Morris 1957, 540)....

What do I see when I look in the mirror? A female body, though scarred and missing some important genital parts. When I interact in daily life with others, though, I experience a strange sort of bodily dissociation; my perception of myself is as a disembodied entity, without sex or gender. I view healing this split as an important element of personal growth that will allow me to reclaim my sexuality and to be more effective as an intersex advocate. My body is not female; it is intersexed. Nonconsensual surgery cannot erase intersexuality and produce whole males and females; it produces emotionally abused and sexually dysfunctional intersexuals. If I label my post-surgical anatomy female, I ascribe to surgeons the power to create a *woman* by removing body parts. I accede to their agenda of "woman as lack." I collaborate in the prohibition of my intersexual identity. Kessler quotes an endocrinologist who specializes in treating intersexed infants: "In the absence of maleness, you have femaleness.... It's really the basic design" (Kessler 1990, 15).

Must things be this way? In all cultures, at all times? Anthropologist Clifford Geertz contrasted the conceptualization of intersexuals by the

Navajo and the Kenyan Pokot ("a product, if a somewhat unusual product, of the normal course of things") with the American attitude. "Americans . . . regard femaleness and maleness as exhausting the natural categories in which persons can conceivably come: What falls between is a darkness, an offense against reason" (Geertz 1984, 85). The time has come for intersexuals to denounce our treatment as abuse, to embrace and openly assert our identities as intersexuals, to intentionally affront that sort of reason which requires that we be mutilated and silenced. . . .

When I first began to seek out other intersexuals, I expected and wanted to find people whose experience exactly matched mine. What I have discovered is that in one sense we are very different: the range of personalities, politics, and anatomies in our nascent intersexual movement is broad. Some of us live as women, some as men, some as open intersexuals. Many of us are homosexual, if that term is narrowly understood in terms of the social gender roles of the partners. Some of us have never been sexual. But in another sense our experiences are surprisingly coherent: Those of us who have been subjected to medical intervention and invisibility share our experience of it as abuse.

I claim lesbian identity because women who feel desire for me experience that desire as lesbian, because I feel most female when being sexual, and because I feel desire for women as I do not for men. Many intersexuals share my sense of queer identity, even those who do not share this homosexual identity. One, assigned female at birth and lucky enough to escape genital surgery through a fluke, has said that she has enjoyed sex with both women and men, but never with another intersexual. "I'm a heterosexual in the truest sense of the word" (Angier 1996).

Healing is a process without end. The feeling of being utterly alone may be the most damaging part of what has been done to us. My work as an activist, listening to, counseling, and connecting other intersexuals, and working to save children born every day from having to repeat our suffering, has been an important part of my own healing, of feeling less overwhelmed by grief and rage.

Notes

1. Melanie Blackless, Anthony Charuvastra, Amanda Derryck, Anne Fausto-Sterling, Karl Lauzanne, and Ellen Lee, "How Sexually Dimorphic Are We? Review and Synthesis," *American Journal of Human Biology* 12 (2000): 151–66.

2. Intersex Society of North America, 979 Golf Course Drive, #282, Rohnert Park, CA 94928. www.isna.org.

3. Although this statement was written in connection with an article about "clitoroplasty without loss of sensitivity," the authors provide no evidence that this standard procedure, which removes nearly the entire clitoris and relocates the remainder, leaves sexual sensation intact. On the other hand, Morgan Holmes, who was subjected to it as a child, characterizes it as a "partial clitorectomy"

(Holmes 1994). Another woman, who had the procedure performed as an adult and is able to contrast her sexual experience before and after the surgery, calls it "incredibly desensitizing" (Chase 1994).

References

Angier, Natalie. 1996. Intersexual healing: An anomaly finds a group. *New York Times*, 4 February, E14.

Bailez, M. M., John P. Gearhart, Claude Migeon, and John Rock. 1992. Vaginal reconstruction after initial construction of the external genitalia in girls with salt-wasting adrenal hyperplasia. *Journal of Urology* 148:680–84.

Chase, Cheryl. 1996. Re: Measurement of evoked potentials during feminizing genitoplasty: Techniques and applications (letter). *Journal of Urology* 156(3): 1139–40.

Edgerton, Milton T. 1993. Discussion: Clitoroplasty for clitoromegaly due to adrenogenital syndrome without loss of sensitivity (by Nobuyuki Sagehashi). *Plastic and Reconstructive Surgery* 91(5):956.

Fausto-Sterling, Anne. 1993. The five sexes: Why male and female are not enough. *The Sciences* 33(2):20–25.

Foucault, Michel. 1980a. *Herculine Barbin, being the recently discovered memoirs of a nineteenth-century hermaphrodite*, translated by Richard McDougall. New York: Colophon.

Geertz, Clifford. 1984. *Local Knowledge*. New York: Basic Books.

Hendricks, Melissa. 1993. Is it a boy or a girl? *Johns Hopkins Magazine* (November): 10–16.

Holmes, Morgan. 1994. Medical politics and cultural intersexuality beyond pathology and erasure. Master's thesis, York University.

Kessler, Suzanne. 1990. The medical construction of gender: Case management of intersexual infants. *Signs: Journal of Women in Culture and Society* 16(1):3–26.

Kessler, Suzanne J., and Wendy McKenna. 1978. *Gender: An Ethnomethodological Approach*. New York: John Wiley and Sons.

Lee, Ellen Hyun-Ju. 1994. Producing sex: An interdisciplinary perspective on sex assignment decisions for intersexuals. Senior thesis, Brown University.

Money, John. 1991. *Biographies of Gender and Hermaphroditism in Paired Comparisons*, edited by John Money and H. Musaph. *Clinical Supplement to the Handbook of Sexology*. New York: Elsevier.

Morris, John McL. 1957. Intersexuality. *Journal of the American Medical Association* 163(7):538–42.

Pool, Robert E. 1994. *Eve's rib: The biological roots of sex differences*. New York: Crown Publishers.

Slijper, Froukje M. E., S. L. S. Drop, J. C. Molenaar, and R. J. Scholtmeijer. 1994. Neonates with abnormal genital development assigned the female sex: Parent counseling. *Journal of Sex Education and Therapy* 20(1):9–17.

Walker, Alice. 1992. *Possessing the Secret of Joy*. New York: Simon and Schuster.

6

Foucault, Femininity, and the Modernization of Patriarchal Power

Sandra Lee Bartky

Early feminist scholars often emphasized how social organizations and institutions such as churches, police, schools, and medicine controlled women's behavior by rewarding girls and women who conformed to social expectations and punishing those who did not. In contrast, the highly influential philosopher Michel Foucault emphasized how modern society instead creates "docile bodies"—bodies that meet social expectations without complaint or resistance—not through punishment, but by teaching individuals to accept those expectations as their own and to live as if they might *be punished at any moment.*

Foucault developed his ideas about the social creation of docile bodies through his research on the history of prisons. In the premodern world, kings and churches instilled obedience in the population by gruesomely and publicly torturing criminals and burning heretics at the stake. In contrast, according to Foucault, modern societies use a very different approach to instill obedience. This approach is encapsulated in the idea of the Panopticon. The Panopticon was a proposed "modern" prison design in which a single prison guard, out of sight of the prisoners, would staff a central guard tower. Because the guard could see anywhere in the prison, but the prisoners could never tell if the guard was watching them, the prisoners (at least in theory) would never dare to revolt. Similarly, Foucault argues, workers in factories and students in schools come to believe that they are always under surveillance and therefore come to accept the rules and to discipline themselves.

In "Foucault, Femininity, and the Modernization of Patriarchal Power," philosopher Sandra Lee Bartky extends Foucault's ideas to female bodies. She describes how women internalize men's social expectations regarding female appearance and behavior and then strive to meet those expectations, through such "disciplinary practices" as dieting, sitting with knees together, and wearing high heels.

Bartky further argues that these disciplinary practices, or "disciplines of femininity," keep women smaller, weaker, less powerful, and constantly struggling with shame when they cannot meet impossible appearance goals (especially if they are poor or minority). As a result, these disciplines not only reflect women's subordination to men's expectations but also reinforce that subordination. Yet because women seem to accept these disciplines willingly—as she writes, "no one is ever marched off for electrolysis at gunpoint"—we rarely recognize the subtle process through which women are pressed to accept those disciplines. Nevertheless, Bartky suggests, the clash between women's increasing economic and social freedom, on the one hand, and their increasing bodily disciplines, on the other, may eventually lead more women to resist their subordination and the disciplines of femininity.

I.

In a striking critique of modern society, Michel Foucault (1979) has argued that the rise of parliamentary institutions and of new conceptions of political liberty was accompanied by a darker counter-movement, by the emergence of a new and unprecedented discipline directed against the body. More is required of the body now than mere political allegiance or the appropriation of the products of its labor: the new discipline invades the body and seeks to regulate its very forces and operations, the economy and efficiency of its movements.

The disciplinary practices Foucault describes are tied to peculiarly modern forms of the army, the school, the hospital, the prison, and the manufactory; the aim of these disciplines is to increase the utility of the body, to augment its forces:

> What was then being formed was a policy of coercions that act upon the body, a calculated manipulation of its elements, its gestures, its behaviour. The human body was entering a machinery of power that explores it, breaks it down and rearranges it. A "political anatomy," which was also a "mechanics of power," was being born; it defined how one may have a hold over others' bodies, not only so that they may do what one wishes, but so that they may operate as one wishes, with the techniques, the speed and the efficiency that one determines. Thus, discipline produces subjected and practiced bodies, "docile" bodies. (1979, 138)

The production of "docile bodies" requires that an uninterrupted coercion be directed to the very processes of bodily activity, not just their result; this "micro-physics of power" fragments and partitions the body's time, its space, and its movements (Foucault 1979, 28).

The student, then, is enclosed within a classroom and assigned to a desk he cannot leave; his ranking in the class can be read off the position of his desk in the serially ordered and segmented space of the classroom itself. Foucault (1979, 147) tells us that "Jean-Baptiste de la Salle dreamt of a classroom in which the spatial distribution might provide a whole series of distinctions at once, according to the pupil's progress, worth, character, application, cleanliness and parent's fortune." The student must sit upright, feet upon the floor, head erect; he may not slouch or fidget; his animate body is brought into a fixed correlation with the inanimate desk.

The minute breakdown of gestures and movements required of soldiers at drill is far more relentless:

> Bring the weapon forward. In three stages. Raise the rifle with the right hand, bringing it close to the body so as to hold it perpendicular with the right knee, the end of the barrel at eye level, grasping it by striking it with the right hand, the arm held close to the body at waist height. At the second stage, bring the rifle in front of you with the left hand, the barrel in the middle between the two eyes, vertical, the right hand grasping it at the small of the butt, the arm outstretched, the triggerguard resting on the first finger, the left hand at the height of the notch, the thumb lying along the barrel against the moulding. At the third stage . . . . (Foucault 1979, 153)[1]

These "body-object articulations" of the soldier and his weapon, the student and his desk effect a "coercive link with the apparatus of production." We are far indeed from older forms of control that "demanded of the body only signs or products, forms of expression or the result of labour" (Foucault 1979, 153).

The body's time, in these regimes of power, is as rigidly controlled as its space: the factory whistle and the school bell mark a division of time into discrete and segmented units that regulate the various activities of the day. The following timetable, similar in spirit to the ordering of my grammar school classroom, is suggested for French "écoles mutuelles" of the early nineteenth century:

> 8:45 entrance of the monitor, 8:52 the monitor's summons, 8:56 entrance of the children and prayer, 9:00 the children go to their benches, 9:04 first slate, 9:08 end of dictation, 9:12 second slate, etc. (Foucault 1979, 150)

Control this rigid and precise cannot be maintained without a minute and relentless surveillance.

Jeremy Bentham's design for the Panopticon, a model prison, captures for Foucault the essence of the disciplinary society. At the periphery of the Panopticon, a circular structure; at the center, a tower with wide windows that opens onto the inner side of the ring. The structure on the periphery is divided into cells, each with two windows, one facing the windows of the tower, the other facing the outside, allowing an effect of backlighting to make any figure visible within the cell. "All that is needed, then, is to place a supervisor in a central tower and to shut up in each cell a madman, a patient, a condemned man, a worker or a schoolboy" (Foucault 1979, 200). Each inmate is alone, shut off from effective communication with his fellows, but constantly visible from the tower. The effect of this is "to induce in the inmate a state of conscious and permanent visibility that assures the automatic functioning of power"; each becomes to himself his own jailer (Foucault 1979, 201). This "state of conscious and permanent visibility" is a sign that the tight, disciplinary control of the body has gotten a hold on the mind as well. In the perpetual self-surveillance of the inmate lies the genesis of the celebrated "individualism" and heightened self-consciousness that are hallmarks of modern times. For Foucault (1979, 228), the structure and effects of the Panopticon resonate throughout society: Is it surprising that "prisons resemble factories, schools, barracks, hospitals, which all resemble prisons"?

Foucault's account in *Discipline and Punish* of the disciplinary practices that produce the "docile bodies" of modernity is a genuine *tour de force*, incorporating a rich theoretical account of the ways in which instrumental reason takes hold of the body with a mass of historical detail. But Foucault treats the body throughout as if it were one, as if the bodily experiences of men and women did not differ and as if men and women bore the same relationship to the characteristic institutions of modern life. Where is the account of the disciplinary practices that engender the "docile bodies" of women, bodies more docile than the bodies of men? Women, like men, are subject to many of the same disciplinary practices Foucault describes. But he is blind to those disciplines that produce a modality of embodiment that is peculiarly feminine. To overlook the forms of subjection that engender the feminine body is to perpetuate the silence and powerlessness of those upon whom these disciplines have been imposed. Hence, even though a liberatory note is sounded in Foucault's critique of power, his analysis as a whole reproduces that sexism which is endemic throughout Western political theory.

We are born male or female, but not masculine or feminine. Femininity is an artifice, an achievement, "a mode of enacting and reenacting received gender norms which surface as so many styles of flesh" (Butler 1985, 11). In what follows, I shall examine those disciplinary practices that produce a body which in gesture and appearance is recognizably feminine. I consider three categories of such practices: those that aim to produce a body of a certain size and general configuration; those that bring forth from this body a specific repertoire of gestures, postures, and movements; and those that are directed toward the display of this body as an ornamented surface. I shall examine the nature of these disciplines, how they are imposed and by whom. I shall probe the effects of the imposition of such discipline on female identity and subjectivity. In the final section I shall argue that these disciplinary practices must be understood in the light of the modernization of patriarchal domination, a modernization that unfolds historically according to the general pattern described by Foucault.

II.

Styles of the female figure vary over time and across cultures: they reflect cultural obsessions and preoccupations in ways that are still poorly understood. Today, massiveness, power, or abundance in a woman's body is met with distaste. The current body of fashion is taut, small-breasted, narrow-hipped, and of a slimness bordering on emaciation; it is a silhouette that seems more appropriate to an adolescent boy or a newly pubescent girl than to an adult woman. Since ordinary women have normally quite different dimensions, they must of course diet.

Mass-circulation women's magazines run articles on dieting in virtually every issue. The *Ladies' Home Journal* of February 1986 carries a "Fat Burning Exercise Guide," while *Mademoiselle* offers to "Help Stamp Out Cellulite" with "Six Sleek-Down Strategies." After the diet-busting Christmas holidays and, later, before summer bikini season, the titles of these features become shriller and more arresting. The reader is now addressed in the imperative mode: Jump into shape for summer! Shed ugly winter fat with the all-new Grapefruit Diet! More women than men visit diet doctors, while women greatly outnumber men in such self-help groups as Weight Watchers and Overeaters Anonymous—in the case of the latter, by well over 90 percent (Millman 1980, 46).

Dieting disciplines the body's hungers: appetite must be monitored at all times and governed by an iron will. Since the innocent need of the organism for food will not be denied, the body becomes one's enemy, an alien being bent on thwarting the disciplinary project. Anorexia nervosa, which has now assumed epidemic proportions, is to women of the late twentieth century what hysteria was to women of an earlier day: the crystallization in a pathological mode of a widespread cultural obsession (Bordo 1985–86). A survey taken recently at UCLA is astounding: of 260 students interviewed, 27.3 of women but only 5.8 percent of men said they were "terrified" of getting fat; 28.7 percent of women but only 7.5 percent of men said they were obsessed or "totally preoccupied" with food. The body images of women and men are strikingly different as well: 35 percent of women but only 12.5 percent of men said they felt fat though other people told them they were thin. Women in the survey wanted to weigh ten pounds less than their average weight; men felt they were within a pound of their ideal weight. A total of 5.9 percent of women and no men met the psychiatric criteria for anorexia or bulimia (*USA Today* 1985).

Dieting is one discipline imposed upon a body subject to the "tyranny of slenderness"; exercise is another (Chernin 1981). Since men as well as women exercise, it is not always easy in the case of women to distinguish what is done for the sake of physical fitness from what is done in obedience to the requirements of femininity. Men as well as women lift weights and do yoga, calisthenics, and aerobics, though "jazzercise" is largely a female pursuit. Men and women alike engage themselves with a variety of machines, each designed to call forth from the body a different exertion: there are Nautilus machines, rowing machines, ordinary and motorized exercycles, portable hip and leg cycles, belt massagers, trampolines, treadmills, and arm and leg pulleys. However, given the widespread female obsession with weight, one suspects that many women are working out with these apparatuses in the health club or at the gym with an aim in mind and in a spirit quite different from men's.

But there are classes of exercises meant for women alone, these designed not to firm or reduce the body's size overall, but to resculpture its various parts on the current model. M. J. Saffon (1981), "international beauty expert," assures us that his twelve basic facial exercises can erase frown lines, smooth the forehead, raise hollow cheeks, banish crow's feet, and tighten the muscles under the chin. There are exercises to build the breasts and exercises to banish "cellulite," said by "figure consultants" to be a special type of female fat. There is "spot-reducing," an umbrella term that covers dozens of punishing exercises designed to reduce "problem areas" like thick ankles or "saddlebag" thighs. The very idea of "spot-reducing" is both scientifically unsound and cruel, for it raises expectations in women that can never be realized—the pattern in which fat is deposited or removed is known to be genetically determined.

It is not only her natural appetite or unreconstructed contours that pose a danger to woman: the very expressions of her face can subvert the disciplinary project of bodily perfection. An expressive face lines and creases more readily than an inexpressive one. Hence, if women are unable to suppress strong emotions, they can at least learn to inhibit the tendency of the face to register them. Sophia Loren (1984, 57) recommends a unique solution to this problem: a piece of tape applied to the forehead or between the brows will tug at the skin when one frowns and act as a reminder to relax the face. The tape is to be worn whenever a woman is home alone.

III.

There are significant gender differences in gesture, posture, movement, and general bodily comportment: women are far more restricted than men in their manner of movement and in their spatiality. In her classic paper on the subject, Iris Young (1980) observes that a space seems to surround women in imagination that they are hesitant to move beyond: this manifests itself both in a reluctance to reach, stretch, and extend the body to meet resistances of matter in motion—as in sport or in the performance of physical tasks—and in a typically constricted posture and general style of movement. Woman's space is not a field in which her bodily intentionality can be freely realized but an enclosure in which she feels herself positioned and by which she is confined (Wex 1979). The "loose woman" violates those norms: her looseness is manifest not only in her morals, but in her manner of speech and quite literally in the free and easy way she moves.

In an extraordinary series of over two thousand photographs, many candid shots taken in the street, the German photographer Marianne Wex (1979) has documented differences in typical masculine and feminine body posture. Women sit waiting for trains with arms close to the body, hands folded together in their laps, toes pointing straight ahead or turned inward, and legs pressed together. The women in these photographs make themselves small and narrow, harmless; they seem tense; they take up little space. Men, on the other hand, expand into the available space; they sit with legs far apart and arms flung out at some distance from the body. Most common in these sitting male figures is what Wex calls the "proffering position": the men sit with legs thrown wide apart, crotch visible, feet pointing outward, often with an arm and a casually dangling hand resting comfortably on an open, spread thigh.

In proportion to total body size, a man's stride is longer than a woman's. The man has more spring and rhythm to his step; he walks with toes pointed outward, holds his arms at a greater distance from his body and swings them farther; he tends to point the whole hand in the direction he is moving. The woman holds her arms closer to her body, palms against her sides; her walk is circumspect. If she has subjected herself to the additional constraint of high-heeled shoes, her body is thrown forward and off balance: the struggle to walk under these conditions shortens her stride still more.

But women's movement is subjected to a still finer discipline. Feminine faces, as well as bodies, are trained to the expression of deference. Under male scrutiny, women will avert their eyes or cast them downward; the female gaze is trained to abandon its claim to the sovereign status of seer. The "nice" girls learns to avoid the bold and unfettered staring of the "loose" woman who looks at whatever and whomever she pleases. Women are trained to smile more than men, too. In the economy of smiles, as elsewhere, there is evidence that women are exploited, for they give more than they receive in return; in a smile elicitation study, one researcher found that the rate of smile return by women was 93 percent, by men only 67 percent (Henley 1977, 176). In many typical women's jobs, graciousness, deference, and the readiness to serve are part of the work; this requires the worker to fix a smile on her face for a good part of the working day, whatever her inner state (Hochschild 1983). The economy of touching is out of balance, too: men touch women more often and on more parts of the body than women touch men: female secretaries, factory workers, and waitresses report that such liberties are taken routinely with their bodies (Henley 1977, 108).

Feminine movement, gesture, and posture must exhibit not only constriction, but grace and a certain eroticism restrained by modesty: all three. Here is field for the operation for a whole new training: a woman must stand with stomach pulled in, shoulders thrown slightly back and chest out, this to display her bosom to maximum advantage. While she must walk in the confined fashion appropriate to women, her movements must, at the same time, be combined with a subtle but provocative hip-roll. But too much display is taboo: women in short, low-cut dresses are told to avoid bending over at all, but if they must, great care must be taken to avoid an unseemly display of breast or rump. From time to time, fashion magazines offer quite precise instructions on the proper way of getting in and out of cars. These instructions combine all three imperatives of women's movements: a woman must not allow her arms and leg to flail about in all directions, she must try to manage her movements with the appearance of grace—no small accomplishment when one is climbing out of the back seat of a Fiat—and she is well-advised to use the opportunity for a certain display of leg.

All the movements we have described so far are self-movements; they arise from within the woman's own body. But in a way that normally goes unnoticed, males in couples may literally steer a woman everywhere she goes: down the street, around corners, into elevators, through doorways, into her chair at the dinner table, around the dance floor. The man's movement "is not necessarily heavy and pushy or physical in an ugly way; it is light and gentle but firm in the way of the most confident equestrians with the best trained horses" (Henley 1977, 149).

IV.

We have examined some of the disciplinary practices a woman must master in pursuit of a body of the right size and shape that also displays the proper styles of feminine motility. But woman's body is an ornamented surface too, and there is much discipline involved in this production as well. Here, especially in the application of makeup and the selection of clothes, art and discipline converge, though, as I shall argue, there is less art involved than one might suppose.

A woman's skin must be soft, supple, hairless, and smooth; ideally, it should betray no sign of wear, experience, age, or deep thought. Hair must be removed not only from the face but from large surfaces of the body as well, from legs and thighs, an operation accomplished by shaving, buffing with fine sandpaper, or applying foul-smelling depilatories. With the new high-leg bathing suits and leotards, a substantial amount of pubic hair must be removed too. The removal of facial hair can be more specialized. Eyebrows are plucked out by the roots with a tweezers. Hot wax is sometimes poured onto the mustache and cheeks and then ripped away when it cools. The woman who wants a more permanent result may try electrolysis: this involves the killing of hair root by the passage of an electric current down a needle that has been inserted into its base. The procedure is painful and expensive.

The development of what one "beauty expert" calls "good skincare habits" requires not only attention to health, the avoidance of strong facial expressions, and the performance of facial exercises, but the regular use of skincare preparations, many to be applied more often than once a day: cleansing lotions (ordinary soap and water "upsets the skin's acid and alkaline balance"), wash-off cleansers (milder than cleansing lotions), astringents, toners, makeup removers, night creams, nourishing creams, eye creams, moisturizers, skin balances, body lotions, hand creams, lip pomades, suntan lotions, sunscreens, and facial masks. Provision of the proper facial mask is complex: there are sulfur masks for pimples; oil or hot masks for dry areas; if these fail, then tightening masks; conditioning masks; peeling masks; cleansing masks made of herbs, cornmeal, or almonds; and mudpacks. Black women may wish to use "fade creams" to "even skin tone." Skincare preparations are never just sloshed onto the skin, but applied according to precise rules: eye cream is dabbed on gently in movements toward, never away from, the nose; cleansing cream is applied in outward directions only, straight down the nose and up and out on the cheeks (Klinger and Rowes 1978).

The normalizing discourse of modern medicine is enlisted by the cosmetics industry to gain credibility for its claims. Dr. Christian Barnard lends his enormous prestige to the Glycel line of "cellular treatment activators"; these contain "glycosphingolipids" that can "make older skin behave and look like younger skins" (ads in *Chicago Magazine*, March 1986). The Clinique computer at any Clinique counter will select a combination of preparations just right for you. Ultima II contains "procollagen" in its anti-aging eye cream that "provides hydration" to "demoralizing lines." "Biotherm" eye cream dramatically improves the "biomechanical properties of the skin" (*Chicago Magazine* 1986). The Park Avenue clinic of Dr. Zizmor, "chief of dermatology at one of New York's leading hospitals," offers not only such medical treatment as derma-brasion and chemical peeling, but "total deep skin cleansing" as well (ad in *Essence* magazine, April 1986, 25).[2]

Really good skincare habits require the use of a variety of aids and devices: facial steamers, faucet filters to collect impurities in the water, borax to soften it, a humidifier for the bedroom, electric massagers, backbrushes, complexion brushes, loofahs, pumice stones, and blackhead removers. I will not detail the implements or techniques involved in the manicure or pedicure.

The ordinary circumstances of life as well as a wide variety of activities cause a crisis in skincare and require a stepping-up of the regimen as well as an additional laying-on of preparations. Skincare discipline requires a specialized knowledge: a woman must know what to do if she has been skiing, taking medication, doing vigorous exercise, boating, or swimming in chlorinated pools; or if she has been exposed to pollution, heated rooms, cold, sun, harsh weather, the pressurized cabins on airplanes, saunas or steam rooms, fatigue, or stress. Like the schoolchild or prisoner, the woman mastering good skincare habits is put on a timetable: Georgette Klinger requires that a shorter or longer period of attention be paid to the complexion at least four times a day (Klinger and Rowes 1978, 137–40). Haircare, like skincare, requires a similar investment of time, the use of a wide variety of preparations, the mastery of a set of techniques, and, again, the acquisition of a specialized knowledge.

The crown and pinnacle of good haircare and skincare is, of course, the arrangement of the hair and the application of cosmetics. Here the regimen of haircare, skincare, manicure, and pedicure is recapitulated in another mode. A woman must learn the proper manipulation of a large number of devices—the blow dryer, styling brush, eyelash curler, and mascara brush. And she must learn to apply a wide variety of products—foundation, toner, covering stick, mascara, eyeshadow, eyegloss, blusher, lipstick, rouge, lip gloss, hair dye, hair rinse, hair lightener, hair "relaxer," and so on.

In the language of fashion magazine and cosmetic ads, making-up is typically portrayed as an aesthetic activity in which a woman can express her individuality. In reality, while cosmetic styles change every decade or so, and while some variation in makeup is permitted depending on the occasion, making-up the face is, in fact, a highly stylized activity that gives little rein to self-expression. Painting the face is not like painting a picture; at best, it might be described as painting the same picture over and over again with minor variations. Little latitude is permitted in what is considered appropriate makeup for the office and for most social occasions; indeed, the woman who used cosmetics in a genuinely novel and imaginative way is liable to be seen not as an artist but as an eccentric. Furthermore, since a properly made-up face is, if not a card of entree, at least a badge of acceptability in most social and professional contexts, the woman who chooses not to wear cosmetics at all faces sanctions of a sort that will never be applied to someone who chooses not to paint a watercolor.

V.

Are we dealing in all this merely with sexual *difference?* Scarcely. The disciplinary practices I have described are part of the process by which the ideal body of femininity—and hence the feminine body-subject—is constructed; in doing this, they produce a "practiced and subjected" body, that is, a body on which an inferior status has been inscribed. A woman's face must be made-up, that is to say, made-over, and so must her body: she is ten pounds overweight; her lips must be made more kissable, her complexion dewier, her eyes more mysterious. The "art" of makeup is the art of disguise, but this presupposes that a woman's face, unpainted, is defective. Soap and water, a shave, and routine attention to hygiene may be enough for *him*; for *her* they are not. The strategy of much beauty-related advertising is to suggest to women that their bodies are deficient; but even without such more or less explicit teaching, the media images of perfect female beauty that bombard us daily leave no doubt in the minds of most women that they fail to measure up. The technologies for femininity are taken up and practiced by women against the background of a pervasive sense of bodily deficiency; this accounts for what is often their compulsive or even ritualistic character.

The disciplinary project of femininity is a "setup": it requires such radical and extensive measures of bodily transformation that virtually every woman who gives herself to it is destined in some degree to fail. Thus, a measure of shame is added to a woman's sense that the body she inhabits is deficient: she ought to take better care of herself; she might after all have jogged that last mile. Many women are without the time or resources to provide themselves with even the minimum of what such a regimen requires, for example, a decent diet. Here is an additional source of shame for poor women, who must bear what our society regards as the more general shame of poverty. The burdens poor women bear in this regard are not merely psychological, since conformity to the prevailing standards of bodily acceptability is a known factor in economic mobility.

The larger disciplines that construct a "feminine" body out of a female one are by no means race- or class-specific. There is little evidence that women of color or working-class women are in general less committed to the incarnation of an ideal femininity than their more privileged sisters: this is not to deny the many ways in which factors of race, class, locality, ethnicity, or personal taste can be expressed within the kinds of practices I have described. The rising young corporate executive may buy her cosmetics at Bergdorf-Goodman, while the counter-server at McDonald's gets her at the K-Mart; the one may join an expensive "upscale" health club, while the other may have to make do with the $9.49 GFX Body-Flex II Home-Gym advertised in the *National Enquirer*: both are aiming at the same general result.

In the regime of institutionalized heterosexuality, woman must make herself "object and prey" for the man: it is for him that these eyes are limpid pools, this cheek baby-smooth (de Beauvoir 1968, 642). In contemporary patriarchal culture, a panoptical male connoisseur resides within the consciousness of most women: they stand perpetually before his gaze and under his judgment. Woman lives her body as seen by another, by an anonymous patriarchal Other. We are often told that "women dress for other women." There is some truth in this: who but someone engaged in a project similar to my own can appreciate the panache with which I bring it off? But women know for whom this game is played: they know that a pretty young woman is likelier to become a flight attendant than a plain one, and that a well-preserved older woman has a better chance of holding onto her husband than one who has "let herself go."

Here it might be objected that performance for another in no way signals the inferiority of the performer to the one for whom the performance is intended: the actor, for example, depends on his audience but is in no way inferior to it; he is not demeaned by his dependency. While femininity is surely something enacted, the analogy to theater breaks down in a number of ways. First, as I argued earlier, the self-determination we think of as requisite to an artistic career is lacking here: femininity as spectacle is something in which virtually every woman is required to participate. Second, the precise nature of the criteria by which women are judged, not only the inescapability of judgment itself, reflects gross imbalances in the social power of the sexes that do not mark the relationship of artists and their audiences. An aesthetic of femininity, for example, that mandates fragility and a lack of muscular strength produces female bodies that can offer little resistance to physical abuse, and the physical abuse of women by men, as we know, is widespread. It is true that the current fitness movement has permitted women to develop more muscular strength and endurance than was heretofore allowed; indeed, images of women have begun to appear in the mass media that seem to eroticize this new muscularity. But a woman may by no means develop more muscular strength than her partner; the bride who would tenderly carry her groom across the threshold is a figure of comedy, not romance.

Under the current "tyranny of slenderness" women are forbidden to become large or massive; they must take up as little space as possible. The very contours a woman's body takes on as she matures—the fuller breasts and rounded hips—have become distasteful. The body by which a women feels herself judged and which by rigorous discipline she must try to assume is the body of early adolescence, slight and unformed, a body lacking flesh or substance, a body in whose very contours the image of immaturity has been inscribed. The requirement that a woman maintain a smooth and hairless skin carries further the theme of inexperience, for an infantilized face must accompany her infantilized body, a face that never ages or furrows its brow in thought. The face of the ideally feminine woman must never display the marks of character, wisdom, and experience that we so admire in men.

To succeed in the provision of a beautiful or sexy body gains a woman attention and some admiration but little real respect and rarely any social power. A woman's effort to master feminine body discipline will lack importance just because she does it: her activity partakes of the general depreciation of everything female. In spite of unrelenting pressure to "make the most of what she has," women are ridiculed and dismissed for their interest in such "trivial" things as clothes and makeup. Further, the narrow identification of woman with sexuality and the body in a society that has for centuries displayed profound suspicion toward both does little to raise her status. Even the most adored female bodies complain routinely of their situation in ways that reveal an implicit understanding that there is something demeaning in the kind of attention they receive. Marilyn Monroe, Elizabeth Taylor, and Farrah Fawcett have all wanted passionately to become actresses-artists—and not just "sex objects."

But it is perhaps in their more restricted motility and comportment that the inferiorization of women's bodies is most evident. Women's typical body-language, a language of relative tension and constriction, is understood to be a language of subordination when it is enacted by men in male status hierarchies. In groups of men, those with higher status typically assume looser and more relaxed postures: the boss lounges comfortably behind the desk, while the applicant sits tense and rigid on the edge of his seat. Higher status individuals may touch their subordinates more than they themselves get touched; they initiate more eye contact and are smiled at by their inferiors more than they are observed to smile in return (Henley 1977). What is announced in the comportment of superiors is confidence and ease, especially ease of access to the Other. Female constraint in posture and movement is no doubt overdetermined: the fact that women tend to sit and stand with legs, feet, and knees close or touching may well be a coded declaration of sexual circumspection in a society that still maintains a double standard, or an effort, albeit unconscious, to guard the genital area. In the latter case, a woman's tight and constricted posture must be seen as the expression of her need to ward off real or symbolic sexual attack. Whatever proportions must be assigned in the final display to fear or deference, one thing is clear: woman's body language speaks eloquently, though silently, of her subordinate status in a hierarchy of gender.

VI.

If what we have described is a genuine discipline—a system, in Foucault's words (1979, 222), of "micro-power" that is "essentially non-egalitarian and asymmetrical"—who then are the disciplinarians? Who is the top sergeant in the disciplinary regime of femininity? Historically, the law has had some responsibility for enforcement: in times gone by, for example, individuals who appeared in public in the clothes of the other sex could be arrested. While cross-dressers are still liable to some harassment, the kind of discipline we are considering is not the business of the police or the courts. Parents and teachers, of course, have extensive influence, admonishing girls to be demure and ladylike, to "smile pretty," to sit with their legs together. The influence of the media is pervasive, too, constructing as it does an image of the female body as spectacle, nor can we ignore the role played by "beauty experts" or by emblematic public personages such as Jane Fonda and Lynn Redgrave.

But none of these individuals—the skincare consultant, the parent, the policeman—does in fact wield the kind of authority that is typically invested in those who manage more straightforward disciplinary institutions. The disciplinary power that inscribes femininity in the female body is everywhere and it is nowhere; the disciplinarian is everyone and yet no one in particular. Women regarded as overweight, for example, report that they are regularly admonished to diet, sometimes by people they scarcely know. These intrusions are often softened by reference to the natural prettiness just waiting to emerge: "People have always said that I had a beautiful face, and 'if you'd only lose weight you'd be really beautiful'" (Millman 1980, 80). Here, "people"—friends and casual acquaintances alike—act to enforce prevailing standards of body size.

Foucault tends to identify the imposition of discipline upon the body with the operation of specific institutions, for example, the school, the factory, the prison. To do this, however, is to overlook the extent to which discipline can be institutionally *unbound* as well as institutionally bound.[3] The anonymity of disciplinary power and its wide dispersion have consequences that are crucial to a proper understanding of the subordination of women. The absence of a formal institutional structure and of authorities invested with the power to carry out institutional directives creates the impression that the production of femininity is either entirely voluntary or natural. The several senses of "discipline" are instructive here. On the one hand, discipline is something imposed on subjects of an "essentially non-egalitarian and asymmetrical" system of authority. Schoolchildren, convicts, and draftees are subject to discipline in this sense. But discipline can be sought voluntarily as well—for example, when an individual seeks initiation into the spiritual discipline of Zen Buddhism. Discipline can, of course, be both at once: the volunteer may seek the physical and occupational training offered by the army without the army's ceasing in any way to be the instrument by which he and other members of his class are kept in disciplined subjection. Feminine bodily discipline has this dual character: on the one hand, no one is marched off for electrolysis at gunpoint, nor can we fail to appreciate the initiative and ingenuity displayed by countless women in an attempt to master the rituals of beauty. Nevertheless, insofar as the disciplinary practices of femininity produce a "subjected and practiced," an inferiorized, body, they must be understood as aspects of a far larger discipline, an oppressive and inegalitarian system of sexual subordination. This system aims at turning women into the docile and compliant companions of men just as surely as the army aims to turn its raw recruits into soldiers.

Now the transformation of oneself into a properly feminine body may be any or all of the following: a rite of passage into adulthood, the adoption and celebration of a particular aesthetic, a way of announcing one's economic level and social status, a way to triumph over other women in the competition for men or jobs, or an opportunity for massive narcissistic indulgence (Bartky 1982). The social construction of the feminine body is all these things, but at its base it is discipline, too, and discipline of the inegalitarian sort. The absence of formally identifiable disciplinarians and of a public schedule of sanctions only disguises the extent to which the imperative to be "feminine" serves the interest of domination. This is a lie in which all concur: making-up is merely artful play; one's first pair of high-heeled shoes is an innocent part of growing up, not the modern equivalent of foot-binding.

Why aren't all women feminists? In modern industrial societies, women are not kept in line by fear of retaliatory male violence; their victimization is not that of the South African black [under the former system of apartheid]. Nor will it suffice to say that a false consciousness engendered in women by patriarchal ideology is at the basis of female subordination. This is not to deny that women are often subject to gross male violence or that women and men alike are ideologically mystified by the dominant gender arrangements. What I wish to suggest instead is that an adequate understanding of women's oppression will require an appreciation of the extent to which not only women's lives but their very subjectivities are structured within an ensemble of systematically duplicitous practices. The feminine discipline of the body is a case in point: the practices that construct this body have an overt aim and character far removed, indeed, radically distinct, from their overt function. In this regard, the system of gender subordination, like the wage-bargain under capitalism, illustrates in its own way the ancient tension between what-is and what-appears: the phenomenal forms in which it is manifested are often quite different from the real relations that form its deeper structure.

VII.

The lack of formal public sanctions does not mean that a woman who is unable or unwilling to submit herself to the appropriate body discipline will face no sanctions at all. On the contrary, she faces a very severe sanction indeed in a world dominated by men: the refusal of male patronage. For the heterosexual woman, this may mean the loss of a badly needed intimacy; for both heterosexual women and lesbians, it may well mean the refusal of a decent livelihood.

As noted earlier, women punish themselves too for the failure to conform. The growing literature on women's body size is filled with wrenching confessions of shame from the overweight:

> I felt clumsy and huge. I felt that I would knock over furniture, bump into things, tip over chairs, not fit into VW's especially when people were trying to crowd into the back seat. I felt like I was taking over the whole room. . . . I felt disgusting and like a slob. In the summer I felt hot and sweaty and I knew people saw my sweat as evidence that I was too fat.

> I feel so terrible about the way I look that I cut off connection with my body. I operate from the neck up. I do not look in mirrors. I do not want to spend time buying clothes. I do not want to spend time with make-up because it's painful for me to look at myself. (Millman 1980, 80, 195)

> I can no longer bear to look at myself. . . . Whenever I have to stand in front of a mirror to comb my hair I tie a large towel around my neck. Even at night I slip my nightgown on before I take off my blouse and pants. But all this has only made it worse and worse. It's been so long since I've really looked at my body. (Chernin 1981, 53)

The depth of these women's shame is a measure of the extent to which all women have internalized patriarchal standards of bodily acceptability. A fuller examination of what is meant here by "internalization" may shed light on a question posed earlier: Why isn't every woman a feminist?

Something is "internalized" when it gets incorporated into the structure of the self. By "structure of the self" I refer to those modes of perception and of self-perception that allow a self to distinguish itself both from other selves and from things that are not selves. I have described elsewhere (Bartky 1982) how a generalized male witness comes to structure woman's consciousness of herself as a bodily being. This, then, is one meaning of "internalization." The sense of oneself as a distinct and valuable individual is tied not only to the sense of how one is perceived, but also to what one knows, especially to what one knows how to do; this is a second sense of "internalization." Whatever its ultimate effect, discipline can provide the individual upon whom it is imposed with a sense of mastery as well as a secure sense of identity. There is a certain contradiction here: while its imposition may promote a larger disempowerment, discipline may bring with it a certain development of a person's powers. Women, then, like other individuals, have a stake in the perpetuation of their skills, whatever it may have cost to acquire them and quite apart from the question whether, as a gender, they would have been better off had they never had to acquire them in the first place. Hence, feminism, especially a genuinely radical feminism that questions the patriarchal construction of the female body, threatens women with a certain de-skilling, something people normally resist: beyond this, it calls into question that aspect of personal identity that is tied to the development of a sense of competence.

Resistance from this source may be joined by a reluctance to part with the rewards of compliance; further, many women will resist the abandonment of an aesthetic that defines what they take to be beautiful. But there is still another source of resistance, one more subtle, perhaps, but tied once again to questions of identity and internalization. To have a body felt to be "feminine"—a body socially constructed through the appropriate practices—is in most cases crucial to a woman's sense of herself as female and, since persons currently can *be* only as male or female, to her sense of herself as an existing individual. To possess such a body may also be essential to her sense of herself as a sexually desiring and desirable subject. Hence, any political project that aims to dismantle the machinery that turns a female body into a feminine one may well be apprehended by a woman as something that threatens her with desexualization, if not outright annihilation.

The categories of masculinity and femininity do more than assist in the construction of personal identities; they are critical elements in our informal social ontology. This may account to some degree for the otherwise puzzling phenomenon of homophobia and for the revulsion felt by many at the sight of female bodybuilders; neither the homosexual nor the muscular woman can be assimilated easily into the categories that structure everyday life. The radical feminist critique of femininity, then, may pose a threat not only to a woman's sense of her own identity and desirability but to the very structure of her social universe.

Of course, many women *are* feminists, favoring a program of political and economic reform in the struggle to gain equality with men. But many "reform," or liberal, feminists (indeed, many orthodox Marxists) are committed to the idea that the preservation of a woman's femininity is quite compatible with her struggle for liberation (Markovic 1976). These thinkers have rejected a normative femininity based upon the notion of "separate spheres" and the traditional sexual division of labor, while accepting at the same time conventional standards of feminine body display. If my analysis is correct, such a feminism is incoherent. Foucault has argued that modern bourgeois democracy is deeply flawed in that it seeks political micropowers that lie beyond the realm of what is ordinarily defined as the "political." "The man described for us whom we are invited to free," he says, "is already in himself the effect of a subjection much more profound than himself" (Foucault 1979, 30). If, as I have argued, female subjectivity is constituted in any significant measure in and through the disciplinary practices that construct the feminine body, what Foucault says here of "man" is perhaps even truer of "woman." Marxists have maintained from the first the inadequacy of a purely liberal feminism: we have reached the same conclusion through a different route, casting doubt at the same time on the adequacy of traditional Marxist prescriptions for women's liberation as well. Liberals call for equal rights for women, traditional Marxists for the entry of women into production on an equal footing with men, the socialization of housework, and proletarian revolution; neither calls for the deconstruction of the categories of masculinity and femininity. [Some radical feminists such as Wittig (1976), however, have called for just such a deconstruction.] Femininity as a certain "style of the flesh" will have to be surpassed in the direction of something quite different—not masculinity, which is in many ways only its mirror opposite, but a radical and as yet unimagined transformation of the female body.

VIII.

Foucault (1979, 44) has argued that the transition from traditional to modern societies has been characterized by a profound transformation in the exercise of power, by what he calls "a reversal of the political axis of individualization." In older authoritarian systems, power was embodied in the person of the monarch and exercised upon a largely anonymous body of subjects; violation of the law was seen as an insult to the royal individual. While the methods employed to enforce compliance in the past were often quite brutal, involving gross assaults against the body, power in such a system operated in a haphazard and discontinuous fashion; much in the social totality lay beyond its reach.

By contrast, modern society has seen the emergence of increasingly invasive apparatuses of power: these exercise a far more restrictive social and psychological control than was heretofore possible. In modern societies, effects of power "circulate through progressively finer channels, gaining access to individuals themselves, to their bodies, their gestures and all their daily actions" (Foucault 1980, 151). Power now seeks to transform the minds of those individuals who might be tempted to resist it, not merely to punish or imprison their bodies. This requires two things: a finer control of the body's time and of its movements—a control that cannot be achieved without ceaseless surveillance and a better understanding of the specific person, of the genesis and nature of his "case." The power these new apparatuses seek to exercise requires a new knowledge of the individual: modern psychology and sociology are born. Whether the new modes of control have charge of correction, production, education, or the provision of welfare, they resemble one another; they exercise power in a bureaucratic mode—faceless, centralized, and pervasive. A reversal has occurred: power has now become anonymous, while the project of control has brought into being a new individuality. In fact, Foucault believes that the operation of power constitutes the very subjectivity of the subject. Here, the image of the Panopticon returns: knowing that he may be observed from the tower at any time, the inmate takes over the job of policing himself. The gaze that is inscribed in the very structure of the disciplinary institution is internalized by the inmate: modern technologies of behavior are thus oriented toward the production of isolated and self-policing subjects (Dews 1984, 77).

Women have their own experience of the modernization of power, one that begins later but follows in many respects the course outlined by Foucault. In important ways, a woman's behavior is less regulated now than it was in the past. She has more mobility and is less confined to domestic space. She enjoys what to previous generations would have been an unimaginable sexual liberty. Divorce, access to paid work outside the home, and the increasing secularization of modern life have loosened the hold over her of the traditional family and, in spite of the current fundamentalist revival, of the church. Power in these institutions was wielded by individuals known to her. Husbands and fathers enforced patriarchal authority in the family. As in the ancient regime, a woman body was subject to sanctions if she disobeyed. Not Foucault's royal individual but the Divine Individual decreed that her desire be always "unto her husband," while the person of the priest made known to her God's more specific intentions concerning her place and duties. In the days when civil and ecclesiastical authority were still conjoined, individuals formally invested with power were charged with the correction of recalcitrant women whom the family had somehow failed to constrain.

By contrast, the disciplinary power that is increasingly charged with the production of a properly embodied femininity is dispersed and anonymous; there are no individuals formally empowered to wield it; it is, as we have seen, invested in everyone and in no one in particular. This disciplinary power is peculiarly modern: it does not rely upon violent or public sanctions, nor does it seek to restrain the freedom of the female body to move from place to place. For all that, its invasion of the body is well-nigh total: the female body enters "a machinery of power that explores it, breaks it down and rearranges it" (Foucault 1979, 138). The disciplinary techniques through which the "docile bodies" of women are constructed aim at a regulation that is perpetual and exhaustive—a regulation of the body's size and contours, its appetite, posture, gestures and general comportment in space, and the appearance of each of its visible parts.

As modern industrial societies change and as women themselves offer resistance to patriarchy, older forms of domination are eroded. But new forms arise, spread, and become consolidated. Women are no longer required to be chaste or modest, to restrict their sphere of activity to the home, or even to realize their properly feminine destiny in maternity: normative femininity is coming more and more to be centered on woman's body—not its duties and obligations or even its capacity to bear children, but its sexuality, more precisely, its presumed heterosexuality and its appearance. There is, of course, nothing new in women's preoccupation with youth and beauty. What is new is the growing power of the image in a society increasingly oriented toward the visual media. Images of normative femininity, it might be ventured, have replaced the religiously oriented tracts of the past. New too is the spread of this discipline to all classes of women and its deployment throughout the life cycle. What was formerly the specialty of the aristocrat or courtesan is now the routine obligation of every woman, be she a grandmother or a barely pubescent girl.

To subject oneself to the new disciplinary power is to be up-to-date, to be "with it"; as I have argued, it is presented to us in ways that are regularly disguised. It is fully compatible with the current need for women's wage labor, the cult of youth and fitness, and the need of advanced capitalism to maintain high levels of consumption. Further, it represents a saving in the economy of enforcement: since it is women themselves who practice this discipline on and against their own bodies, men get off scott-free.

The woman who checks her makeup half a dozen times a day to see if her foundation has caked or her mascara has run, who worries that the wind or the rain may spoil her hairdo, who looks frequently to see if her stockings have bagged at the ankle or who, feeling fat, monitors everything she eats, has become, just as surely as the inmate of the Panopticon, a self-policing subject, a self committed to a relentless self-surveillance. This self-surveillance is a form of obedience to patriarchy. It is also the reflection in woman's consciousness of the fact that *she* is under surveillance in ways that *he* is not, that whatever else she may become, she is importantly a body designed to please or to excite. There has been induced in many women, then, in Foucault's words (1979, 201), "a state of conscious and permanent visibility that assures the automatic functioning of power." Since the standards of female bodily acceptability are impossible fully to realize, requiring as they do a virtual transcendence of nature, a woman may live much of her life with a pervasive feeling of bodily deficiency. Hence a tighter control of the body has gained a new kind of hold over the mind.

Foucault often writes as if power constitutes the very individuals upon whom it operates:

> The individual is not to be conceived as a sort of elementary nucleus, a primitive atom, a multiple and inert material on which power comes to fasten or against which it happens to strike.... In fact, it is already one of the prime effects of power that certain bodies, certain gestures, certain discourses, certain desires, come to be identified and constituted as individuals. (Foucault 1980, 98)

Nevertheless, if individuals were wholly constituted by the power-knowledge regime Foucault describes, it would make no sense to speak of resistance to discipline at all. Foucault seems sometimes on the verge of depriving us of a vocabulary in which to conceptualize the nature and meaning of those periodic refusals of control that, just as much as the imposition of control, mark the course of human history.

Peter Dews (1984, 92) accuses Foucault of lacking a theory of the "libidinal body," that is, the body upon which discipline is imposed and whose bedrock impulse toward spontaneity and pleasure might perhaps become the locus of resistance. Do women's "libidinal" bodies, then, not rebel against the pain, constriction, tedium, semistarvation, and constant self-surveillance to which they are currently condemned? Certainly they do, but the rebellion is put down every time a woman picks up her eyebrow tweezers or embarks upon a new diet. The harshness of a regime alone does not guarantee its rejection, for hardships can be endured if they are thought to be necessary or inevitable.

While "nature," in the form of a "libidinal" body, may not be the origin of a revolt against "culture," domination (and the discipline it requires) are never imposed without some cost. Historically, the forms and occasions of resistance are manifold. Sometimes, instances of resistance appear to spring from the introduction of new and conflicting factors into the lives of the dominated: the juxtaposition of old and new and the resulting incoherence or "contradiction" may make submission to the old ways seem increasingly unnecessary. In the present instance, what may be a major factor in the relentless and escalating objectification of women's bodies—namely, women's growing independence—produces in many women a sense of incoherence that calls into question the meaning and necessity of the current discipline. As women (albeit a small minority of women) begin to realize an unprecedented political, economic, and sexual self-determination, they fall ever more completely under the dominating gaze of patriarchy. It is this paradox, not the "libidinal body," that produces, here and there, pockets of resistance.

In the current political climate, there is no reason to anticipate either widespread resistance to currently fashionable modes of feminine embodiment or joyous experimentation with new "styles of the flesh"; moreover,

such novelties would face profound opposition from material and psychological sources identified earlier in this essay (see section VII). In spite of this,
a number of oppositional discourses and practices have appeared in recent
years. An increasing number of women are "pumping iron," a few with little
concern for the limits of body development imposed by current canons of
femininity. Women in radical lesbian communities have also rejected hegemonic images of femininity and are struggling to develop a new female
aesthetic. A striking feature of such communities is the extent to which they
have overcome the oppressive identification of female beauty and desirability
with youth: here, the physical features of aging—"character" lines and graying hair—not only do not diminish a woman's attractiveness, they may even
enhance it. A popular literature of resistance is growing, some of it analytical
and reflective, like Kim Chernin's [1981 book] *The Obsession*, some oriented
toward practical self-help, like Marcia Hutchinson's (1985) *Transforming
Body Image, Learning to Love the Body You Have*. This literature reflects a
mood akin in some ways to that other and earlier mood of quiet desperation
to which Betty Friedan gave voice in *The Feminine Mystique*. Nor should we
forget that a mass-based women's movement is in place in this country that
has begun a critical questioning of the meaning of femininity, if not yet in
the corporeal presentation of self, then in other domains of life. We women
cannot begin the re-vision of our own bodies until we learn to read the cultural messages we inscribe upon them daily and until we come to see that
even when the mastery of the disciplines of femininity produces a triumphant
result, we are still only women.

Notes

An earlier version of this paper was read to the Southwestern Philosophical Society,
November 1985. Subsequent versions were read to the Society of Women in Philosophy, March 1986, and to the American Philosophical Association, May 1986. Many
people in discussion at those meetings offered incisive comments and criticisms. I
would like to thank in particular the following persons for their critiques of earlier
drafts of this paper: Nancy Fraser; Alison Jaggar; Jeffner Allen; Laurie Shrage; Robert
Yanal; Martha Gimenez; Joyce Trebilcot, Rob Crawford, and Iris Young.

1. Foucault is citing an eighteenth-century military manual, "Ordonnance du Ier
   janvier 1766..., title XI, article 2."
2. I am indebted to Laurie Shrage for calling this to my attention and for providing
   most of these examples.
3. I am indebted to Nancy Fraser for the formulation of this point.

References

Bartky, Sandra Lee. 1982. Narcissism, femininity and alienation. *Social Theory and
    Practice* 8:127–43.

Bordo, Susan. 1985–86. Anorexia nervosa: Psychopathology as the crystallization of culture. *Philosophical Forum* 17:73–104.

Butler, Judith. 1985. Embodied identity in de Beauvoir's *The Second Sex*. Paper presented at the American Philosophical Association, Pacific Division, March 22, 1985.

Chernin, Kim. 1981. *The Obsession: Reflections on the Tyranny of Slenderness*. New York: Harper and Row.

de Beauvoir, Simone. 1968. *The Second Sex*. New York: Bantam Books.

Dews, Peter. 1984. Power and subjectivity in Foucault. *New Left Review* 144(March–April):17.

Foucault, Michel. 1979. *Discipline and Punish: The Birth of the Prison*. New York: Vintage.

———. 1980. *Power/Knowledge: Selected Interviews and Other Writings, 1972–1977*, edited by Colin Gordon. New York: Pantheon.

Henley, Nancy. 1977. *Body Politics*. Englewood Cliffs, NJ: Prentice Hall.

Hochschild, Arlie. 1983. *The Managed Heart: The Commercialization of Human Feeling*. Berkeley: University of California Press.

Hutchinson, Marcia. 1985. *Transforming Body Image: Learning to Love the Body You Have*. Trumansburg, NY: Crossing Press.

Klinger, Georgette, and Barbara Rowes. 1978. *Georgette Klinger's Skincare*. New York: William Morrow.

Loren, Sophia. 1984. *Women and Beauty*. New York: William Morrow.

Markovic, Mihailo. 1976. Women's liberation and human emancipation. In *Women and Philosophy*, edited by Carol C. Gould and Marx W. Wartofsky. New York: G. P. Putnam.

Millman, Marcia. 1980. *Such a Pretty Face: Being Fat in America*. New York: W. W. Norton.

Saffon, M. J. 1981. *The 15-Minute-A-Day Natural Face Life*. New York: Warner Books.

USA Today. 1985. 30, May.

Wex, Marianne. 1979. *Let's Take Back Our Space: "Female" and "Male" Body Language as a Result of Patriarchal Structures*. Berlin: Frauenliteraturverlag Hermine Fees.

Wittig, Monique. 1976. *The Lesbian Body*. New York: Avon Books.

Young, Iris. 1980. Throwing like a girl: A phenomenology of feminine body comportment, motility and spatiality. *Human Studies* 3:137–56.

II

THE POLITICS OF SEXUALITY

Sexuality is an integral part of everyone's life. Even those who are celibate generally retain sexual feelings, whether of longing or revulsion, and still define themselves in terms of their sexual history and sexual orientation. Moreover, sexual activity provides a broad canvas on which individuals express their personalities and values. For these reasons, both individuals and societies have found that controlling women's sexuality is an effective way to control women's lives.

The articles in this section address the link between women's bodies, women's sexuality, and the control of women's lives. In the first article, "Menarche and the (Hetero)sexualization of the Female Body," Janet Lee describes how girls' early experiences of menstruation lead them to feel alienated from their bodies and to both value and fear the male attention their bodies can bring them. Similarly, Deborah L. Tolman's article, "Daring to Desire: Culture and the Bodies of Adolescent Girls," discusses young women's feelings about both sexual desire and sexual danger, as well as discussing how social privilege (based on race or social class) affects those feelings.

This topic is explored from a different angle in the next two articles. In "Get Your Freak On," Patricia Hill Collins analyzes contemporary media messages about African American women's bodies and sexuality, while in "Brain, Brow, and Booty: Latina Iconicity in U.S. Popular Culture," Isabel

Molina Guzmán and Angharad N. Valdivia look at the portrayal of Latinas in U.S. media.

Whereas African American and Latina women are often marginalized by other Americans and mainstream U.S. culture, other young women choose to place themselves outside the mainstream. The final article in this section, " 'So Full of Myself as a Chick' ": Goth Women, Sexual Independence and Gender Egalitarianism," by Amy C. Wilkins, looks at the "polyamorous" culture of Goths, in which both men and women are expected to have "open" sexual and romantic relationships.

7

Menarche and the (Hetero)sexualization of the Female Body

JANET LEE

Janet Lee's article, "Menarche and the (Hetero)sexualization of the Female Body," uses women's narratives of menstruation, beginning with menarche (first menstruation), to show how these experiences socialize women to think of their bodies and sexuality in ways demanded by our culture. Through these experiences, Lee explains, young women learn to think of their bodies as contaminating and embarrassing. They become alienated from their bodies—learning to think of the changes in their bodies as something happening to them rather than something they are doing, and learning to think of their appearance and sexuality as things designed for men's viewing and pleasure rather than something they themselves can take pleasure in. Similarly, young women at menarche learn to fear both that they will not attract male attention and that they will attract unwanted male attention.

Finally, Lee takes up the issue of resistance introduced in the previous article by Bartky. Compared to Bartky (and Foucault), however, Lee appears more optimistic about the possibilities for agency—exerting control over one's life and actions—and for resistance, as well as more willing to define a broad range of activities as resistance. Lee ends her article with a discussion of how women resist the cultural restrictions placed on menstruating women, by, for example, accepting those cultural restrictions, using them to their advantage, and using their stories to reframe their experiences in a more positive light.

In high school I wanted to be a beatnik. I too wanted to go on
the road, but I could never figure out what would happen if,
travelling in Mexico in 1958, I got my period. Were you
supposed to carry a supply of Kotex with you? How many
could you carry? If you took all you needed, there wouldn't be
any room for all those nice jugs of wine in Jack Kerouac's car.
The only beatnik I know who even considered this question
was Diana diPrima in *Memoirs of a Beatnik*. She describes her
first big orgy, the one with the works, including Allen
Ginsburg. As she takes a deep breath and decides to plunge in,
so to speak, she pulls out her Tampax and flings it across the
room where somehow it gets irretrievably lost. A grand
moment, that. Do I hear you thinking, How gross? Or, How
irrelevant? Gross, yes; irrelevant, no. And that's the point.
Having to worry about the gross mess becomes a part of life
from puberty on.

Dimen, 1986, p. 32–33

Menstruation is a biological act fraught with cultural implications, helping
to produce the body and women as cultural entities. The body is a "text" of
culture; it is a symbolic form upon which the norms and practices of society
are inscribed (Bartky 1992; Bordo 1989; Haug 1987). Male desire and policy
have been scripted onto the female body at the same time that "woman" has
been overdetermined and overrepresented in contemporary art, social science
and politics, as well as scientific and medical discourses. In this article I share
stories of the body in an analysis of the menarche (or first period) experiences
of ordinary women who participated in an ongoing oral and written history
project. It is primarily through the body that women are inserted, and insert
themselves, into the hierarchical ordering of the sexual.

I explore menarche as a central aspect of body politics since it is loaded
with the ambivalence associated with being a woman in Western society
today. Menarche represents the entrance into womanhood in a society that
devalues women through cultural scripts associated with the body. Overwhelmingly, messages associated with menarche in a wide range of cultural
and historical contexts are ambivalent (Buckley and Gottlieb 1988; Delaney
et al. 1988; Golub 1983, 1992; Lander 1988). Even those women who
have reflected on this experience with positive thoughts and memories have
been found to articulate its negative and shameful aspects (Hays 1987;
Jackson 1992; Koff et al. 1981; Martin 1987; Weideger 1976; Whisnant and
Zegans 1975). To talk of menstruation in contemporary Western culture is
to articulate its secretive, emotionally laden, and shame filled aspects (Thorne
1993)....

While women's bodies are produced discursively within misogynist
societies (Bartky 1992; Foucault 1978; Scott 1992), women's everyday experiences negotiating adolescence are concretely lived in ways that not only

internalize and maintain such discourses, but also actively resist them through appropriation and/or the integration of more positive discourses of the body (Martin 1987).... Narratives of women's memories of menarche highlight this interactive nature of discourse and agency; when women remember their first menses, their memories are framed by many competing discourses, having become subjects through the sifting and making meaning out of their experiences.

My methodological focus is phenomenological. I explore the meanings women attribute to menarche, what they think and feel, and the significance of this event as represented in what they say and write. I analyzed forty narratives (twenty-eight oral and twelve written narratives), listening and reading for interpretations of menarche embedded within the everyday, lived experience of women.... Participants were volunteers who had agreed to participate as word of the project spread through presentations made in classes, flyers in a local physician's office, and through contact with colleagues, students, and friends and the Extended Education Office at Oregon State University.

This local sample was Eurocentric, including thirty white women, three Jews, two African Americans, one biracial woman, three Asian Americans, two Mexican Americans, and three women each from Nepal, Malaysia, and Iran. Since three-quarters of the participants were white, reflecting the general lack of racial and ethnic diversity in Oregon, where this study was done, I must emphasize its limitations and the dangers of over-generalization. The age range spanned from 18 to 80 years. Five women identified themselves as lesbians and three as bisexuals, although none said they identified as such during early adolescence. Nineteen of the participants are working class and twenty-one are middle class, all residing in the Willammette Valley and south and central Oregon.

I suggest here that menarche is an important time when young women become inserted and insert themselves into the dominant patterns of sexuality. As a crucial signifier of reproductive potential and thus embodied womanhood, menarche becomes intertwined with sexuality. Certain orifices and their secretions take on sexual significance and menarche marks a simultaneous entry into adult womanhood and adult female sexualization. I will share excerpts from the narratives to illustrate themes associated with female sexualization at menarche, exploring the ways these women relate to the female body and menstrual blood. I focus on issues of contamination and alienation, and the relationship between menarche, boys, and developing bodies. Finally, I will discuss issues of consciousness and resistance, exploring ways women have coped with menarche in their everyday lives.

Contaminating Bodies

Historically and cross-culturally, menstrual blood has been considered both magical and poisonous, and menstrual taboos have structured and restricted women's lives (Buckley and Gottlieb 1988; Golub 1992). Since women are associated with the body, earth, and nature, and men with the abstract powers of reason, women's bodies connote words like *earthy*, *fleshy*, and *smelly*, reminding humans of their mortality and vulnerability. Dorothy Dinnerstein (1976) captures this in her discussion of the deep-seated cultural perceptions of the female body as corrupting, contaminating, unclean, and sinful. On the one hand, woman is associated with life, while on the other, her bleeding and oozing body is met with disgust, reminiscent of earthly vulnerabilities. Male bodies are not so symbolically marked with such connotations; men are more easily able to imagine their bodies free of such constraints, and they are allowed to project their fears and hatred onto women's flesh. Cultural contexts provide mythologies and images of disgust for women's bleeding that are deeply internalized into the psyche, encouraging women to hate their bodies and men to hate things they recognize as feminine in themselves (Ussher 1989).

Repeatedly, women in this study stated that their monthly bleeding made them feel ambivalent about their bodies, menarche being clouded by negativity. Almost half the sample specifically mentioned "the curse" as a term they and others had used to describe menstruation. Edith, a 66-year-old mother and grandmother emphasized the gloom associated with menarche:

> It's so long ago...I guess it was mid-winter, and waking after dozing to sleep, briefly, having had a "funny" tummy ache, to a sticky, nasty uncomfortable feeling between my legs; slightly smelly too, if I really think deeply, ugh.... There was this dark, clammy, gloominess and sort of "dread" accompanying it.

Others also stated that their first menstrual blood made them feel dirty and unclean, ashamed and fearful. Bertha, a Jewish woman in her forties, remembered her menarche as similar to "a feeling I used to feel when I was young and wet my pants.... It was a feeling of having soiled myself." Such feelings affect women's sense of self and worth, establishing female bodies and sexuality as bad and corrupting. These memories of shame and embarrassment were shared by Northstar, a Chinese American woman in her late twenties who grew up in Taiwan:

> I feel I have a big diaper. I feel everyone can see me...very embarrassed....I know sometimes when I went to my uncle's house that sometimes my aunt would forbid my uncle to take garbage out because she said that we have "women's mess" inside so men cannot carry the garbage out because there are women's pads inside.

With similar sentiment, a white working-class woman in her thirties named Anna wrote that she was "mortified," and felt she needed to hide her shame and embarrassment:

When I first started menstruating (the very first time) I had experienced incredible stomach pains the night before. I stayed in bed all night and was the first one up in the morning. I went to the bathroom and lo and behold there was blood. I felt mortified because I knew what had happened. I felt incredibly ashamed and didn't tell anyone for a year (I used tissue paper). Now I was like my mother, a woman who had a bad smelly part of her. This, for the most part, is also how men see menstruation, as something filthy belonging to a woman that makes them mentally unstable.

The disdain associated with menstrual blood encouraged many women to go to great lengths to hide such evidence of their contamination from the potentially disapproving gaze of others. There was overwhelming evidence of women's fears of showing evidence of wearing pads or staining garments or sheets. Three-quarters of all women in the sample specifically shared a story of the embarrassment associated with staining, or a fear that it might happen to them. This illustrates how the bulge or stain becomes a visible emblem of their contamination and shame, announcing their "condition" for all to see. It also symbolizes a lapse in women's task of maintaining the taboo, concealing the evidence and preventing the embarrassment of others (Laws 1990). Seventy-four-year-old Laverne shared the following:

A problem with menstruating at that time was the napkin pads. They were made out of absorbent cotton with a cotton mesh cover (no shields). They soaked through easily and you often stained your underwear. I always worried that my skirt might be stained and would sometimes wear my coat in school all day long. At Girls High, it was the custom for the Seniors to wear all white every Friday. When I was a Junior, I happened to notice that one of the Seniors was wearing a thin white skirt which showed the outline of her sanitary pad so when I had my Senior skirt made I bought rather heavy material and had a double panel put in the back.

Women tended to see themselves as becoming more visible at the same time that they felt the pressure to conceal evidence of menstruation. Many women talked about wearing baggy clothes or coats to hide evidence of menstruation. Other research has also reported such findings, with women sharing feelings of being afraid of being found out with a strong desire to hide any traces of their period (Patterson and Hale 1985). One study found that it was only after several menstrual periods that girls would share their experiences with anyone other than their mothers (Brooks-Gunn and Ruble 1983). Similar results were found here, with several women using tissue and toilet paper for months, or hiding soiled underwear at the back of drawers and closets.

The most intense and poignant stories of contamination came from childhood survivors of violence. Of the 10 women who shared experiences of incest or child sexual abuse, all connected the violation of their bodies to menarche as a contaminating experience and said that they felt their bodies were dirty and shameful. Hannah, a young, white lesbian spoke poignantly of the way her feelings about her contaminated body as a survivor coincided with her feelings about her menstrual flow:

> The abuse made me feel awful. It colored everything, so much of what I did, how I felt about my body and my self-esteem. . . . I felt really dirty and you know because I was on my period, and I would cramp more and I just felt dirty, I felt icky, I felt horrible, like people could smell me and I just felt subhuman. . . . I felt kind of shameful to be around men and I don't want to be around people and I don't want people to know at all. . . . I hated the feeling of flowing, I hated just that warm feeling whenever. . . . I felt as if it was something dirty, something horrible coming out and I wanted to not flow as much as possible and if I got really active I would flow more and I didn't want to flow. I just wanted it to stop.

Child sexual abuse survivors' words illustrate the way the vulnerabilities associated with women's emerging sexuality (and in these cases, the exploitation of what these little girls' bodies signified in the context of a society that exploits female sexuality) become integrated so that the body becomes and is experienced by girls as something acted upon, used, and soiled.

Alienated Bodies

Many of the women interviewed experienced menarche as something that was happening to them, as something outside of themselves and frequently referred to as "it," giving an illusion of a self that was fragmented. Overwhelmingly, women used the passive voice to describe menarche. Examples include: "I couldn't believe it was happening to me," "we called it 'the visitor,' " "I got it when I was fourteen," "I remember exactly when it started," "this monthly event," and (my favorite) "when it came I was at home."

Karin, a 22-year-old white woman, shared the following:

> I mean she [her sister] had no problem with it. I don't know if she was happy about it but she was on good terms with it. . . . I guess I'm not really in control of it because I just felt like it happened to me, I didn't ask for it, it just suddenly happened.

Similarly, Barbara, a 19-year-old lesbian, also clearly illustrates this sense of bodily alienation: "It was unknown and I really didn't understand it and it was something I couldn't control so it seemed kind of abstract and not within me."

With their passive construction and image, these quotes suggest a fragmentation between self and body, a sense of menarche as something a woman has to cope with, adjust to, and manage. Menarche is something that seems to appear from the outside, invading the self. Such findings were also reported by Martin (1987), who wrote of the women she interviewed as seeing menstruation as something that happened to them, rather than seeing the process as being a part of them. While she explained this in terms of the medicalization of the female body and the way a scientifically based society produces images of human bodies as machines, I suggest that there is more at work here, since many women framed menarche as happening "to them" in the context of their emerging understandings of sexuality. Charlotte, a white bisexual mother in her late thirties, shared her feelings about this fragmentation and lack of control, illustrating how menarche is intimately connected to feelings about sexual alienation and objectification (the "it" is her first period):

> When it came, I was a high school exchange student in Europe, staying with the family of a friend. I felt like I was out of control, that something was happening to me that I couldn't stop. I bled terribly all over the sheets and was horribly embarrassed telling my friend's aunt (especially since I didn't know the right words, menstruation is hardly one of the common vocabulary words you have to learn). I remember distinctly being embarrassed because this blood seemed like an emblem of my sexuality, like somehow it indicated that I might run out and have sex, yet really I felt like it was all happening to someone else, not me, like I was watching myself in a movie and now was this sexual being.

The passive, indirect, fragmented language of menarche and menstruation is about sexual objectification and alienation. This sense of bodily alienation is entwined with women's object status in patriarchal societies that allow men subjectivity but construct femininity as a mirror through which men see themselves as human (Irigaray 1985). Adolescence and the journey from girlhood to womanhood involve forms of self-silencing whereby girls become preoccupied with how they are perceived by others (Brown and Gilligan 1992; Gilligan et al. 1990). Femininity means moving from assertive actor to developing woman, learning to respond to the world indirectly through the filter of relationships. Women are encouraged to accommodate male needs, understand themselves as others see them, and feel pleasure through their own bodily objectification, especially being looked at and identified as objects of male desire (Connell 1987). Again, the voice of a survivor, this time Susan, is especially poignant in illustrating this objectification:

> Becoming a woman kind of opened the avenues which I think I unconsciously kind of knew that men would start looking at me more which was, I think, a little bit scary in a sense. I mean I was confused, I think I wanted to be accepted by the male gender, but yet with this experience [incest] it was a frightening thing because, it wasn't even me, it was like my body, and it was happening to my body. . . . It was no longer my mind or who I was, I mean it was like I was nothing. But yet my body was something, a sex object or something and I couldn't have said it, I didn't think that my body was like a

sex object. I mean I couldn't clarify what was a norm, but, to look back now, that is what it was, my body was a sex object and the menstruation process was, just defined it that much more that I was a woman.... You know what I am saying? Because I related the menstrual cycle, I connected it directly with all this.... So there is a connection there, one part of me, I wanted to be that woman for the opposite sex, because it was kind of like expected of me, you know, that I be pleasing to look at and starting that menstrual cycle was my direct link with that, wow, I am a woman. But then there is this bad incident that I don't think had a lot of negative influence on that, but yet it must have somehow, you know, been buried there.

Anxious Bodies

Adolescence is a difficult and vulnerable time when girls focus attention on their bodies (Koff 1983; Koff et al. 1978; Rierdan and Koff 1980; Ussher 1989) in the context of a culture that demands perfect female bodies (Brownmiller 1984; Coward 1985). In a study that asked pre- and post-menarcheal girls to draw pictures of women, Koff found that girls who had experienced menarche drew considerably more sexually differentiated bodies. She writes about how girls come to experience themselves as more sexually mature at menarche: "It appears that regardless of the actual physical changes that are taking place, the girl at menarche anticipates and experiences a reorganization of her body image in the direction of greater sexual maturity and feminine differentiation" (1983, 83).

For many women, the increasing focus on their bodies was associated with painful cramps or even severe dysmenorrhea or painful periods. For example, Mehra, a young Iranian woman, spoke of how she noticed her body more at this time: "Yes, I felt like I paid more attention to my body, how it looked, felt, but also about where the pain comes from.... I would focus on that because of the pain." Some, like Laurence, a 20-year-old Malaysian student, started tuning into their body at menarche, becoming more self-conscious generally: "Yes, I guess mentally I became more aware of my body and what you would say 'the journey to womanhood,' yeah, and I became more self-conscious when I had my period.... I did become more self-conscious."

Others, like Robin, a young, lesbian, biracial woman, were aware that other people treated their bodies differently, and felt that this contributed to their interpretations of menarche:

Then they [her brothers] started becoming critical of the way I dressed, and my hair and the way I spoke... and criticizing and saying you need to go over that way and you need to start wearing skirts and you need to start doing your hair, and you need to care about what you look like and not talk like this or that. So, I think there was a definite change in how they saw me.... I think it did set inside their heads "she is woman, I mean, she is not a boy. Yeah, she is different other."

For most women, anxieties about their developing bodies at menarche concerned the way these bodies looked and might be interpreted by others, rather than how they looked or felt to themselves. Breast development seemed especially fraught with such anxiety. When recounting their first period stories, many women described their feelings toward their breasts, emphasizing how menarche is so often framed within the discourse of the sexual. Although enlarging breasts and hips are visual representations of femaleness, they are also highly constituted in our culture as objects of male desire (to be gazed at) and contribute to the experience of menarche as connected to the process of sexualization. As Haug et al. (1987, 139) suggest, "female breasts are never innocent." The excerpt below from Madeleine, a white woman in her thirties, illustrates the anxiety and self-consciousness associated with the developing body at menarche; a body that is being increasingly viewed as sexual, and, given the patriarchal context, a body that is becoming increasingly objectified:

> I remember when I was in 6th grade and this boy called me "stuffy," in other words he was accusing me of stuffing my bra, because I wore a sweater that was, you know, more fitted than the day before and I was developing very early as a 6th grader and I didn't like my body at all, in fact I had a breast reduction when I was in 10th grade.... But so, I had a lot of hang-ups about that and they were very painful to me and so it just, my boobs were just so big that, I mean, I am still busty and I mean, they are huge and I was a small person and they got in my way (long laugh) and I really hated them.... I just remember feeling that I was going to grow up and the only thing that I would be good for was something like a Playboy bunny or something really you know... disgusting or just to be a housewife which was like a fate worse than death.... So, I guess that maybe that's why I felt so angry about my period because I associated it with these feelings about my boobs, you know.

At menarche, women say that their physical bodies are becoming problematic; women report that their breasts are too small or too big, hips tend to become enemy sites and there is the overwhelming fear of fat. These reports spanned generations as Florence, an 80 year-old Jewish woman remembered feeling "ugly and fat," just as did 18-year-old Marie, who, when asked how she felt about her body, responded: "I had a really low self-esteem about my physical appearance and stuff... it was pretty heavy dislike." Ambivalence is a good word to describe the feeling that many women report since, while many felt okay about their developing bodies (especially in the context of competition with female friends and the relief from the embarrassment that goes along with being undeveloped—of not "measuring up," so to speak), these were accompanied by strong negative experiences of self-consciousness and embarrassment, and the internalization of ambivalence about women's flesh and sexuality. The relationship here between menarche and sexuality is illustrated by several women who commented that friends of theirs whose bodies had developed early were somehow seen as promiscuous, even though they were just young girls with no active sexual relationships. The use of the term "precocious puberty" in the literature to describe girls with early puberty and onset of menarche is also an example of this issue. Robin shares the following:

> Oh, there was one person I knew who had it before any of us you know... this is really terrible, but I think that I thought that she was just a little more ahead of us sexually. I am positive the woman wasn't sexual, but I knew that was a part of getting older, and I knew that getting older meant having sex, and I think seeing someone else with their period made me feel that they were a lot further ahead than I was.... I am sure they probably weren't having sex, I don't know, but I saw them as more promiscuous.

Bodies and Boys

Women also make a clear association between menarche and changing relationships with boys through the language of the body. Many were distressed that their camaraderie with boys dissipated. They felt they could no longer be "one of the boys" or their friendships became infused with the sexual tensions of early adolescence and its budding compulsory heterosexuality. Barbara, a strong athlete during adolescence, illustrates this:

> Yeah, I think it was in the sense that it [her menarche] separated me from the boys, and so I felt like I was going to have to dress up and just drop sports by the wayside because now it was like some way of being notified that well, you have had your fun as a tomboy but it is time to really do what you are "supposed" to do.

Women worried about what boys might think, if boys noticed them, if they didn't. Sixty-two-year-old Rowena remembered distinctly how her behavior changed. She wrote, "I began to 'be careful' at school, to not act 'too smart' although I continued to get straight A's. That was stupid."

Women remembered being embarrassed around boys, and especially remembered the teasing and crude comments about menstruation. Urmila, in her twenties and raised in Nepal, shared her memories of such teasing:

> Maybe they [boys] don't understand it, so the only way of doing it is by laughing, making fun... they just laugh, making it feel for the girls that they do know, so it sort of makes them dominant and makes the girls feel like "oh, my goodness, I have done something wrong."

Women reported that they learned early that they must hide all evidence of menstruation from boys and men, brothers and fathers. This set up a self-consciousness for girls who were used to playing with boys. Crystal, a young, white, bisexual woman, summed this best: "When I didn't have my period I didn't mind playing with the guys, but when I did, I was afraid someone would see me, like something might leak through or things like that."

In terms of potential sexual relationships with boys, the risk of pregnancy that sets in at menarche influences family dynamics. Research suggests that parents tend to see their daughter's emerging sexuality as more problematic than their son's, with early sexual maturation being associated with greater independence and achievement from parents for boys, and to a lesser extent for girls (Fine 1988; Hill and Lynch 1983; Ussher 1989). Hill and Holmbeck (1987) found that menarche was accompanied by intense family turmoil for a large number of the girls in their sample, with daughters reporting more parental control in the first six months after menarche than at any other time. The comments of Elizabeth, a white woman in her forties who grew up in a Catholic home with thirteen brothers and sisters, is illustrative of this:

> When I hit my adolescent years our relationship [with her mother] really split because my mother all of a sudden was very suspicious of everything I did. . . . I still remember her just all of a sudden, a suspicion about me, maybe I was becoming sexual.

In predictable ways the double standard of sexual conduct plays itself out as boys are encouraged to sow their wild oats and girls are chastised for similar behavior, resulting in closer monitoring. "I was told by my mother that I was a lady now, so that I had to act like one, and not play with the boys anymore," recalled Darlene, a white working-class woman in her forties. She followed this statement with:

> I started to cry. I said, "I'm not ready to be a lady and I like playing with the boys." I guessed the reason I couldn't play with them anymore is that they would smell me too and know my horrible secret. I felt dirty, humiliated and angry.

Finally, the remarks of 77-year-old Gerta, a widow and retired teacher, illustrate the responsibilities of potential sexual relations that girls have to assume at menarche:

> During the "curse" as we termed it, I was concerned about odor and spotting. My mother made it clear that now necking and petting could have serious results if we went "all the way"—which could happen if emotions got out of hand.

Consciousness and Resistance

To study menarche is to study the female body as it is contextualized through the sociopolitical constructs of specific societies. In this study, the words that women used to describe menarche are those that symbolize the relationship of women to their bodies in a misogynist society: fear, shame, embarrassment, humiliation, preoccupation, mess, hassle, and so on; however, running through these stories are also tales of consciousness, agency, and resistance.

Women are not merely acted upon, nor are they merely powerless pawns embedded in the discursive struggles that determine existence. While these discourses do frame the body, the woman in the body does resist, as Martin (1987) has suggested. Women show their resistance to the destructive and alienating discourses associated with menarche through insight and analysis, through telling their stories, and through the many ways that women have learned to cope. Some spoke of increasing solidarity with girls, of using menstruation as a way to manipulate and get their way; many spoke of having done or having a desire to do things differently when their own daughters start to menstruate. It is to these forms of consciousness and resistance that I now turn.

Telling the Story

Since this project involved participants who were volunteers, the women's voices I share here are all those who wanted to have the opportunity to tell their stories. Usually, when the tape had been switched off and women were leaving, they would comment on the benefits of speaking about something that they had never really spoken of in any public way before, something that was an important experience in their lives, but which the society in which they lived, as well as academia, has tended to ignore. "I don't know if it's making any real sense, but it is starting to make more sense to me when I talk about it" was a comment often heard.

For many, the telling of their stories took the form of ongoing analysis and commentary on those experiences, speaking or writing with insight into body politics and the effects of those politics on women's everyday lives. Kay, a white mother and student in her thirties wrote the following, nicely illustrating this consciousness and insightful analysis:

> First, in fifth or sixth grade, at my elementary school, we were separated from the boys and shown a film about menstruation. Next we were given a packet which contained some kind of feminine hygiene products and propaganda. We considered this whole affair hilarious, embarrassing and yet it took the place of what could be considered a puberty ritual for us girls. We never knew what the boys talked about or what they were told about us, reproductively, etc. But I always somehow felt that they had been given some important secret that day, that we, as girls, were not privy to, and that this was just some kind of weird, divisive act on the part of the administration to distract and codify us. I suppose that sounds like a true paranoid at work, or perhaps hindsight talking, eh? But it's true I did feel that way. . . . I also believe that most of what I experienced, or did not experience, were [sic] consistent with much of the cultural conditioning that women receive from the media and the medical establishment.

Many women revealed a form of resistance in the contradictory voices used to tell their stories. Women moved between the anxious, hesitant and fearful disclosure complete with multiple "umms" and "you knows" to the staging of their stories as a series of adventures, gaining control over the experience and framing it in hindsight as ridiculous. In so doing, they claimed control over events, appropriating them and defusing the pain and anguish. This emphasizes the sometimes contradictory ways gender is negotiated, discourses of resistance being crucial components of this negotiation. Virginia, a 38-year-old white student, illustrates this as she jokes about the story of her first period, laughing and describing the event as a funny experience:

> So I was 10 years old and didn't understand any of it. In fact I misunderstood most of it. What I remember about it from the book was that somehow the menstrual blood came out on the outside of your lower abdomen somehow like it seeped through your skin! (laugh)...and so here's the book telling me that these napkins don't show and I'm holding them up to my stomach and saying, yeah, right (laugh), that is going to show, you can't tell me that is not going to show....So I told my mother and it was like "oh," she did seem rather pleased but it wasn't like the kind of pleased where if I got a really good grade or you know, gotten the solo in the school play (laugh)....She pulls out the Kotex kit and that is when I begin to connect, this is what it is, it doesn't come out of your stomach!

Hannah, an incest survivor, spoke very poignantly about her first menses. Despite her sadness she tells funny stories of menarche, her humor helping her gain control over her pain:

> I saw blood in my underwear and it was like I just sat on the toilet (laugh) and I am like "mom." She comes in and she was like, "What? Well honey, congratulations, you are a little lady now." I am like, "Say what?!!" I was cramping really bad and I was given medication. It was to get me regulated....I remember lying on the floor and my mom, she used to have bad cramps because she had a tipped uterus, so my grandfather used to buy her a pint of alcohol because they didn't have medication then, and she would drink it and she would pass out and she would be out for a day, so my mom gave me some brandy because she thought it would solve it! (laugh) Well, after I had the brandy I just started to york it, I was throwing up left and right, so it seems like after that time every period I ever had I would throw up!

Acceptances, Coping, and Appropriation

For some women, especially those at midlife and beyond, there was a general sense of acceptance or resignation to the politics of menarche that was apparent in the narratives. I had never thought of this as a form of resistance until I read Emily Martin's discussion of acceptance, lament, and nonaction as a way of responding to women's reproductive restrictions (Martin 1987, 184–86); yet these ways of coping and surviving are important, and they also subvert the masculinist idea of resistance as oppositional action and behavior.

When asked about the specifics of their menarche, many women responded with such comments as "people didn't talk about such things back then," "it was just something I had to endure," "that's the way it was back then." The comments of Alex, an 80-year-old white woman, were typical:

> And in those days we didn't have the sanitary napkins we have today, or even now the Tampax and so on, but you always had that laundry to do. That was just not very pleasant, but it was a thing you did. I mean, that was the way it went.

This acceptance did not always take the form of resignation. Many women, such as Yvonne, an African American woman in her thirties, were angry that they had had to endure certain experiences. "I was pissed" was among Yvonne's comments. Some tempered their frustrations with observations such as "Well, that's just the way it was then you see." The important point is that these were survival and coping mechanisms.

Louie, age 73, talked about the hardships associated with menstruation before the onset of disposable sanitary supplies. She remembers being in a tight spot with no menstrual cloths: "I had a jackknife and I cut up one of my blankets for pads and used those." Women of all ages reported using toilet paper, tissue, and underwear to help them hide their bleeding and cope with their first menses. Some hid evidence, some threw it away, some washed it out when no one was around. Many worked out ways to avoid going to a grocery store where they might be recognized, and others modified their clothes and activities to avoid embarrassment.

Many women told stories of using menstruation as a way to manipulate and have some control over situations. A Mexican American woman in her thirties was not alone in sharing how she avoided showers in school by telling the teacher she had her period, and also telling her boyfriend the same to avoid sexual contact. Gerta spoke for many as she wrote:

> As far as school was concerned—during Physical Education, we were benched for three days. CLUB members [those girls who had already started their periods] often considered this a plus as we were not required to wear gym attire.

Bonding and Solidarity

Some women found that the experience of menarche helped girls identify and bond with each other, providing support and solidarity. Amy, an African American student and mother, told how she had pretended to have her period for several months before she actually experienced it in order to feel accepted by her friends. She said: "I was happy because I didn't have to lie anymore, now I was one of the girls.... It was important for me to be accepted as one of the group, it was a significant event for that reason." Gerta, almost 40 years Amy's senior, talked about how friends who had "joined the Club" were closer and held in a higher regard by other girls. For many women, then, first menses was an ambivalent time; it was framed by negativity, but at the same time, symbolic of maturation, it brought status. This was usually acted out in the context of sisters and peers, where girls wanted very much to be included in the group. As Thorne (1993) suggests, the "popular" girls set the stage; if they were perceived as having started their period, then this development was seen as desirable. Since this status is intertwined with their sexual status, it is complex: girls do not want to start too soon and be seen as too advanced or promiscuous, but they do not want to start last and be branded a less mature child. Timing is definitely of the essence.

The importance such a personal event held within girls' groups was illustrated by Robin, who reported that she was obsessed with the idea of starting her period and looked forward to the drama of it all: "Blood would run down your leg and you would have to run out of class!" She was not daunted by this thought and said, "I wanted very much for it to begin at school. . . . Just for the attention I guess. . . . It was a social thing. All my friends were going to get their period and I wanted to be social."

While most girls suffered the embarrassment of menarche alone, some reported how friends had supported and helped them. Laurence, a young Malaysian woman, spoke of the support and solidarity received from friends when she started her period while away at boarding school:

> It was during choir practice, we were just singing and I felt something weird and so a girl said "you have a little stain on your skirt." The girls' side of the choir was really restless and the guys had no idea what was happening. A bunch of girls, about three of them my close friends, escorted me to the bathroom and everything happened, they got me the pads, told me what to do, everything.

Others also talked and wrote about friends and older sisters who helped them figure out what was happening to their bodies, as well as helped them access and use menstrual products. Karin emphasized how she felt closer to her friends after she started her period:

> I think it kind of brought me closer to girls in a certain way because when you talk about things that are personal it really kind of strengthens your friendships I think, and I think it makes it a very intimate friendship. So I realize that [with] some of my girlfriends I was really closer, I felt very close to them.

Changing the Scripts

For many women, the framing of womanhood at menarche occurred within the context of the complex dynamic of their relationship with their mothers. Scholars have suggested (and the data here certainly support this) that since girls rely on their mothers at menarche, they report either increased conflict or closeness, depending on the relationship and communication patterns before puberty (Brooks-Gunn and Petersen 1983; Danza 1983; Orbach 1986). Mothers often socialize their daughters into the same restrictions associated with femininity that they have endured, ensuring that their daughters will fit into society and maintaining a shared compliance in the development of a submissive femininity and gendered sexual identity. Girls may grow to resent their mothers for their role in this at the same time that they may fear becoming what they perceive their mothers have become; however, there is much evidence here to suggest that these patterns are being disrupted. Many of the women who had negative experiences with their mothers at menarche also said that they would never want that to happen to their own daughters, and several went on to tell stories of positive experiences of menarche with adolescent children. Nonetheless, several women also emphasized that even though they had prepared their children and made it a positive experience, their daughters still felt some shame and embarrassment. The values of the culture are strong; children are not raised in a vacuum and quickly internalize the negative messages associated with menstruation.

Judy, a Japanese American in her twenties, shared her desire for a better experience for any future daughters:

> If I have daughters of my own in the future, I will tell them more positive things about periods, such as that it's not something you should be ashamed of or something dirty. I would make sure that they'll have some knowledge about menstruation before it starts because, when my period started, I didn't have any knowledge why women have [a] period or how it starts or anything.

Ann, a white mother of two daughters and a grandmother, spoke with regret that she acted very much like her own mother and was not able to give information and help her daughters feel good about their first menses. She is, however, committed to undoing this piece of family history with her granddaughter:

> My mother neglected telling me and I neglected telling my girls and I wouldn't want that to happen to my granddaughter... because I wouldn't want it to come from an outside source like from girls at school. I feel that my daughter really should do this, but like I said, if she doesn't I am prepared to do it for her.

Conclusion

Although women's bodies have been the object of derogation and admiration, women themselves have not had the power to control how their bodies might look, act, and feel. Menarche is an event that symbolizes both reproductive and sexual potential and centers attention on the body. Since "woman" is overrepresented through the practices and values of sexuality, menarche takes on loaded meanings that have consequences for women and their everyday lives, scripting relations of power into the discourses and practices that surround women's bodies. The women who participated in the study remembered menarche as an important experience and, for most, this experience provoked anxiety, reminding them of their contaminating natures and encouraging them to hide evidence of their bleeding, while focusing attention on the sexualized body and changing relationships with others. Bodies are contextualized in a society that devalues and trivializes women; however, while adult women have internalized the stigma and shame associated with having bodies that bleed and all that this entails in terms of restrictions on body, mind, and soul, they have responded as active agents, and have resisted these discourses through a variety of means. They continue to resist them as they reminisce about their first menses, viewing their experiences retrospectively, framing and reframing them, hoping to neutralize the pain, perhaps taking back their power.

Menarche is a physiological happening, framed by the biomedical metaphors of current scientific knowledge, yet also a gendered sexualized happening, a transition to womanhood as objectified other. What is crucial here is that this juncture, menarche, is a site where girls become women and gender relations are reproduced. Such relations are about power and its absence; power to define the body and live in it with dignity and safety; power to move through the world with credibility and respect. May this be in our futures.

References

Bartky, Sandra. 1992. Foucault, femininity, and the modernization of patriarchal power. In *Feminist Philosophies: Problems, Theories and Applications*, edited by Janet J. A. Kourany, James J. P. Sterba, and Rosemarie R. Tong. Englewood Cliffs, NJ: Prentice Hall.

Bordo, Susan R. 1989. The body and the reproduction of femininity: A feminist appropriation of Foucault. In *Gender/body/knowledge: A Feminist Reconstruction of Being and Knowing*, edited by Alice M. Jaggar and Susan R. Bordo. New Brunswick, NJ: Rutgers University Press.

Brooks-Gunn, Jeanne, and Anne C. Petersen. 1983. The experience of menarche from a developmental perspective. In *Girls at Puberty*, edited by Jeanne Brooks-Gunn and Anne C. Petersen. New York: Plenum.

Brooks-Gunn, Jeanne, and Diane N. Ruble. 1983. Dysmenorrhea in adolescence. In *Menarche: The Transition from Girl to Woman*, edited by Sharon Golub. Lexington, MA: D. C. Heath.

Brown, Lyn Mikel, and Carol Gilligan. 1992. *Meeting at the Crossroads: Women's Psychology and Girls' Development*. Cambridge, MA: Harvard University Press.

Brownmiller, Susan. 1984. *Femininity*. New York: Ballantine.

Buckley, Thomas, and Alma Gottlieb. 1988. *Blood Magic: The Anthropology of Menstruation*. Berkeley: University of California Press.

Connell, R. W. 1987. *Gender and Power*. Stanford, CA: Stanford University Press.

Coward, Rosalind. 1985. *Female Desires: How They Are Sought, Bought and Packaged.* New York: Grove Press.

Danza, Roberta. 1983. Menarche: Its effects on mother-daughter and father-daughter interactions. In *Menarche: The Transition from Girl to Woman*, edited by Sharon Golub. Lexington, MA: D. C. Heath.

Delaney, Janice, Mary Jane Lupton, and Emily Toth. 1988. *The Curse: The Cultural History of Menstruation.* Urbana: University of Illinois.

Dimen, Muriel. 1986. *Surviving Sexual Contradiction: A Startling and Different Look at a Day in the Life of a Contemporary Professional Woman.* New York: Macmillan.

Dinnerstein, Dorothy. 1976. *The Mermaid and the Minotaur: Sexual Arrangements and Human Malaise.* New York: Harper & Row.

Fine, Michelle. 1988. Sexuality, schooling and adolescent females: The missing discourse of desire. *Harvard Educational Review* 58:29–53.

Foucault, Michel. 1978. *The History of Sexuality, Volume 1: An Introduction.* New York: Pantheon.

Gilligan, Carol, Nona P. Lyons, and Trudy J. Hanner, eds. 1990. *Making Connections: The Relational Worlds of Adolescent Girls at Emma Willard School.* Cambridge, MA: Harvard University Press.

Golub, Sharon, ed. 1983. *Menarche: The Transition from Girl to Woman.* Lexington, MA: D. C. Heath.

———. 1992. *Periods: From Menarche to Menopause.* Newbury Park, CA: Sage.

Haug, Frigga 1987. *Female Sexualization.* London: Verso.

Hays, Terence E. 1987. Menstrual expression and menstrual attitudes. *Sex Roles* 16:605–14.

Hill, John P., and Grayson N. Holmbeck. 1987. Familial adaptation to biological change during adolescence. In *Biological-psychological Interactions of Early Adolescence*, edited by Richard M. Lerner and Terryl T. Foch. Hillsdale, NJ: Lawrence Erlbaum.

Hill, John P., and Mary Ellen Lynch. 1983. The intensification of gender-related role expectations during early adolescence. In *Girls at Puberty*, edited by Jeanne Brooks-Gunn and Anne C. Petersen. New York: Plenum.

Irigaray, Luce. 1985. *Speculum of the Other Woman.* Ithaca, NY: Cornell University Press.

Jackson, Beryl B. 1992. Black women's responses to menarche and menopause. In *Menstrual Health in Women's Lives*, edited by Alice J. Dan and Linda L. Lewis. Urbana: University of Illinois Press.

Koff, Elissa. 1983. Through the looking glass of menarche: What the adolescent girl sees. In *Menarche: The Transition from Girl to Woman*, edited by Sharon Golub. Lexington, MA: D. C. Heath.

Koff, Elissa, Jill Rierdan, and S. Jacobson. 1981. The personal and interpersonal significance of menarche. *Journal of the American Academy of Child Psychiatry* 20:148–58.

Koff, Elissa, Jill Rierdan, and Ellen Silverstone. 1978. Changes in representation of body image as a function of menarcheal status. *Developmental Psychology* 14: 635–42.

Lander, Louise. 1988. *Images of Bleeding: Menstruation as Ideology.* New York: Orlando Press.

Laws, Sophie. 1990. *Issues of Blood.* London: Macmillan.

Martin, Emily. 1987. *The Woman in the Body: A Cultural Analysis of Reproduction.* Boston: Beacon Press.

Orbach, Susie. 1986. *Hunger Strike.* London: Faber and Faber.

Patterson, Ellen T., and Ellwyn S. Hale. 1985. Making sure: Integrating menstrual care practices into activities of everyday living. *Advances in Nursing Science* 7:18–31.

Rierdan, Jill, and Elissa Koff. 1980. Representation of the female body by early and late adolescent girls. *Journal of Youth and Adolescence* 9:339–96.

Scott, Joan W. 1992. Experience. In *Feminists Theorize the Political*, edited by Judith Butler and Joan W. Scott. New York: Routledge.

Thorne, Barrie. 1993. *Gender Play: Girls and Boys in School.* New Brunswick, NJ: Rutgers University Press.

Ussher, Jane. 1989. *The Psychology of the Female Body.* New York: Routledge.

Weideger, Paula. 1976. *Menstruation and Menopause: The Physiology and Psychology: The Myth and Reality.* New York: Knopf.

Whisnant, Lynn, and Leonard Zegans. 1975. A study of attitudes towards menarche in white, middle-class American adolescent girls. *American Journal of Psychiatry* 132:809–14.

8

Daring to Desire

Culture and the Bodies of Adolescent Girls

DEBORAH L. TOLMAN

*Deborah L. Tolman's article "Daring to Desire: Culture and the Bodies of Ado-
lescent Girls" offers a groundbreaking analysis of how teenage girls think about
their own sexual desires. This research challenges the commonly held idea that
teenage girls engage in sexual activity because they want intimate relationships
rather than because they feel sexual desire. In contrast, among the (small and
nonrandom) group of adolescents Tolman interviewed, more than half clearly
articulated feelings of desire: intense bodily sensations that demanded a response
of some sort.*

*In addition, by contrasting the experiences and voices of urban and subur-
ban girls, Tolman shows how teens' feelings of sexual desire are shaped both by the
promise of sexual pleasure and the threat of sexual dangers. The "urban girls" in
her study live in an environment in which the dangers of sexuality—unwanted
pregnancy, sexual violence, the social stigma of having a "bad reputation"—
are apparent. Consequently, most consciously work to silence their desires. In
contrast, the "suburban girls," who live in a physically and emotionally safer
environment, feel far freer to acknowledge and enjoy their sexual desires,
although they struggle with the conflict between those desires and the desire to
maintain their image as "good girls." Thus Tolman's research both demonstrates that young girls experience sexual desire and shows how social context
substantially limits girls' ability to acknowledge and enjoy those feelings.*

This culture's story about adolescent girls and sexuality goes like this: girls do not want sex; what girls really want is intimacy and a relationship. This concept of girls' sexuality, which permeates education and psychology, focuses on girls' emotional feelings and desire for intimacy and excludes their sexual feelings and their bodies. Statistics indicate that girls do in fact have sex (that is, sexual intercourse) and are beginning to have sex at younger and younger ages.[1] Keeping within the terms of the cultural story, the fact of girls' sexual activity is explained in terms of relationships: girls have sex in the service of relationships. However, the assumption that girls are having sex for the sake of relationships rather than in relation to their own desire has precluded empirical explorations of this aspect of girls' experiences of adolescence. The most striking feature of a review of the psychological research on adolescent girls' sexual desire is that there is virtually none....

Recent research in the psychology of women's development reveals that at adolescence girls come into a different and more problematic relation with themselves, with others, and with the culture(s) in which they are growing.[2] In essence, many girls appear to face a relational impasse or crisis. Carol Gilligan has characterized this crisis as a division between what girls know through experience and what is socially constructed as "reality." It is also at adolescence that girls come into relationship with their social contexts as sexual beings. As the unmistakable contours of a female body emerge, a girl's body becomes defined in cultural terms as an object of men's fantasies and desires.[3] When breasts grow and hips form, girls' bodies are rendered sexual, and the relationship between internal and external, the subjective experience of desire and the objective experience of finding oneself objectified, is essentially confusing and problematic for girls.[4] This psychologically difficult yet very real psychological challenge, coupled with the fact that adolescent girls are sexually active, makes the question of how adolescent girls experience sexual desire especially pressing....

The Missing Discourse of Desire in the Literature of Developmental Psychology

Why have psychologists maintained this silence on girls' sexual desire? Feminist analyses of patriarchal culture offer some insight. Feminist scholars have observed that the cultural context of women's lives denies female sexual desire or acknowledges it only to denigrate it, suppressing women's voices and bodies by making it socially, emotionally, and often physically dangerous for women to be in touch with or to speak openly about their own sexual feelings.[5] The absence of inquiry about girls' sexual desire occurs within this dominant culture that denigrates and suppresses female sexual desire. Yet even in feminist analyses of female sexual desire, a subject heavily theorized by feminist scholars outside of psychology, scant attention is paid to female adolescents. A handful of feminist researchers have studied female adolescent sexuality; since they did not inquire directly about girls' sexual desire, their occasional observations regarding girls' sexual desire, their occasional observations regarding girls' sexual desire are grounded in what girls do not say[6] or in sparse, vague quotes from girls that are difficult to interpret.[7] That few feminists have explicitly identified adolescent girls' sexual desire as a domain of theory or research suggests the extent to which girls' own sexual feelings are resisted in the culture at large.

At best, psychologists seem to be colluding with the culture in simply assuming that adolescent girls do not experience sexual desire; at worst, by not using the power and authority conferred upon them to say what is important in human experience and growth, psychologists participate in the larger cultural resistance to this feature of female adolescence and thus reify and perpetuate this resistance. If desire is not theorized as a potentially relevant aspect of female experience or development, then what adolescent girls may know and feel about their desire and about the place of their bodies in their experiences of desire can and will remain unknown. The very existence of this silence about girls' sexual desire within the culture in which girls develop may have psychological, physical, and material consequences for girls and also for women. The aim of my study was to ask girls directly, in no uncertain terms, about their experiences of sexual desire and about the place of their bodies in those experiences.

The Study

My study was framed by basic questions: Do adolescent girls speak of themselves as experiencing sexual desire? What do they say about it and about their bodies? In this study, I asked thirty girls—fourteen from an urban school, fourteen from a suburban school, and two from a gay and lesbian youth group—about their experiences of sexual desire. To "interrupt" the cultural story that denies girls their bodies, that says girls are interested solely in relationships and not in exploring or expressing their sexual feelings, I made a particular effort to include questions about if and how their bodies figure in these sexual experiences. The thirty young women who took part in my study brought many differences to my project—structural differences, such as class, culture, educational privilege, race, and religion, and individual differences in family situation, history of sexual abuse or violence, history of closeness and safety, physical appearance, and sexual experience. I interviewed each of these girls in a clinical interview between one and two hours long; in this explicitly relational approach to psychological inquiry the interviewer attends to the participant's experience as the guide for inquiring, using a flexible protocol. . . .

Three Voices of Desire

While many of the girls in this study found it odd, uncomfortable, or unusual for an adult woman to want to know about their experiences of sexual desire, all of the girls who participated knew that sexual desire was something that adolescent girls could and did experience, even if they themselves said they did not feel sexual desire. Of the thirty girls I interviewed, eighteen said they did feel sexual desire; four of these eighteen girls said they felt desire but also said they were confused about their sexual feelings. Three of the thirty said they did not feel desire, and four said, "I don't know," when I asked them if they experienced sexual desire. For seven of the thirty girls who answered my questions, I could not tell by what they told me whether they felt sexual desire. The distribution of these answers is remarkably similar across the race and class differences embedded in my study. Although I realize that this is a small sample, this pattern suggests the ways girls speak about their sexual desire may be distributed consistently across some structural differences.

When these girls spoke to me about their desire, they described their relationships with themselves—a relationship embedded in a web of other relationships, with other people, with the social world in which they lived. I discerned three distinct themes, or voices, in what they said: an erotic voice, a voice of the body, and a response voice.[8] For them, sexual desire is a feature of a relationship; the three voices of desire are relational voices. However, these girls make a key distinction between their sexual desire and their wish for a relationship. While their feelings of sexual desire most often arise in the context of relationships, they are not the same as or a substitute for wanting relationships. Rather, these girls say that sexual desire is a specific "feeling," a powerful feeling of wanting that the majority of these girls experience and describe as having to do with sex and with their bodies, a feeling to which they respond in the context of the many relationships that constitute their lives.

An Erotic Voice

In her essay, "Uses of the Erotic: The Erotic as Power," Audre Lorde has described what she calls the power of the erotic as "the *yes* within ourselves, our deepest cravings," and "how fully and acutely we can feel in the doing."[9] Lorde writes that in this culture, women have been systematically kept from this power in themselves because, she surmises, the power of the erotic makes women dangerous. She encourages women to reclaim and reconnect with this affirmative force that resides in them to enable them to glean pleasure in their work and in their existence. Lorde does not characterize the erotic as an explicitly sexual force but conceptualizes it more expansively; when she does speak of the connection between the sexual and the erotic, she observes how the erotic has often been reduced to the merely sexual in ways that have traditionally exploited and denigrated women, in ways, she says, that are in fact pornographic rather than sexual or erotic. In listening to the girls in my study, I was struck by the gap between how adolescent girls are portrayed, studied, and discussed and what they were saying. Out of sync with the cultural story about girls' sexuality, their words when speaking specifically about the sexual expressed the power, intensity, and urgency of their feelings and resonated with Lorde's description of the erotic. This resonance led me to call these ways that girls speak about their sexual desire an erotic voice.

What comes across powerfully in the narratives of the girls who say they feel sexual desire is that they experience it as having an unmistakable intensity. Inez knows she is feeling desire when "my body says yes yes yes yes." Lily calls feeling desire "amazing." Rochelle feels it "so, so bad ... I wanna have sex so bad, you know"; she explains, "you just have this feeling, you just have to get rid of it." Liz explains, "I just wanted to have sex with him really badly and I just ... and we just took off our bathing suits really fast [with laugh], and, um, it was almost like really rushed and really quick." For Barbara it is "very strong ... an overwhelming longing" and "a wicked urge." Paulina's heart "would really beat fast"; she is "extremely aware of every, every touch and everything." Alexandra speaks of being "incredibly attracted" to her friend. Jane calls the power of her desire "demanding" and says "the feelings are so strong inside you that they're just like ready to burst." These direct acknowledgments of the power of sexual desire as these girls know it resonate across differences of class, race, and sexual orientation. These descriptions suggest a challenge to characterizations of "female" sexual desire as having an essence that is gentle, diffuse, and ephemeral.[10]

Some girls also convey the intensity of their desire by the strength of their voiced resistance to it; in response to her body's "yes yes yes yes," Inez explains that "my mind says no no no; you stop kissing him." Cassandra evidences the strength and the urgency of her feeling in narrating what she does not want to do, "stop": "He just like stopped all of a sudden, and I was like 'What are you doing?' Cause I didn't want to stop at all." She says that for her, desire is "powerful." Lily contrasts not being "in the mood to do anything ... because I just have all my clothes on ... because it's just too inconvenient," with the power of her desire when she feels it "once in a while": "Even though it's inconvenient for me, sometimes I just have this feeling, Well I just don't care if I have to put my pantyhose on or not," the power of her desire overriding the usual paramount concern she has for maintaining a proper appearance. These girls, who express the intensity of their sexual feelings without speaking about them directly, use a kind of code; by not saying explicitly and directly that they have strong sexual feelings, perhaps they retain the power to deny being girls who desire, should they need to exercise that power for their own protection.

A Voice of the Body

I identified a voice of the body when the girls described bodily sensations or parts of their bodies as aspects of their sexual desire. A voice of the body is central in these narratives and often interacts with the erotic voice. Across class differences and also across differences in sexual orientation, the girls who said they did not feel sexual desire also spoke of voiceless, silent bodies, of an absence of feeling in their bodies. The girls who said they did not know if they experienced sexual desire, and the girls who said they felt desire but also voiced confusion about their desire, said they were confused about their bodies; it was unclear to them and to me what their bodily feelings signaled, or they were not sure if they felt feelings in their bodies. That is, the voices of their bodies were muffled, at best. The girls whose experience of sexual desire remained uncertain voiced their bodies in ways that raised questions for me about the presence or absence of desire in their lives. For the girls in this group who said they did not feel desire, the voices of their bodies were audible, rendering their statements about the absence of their desire confusing to me. For those in this group who said they did feel desire, the silence or distress of their bodies made me wonder whether they did in fact feel sexual feelings.

Girls spoke about their bodies in two ways: they named the involvement of their bodies directly, or they signified their bodily feelings in veiled, subtle, and indirect ways. Megan spoke of knowing she was feeling sexual desire for boys because of what she felt in her body; as she said, "Kind of just this feeling, you know? Just this feeling inside my body." The voice of her body is explicitly sexual when she explains how she knows she is feeling desire for a boy: "Well, my vagina starts to kinda like act up, and it kinda like quivers and stuff, and, um, like I'll get like tingles, and you can just feel your hormones [laughing] doing something weird, and you just . . . you get happy, and you just get, you know, restimulated kind of, and it's just . . . and oh! Oh!" And "your nerves feel good." Although these girls spoke about feelings in their stomachs, shoulders, necks, and legs, as well as about all-over bodily sensations, Megan was one of the few girls who connected her desire to her "vagina," naming the sexual nature of her bodily feelings directly. Very few girls named the sexual parts of their bodies in these interviews. As Mary Calderone has observed, girls are not taught the names of the sexual parts of their bodies—"vagina," "labia," and "clitoris" are words that are not said to girls.[11]

Other girls spoke in less direct ways, revealing the embodied nature of their feelings through the logic of their stories rather than in explicit language. Trisha says of her feelings when she sees a boy to whom she is attracted, "And every time I see him, I just, like, just wanna go over and grab him and say, Let's go; I just . . . 'cause I just want him so bad; he just . . . I don't know . . . he just gives me a funny feeling; he's just, like . . . you just wanna go over and grab him" even though "I know it's just gonna be one of those one-night stand type of things." Trisha's "want" is not for a relationship, since she is talking about a potential "one-night stand type of thing"; it is to be sexual in a way that is explicitly physical, to "grab" him. Although Trisha avoids overtly placing the "funny feeling" he gives her in her body, the facts of the story lead to no other conclusion but that this "feeling" is embodied. Not surprisingly, voicing their bodies was not easy for these girls. While many of them did speak about their bodies, they also spoke sparingly and said little. When they voiced their bodies in response to my direct questions, their reticence suggested their knowledge, which I shared, that in speaking about desire itself, we were breaking with culture, resisting a cultural taboo that renders the body, particularly a girl's body and the sexual parts of her body, unspeakable.

Voices of Response

The girls who said they felt sexual desire also described how they responded to their own embodied feelings of sexual desire when they told me narratives about their experiences. All of these girls voiced conflict in speaking of their responses to their sexual desire, conflict between the voices of their bodies and the realities of their lives. Whether they spoke of the reality of physical risk and vulnerability or the reality of getting a bad reputation or of cultural messages that silence or are silent about girls' sexual desire, these girls knew and spoke about, in explicit or more indirect ways, the pressure that they felt to silence the voices of their bodies, to disconnect from the bodies in which they inescapably live. When I asked these girls to speak specifically about their own experiences, a lot of these girls spoke about controlling their own sexual feelings rather than about controlling the sexual feelings of boys, raising the question to what or whom girls are being encouraged to "just say no." When asked what they think and feel, they challenged the cultural story about their sexuality—which frames sexual feelings as male—by describing the conflict they experience between the feelings in their bodies and the cultural taboo on what they want. When they spoke of their responses to their sexual desire, they gave voice to an agency in which they are sexual objects of their own feelings rather than simply objects of the desire of others. This agency is informed by their own embodied erotic voice and the voices of the social world in which they live.

Although an erotic voice and a voice of the body sounded similar across the differences of social context embedded in the study, I began to hear in these girls' descriptions differences between urban girls' and the suburban girls', heterosexual girls' and lesbian/bisexual girls', responses to sexual desire. These differences seemed to be connected to the real differences in the social contexts of these girls' lives that the design of this study highlighted.[12] I noticed distinct tones and characters in their voices that I think are related to the fact that some of these girls were bisexual and lesbian and some straight, that some of them lived in overtly dangerous urban areas, while others lived in the relatively safe environment of the suburbs. One way to characterize these differences is that some girls described an agency in the service of protection, whereas others told of an agency in the service of pleasure. . . .

Urban Girls: Cautious Bodies

The urban girls share an environment in which violence as well as adolescent pregnancy and parenthood are highly visible and an unavoidable part of their daily routines. The urban girls in this study share a social experience in which girls' physical movements and sexual activities are a topic of conversation and gossip, subject to a not-so-subtle and entrenched system of social control.

When the urban girls describe their responses to their own sexual desire, themes of self-control, caution, and conflict predominate. Speaking primarily about a conflict between two real features of their experience, the voices of their bodies and what they know and say about the reality of their vulnerability—physical vulnerability to AIDS and pregnancy, as well as social vulnerability in the form of getting a "bad reputation"—they make explicit connections between their sexual desire and danger. In a social context in which danger and violence, the constant threat of violation, is palpable, visible, and unavoidable, most of these girls make conscious choices to sacrifice pleasure as an attempt to protect themselves from danger, a self-protective strategy that costs them a connection to themselves and to their own bodies and unfortunately provides little real safety.

Inez is a Puerto Rican girl with green eyes, light skin, and a shapely figure. She knows she is feeling desire when "my body gets into the pleasure mood." Connecting her desire to "pleasure," Inez speaks of her sexual desire in terms of her body—she knows she is feeling desire "when my body says yes." She lays out the relationship she experiences between her "mind" and her "body," narrating one resolution to the mind-body split permeating Western culture and alive in Inez: "My body does not control my mind. My mind controls my body, and if my body gets into the pleasure mood, my mind is gonna tell him no . . . tell, tell my body . . . my, my mind's gonna tell my body no. And it can happen, because I said so, because I control you, and my mind is lookin' towards my body." Inez describes what she frames as a general rule for how to resolve the differences between her body and her mind: her response to her sexual desire, to the "yes" she knows in her body, is to "control" her body with her mind, that is, to override the voice of her body with other knowledge. When Inez speaks of her experiences of sexual desire, she speaks of two ways she experiences her sexuality, of knowing and feeling pleasure and of knowing, fearing, and avoiding danger. While she knows that having her breasts touched by a former boyfriend to whom she is still attracted "feels so wonderful," Inez also thinks and speaks about the physical dangers that make her vulnerable: "Let's say you don't have no kind of contraceptives like a condom, and he has AIDS, and you don't know that; you can get AIDS just by having sex with him, because your body said yes, your mind said no, but your body said yes." Inez knows that her own sexual desire can bring both danger and pleasure, knowledge that poses a dilemma for her: whether to pursue pleasure and an embodied sense of self or to avoid the dangers she perceives, sacrificing a part of herself to keep herself safer in a larger sense. Inez speaks about how listening and responding to the "yes" of her body can lead to pregnancy and AIDS and how her "mind is lookin' towards my body," thereby acting as a shield to protect her body from vulnerabilities about which she is very aware. Inez resolves this dilemma by choosing to keep safe from danger, the "no" in her mind drowning out her body's "yes," to protect her from disease and death and from pregnancy or early motherhood at the expense of pleasure.[13] The erotic voice that she recognizes and knows can bring her pleasure and can also make her feel empowered and self-confident and that she feels she must silence is a voice that receives no nurturing or sustenance in her social context. This logic, which implements the disembodied discourses she hears in the school corridors, does not acknowledge or value her ability to know herself or what is happening in her relationship via the information conveyed in her own bodily feelings. At other times in this interview, Inez raises the danger stakes, speaking not only about the physical dangers that her own desire can invoke but also about social risks, about the danger of losing her reputation and of not being "respected," which can lead to physical abuse, and of revealing her true wishes and thereby risking humiliation and a loss of dignity. The erotic voice of her body sounds in a silence, the only response to her body's "yes" she has been offered and now describes is her mind's absolute "no," leaving her seemingly with no safe choice but to silence the voice of her body.

Throughout this interview, Inez voices her knowledge of her own sexual desire and her choice to keep herself out of danger by silencing the voice of her body. She tries to avoid situations in which she will feel desire, keeping herself out of situations in which her desire might be inflamed and lead to danger and minimizing the moments when she will have to cope with this mind-body conflict. Inez derives her knowledge not only from her own experience but also from her observations of other girls:

> Desire? Yes, because she's [a girl] probably in one of those; like let's say she's just drunk, and she doesn't know what she's doin', and she's dancing with this guy—you know how they dance reggae—ever seen somebody dance reggae? How they rubbin' on each other? Well that gets a guy real, I'll say, hard. And it gets a girl very horny. And they could just be dancin' together for like five minutes, and all the sudden [snaps fingers] they just...they...something just snaps in 'em and they say, "Oh, let's go to the bedroom." And, it'll just happen, just because they were dancing. That's why I don't dance reggae with guys.

Interrupting the cultural story about girls and sex, Inez does not frame the danger of dancing reggae as the lure of romance or the promise of a romantic relationship; this kind of dancing is sexually arousing for the girl as well as for the boy—the boy gets "hard"; the girl gets "very horny." In this interview Inez has told me that she enjoys dancing and describes herself as a very good dancer, something about herself that makes her feel proud. However, in order to avoid getting "very horny," Inez does not dance reggae. To keep her body safe, she keeps her body still, not "danc[ing] reggae with guys" so that she will not risk having "something just [snap]" in her.

Barbara is white and has blue eyes framed by long blonde hair that falls across the back of her track jacket, flung over her slight yet athletic frame. In the interview, she speaks of her own sexual desire often in the context of her current relationship. She tells a story about a time with her boyfriend "before [we] had sex, 'cause I wasn't sure how he looked at sex....There was this time he was giving me a backrub, and all I could think about is what I wanted him to do besides have backrubs [with small laugh], and he has to rub my body, forget the back, just do the whole body....It was a very strong desire just to have him rub all over, and that was the one time I can think of I've really had it bad [with laugh].... I'm laying there thinking this, and I didn't want to tell him that, 'cause I didn't know him that well at the time, and its like, noooo, no, we'll just wait [laugh]." Barbara conveys the strength of her sexual feelings as consuming, embodied, and disruptive: "all I could think about," "he has to rub my body," "I...had it bad." Yet Barbara's response to "a very strong desire" is to "wait"; like Inez, she tells herself, "Noooo, no." Her caution is evident in her way of speaking by not speaking directly about her sexual feelings; she seems to rely on my ability to imagine what kinds of sexual things she "wanted him to do besides have backrubs" and what she means by "do the whole body," and thereby she does not have to risk the embarrassment, the indictment, or saying explicitly what she wanted. Her response is shaped by the fact that feeling desire is a risky proposition for a girl, as she makes clear in her explanation of how she comes to her decision not to express her desire at this moment in this relationship, not to say or act in conformity with what she is feeling and wanting: "I didn't know him well enough. I subtly like to initiate; I don't like to come outright and say, Oh let's go do this; I just like doing things very subtly, 'cause I'm not a very... when it comes to sex, the first few times with the person, I'm not very forthright about anything, until after I've gotten to know them, and I trust them a little bit more, and I know that they're not going to look at me funny when I say I want to do something like this."

Barbara is keenly aware that if she is "forthright," if she says what she wants to do—that is, if she reveals her desire—boys might "look at [her] funny," a precursor perhaps to humiliation and even to loss of the relationship. Because she does not know if she can "trust" this boy, because she "didn't know him well enough," Barbara's way of dealing with this identified risk is to be "subtle"—to "initiate" and "[do] things," to be an agent of her own feelings, but to be a kind of secret agent, to behave in a way that is veiled and not readily identifiable, similar to her cautious choice of words in telling her story to me. Yet in this particular situation, she chose not to act on her feelings but to stay still, to "[lie] there thinking," to "wait" to act on her feelings. The logic of her choice resonates with Gilligan's observation that, at adolescence, some girls seem to move into what she has called a female "underground." She suggests that some girls make a conscious psychic retreat within relationships, being aware of their true thoughts and feelings but choosing to protect themselves by keeping their authentic voices out of their relationships, essentially silencing themselves[14] by not acting on their own knowledge or by keeping what they know from view.[15] Girls make this choice because saying what they really think and feel can be dangerous; that is, their authentic thoughts and feelings could threaten relationships or make them vulnerable to physical or psychic attack. Barbara knows that she is feeling desire; she chooses not "to tell him," to keep her genuine feeling out of this relationship, as a way of protecting herself from the possibility that her boyfriend might "look at me funny when I say what I want." This response is a conscious choice not to be "very forthright," which she is fully capable of being and which she decided not to be in this moment. She will "wait" until she "[knows] him well enough." Why is she so cautious, and why might this caution be problematic?

Barbara goes on to explain her choice. Her sense that she needs to keep herself from "com[ing] outright and say[ing], Oh let's go do this," from being known as a young woman who "[wants] to do something," who knows and wants to act in response to her own desire, is a result of her own experience of making her desires known, of letting herself be known as a girl who has sexual wants:

> That was like with oral sex, I never thought I would meet a guy that didn't like oral sex, and I met a guy. 'Cause I hadn't had oral sex with this boyfriend, but the boyfriend before that I was wanting to attempt that, and he would have no part in that. And so I was kind of...you feel really embarrassed after you've asked to do something, and it's like...and then they're, "Oh no, no, no, get away." And so I came to this boyfriend I'm thinking; I was very [with laughter] subtle about doing this 'cause I wanted to make sure I wasn't going to make a fool of myself. It depends on the guy, if I'll be forthright or not.

Having been "embarrassed" and "[made] a fool of" when she expressed her curiosity and desire to have oral sex with a boy, Barbara has learned that voicing her sexual wishes can lead to humiliation. The relational context in which she feels and expresses her desires is paramount: how she will respond to her own sexual feelings "depends on the guy." By being "subtle," Barbara takes great care to try to balance expression of her desire and avoidance of making a fool of herself. This subtlety incurs the risk of not having her desire met.

Although both Inez and Barbara tell narratives about deciding not to voice their desires, there is an important difference in how they respond to their own sexual feelings. In contrast to Inez, Barbara does not silence the "yes" in her body, drowning out the erotic voice with the dangers of desire in the way that Inez describes. While she chooses not to express her desire, Barbara continues to feel it, keeping it alive in the underground world of her real thought and feelings. And this solution has a psychological cost for Barbara to which she gives voice: "It's kinda depressing in its own way afterwards, 'cause you're like sitting there, Well I, you know, I should have said something, or, you know, actually left and gone home. You're laying there, Well I should have said something [with small laugh], 'cause later on it's like, well, I didn't fulfill it [moan, laugh]." Barbara's voice is filled with regret and frustration at having silenced herself. Perhaps precisely because Barbara does not silence her body, she understands the costs of her choice, making it possible for her to know and bemoan the frustration she now feels in the wake of her choice not to respond to her own sexual feelings and curiosity. In telling this desire narrative, Barbara describes the doubt and sense of loss surrounding her choice to respond to her desire by silencing her body and sacrificing her pleasure and herself. What is key about Barbara's dilemma is how very real it is: How can she express her desire and protect herself from potential punishment through humiliation or desertion?

The urban girls in this study describe a self-silencing and portray a vigilant caution regarding their own sexual desire. Because they are in fact experiencing sexual desire, this response requires a substantial investment of energy in what they feel are efforts to ensure their physical and social safety. Missing from these narratives are positive descriptions of sexual curiosity or sexual exploration as responses to their desire; rather, I heard girls tempering or disconnecting from any curiosity they felt. I began to notice what was not said in what they did say. I wondered whether curiosity and the pleasure of feeling and learning about themselves and others in sexual interactions and relationships, whether staying in connection with the power of the erotic in their bodies, were luxuries for these girls, ones they could ill afford. The one exception among the urban girls was Paulina, a young woman who immigrated from Eastern Europe several years ago, who describes a response to her sexual desire in which caution and curiosity intermingle: "[That feeling] makes me like really aware of what somebody's doing.... You're like aware of every move he makes—you just know it.... I don't mind touching the other person; I mean, I don't feel like any part of the other person is dirty in any way. And like, I like guys' chests especially, especially if it's broad, and I like touching the chest, especially if it smells nice; I like it. And I like playing just like especially if it's like little hairs; I just like playing with it; I don't mind." Paulina speaks clearly about responding to her desire by doing what she wants and "likes." In knowing what she likes sexually, she develops her knowledge of herself. She knows and says exactly what she "likes," giving voice to how she comes to this knowledge about herself through her own senses of "touch" and "smell," through her willingness to "play."

But there is a distinct note of caution in how Paulina speaks about her enjoyment, a certain defensiveness woven into her description of pleasure. I am struck by Paulina's repeated caveat that, in exploring a man's body, she "[doesn't] mind" doing what she likes and that she "[doesn't] feel like any part of the other person is dirty in any way." The extremes of her parenthetical commentary suggest to me that she knows or feels that she should mind and that she should find "the other person" to be "dirty." When I tell her

I am curious that she is telling me that she does not mind something that she has also said she likes, she explains that she knows—as do I—that girls are "aware" of how others view and judge them if they explore and express sexual desire: "Because there's a lot of girls that I know who just wouldn't do it; they're kind of like . . . they wouldn't have oral sex with somebody because the person might think something of them. And I don't really care what the person will think, because the person will know me well enough, so I just do it." Paulina seems to be engaged in another conversation with a voice she and I both know well, the social voice that says girls who have oral sex are thought about and spoken about in denigrating ways. Paulina's words suggest that she is aware that she is resisting a social imperative to curb her actions in order to keep other people from judging her to be a bad girl. Knowing the power of this voice, I ask her why she "just [does] it." Her answer provides the linchpin to the logic of Paulina's actions: her own desire. She says she defies conventions intended to keep her from exploring her sexual feelings "because I would want to"—because of her insistence on staying connected with and acting on her own desire. Paulina voices a resistance to "what other people will think," not "really car[ing]" if "something" is thought or said about her if she is exploring her desire by having oral sex, doing what she wants to do. Yet her editorial comments on her own statements of desire, that she "[doesn't] mind" and that a man's body is not "dirty," belies the fact that she is under pressure to modulate her desire and her response to it. In order to stay with the knowledge and pleasure of her senses, Paulina maintains an active program of not caring about the potentially painful social stigma of being talked about—or shunned—which constantly threatens her ability to stay connected with the power of the erotic. If she is to stay connected with the erotic voice, the voice of her body, she must engage in an active resistance to the social pressure she feels to silence herself. . . .

Suburban Girls: Curious Bodies

When the suburban girls told me about their responses to sexual desire, they spoke frequently of a sexual curiosity that was hardly audible among the urban girls and that sometimes challenged their wish to control themselves when they felt desire, a wish that echoed that of the urban girls. Like the urban girls, they too spoke of conflict when speaking of desire, of the power of the erotic and the voices of their bodies. Rather than speak directly about the problems of physical or social vulnerability, these suburban girls voiced a more internal conflict in relation to their sexual desire, a discrepancy between what they described feeling in their bodies and the cultural messages about female sexuality and appropriate female sexual behavior that they have internalized. Instead of silencing their bodies in respones to this conflict, these suburban girls described their often failed struggle to stay in connection with themselves and their bodies and at the same time to maintain a positive sense of themselves as good girls and daughters.

For some, confusion dominates their responses to my questions as they describe their experiences of desire to me.[16] Zoe is white, blond-haired, and blue-eyed, clad in a suit that gives her an air of maturity and also a prim bearing. She sounds very confused, though this confusion is punctuated by moments of intense clarity, when she tells me about her experience: "I guess [three second pause]... I can't, I mean, I can't think of what I... it feels like; I don't know; I think about it; it feels like to me that I want to do something I'm longing to do, but, I mean, I don't know that; I don't know; I don't know what it feels like really." Zoe is, frankly, tongue-tied when she tries to describe her feelings. The fact that she is capable of a clear description of what desire feels like for her—"it feels like to me I want to do something I'm longing to do"—suggests that her struggle to find her voice holds meaning. Perhaps she is embarrassed; perhaps finding the words to articulate her feelings is a challenge. Another way to think about her flustered response is that she is resisting her own knowledge or resisting bringing this knowledge about herself into relationship with me. That I may have met in Zoe or inspired in Zoe a moment of resistance is suggested as I listen to her undo her own knowledge: after telling me that her sexual desire is "that I want to do something I'm longing to do," she immediately undoes her knowledge by telling me, "I don't know what it feels like really." This knowing and then not knowing is typical of the way many girls of Zoe's age, race, and class speak about aspects of their own experience that they, as "good" or "perfect" girls coming of age in a patriarchal culture, are pressured not to know or speak about.[17]

As Zoe describes her response to her own sexual desire, she describes how her wish and effort to be a "good" young woman results in a tenuous connection to her sexual feelings. When Zoe speaks of herself, the voice of the culture that demands capitulation to feminine conventions of passivity is audible, as is the conflict within herself that this norm creates. She says she is someone who has "to wait for other people to do things," yet she has sexual feelings that make her "want to do it." Zoe's response to this "want" is that she "just... can't for some reason."

D: What do you do in a situation you've just described, when you're kissing and you feel like you want to do more; what do you do?

Z: What do I do? I don't know; I don't really; I'm not the person who is initiating things as much [laugh]. I don't know, I guess. I mean, I guess, I know it happens to both of us at the same time, because I don't know—well, I mean, do you mean—like, do I say something? I mean, he's usually the one who will like start more things. I mean, I don't take the initiative; like, I don't—I don't know—start something.

D: Because?

Z: I don't know; I've never been able to, like—I'm not an outgoing person—I've never been able to start things as much; I don't know what it is. I have to wait for other people to do things.

D: Would you like to be able to start things more in that kind of situation?

Z: Yeah.

D: What do you think might make that possible?

Z: I don't know. I have to be sure of myself in that way more. I mean, maybe sometimes I'm afraid that the other person doesn't want to do something, and so I wait until they want to, and then I'll say, Okay, I'm ready now.

D: What gets in the way of your doing that?

Z: Well, I have always worried about what other people think. I'll just wait or something. I mean, I want to do it, but I just . . . I can't for some reason; I don't like physically just do it, you know.

D: How does that make you feel?

Z: Frustrated.

D: What kinds of things are you wanting to do that you don't do?

Z: I don't know. I mean, at first, it's like little things like, I don't know, just like starting to kiss or something like that, instead of them, having them coming to you to, you know; I mean little things like that. I don't know.

Zoe describes a conflict between what she wants to do when she feels desire and what she does—"I'll just wait"—which leads to her feeling "frustrated." When she feels desire, other feelings as well are aroused in Zoe. She feels a moral imperative not to act on her desire. She experiences distress and fear—she feels "worried" and "afraid that the other person doesn't want to do something." To respond to her own sexual feelings passively, "to wait for other people to do things," is one way to lessen or avoid the uncomfortable feelings that her desire incites. She associates the way she responds to her desire with how she behaves in relationship with others in general: she is not "the person who is initiating things" because she is "not an outgoing person," she has "never been able to start things as much," and she has "to wait for other people to do things." When I ask her specifically about her own thoughts and feelings, she undercuts her analysis repeatedly, interrupting her lucid explanations of her behavior by telling me, "I don't know," over and over again, making us both spin. I wonder what it is that she does not know about. Is it an unsureness or a curiosity about this understanding of herself? Is it doubt about being a person who is "not outgoing," "never . . . able to start things much"? Zoe knows there is "some reason" she cannot do what she wants; she knows that she does not "take the initiative" and is "worried about what other people think," but she speaks of having no sense that her behavior or feelings are at odds with larger social forces that may be at play in her psyche. This description of herself echoes the ways that a "good" girl or woman should behave. By definition, to be an acceptable young woman within her social context, she must not know or exercise her own agency, a lesson in being appropriately feminine that Zoe has learned to apply to her sexuality. When I listen to Zoe's story, I hear that she may in part be engaged in a struggle that is shaped by social norms rendering problematic a girl's agency in general and her sexual agency in particular. Yet Zoe also knows that this way of behaving leaves out her desire; knowing that she should not act, yet also experiencing sexual feelings and frustration that contradict this ban on agency, seems to fuel her confusion.

Emily, who is white, has distinctly Jewish features. In our interview she seems to be trying to appear comfortable, and she is also obviously eager to talk to me. Emily tells of an experience of exploring her desire, when her boyfriend, "tan and great looking," came to her house for a family dinner upon his return from a vacation in Florida. Riveted by a renewed realization of how attractive she found him, she was "just staring at him across the table. It was almost fun, because I knew that we were going out later and I would be able to kiss him and stuff, but it was like, I mean, all through dinner I was just like looking at him and just... I was almost trying myself to increase it, so that the fulfillment would be better at the end, when we were alone."

Two things stand out about the way that Emily characterizes her experience of sexual desire. First, her desire seems to be an aspect of herself with which she experiments, interacts, even plays; through trying to manipulate her own desire, she is in fact finding out about herself, how her embodied feelings work, and ways in which she can and cannot control them. Second, the tentative quality in the way that Emily describes her experience—"almost fun" and "almost trying myself to increase it"—makes me wonder if Emily, while speaking about playing with her desire, is also holding herself back. Her reference to her desire as "it," more a way to speak about a foreign body than about a part of oneself, also suggests some distance between her sense of self and her desire. As she continues to describe how her desire "escalates," she seems to recede even further: "You're like very excited and revved up, and then, it's like it starts when you're fooling around at a higher level, like you don't have to work up to anything. It doesn't get you in the mood; you're already in the mood. And you start at a higher level, which means you probably escalate to an even higher level, and that's like cool; I mean, it's fun." When I ask Emily to speak specifically about "it," her words shift from the particulars of her own feelings and behavior to an abstract description of a mechanistic process that I can hardly follow. The "I" of Emily's story has been supplanted by a less direct and clear "you," which makes this description sound more distant from herself. I am puzzled by this shift, and so I ask her about it. Shifting back to "I," Emily begins to speak about her sexual desire in another way:

E: I hadn't thought about it, you know; maybe I feel self-conscious using "I," perhaps.

D: How come?

E: I don't know; I just thought about myself; *I* get to a higher level, and then I was saying, oh, that sounds a little . . .

D: Sounds a little what?

E: Well I guess, just going back, I don't like to think of myself as feeling really sexual. I guess that's probably the whole thing—I think I just hit it—that I don't like to think of myself as being like someone who needs to have their desires fulfilled; that's it. That's what it is.

D: Hm. What do you think about that?

E: I mean, I understand that it's wrong and that everybody has needs, but I just feel like self-conscious when I think about it, and I don't feel self-conscious when I say that we do these things, but I feel self-conscious about saying, I need this kind of a thing.

D: What do you think about that?

E: I don't know what to blame it on. Maybe my family. Maybe I see my father as the more sexual part of my family, and my mom as more just the fun member of my family. Maybe it's that all through growing up, he's gonna try to get this off you, and he's gonna try to do—you know, when you're little and he's gonna try to kiss you and you have to say no, you know—stuff like that, not that you have to say no, but be prepared for that, and stuff like that. I mean, it could be societal, it could be family, it could be, it could be me, I don't know.

When I ask Emily about her shift from "I" to "you," she tells me another story about her experience of sexual desire, how acknowledging her own desire makes her feel. She is self-conscious when she says that she "needs this," and she does not like to think of herself as "feeling really sexual," as "being like someone who needs to have their desires fulfilled." By speaking as a "you" rather than an "I," Emily is able to speak about her desire without explicitly having to acknowledge that the sexual feelings she is describing are her own, thus enabling her to protect herself from feeling self-conscious. She is aware that her feeling self-conscious contradicts what she "understands" about her sexual desire, that "everyone has needs," that she does in fact feel "really sexual." Emily knows and can speak about the source of this contradiction and offers a comprehensive description of how her socialization makes it difficult for her to be in connection with her body and her own desire. She explains that "all through growing up" she learned that "you [the girl] have to say no," that men are "sexual" and will "try to get this off you," and that girls "have to say no . . . [and] be prepared for that." Having taken in a story that does not acknowledge her sexual feelings, it is no wonder that Emily feels self-conscious when she speaks about and claims her "sexual needs." Emily remembers hearing that "he's gonna try to kiss you"; she does not speak of hearing that she might want to kiss him. The disjuncture between the sexual feelings that she does experience and the ways that male and female sexuality have and have not been spoken about makes it hard for Emily to speak about and to know or respond to her "needs." While still unsure "what to blame it on," Emily demonstrates a sophisticated understanding of how she has been guided through "societal" means out of her body and into self-consciousness.

Sophie's blue eyes sparkle impishly, her lithe body clothed casually; yet also perhaps in a studied fashion, in T-shirt and jeans. She is white. In speaking about a time when she experienced sexual desire, Sophie describes an experience that evokes an episode from a romance novel or a soap opera:

> My friend [Eugenia] was on the phone, and he was like chasing me around, like we were totally joking. He was like chasing me with some like bat or something like that? And I like went to get away, and he like more like pinned me down. It sounds like cruel and like ferocious, but he was like holding me down, and I was like [calling to my friend], Eugenia! But I was literally like, I was like, Eugenia! But she knew that I liked him [laughing], so she was just staying on the phone. And he was just right above me and had both my arms down, and it was like I knew that I was acting like I just wanted to get away, but really I just would've wanted to just totally kiss him or something? And it is those great brown eyes again, he just looked right at me, and he's just so—it's that sexual desire thing, you just feel a certain way, and it was just like it's almost like a waiting feeling?

Sophie is narrating a story of how she disguised her true feelings but also of how she enjoyed the pleasure of "the waiting feeling" that her feigning resistance incited. She is direct about how she has acted her part—"I knew that I was acting like I just wanted to get away"—the role of the good girl who does not feel desire. This "act" is in fact just the opposite of what she is really feeling, "that sexual desire thing I said"; in fact, her desire is unequivocally clear to her and suggests a wish to take action—she "would've wanted to just totally kiss him or something?" Although Sophie played the prescribed role of ingenue, I am struck that what she pretended was "want[ing] to get away." This phrase evokes fear and distress, suggesting that Sophie has an awareness of a link between fear and desire that is not conscious but that may shape her actions and responses. In speaking about desire, Sophie outlines a complicated response to the link between pleasure and danger that she does not identify explicitly but that appears just beneath the surface of her words.

For Sophie, desire is connected to "waiting." In her explanation of why she waits rather than acts in this situation, she reveals that she is cognizant of, though somewhat confused about, a connection between her passivity and her gender: "Maybe that's because I'm a female, and usually guys make the first move. That isn't always the way, but a lot of times it's that way.... But, it's not so much because I would be intimidated to; it just tends to happen that way? Like, they tend to ... maybe they tend to just get to it faster or ... I don't know." Sophie associates with being "female" her feeling of "waiting" and her conscious decision to "act" as if she wanted to escape, when in fact she wants to "totally kiss him or something." She has taken in the cultural message that the prerogative of sexual action is male—"guys usually make the first move." Sophie says she does not know why this is so. While she senses that how she acts and waits has to do with being a girl, she has no logical explanation for why girls wait and boys "make the first move"; she does not seem satisfied by her own explanation that boys "just get to it faster." Yet Sophie seems also to hold subliminal knowledge that her actions reflect a vulnerability to being "intimidated."

The passive role that creates excitement and anticipation—"a waiting feeling" that Sophie likes—also creates vulnerability. In raising the question of intimidation, Sophie suggests that she is not entirely unaware of the potential violence that pervades her story. Sophie gives words to the violent undertones of her experience, saying that there is something "cruel" and "ferocious" about a young man chasing her with a bat, even though they are merely friends engaged in a charged flirtation. The fuzzy overlap between fear and excitement, desire and danger, is captured in Sophie's description of her own vulnerability. Because she is safe in this particular situation—her friend does not respond to Sophie's cries but is in fact in full view—Sophie can enjoy this play. However, Sophie voices the possibility that she is being intimidated only to discount that possibility, suggesting that she both does and does not know (or does not wish to know) or speak about the potential for danger that is braided into "that sexual desire thing."

Although I was struck by the struggle in the voices of these suburban girls to find ways to stay connected to their sexual desire within the contours of womanhood available to them, when I brought the voices of the urban girls into relation with the voices of the suburban girls, I began to notice what the suburban girls did not say: the suburban girls did not speak overtly about danger when they voiced their sexual desire, a striking contrast to how the urban girls spoke. Getting a reputation was not much of a concern among the suburban girls, and few of them spoke about fears of getting pregnant or getting AIDS. A few of these girls, like Sophie, spoke, yet did not directly acknowledge, an association between their sexual desire and the potential for physical violence or violation by men; their narratives were structured by the romance plot alive in the culture and in their lives that plays subtly with, but does not distinctly define, the connection between pleasure and danger.[18] These suburban girls seemed to know subconsciously about a real danger that they could encounter, in fact, that many of them *had* encountered. In this study, one-third of these thirty girls told me that they had experienced sexual abuse or sexual violence, in childhood or in adolescence; what was striking about the occurrence of violation is that it did not matter whether a girl lived in the city or in the suburbs—abuse and violence were distributed evenly, regardless of social context, in this sample. Beyond this small sample, statistics indicate that sexual violence is prevalent and real in the lives of all female adolescents. Sexual harassment is prevalent in high schools.[19] Research has shown that one out of ten female adolescents has experienced physical violence while dating in high school. FBI statistics reveal that 20 percent of female homicide victims are between fifteen and twenty-four and that many young women are murdered by their boyfriends; conflicts about sex often lead to such violence.[20] Although I found that the suburban girls seemed more able to know themselves through exploring their sexual desire, more able to be enlivened by the power of the erotic voice in their own bodies than the urban girls were, I also became concerned that these girls did not know—or at least did not speak to me in direct ways—about the real risks they faced in exploring their sexual curiosity, in staying connected to their own bodies in a social context in which sexual and physical violence against women is a real threat....

Desire for the Future

When these girls spoke to me about their sexual desire, they talked about their bodies, the power of the erotic as it surged through their bodies, and how to respond to these embodied feelings. The differences in the ways these girls spoke about their responses to their sexual desire, embedded in the different social contexts in which they live, enabled me to know and articulate one of the most powerful findings of this inquiry: that their responses to these sexual feelings are deeply informed and shaped by the social contexts in which they live—inevitably, inescapably—in female bodies, bodies that hold the possibility of pleasure and also the potential for violation. Developing an ability to know and balance both pleasure and danger may be a way for girls and women to enhance their psychological well-being and to protect themselves from danger within the current social landscape of women's lives. However, this "solution" falls short on several counts. Such a balance was very rare among these girls; girls seemed to align with pleasure or with danger rather than strike a balance. Their voices suggest that when girls align with danger, acknowledgment of pleasure may be impossible or implausible, and that if girls align with pleasure, this move may necessitate that they obscure danger. Knowing only danger seems to deny girls access to important knowledge about themselves and their relationships. While "not knowing" danger may be a necessary psychic strategy in order for a girl or woman to pursue her desire, the cost of this denial of a frightening and enraging aspect of reality may also serve to perpetuate violence against women and to keep women's sexual desire unnecessarily dangerous. If women do not know they are in danger, they will not feel compelled to combat it.

Thus, what these girls say and do not say when they speak about their experiences of sexual desire raises a psychological question and gives shape to the dilemma that women's sexual desire, in the context of patriarchal culture, poses. It is a dilemma that raises unavoidable psychological implications: How can girls and women experience pleasure and know about and protect themselves from, as well as fight against, danger? What are the psychological ramifications and adaptations that girls and women make in light of the fact that they live in female bodies, through which the erotic has the potential to flow, in the context of a culture in which their bodies are subjected to the violence of objectification and physical violation as well as the possibility of pleasure? In the context of these bodies and this culture, what does it mean, then, for girls and women to know their sexual desire or, for that matter, any desire at all? The voices of these girls speaking about their sexual feelings suggest a complexity that sexual desire poses for girls in adolescence, as well as for adult women. Whether these girls say they feel desire, are confused about their desire, do not feel desire, or speak about desire in contradictory ways, sexual desire is a key feature of adolescence for them. Their voices are out of harmony with what is and is not said about them in the literature and in the dominant cultural story about girls and sexuality. By resisting and interrupting the accepted notion that girls do not want sex, that they just want relationships, and by asking girls direct questions—that is, engaging in an empirical endeavor—about their experiences of sexual desire, I discovered that sexual desire is something that girls know. . . .

Notes

This research was supported in part by the Henry A. Murray Dissertation Award through the Murray Center for Research at Radcliffe College.

1. The national average age at first intercourse is 16.2 years for girls. See Melvin Zelnik and John Kantner, "Sexual and Contraceptive Experience of Young Unmarried Women in the United States, 1976 and 1978," in *Teenage Sexuality, Pregnancy, and Childbearing*, ed. Frank Furstenburg, Richard Lincoln, and Jane Menken (Philadelphia: University of Pennsylvania Press, 1981), 68–92. In addition, Lillian Rubin observes that recent studies show that girls are having sex at younger and younger ages. See Lillian Rubin, *Erotic Wars* (New York: Harper Collins, 1990).

2. Carol Gilligan, "Joining the Resistance: Psychology, Politics, Girls, and Women," *Michigan Quarterly Review* 29, no. 4 (1990): 501–36; Lyn Mikel Brown, "Narratives of Relationship: Development of a Care Voice in Girls Ages Seven to Sixteen" (Ed.D. diss., Harvard University, 1989); idem, "Telling a Girl's Life: Self-Authorization as a Form of Resistance," in *Women, Girls, and Psychotherapy: Reframing Resistance*, ed. Carol Gilligan, Annie Rogers, and Deborah L. Tolman (New York: Haworth Press, 1992), 71–86.

3. Susan Bordo, "The Body and the Reproduction of Femininity: A Feminist Appropriation of Foucault," in *Gender/Body/Knowledge*, ed. Alison Jaggar and Susan Bordo (New Brunswick, N.J.: Rutgers University Press, 1989), 13–33.

4. Carol Gilligan, "Joining the Resistance"; Elizabeth Debold and Lyn Brown, "Losing the Body of Knowledge: Conflicts Between Passion and Reason in the Intellectual Development of Adolescent Girls" (Paper presented at the annual meeting of the Association for Women in Psychology, March 1991); Deborah L. Tolman and Elizabeth Debold, "Conflicts of Body and Image: Female Adolescents, Desire, and the No-Body Body," in *Feminist Treatment and Therapy of Eating Disorders*, ed. Melanie Katzman, Pat Fallon, and Susan Wooley (New York: Guilford Press, 1994).

5. See, for example, *Powers of Desire: The Politics of Sexuality*, ed. Ann Snitow, Christine Stansell, and Sharon Thompson (New York: Monthly Review Press, 1983); *Pleasure and Danger: Exploring Female Sexuality*, ed. Carole S. Vance (Boston: Routledge and Kegan Paul, 1984); and Janice Irvine, *Disorders of Desire: Sex and Gender in Modern American Sexology* (Philadelphia: Temple University Press, 1990).

6. Mica Nava, " 'Everybody's Views Were Just Broadened': A Girls' Project and Some Responses to Lesbianism," *Feminist Review* 10 (1982): 37–59; Michelle Fine, "Sexuality, Schooling, and Adolescent Females: The Missing Discourse of Desire," *Harvard Educational Review* 58, no. 1 (1988): 29–53; Pat Macpherson and Michelle Fine, "Hungry for an Us: Adolescent Women Narrating Sex and Politics" (Unpublished manuscript, Philadelphia, 1991); Michelle Fine and Pat Macpherson, "Over Dinner: Feminism and Adolescent Female Bodies" (Unpublished manuscript, Philadelphia, 1991); Sharon Thompson, "Search for Tomorrow: On Feminism and the Reconstruction of Teen Romance," in *Pleasure and Danger: Exploring Female Sexuality*, 250–84; idem, " 'Drastic Entertainments': Teenage Mothers' Signifying Narratives," in *Uncertain Terms*, ed. Faye Ginsberg and A. Tsing (Boston: Beacon Press, 1991); Celia Cowie and Susan Lees, "Slags or Drags," in *Sexuality: A Reader*, ed. Feminist Review (London: Virago, 1987); Susan Lees, *Losing Out: Sexuality and Adolescent Girls* (London: Hutchinson, 1986); idem, "Sexuality, Reputation, Morality, and the Social Control of Girls: A British Study," in *Aspects of School Culture and the Social Control of Girls* (European University Institute, no. 87/301), 1–20; Jane Ussher, *The Psychology of the Female Body* (London: Routledge and Kegan Paul, 1989).

7. Fine, "Sexuality, Schooling, and Adolescent Females," 1988.

8. For descriptions of these voices and how I articulated them, see Tolman, "Voicing the Body: A Psychological Study of Adolescent Girls' Sexual Desires" (Ph.D. diss., Harvard University, 1992).

9. Audre Lorde, "Uses of the Erotic: The Erotic as Power," in *Sister Outsider* (Freedom, Calif.: Crossing Press, 1984), 54.

10. Susan Griffin, *Pornography and Silence: Culture's Revenge Against Nature* (New York: Harper Colophon Press, 1981); Jana Sawicki, "Identity Politics and Sexual Freedom: Foucault and Feminism," in *Feminism and Foucault: Reflections on Resistance*, ed. Irene Diamond and Lee Quinby (Boston: Northeastern University Press, 1988), 177–92.

11. Mary Calderone, "One the Possible Prevention of Sexual Problems in Adolescence," *Hospital and Community Psychiatry* 34, no. 6 (1983): 528–30.

12. I do not think that these are the only, or even necessarily the most important, differences among this group of girls regarding their experiences of sexual desire. My initial readings of these data suggest that other, more psychological differences, such as the presence or absence of a history of sexual abuse, or whether or not a girl has a critical perspective on messages about girls' sexuality, may also differentiate how these girls experience sexual desire.

13. A question that emerges from Inez's fears is why contraception to protect her from pregnancy and why the use of condoms to protect against AIDS do not appear to salve her fears or make it possible to avoid these dangers in a way that might include her desire. The issue of access to contraception for poor girls, norms regarding female sexuality, and the use of contraception in the Hispanic community and how effective a girl's wish or demand for the use of condoms by boys really may explain her feelings.

14. Lori Stern, "Disavowing the Self in Female Adolescence," in *Women, Girls, and Psychotherapy*, 105–18.

15. Carol Gilligan, "Teaching Shakespeare's Sister," in *Making Connections: The Relational World of Adolescent Girls at the Emma Willard School*, ed. Carol Gilligan, Nona Lyons, and Trudy Hanmer (Cambridge: Harvard University Press, 1989), 6–29.

16. Two urban girls voiced confusion as well; see Tolman, "Voicing the Body," for in-depth analyses.

17. See, for example, Gilligan, "Joining the Resistance," and Lyn Mikel Brown, "Telling a Girl's Life," in *Women, Girls, and Psychotherapy*, 71–86.

18. Linda K. Christian-Smith, *Becoming a Woman Through Romance* (New York: Routledge and Kegan Paul, 1990).

19. Eleanor Linn, Nan Stein, and J. Young, "Bitter Lessons for All: Sexual Harassment in Schools," in *Sexuality and the Curriculum*, ed. Sears.

20. Liz Kelly, *Surviving Sexual Violence* (Minneapolis: University of Minnesota Press, 1991).

9

"Get Your Freak On"

Sex, Babies, and Images of Black Femininity

PATRICIA HILL COLLINS

For most of American history, racist prejudice and discrimination were overt. African Americans were restricted to segregated housing, kept from higher education and professional jobs, described by politicians and ministers as morally and physically inferior, and so on. These days, such explicit racism is rarely voiced publicly. At the same time, many scholars argue, a new kind of racism has emerged. Under this new racism, many white Americans now declare both that all races are created equal and that racial equality has been achieved. Thus, they conclude, there is no longer any need for policies that combat racism, and any African Americans who do not succeed have only themselves to blame.

In this article, Patricia Hill Collins explores the popular images of African American women that have emerged under this new racism and discusses both how these images reinforce racism and how African American women use these images to assert control over their bodies and lives. So, for example, male rappers (both white and black) may stereotype African American women as hypersexual, manipulative bitches, thus simultaneously reinforcing both sexism and racism. Meanwhile, some female rappers have adopted the bitch *label as a way to declare their sexual independence. At the same time, Hill Collins argues, the popular image of the "Bad Black Mother" (which appears in Hollywood films about female drug addicts, news stories about "welfare queens," and elsewhere) also reinforces gendered social class stereotypes. Taken together, these various stereotypes help white Americans to conclude that the troubles experienced by poor African American women stem from the women's inherent moral failings, rather than from racist, classist, and sexist prejudice and discrimination.*

2001: Established songwriter, producer, rapper, and singer
Missy Elliott's smash hit "Get Your Freak On" catapults her
third album to the top of the charts. Claiming that she can last
20 rounds with the "Niggahs," Missy declares that she's the
"best around" because she has a "crazy style." In tribute to
and in dialogue with Elliott, singer Nelly Furtado also records
her version of "Get Your Freak On." Describing Elliott,
Furtado sings "she's a freak and I'm a chief head banger." In
case listeners might think Furtado is not as down as Elliott,
Furtado sings "Who's that bitch? Me!" Elliott's song becomes
so popular that a series of websites offer its mesmerizing sitar
tones as ringers for cell phones. They ring in Burger King.
"Get your freak on" . . . "Hello?"

. . . [Singer] Missy Elliott's "Get Your Freak On" may have appeared to
come from nowhere, but the differing meanings associated with the term
freak are situated at the crossroads of colonialism, science, and entertainment. Under colonialism, West African people's proximity to wild animals,
especially apes, raised in Western imaginations the specter of "wild" sexual
practices in an uncivilized, inherently violent wilderness.[1] Through colonial
eyes, the stigma of biological Blackness and the seeming primitiveness of
African cultures marked the borders of extreme abnormality. For Western
sciences that were mesmerized with body politics, White Western normality became constructed on the backs of Black deviance, with an imagined
Black hyper-heterosexual deviance at the heart of the enterprise. . . .[2] Entertainment contributed another strand to the fabric enfolding contemporary
meanings of freak. In the nineteenth century, the term *freak* appeared in
descriptions of human oddities exhibited by circuses and sideshows. Individuals who fell outside the boundaries of normality, from hairy women to
giants and midgets, all were exhibited as freaks of nature for the fun and
amusement of live audiences. . . .

"Freaky" sex consists of sex outside the boundaries of normality. . . .
As boundaries of race, gender, and sexuality soften and shift, so do the
meanings of *freaky* as well as the practices and people thought to engage
in them. The term initially invoked a sexual promiscuity associated with
Blackness, but being freaky is no longer restricted to Black people. As
Whodini raps, "freaks come in all shapes, sizes and colors, but what I
like about 'em most is that they're real good lovers." . . . African American
artists may have led the way, but the usages of *freak* have traveled far
beyond the African American experience. The term has shown a stunning
resiliency, migrating onto the dance floor as a particular dance (*Le Freak*)
and as a style of dancing that signaled individuality, sexual abandon, crazi-
ness, wildness, and new uses of the body. "Get your freak on" can mean
many things to many people. To be labeled a freak, to be a freak, and to

freak constitute different sites of race, gender, and sexuality within popular culture....

In modern America where community institutions of all sorts have eroded, popular culture has increased in importance as a source of information and ideas. African American youth, in particular, can no longer depend on a deeply textured web of families, churches, fraternal organizations, school clubs, sports teams, and other community organizations to help them negotiate the challenges of social inequality. Mass media fills this void, especially movies, television, and music that market Black popular culture aimed at African American consumers. With new technologies that greatly expand possibilities for information creation and dissemination, mass media needs a continuing supply of new cultural material for its growing entertainment, advertising, and news divisions. Because of its authority to shape perceptions of the world, global mass media circulates images of Black femininity and Black masculinity and, in doing so, ideologies of race, gender, sexuality, and class.

In the 1990s, Black popular culture became a hot commodity. Within mass media influenced social relations, African American culture is now photographed, recorded, and/or digitalized, and it travels to all parts of the globe. This new commodified Black culture is highly marketable and has spurred a Black culture industry, one that draws heavily from the cultural production and styles of urban Black youth. In this context, representations of African American women and African American men became increasingly important sites of struggle. The new racism [which replaces overt racism with covert racism, assumes that racial equality already exists, and therefore rejects policies designed to increase racial equality] requires new ideological justifications, and the controlling images of Black femininity and Black masculinity participate in creating them. At the same time, African American women and men use these same sites within Black popular culture to resist racism, class exploitation, sexism, and/or heterosexism.

Because racial desegregation in the post–civil rights era needed new images of racial difference for a color-blind ideology, class-differentiated images of African American culture have become more prominent. In the 1980s and 1990s, historical images of Black people as poor and working-class Black became supplemented by and often contrasted with representations of Black respectability used to portray a growing Black middle class. Poor and working-class Black culture was routinely depicted as being "authentically" Black whereas middle- and upper-middle class Black culture was seen as less so. Poor and working-class Black characters were portrayed as the ones who walked, talked, and acted "Black," and their lack of assimilation of American values justified their incarceration in urban ghettos. In contrast, because middle- and upper-middle-class African American characters lacked this authentic "Black" culture and were virtually indistinguishable from their White middle-class counterparts, assimilated, propertied Black people were shown as being ready for racial integration. This convergence of race and class also sparked changes in the treatment of gender and sexuality. Representations of poor and working-class authenticity and middle-class respectability increasingly came in gender-specific form. As Black femininity and Black masculinity became reworked through this prism of social class, a changing constellation of images of Black femininity appeared that reconfigured Black women's sexuality and helped explain the new racism.

"Bitches" and Bad (Black) Mothers: Images of Working-Class Black Women

Images of working-class Black women can be assembled around two main focal points. The controlling image of the "bitch" constitutes one representation that depicts Black women as aggressive, loud, rude, and pushy. Increasingly applied to poor and/or working-class Black women, the representation of the "bitch" constitutes a reworking of the image of the mule of chattel slavery. Whereas the mule was simply stubborn (passive aggressive) and needed prodding and supervision, the bitch is confrontational and actively aggressive. The term *bitch* is designed to put women in their place. Using *bitch* by itself is offensive, but in combination with other slurs, it can be deadly. Randall Kennedy reports on the actions of a 1999 New Jersey state court that removed a judge, in part, for his actions in one case. The judge had attempted to persuade the prosecutor to accept a plea bargain from four men indicted for robbing and murdering a sixty-seven-year-old African American woman. The judge told the prosecutor not to worry about the case since the victim had been just "some old nigger bitch."[3]

Representations of Black women as bitches abound in contemporary popular culture, and presenting Black women as bitches is designed to defeminize and demonize them. But just as young Black men within hip-hop culture have reclaimed the term *nigger* and used it for different ends, the term *bitch* and the image of Black women that it carries signals a similar contestation process. Within this representation, however, not all bitches are the same. Among African American Studies undergraduate students at the University of Cincinnati, the consensus was that "bitch" and "Bitch" referenced two distinctive types of Black female representations. All women potentially can be "bitches" with a small "b." This was the negative evaluation of "bitch." But the students also identified a positive valuation of "bitch" and argued (some, vociferously so) that only African American women can be "Bitches" with a capital "B." Bitches with a capital "B" or, in their language, "Black Bitches," are super-tough, super-strong women who are often celebrated....

Ironically, Black male comedians have often led the pack in reproducing derisive images of Black women as being ugly, loud "bitches." Resembling Marlon Riggs' protestations about the "sissy" and "punk" jokes targeted toward Black gay men, "bitches" are routinely mocked within contemporary Black popular culture. For example, ridiculing African American women as being like men (also, a common representation of Black lesbians) has long been a prominent subtext in the routines of Redd Foxx, Eddie Murphy, Martin Lawrence, and other African American comedians. In other cases, Black male comedians dress up as African American women in order to make fun of them. Virtually all of the African American comics on the popular show *Saturday Night Live* have on occasion dressed as women to caricature Black women. Through this act of cross-dressing, Black women can be depicted as ugly women who too closely resemble men (big, Black, and short hair) and because they are aggressive like men, become stigmatized as "bitches." . . .

In the universe of Black popular culture, the combination of sexuality and bitchiness can be deadly. Invoking historical understandings of Black women's assumed promiscuity, some representations of the "bitch" draw upon American sexual scripts of Black women's wildness. Here, the question of who controls Black women's sexuality is paramount. One sign of a "Bitch's" power is her manipulation of her own sexuality for her own gain. Bitches control men, or at least try to, using their bodies as weapons. . . .

This theme of the materialistic, sexualized Black woman has become an icon within hip-hop culture. The difficulty lies in telling the difference between representations of Black women who are sexually liberated and those who are sexual objects, their bodies on sale for male enjoyment. On the one hand, the public persona of rap star Lil' Kim has been compared to that of a female hustler. Resembling representations of her male counterpart who uses women for financial and sexual gain, the public performance of Lil' Kim brings life to the fictional Winter Santiago. An exposé in *Vibe* magazine describes Kim's public face: "Lil' Kim's mythology is about pussy, really: the power, pleasure, and politics of it, the murky mixture of emotions and commerce that sex has become in popular culture. . . . She is, perhaps, the greatest public purveyor of the female hustle this side of Madonna, parlaying ghetto pain, pomp, and circumstances into main stream fame and fortune."[4] But should we think that Lil' Kim is shallow, the article goes on to describe her "soft center": "Kim's reality, on the other hand, is about love. It is her true currency . . . . Her appeal has much to do with the fact that love—carnal, familial, self-destructive, or spiritual—is the root of who Kim is. Pussy is just the most marketable aspect of it."[5] What do we make of Lil' Kim? Is she the female version of misogynistic rappers? If so, her performance is what matters. To be real, she must sell sexuality as part of working-class Black female authenticity.

On the other hand, many African American women rappers identify female sexuality as part of women's freedom and independence. Being sexually open does not make a woman a tramp or a "ho." When Salt 'n Pepa engage in role reversal in their video "Most Men Are Tramps," they contest dominant notions that see as dangerous female sexuality that is not under the control of men. Lack of male domination creates immoral women. Salt 'n Pepa ask, "Have you ever seen a man who's stupid and rude . . . who thinks he's God's gift to women?" The rap shows a group of male dancers wearing black trench coats. As Salt 'n Pepa repeat "tramp," the men flash open their coats to reveal outfits of tiny little red G-strings. The video does not exploit the men—they are shown for just a second. Rather, the point is to use role reversal to criticize existing gender ideology.[6] In their raps "Let's Talk about Sex," and "It's None of Your Business," the group repeats its anthem of sexual freedom.

This issue of control becomes highly important within the universe of Black popular culture that is marketed by mass media. Some women are bitches who control their own sexuality—they "get a freak on," which remains within their control and on their own terms. Whether she "fucks men" for pleasure, drugs, revenge, or money, the sexualized bitch constitutes a modern version of the jezebel [stereotype of African American women as sexually wanton], repackaged for contemporary mass media. In discussing this updated jezebel image, cultural critic Lisa Jones distinguishes between gold diggers/skeezers (women who screw for status) and crack hos (women who screw for a fix).[7] Some women are the "hos" who trade sexual favors for jobs, money, drugs, and other material items. The female hustler, a materialistic woman who is willing to sell, rent, or use her sexuality to get whatever she wants constitutes this sexualized variation of the "bitch." This image appears with increasing frequency, especially in conjunction with trying to "catch" an African American man with money. Athletes are targets, and having a baby with an athlete is a way to garner income. Black women who are sex workers, namely, those who engage in phone sex, lap dancing, and prostitution for compensation, also populate this universe of sexualized bitches. The prostitute who hustles without a pimp and who keeps the compensation is a bitch who works for herself.

Not only do these images of sexualized Black bitches appear in global mass media, Black male artists, producers, and marketing executives participate in reproducing these images. As cultural critic Lisa Jones points out, "what might make the skeezer an even more painful thorn in your side is that, unlike its forerunners, this type is manufactured primarily by black men."[8] If the cultural production of some African American male artists is any indication, Jones may be on to something.

In the early 1990s, and in conjunction with the emergence of gangsta rap, a fairly dramatic shift occurred within Black popular culture and mass media concerning how some African American artists depicted African American women. In a sense, the *celebration* of Black women's bodies and how they handled them that had long appeared in earlier Black cultural production (for example, a song such as "Brick House" within the rhythm and blues tradition) became increasingly replaced by the *objectification* of Black women's bodies as part of a commodified Black culture. Contemporary music videos of Black male artists in particular became increasingly populated with legions of young Black women who dance, strut, and serve as visually appealing props for the rapper in question. The women in these videos typically share two attributes—they are rarely acknowledged as individuals and they are scantily clad. One Black female body can easily replace another and all are reduced to their bodies. Ironically, displaying nameless, naked Black female bodies has a long history in Western societies, from the display of enslaved African women on the auction block under chattel slavery to representations of Black female bodies in contemporary film and music videos. Describing the placement and use of primitive art in Western exhibits, one scholar points out, " 'namelessness' resembles 'nakedness': it is a category always brought to bear by the Westerner on the 'primitive' and yet a phony category insofar as the namelessness and nakedness exist only from the Euro-American point of view."[9]

Not only can the entire body become objectified but also parts of the body can suffer the same fate. For example, music videos for Sir Mix A Lot's "Baby Got Back," the film clip for "Doing Da Butt" from Spike Lee's film *School Daze*, and the music video for 2LiveCrew's "Pop That Coochie" all focused attention on women's behinds generally, and Black women's behinds in particular. All three songs seemingly celebrated Black women's buttocks, but they also objectified them, albeit differently. "Baby Got Back" is more clearly rooted in the "Brick House" tradition of celebrating Black women's sexuality via admiring their bodies—in his video, Sir Mix A Lot happily wanders among several booty swinging sisters, all of whom are proud to show their stuff. "Doing Da Butt" creates a different interpretive context for this fascination with the booty. In Lee's party sequence, being able to shake the booty is a sign of authentic Blackness, with the Black woman who is shaking the biggest butt being the most authentic Black woman. In contrast, "Pop That Coochie" contains a bevy of women who simply shake their rumps for the enjoyment of the members of 2LiveCrew. Their butts are toys for the boys in the band. Ironically, whereas European men expressed fascination with the buttocks of the Hottentot Venus as a site of Black female sexuality that became central to the construction of White racism itself, contemporary Black popular culture seemingly celebrates these same signs uncritically.

Objectifying Black women's bodies turns them into canvases that can be interchanged for a variety of purposes. Historically, this objectification had a clear racial motive. In the post-civil rights era, however, this use of Black women's bodies also has a distinctive gender subtext in that African American men and women participate differently in this process of objectification. African American men who star in music videos construct a certain version of manhood against the backdrop of objectified, nameless, quasi-naked Black women who populate their stage. At the same time, African American women in these same videos often objectify their own bodies in order to be accepted within this Black male-controlled universe. Black women now can get hair weaves, insert blue contact lenses, dye their hair blond, get silicone implants to have bigger breasts, and have ribs removed to achieve small waists (Janet Jackson) all for the purpose of appearing more "beautiful."

Whether Black women rappers who use the term *bitch* are participating in their own subordination or whether they are resisting these gender relations remains a subject of debate. Rap and hip-hop serve as sites to contest these same gender meanings. The language in rap has attracted considerable controversy, especially the misogyny associated with calling women "bitches" and "hos."[10] First popularized within rap, these terms are now so pervasive that they have entered the realm of colloquial, everyday speech. Even White singer Nelly Furtado proudly proclaims, "Who's that bitch? Me!" Yet because rap is a sphere of cultural production, it has space for contestation. For example, in 1994 Queen Latifah's "U.N.I.T.Y." won a Grammy, an NAACP Image Award, and a Soul Train Music Award. Latifah claims that she did not write the song to win awards, but in response to the verbal and physical assaults on women that she saw around her, especially in rap music. As one line from her award-winning song states, "Every time I hear a brother call a girl a bitch or a ho, trying to make a sister feel low, you know all of that's got to go."[11]

Black bitches are one thing. Black bitches that are fertile and become mothers are something else. In this regard, the term *bitch* references yet another meaning. Reminiscent of the association of Africans with animals, the term *bitch* also refers to female dogs. Via this association, the term thus invokes a web of meaning that links unregulated sexuality with uncontrolled fertility. Female dogs or bitches "fuck" and produce litters of puppies. In a context of a racial discourse that long associated people of African descent with animalistic practices, the use of the term bitch is noteworthy. Moreover, new technologies that place a greater emphasis on machines provide another variation on the updated bitch. In contrast to Black female bodies as animalistic, Black female bodies become machines built for endurance. The Black superwoman becomes a "sex machine" that in turn becomes a "baby machine." The thinking behind these images is that unregulated sexuality results in unplanned for, unwanted, and poorly raised children.

The representation of the sexualized bitch leads to another cluster of representations of working-class Black femininity, namely, controlling images of poor and working-class Black women as bad mothers. Bad Black Mothers (BBM) are those who are abusive (extremely bitchy) and/or who neglect their children either in utero or afterward. Ironically, these Bad Black Mothers are stigmatized as being inappropriately feminine because they reject the gender ideology associated with the American family ideal. They are often single mothers, they live in poverty, they are often young, and they rely on the state to support their children. Moreover, they allegedly pass on their bad values to their children who in turn are more likely to become criminals and unwed teenaged mothers.

Reserved for poor and/or working-class Black women, or for women who have fallen into poverty and shame as a result of their bad behavior, a constellation of new images describes variations of the Bad Black Mother. The image of the crack mother illustrates how controlling images of working-class Black femininity can dovetail with punitive social policies. When crack cocaine appeared in the early 1980s, two features made it the perfect target for the Reagan administration's War on Drugs. Crack cocaine was primarily confined to Black inner-city neighborhoods, and women constituted approximately half of its users. In the late 1980s, news stories began to cover the huge increase in the number of newborns testing positive for drugs. But coverage was far from sympathetic. Addicted pregnant women became demonized as "crack mothers" whose selfishness and criminality punished their children in the womb. Fictional treatments followed soon after. For example, in the feature film *Losing Isaiah*, Academy Award–winning actress Halle Berry plays a woman on crack cocaine who is so high that she abandons her baby. A kindly White family takes Isaiah in, and they patiently deal with the host of problems he has due to his biological mother's failures.

Representations such as these contributed to a punitive climate in which the criminal justice system increasingly penalizes pregnancy by prosecuting women for exposing their babies to drugs in the womb and by imposing birth control as a condition of probation. Between 1985 and 1995, thirty states charged approximately 200 women with maternal drug use. Charges included distributing drugs to a minor, child abuse and neglect, reckless endangerment, manslaughter, and assault with a deadly weapon.[12] In virtually all of these cases, the women prosecuted were poor and African American. As legal scholar Dorothy Roberts points out, "prosecutors and judges see poor Black women as suitable subjects for these reproductive penalties because society does not view these women as suitable mothers in the first place."[13]

Drug use is one sure-fire indicator used to create the BBM representation, but simply being poor and accepting public assistance is sufficient. In the 1960s, when African American women successfully challenged the racially discriminatory policies that characterized social welfare programs, the generic image of the "Bad Black Mother" became crystallized into the racialized image of the "welfare mother." These controlling images under went another transformation in the 1980s as part of Reagan/Bush's efforts to reduce social welfare funding for families. Resembling the practice of invoking the controlling image of the Black rapist via the Bush campaign's use of Willie Horton in 1988, the Reagan/Bush administrations also realized that racializing welfare by painting it as a program that unfairly benefited Blacks was a sure-fire way to win White votes. This context created the controlling image of the "welfare queen" primarily to garner support for refusing state support for poor and working-class Black mothers and children. Poor Black women's welfare eligibility meant that many chose to stay home and care for their children, thus emulating White middle-class mothers. But because these stay-at-home moms were African American and did not work for pay, they were deemed to be "lazy." Ironically, gaining rights introduced a new set of controlling images. In a political economy in which the children of poor and working-class African Americans are unwanted because such children are expensive and have citizenship rights, reducing the fertility [of African Americans] becomes critical....

Beyond the efforts to criminalize the pregnancies of crack-addicted women, a series of public policies have been introduced that aim to shrink state and federal social welfare budgets, in part by reducing Black women's fertility. Despite its health risks and unpleasant side effects, Norplant was marketed to poor inner-city Black teenagers. As a coercive method of birth control, users found that they had little difficulty getting their physicians to insert the contraceptive rods into their bodies but, since only physicians were qualified to remove the rods, getting them out was far more difficult. Depo Provera as a birth control shot was also heavily marketed to women who seemingly could not control their fertility and needed medical intervention to avoid motherhood. Finally, welfare legislation that threatens to deny benefits to additional children is designed to discourage childbearing. In a context in which safe, legal abortion is difficult for poor women to obtain, the "choice" of permanent sterilization makes sense. Representations of Bad Black Mothers help create an interpretive climate that normalizes these punitive policies.

Controlling images of working-class Black women pervade television and film, but rap and hip-hop culture constitute one site where misogyny is freely expressed and resisted. Given this context, African American women's participation in rap and hip-hop as writers, producers, and as performers illustrates how African American women negotiate these representations. In a sense, Black female rappers who reject these representations of working-class Black women follow in the footsteps of earlier generations of Black blues women who chose to sing the "devil's music." The 1990s witnessed the emergence of Black women who made music videos that were sites of promotion, creativity, and self-expression. For example, hip-hop artists Salt 'n Pepa, Erykah Badu, Lauryn Hill, and Missy Elliott depict themselves as independent, strong, and self-reliant agents of their own desire. Because rap revolves around self-promotion, female rappers are able to avoid accusations of being self-centered or narcissistic when they use the form to promote Black female power. Rap thus can provide an important forum for women.

Black women's self-representation in rap results in complex, often contradictory and multifaceted depictions of Black womanhood. One study of representations of Black women in popular music videos found that controlling images of Black womanhood occurred simultaneously with resistant images. On the one hand, when music videos focused on Black women's bodies, presented one-dimensional womanhood by rarely depicting motherhood, and showcased women under the aegis of a male sponsor, they did re-create controlling images of Black womanhood. On the other hand, the music videos also contained distinctive patterns of Black women's agency. First, in many videos, Blackness did not carry a negative connotation, but instead served as a basis for strength, power, and a positive self-identity. Second, despite a predominance of traditional gender roles, Black women performers were frequently depicted as active, vocal, and independent. But instead of exhibiting the physical violence and aggression found in men's videos, the music videos sampled in the study demonstrate the significance of verbal assertiveness where "speaking out and speaking one's mind are a constant theme." Another theme concerns achieving independence—Black women may assert independence, but they look to one another for support, partnership, and sisterhood. Black women's music videos may be situated within hip-hop culture, but they reflect the tensions of negotiating representations of Black femininity: "what emerges from this combination of agency, voice, partnership, and Black context is a sense of the construction of Black woman-centered video narratives. Within these narratives, the interests, desires, and goals of women are predominant.... Black women are quite firmly the subjects of these narratives and are able to clearly and unequivocally express their points of view." ...

[In sum,] images of working-class Black femininity all articulate with the social class system of the post–civil rights era. Depicting African American women as bitches; the sexual use of African American women's bodies by circulating images of Black women's promiscuity; [and] derogating the reproductive capacities of African American women's bodies ... all work to obscure the closing door of racial opportunity in the post–civil rights era. On the surface, these interconnected representations offer a plausible explanation for poor and/or working-class African American women's class status: (1) too-strong, bitchy women are less attractive to men because they are not feminine; (2) to compensate, these less-attractive women use their sexuality to "catch" men and hopefully become pregnant so that the men will marry them; and (3) men see through this game and leave these women as single mothers who often have little recourse but to either try and "catch" another man or "hustle" the government. But on another level, when it comes to poor and working-class African American women, this constellation of representations functions as ideology to justify the new social relations of hyper-ghettoization, unfinished racial desegregation, and efforts to shrink the social welfare state. Collectively these representations construct a "natural" Black femininity that in turn is central to an "authentic" Black culture.

Notes

1. Jordan 1968, 3–43.
2. Fausto-Sterling 1995; Giddings 1992.
3. Kennedy 2002, 63.
4. Marriott 2000, 126.
5. Marriott 2000, 126.
6. Roberts 1995.
7. Roberts 1995, 79.
8. Jones 1994, 80.
9. Torgovnick 1990, 90.
10. Cole and Guy-Sheftall 2003, 182–215.
11. Latifah 1999, 3.
12. Roberts 1997, 153.

13. Roberts 1997, 152. Even worse are those who remain on drugs, sell their bodies, and decide to keep their children. Those Black women who engage in sex work in order to support their children are especially chastised. The hoochie mama popularized in Black popular culture constitutes a bad mother who sells sex and neglects her children. The derogated Black mother who is on drugs also fits within this nexus of representations of bad Black mothers.

References

Cole, Johnetta Betsh, and Beverly Guy-Sheftall. 2003. *Gender Talk: The Struggle for Women's Equality in African American Communities.* New York: Ballantine.

Fausto-Sterling, Anne. 1995. Gender, race, and nation: The comparative anatomy of "Hottentot" women in Europe, 1815–1817. *Deviant Bodies: Critical Perspectives on Difference in Science and Popular Culture,* edited by Jennifer Terry and Jacqueline Urla, pp. 19–48. Bloomington: Indiana University Press.

Giddings, Paula. 1992. "The Last Taboo." *Race-ing Justice, En Gendering Power,* edited by Toni Morrison, pp. 441–465. New York: Pantheon.

Jones, Lisa. 1994. *Bullet Diva: Tales of Race, Sex, and Hair.* New York: Doubleday.

Jordan, Winthrop D. 1968. *White Over Black: American Attitudes towards the Negro, 1550–1812.* New York: W. W. Norton.

Kennedy, Randell. 2002. *Nigger: The Stranger Career of a Troublesome Word.* New York: Pantheon.

Latifah, Queen. 1999. *Ladies First: Revelations of a Strong Woman.* New York: Quill.

Marriott, Robert. 2000. "'Blowin' Up." *Vibe* 8:5 (June–July 2000):124–30.

Roberts, Dorothy E. 1997. *Killing the Black Body: Race, Reproduction, and the Meaning of Liberty.* New York: Pantheon Books.

Roberts, Robin. 1995. "Sisters in the Name of Rap: Rapping for Women's Lives." *Black Women in America,* edited by Kim Marie Vaz, pp. 323–333. Thousand Oaks, CA: Sage.

Torgovnick, Marianna. 1990. *Gone Primitive: Savage Intellects, Modern Lives.* Chicago: University of Chicago Press.

10

Brain, Brow, and Booty

Latina Iconicity in U.S. Popular Culture

ISABEL MOLINA GUZMÁN AND ANGHARAD N. VALDIVIA

Latinos and Latinas now comprise approximately 15% of the U.S. population, more than any other U.S. minority group. Not surprisingly, media images of Latinos and Latinas have become considerably more common, as media producers have recognized that they can commodify *them (i.e., turn them into images that can be sold for profit). In this article, Isabel Molina Guzmán and Angharad N. Valdivia describe how Jennifer Lopez, Salma Hayek, and Frida Kahlo have become icons of female Latinidad (that is, their media representations have become symbols of what it means to be Latina).*

The authors illustrate how the women's differing images reflect and reinforce various tropes of Latinidad. Trope, *in film and cultural studies, means a recognizable and recurrent media theme, story-line, or image. For example, both the "Cinderella trope" and the trope of heterosexual romance appear in many films, including* Pretty Woman *and* Maid in Manhattan. *In addition, the authors note, the images of Lopez, Hayek, and Kahlo are both* racialized *and* gendered—*that is, each woman's media image highlights both her racial identity and how she fits gender norms. Although their images vary substantially, in each case they emphasize the women's status as* others *who differ in important ways from dominant American society.*

Finally, Molina Guzmán and Valdivia note that the women's images emphasize their hybridity *(i.e., their status as hybrids).* Hybridity *refers to any new and distinct culture or identity that emerges from the mixing of cultures or identities. The authors suggest that because these women do not fit neatly into the*

Isabel Molina Guzman and Angharad N. Valdivia. 2004. "Brain, Brow, and Booty," *Communication Review* 7: 205–221. Reprinted by permission of the publisher (Taylor & Francis Group, http://www.informaworld.com).

long-standing U.S. racial categories of black and white, they have the potential to threaten U.S. cultural assumptions about race.

We were shooting on the steps of the Metropolitan Museum one night. It was lit romantically, and Jennifer was wearing an evening gown, looking incredibly stunning. Suddenly there must have been a thousand people screaming her name. *It was like witnessing this icon.*

> Ralph Fiennes in the *New York Times*,
> 2002, p. 16 (emphasis added)

This stamp, honoring a Mexican artist who has transcended "la frontera" and *has become an icon to Hispanics, feminists, and art lovers*, will be a further reminder of the continuous cultural contributions of Latinos to the United States.

> Cecilia Alvear, President of National Association of
> Hispanic Journalists (NAHJ) on the occasion of the
> introduction of the Frida Kahlo U.S. postage stamp;
> 2001 (emphasis added)

"Nothing Like the Icon on the Fridge"

> Column about Salma Hayek's *Frida* by Stephanie
> Zacharek in the *New York Times*, 2002

The iconic location of Latinas and their articulation into commodity culture is an inescapable affirmation of the increasing centrality of Latinidad and Latinas to U.S. popular culture. We live in an age when Latinidad, the state and process of being, becoming, and/or appearing Latina/o, is the "It" ethnicity and style in contemporary U.S. mainstream culture. This construction of Latinidad is transmitted primarily, though not exclusively, through the mainstream media and popular culture. We also continue to live in an age when women function as a sign [or icon], a stand-in for objects and concepts ranging from nation to beauty to sexuality (Rakow & Kranich 1991). This article examines the representational politics surrounding three hypercommodified Latinas in contemporary U.S. culture, Salma Hayek, Frida Kahlo, and Jennifer Lopez.... We focus on the contemporary representations of Hayek, Kahlo, and Lopez in order to explore the gendered and racialized signifiers surrounding Latinidad and Latina iconicity and investigate the related processes of producing and policing Latina bodies and identities in mainstream texts such as films and magazines[1]....

The iconic position of Latinas within U.S. popular culture presents a critical space from which to study the racialized and gendered construction of meaning surrounding transnational identities and hybrid bodies. Iconicity, as a form of representation, involves the transformation of meaning that arises through the interactive relationship between an image, the practices surrounding the production of that image, and the social context within which the image is produced and received by audiences. As Giles and Middleton (2000) propose it is not so much that iconic images communicate a specific meaning or message, but that they "resignify" the meanings surrounding a particular image, event, or issue through their circulation in popular culture. Within contemporary U.S. popular culture, three women—Salma Hayek, Frida Kahlo, and Jennifer Lopez—have gained iconic status as representatives of feminine Latinidad. In other words, popular representations of each woman communicate more than the visuals, instead the images are invited to sign-in for mainstream narratives about Latina identity and sexuality....

Jennifer Lopez

At $13 million dollars per movie, Lopez is the highest paid Latina identified actress in Hollywood history.... Unlike Cameron Diaz whose Latinidad remains relatively invisible by virtue of her proximity to and performance of Whiteness, Lopez has explicitly highlighted and in some instances subverted her malleable ethnic and racial identity. In unprecedented fashion Lopez has catapulted her on-screen image to multiple domains most notably the music, clothing, lingerie, perfume, and television industries.... New perfume and fashion lines as well as forthcoming films and albums are part of a carefully orchestrated effort to remain at the forefront of the mainstream....

Salma Hayek

The fall 2002 release of *Frida* by Miramax catapulted its producer and star Salma Hayek onto the cover of U.S. magazines, ranging from *Parade* to *Elle*. Her success in Mexican soap operas inspired Hayek to cross the entertainment border, where her first Hollywood role was a 30-second stint as a sultry and angry Chicana ex-girlfriend in Alison Ender's 1993 film *Mi Vida Loca*. As Hayek's hair has gotten progressively straighter and thus more "Anglo"-looking, her on-screen image also has become less stereotypically ethnic, consequently yielding more complex supporting and leading roles. While not achieving the multimedia profile of Lopez, Hayek is one of the most prolific contemporary Latinas in Hollywood, recently earning an Oscar nomination for her role in *Frida*, a rare achievement perceived as recognition of an actress's skill and talent....

Frida Kahlo

Decades after her death, [Mexican painter Frida] Kahlo is one of the most popular and commodified mainstream images of Latinidad globally, and in the United States particularly. One can find Frida Kahlo stationery, posters, jewelry, hair clips, autobiographies, cookbooks, biographical books, chrono-logical art books, refrigerator magnets, painting kits, wall hangings, and wrapping paper, to mention a few of the items in bookstores and novelty stores throughout the U.S., Mexico, Puerto Rico, and Spain.... Her paint-ings received the highest ever bid for a Latin American artwork auctioned at the prestigious House of Sotheby. Highlighting Kahlo's representational sig-nificance Hayek and Lopez raced to release biopics of the artist. Thus, it is not so much the art works themselves, including her own self-representational images, in which we are interested, but rather how Kahlo the symbol tran-scends the high and low culture divide by signing in for Latina identity and authenticity.

Racializing Latina Bodies and Sexuality in U.S. Popular Culture

One of the most enduring tropes surrounding the signification of Latinas in U.S. popular culture is that of tropicalism (Aparicio & Chavez-Silverman 1997; Perez-Firmat 1994). Tropicalism erases specificity and homogenizes all that is identified as Latin and Latina/o. Under the trope of tropical-ism, attributes such as bright colors, rhythmic music, and brown or olive skin comprise some of the most enduring stereotypes about Latina/os, a stereotype best embodied by the excesses of Carmen Miranda and the hyper-sexualization of Ricky Martin. Gendered aspects of the trope of tropicalism include the male Latin lover, macho, dark-haired, mustachioed, and the spit-fire female Latina characterized by red-colored lips, bright seductive clothing, curvaceous hips and breasts, long brunette hair, and extravagant jewelry. The tropes of tropicalism extend beyond those people with Caribbean roots to people from Latin America, and recently to those in the United States with Caribbean and/or Latin American roots.

Sexuality plays a central role in the tropicalization of Latinas through the widely circulated narratives of sexual availability, proficiency, and desirabil-ity (Valdivia 2000). For centuries the bodies of women of color, specifically their genitals and buttocks, have been excessively sexualized and exoticized by U.S. and European cultures (Gilman 1985). Not surprisingly popular images of Latinas and the Latina body focus primarily on the area below the navel, an urbane corporeal site with sexualized overdetermination (Desmond 1997). Within the Eurocentric mind/body binary, culture is signified by the higher intellectual functions of the mind while nature is signified by the lower biological functions of the body. That is, Whiteness is associated with a dis-embodied intellectual tradition free from the everyday desires of the body, and non-Whiteness is associated with nature and the everyday needs of the body to consume food, excrete waste, and reproduce sexually. Dominant representations of Latinas and African American women are predominantly characterized by an emphasis on the breasts, hips, and buttocks. These body parts function as mixed signifiers of sexual desire and fertility as well as bodily waste and racial contamination.

Contemporary Latina iconicity inherits traces of this dichotomous representational terrain. Despite Jennifer Lopez's multimedia successes, it is her buttocks insured by Lopez for $1 billion that most journalists and Lopez herself foregrounds. Like other popular Latinas, Lopez is simultaneously celebrated and denigrated for her physical, bodily, and financial excess. Whenever she appears in the popular press, whether it is a newspaper, a news magazine, or *People*, Lopez's gorgeous stereotypical Latina butt is glamorized and sexually fetishized. Indeed, she is often photographed in profile or from the back looking over her shoulders—her buttocks becoming the focus of the image, the part of her body that marks Lopez as sexy but different from Anglo female bodies....

Likewise, while news media images of Lopez foreground her buttocks, photographs of Hayek emphasize her bountiful breasts, small waist, and round hips. Hayek's petite yet hyper-curvaceous frame embodies the romanticized stereotypical Latina hourglass shape, a petite ethnic shape that stands in opposition to the resonances of Blackness surrounding Lopez's hyper-buttocks and music video representations. Profile shots of Hayek in movies and magazine covers show both her breasts and her perfectly shaped booty. Frontal shots of Hayek's body highlight her deep cleavage as well as her long dark hair, worn straightened when performing a more glamorous image, and by implication Anglo identity, or curly when performing a more exotic ethnic identity.

Accompanying images of her body are journalistic texts that ultimately frame Hayek's body and identity within narratives of Latinidad, in particular references to her personality, voracious appetite, and loud, talkative nature. Thus, unlike Lopez whose sexualized image primarily foregrounds her racialized booty, sexualized representations of Hayek center on her body as the stereotyped performance of Latina femininity....

The marginalization of Latina bodies is defined by an ideological contradiction—that is, Latina beauty and sexuality is marked as other, yet it is that otherness that also marks Latinas as desirable. In other words, Latina desirability is determined by their signification as racialized, exotic Others. For example, in the movies *Blood and Wine* and *U-Turn* Lopez's body is framed as animalistic, primitive, and irresistibly dangerous to the Anglo American male characters. In both movies, Lopez's body is fetishized through extreme close-ups of her eyes, lips, breasts, legs, and buttocks, visuals that often link her highly sexualized body to the physical environment around her. Similarly, Hayek's characters in *From Dusk Till Dawn* (1996), *54*, and *Timecode* (2000) construct the ethnic feminine other as a temptress, a source of sexual and racial contamination, whose sexuality ultimately destroys her.

Consequently, representations of Hayek's body provide a symbolic bridge between the racialized and sexualized narrative of Lopez's buttocks and the ethnic and desexualized narrative of Kahlo's self-representations of her physically injured body. Whereas Lopez's body, especially her butt, signifies a racialized exotic sexuality, Kahlo's body asserts her ethnicity and foregrounds her identity beyond or outside of her sexuality. Portraits and images of Kahlo emphasize her face, in particular her hyper-eyebrow as a signifier of ethnic-difference, feminine-strength, and intellectual rather than bodily work. Nevertheless, intellectual efforts by Kahlo to complicate both her identity and Latina body do not necessarily transfer into twenty-first century commodifying practices. Instead we get the reification of difference through the everyday commodification of her face in the form of earrings, shirts, and other mainstream products, and her intellectual labor is resignified as aberrant and exotic. Within these popular products, the emphasis on her colorful-ethnic dress and facial hair, both physical markers of ethnic bodies, work to mediate her ethnic identity for capitalist consumption. In the end, the physical representations of all three women are informed by the racializing discourses of ethnic female bodies as simultaneously physically aberrant, sexually desirable, and consumable by the mainstream. These discourses cannot be examined outside of a framework of analysis that allows for fluidity and mixture.

Hybridity, Authenticity and the Latina Body

... Due to their mixed cultural and ethnic heritage, Hayek, Kahlo, and Lopez as hybrid women often problematize and work against the discursive field of popular ethnic and racial categories. While remaining at the margins of representations of Whiteness, they also exist outside the marginalizing borders of Blackness. Instead, they occupy a racialized space in between the dominant U.S. binary of Black or White identities. Given their dark, full-bodied hair, brown eyes, somatically olive skin, and a range of more or less European facial features, they are physically "any-woman"—with the perception of their identity determined both by the context of reception and the relationally encoded setting of production....

Not coincidentally,... Hayek and Lopez have portrayed characters whose ethnic identity is ambiguous and peripheral to the role, text, and narrative action of particular movies. In at least five movies, *Dogma, Enough, Out of Sight, Timecode,* and *Gigli,* Hayek and Lopez perform characters whose ethnic and/or racial identity are "absent" from the text. This narrative absence has proven historically difficult if not impossible for actresses who explicitly identify as African American and are always already marked by the relatively fixed discourse of Blackness in the United States....

Conclusion

Whether we examine women's magazines, television programs, cinematic texts, girl's toys, clothing, pulp fiction, road signs, medical videos, or popular music and dance, it is difficult to avoid the unmistakable presence of Latinidad and its gendered components in mainstream U.S. culture. While these contemporary representations may provide the opportunity for individual Latinas to open spaces for vocality and action, they nevertheless build on a tradition of exoticization, racialization, and sexualization, a tradition that serves to position Latinas as continual foreigners and a cultural threat. As such Latinas occupy a liminal space in U.S. popular culture, that is, we can be both marginal and desired. Recently popular representations of Latina booties as large, aberrant yet sexy, desirable, and consumable contribute to the reification of racial dichotomies where Latinas occupy that in-between space between the White booty (or the pre-adolescent invisible androgynous White booty) and the Black booty whose excess falls beyond the boundary of acceptability and desirability within U.S. popular culture. . . .

Nevertheless, the representational tensions surrounding the three iconic Latinas highlighted in this article present a potentially emancipatory challenge or at least an unsettling intervention to Eurocentric discourses of racial and ethnic purity. Kahlo, Lopez, and Hayek are iconic presences that engage the stereotyped representation of Latinas to sell products and open a space from which Latina bodies can vex notions of racial and national purity and therefore authentic ethnicity. Although historically Latina actresses have been relegated to exist within the racialized binary narrative of virgin and whore, popular discourses surrounding Salma Hayek, Frida Kahlo, and Jennifer Lopez disrupt some of Hollywood's symbolic boundaries surrounding ethnicity, race, gender, and sexuality. The commodification of Latinidad has signaled a homogenization of Latinidad and simultaneously provided access to roles previously unavailable to Latinas. Despite the exoticized nature of the representations surrounding the bodies of Lopez and Hayek, they successfully have marketed themselves in order to sell mainstream movie tickets, music, clothing, and perfume.

Furthermore, as transnational figures these three icons exist within the representational conflict between the hybrid and the authentic that many diasporic cultures occupy. Kahlo, a German-Hungarian-Jewish-Mexican, recuperates female sexuality and indigenous Mexican culture as a way of challenging the imperialistic Western gaze. Mainstream circulation of her image reinscribes difference, especially in terms of the ubiquitous unibrow, but also inescapably represent her head, her face, and, through her intellectual efforts, her brain. As such, given binary tendencies in our culture, one would expect Kahlo to exist outside the realm of the sensual. However Hayek's further representation of Kahlo takes Kahlo into the sensual and sexual thus fully completing her signification as a contemporary iconic Latina. Lopez, a U.S. born Puerto Rican, a Nuyorican, privileges both her U.S. Americanness and her Puerto Ricanness as way of challenging dichotomous discourses and the erasure of Latina bodies in Hollywood films. Repeated affirmations of love and marriage also firmly place her within that Roman Catholic component so predominant in popular constructions of Latinidad. Finally, Hayek, a Lebanese-Mexican, foregrounds the bodies of Latinas themselves as a way of challenging mainstream narratives about women and Latinidad and uses Eurocentric discourses of authenticity to position her self in relation to other iconic Latinas.

Hayek, Kahlo, and Lopez are not simply passive subjects manipulated by the media and popular culture, but transnational women caught in the dialectic between agency and the objectification of identity that operates within many mediated products. Although the stereotypic representation of Latina sexuality continues, the popular representations of Hayek, Kahlo, and Lopez also problematize emerging constructions of Latinas within dominant discourses about gender, ethnicity, and race. As independent, racially and ethnically undetermined, and transnational women, their Latina iconicity ruptures and affirms the borders that surround contemporary popular significations of Latinas. Latinidad and iconic Latinas render Eurocentric discourses of racial and national purity untenable. All three women point to the uneasy harnessing of transnational, hybrid, and gendered bodies that meet the media's demand for the production and consumption of ethnic identity.

Note

The authors would like to thank Cameron McCarthy, Lori Reed, and Kumarini Silva for their comments and suggestions to drafts of this article.

1. We recognize that the category "Latina" is fluid and porous. As such, Penélope Cruz, who is Spanish, is often categorized by both the popular press and websites as "Latina." As well, although Cameron Diaz is currently (February 2004) Hollywood's highest paid actress, only *Latina* magazine claims her as Latina. Neither she nor most coverage of her ever mentions her Latinidad.

References

Aparicio, F. R., and S. Chavez-Silverman eds. 1997. *Tropicalizations: Transcultural Representations of Latinidad*. Hanover, CT: University Press of New England.
Barthes, R. 1973. *Mythologies*. London: Granada.
Desmond, J. C. 1997. *Meaning in Motion: New Cultural Studies of Dance*. Durham, NC: Duke University Press.
Giles, J., and T. Middleton. 2000. *Studying Culture: A Practical Introduction*. London: Blackwell.
Gilman, S. 1985. *Difference and Pathology: Stereotypes of Sexuality, Race, and Madness*. Ithaca, NY: Cornell University Press.
Perez-Firmat, G. 1994. *Life on the Hyphen: The Cuban American Way*. Austin: University of Texas Press.
Rakow, L., and K. Kranich. 1991. Woman as sign in television news. *Journal of Communication* 41, 8–23.
Valdivia, A. 2000. *A Latina in the Land of Hollywood*. Tucson: University of Arizona Press.

11

"So Full of Myself as a Chick"

Goth Women, Sexual Independence, and Gender Egalitarianism

AMY C. WILKINS

The 1960s saw the rise of second wave feminism *(as opposed to the* first wave, *which had focused on getting the right to vote). Within this second wave, liberal feminists emphasized the importance of obtaining equal treatment for women within existing social structures such as the job market and the legal system. Radical feminists, on the other hand, believed that gender inequality and patriarchal oppression lay at the root of all other forms of inequality, and believed that society needed to be radically restructured before it could truly meet women's needs. Among other things, the radical feminist movement was the first to stress the need to combat rape, incest, and other sexual dangers—issues that had received almost no public discussion previously.*

By the 1980s, however, "sex-positive" or "pro-sex" feminists had begun to challenge this position and to argue that the battle for gender equality should shift to celebrating women's sexual freedom and sexual pleasure and away from highlighting sexual dangers. This call was picked up beginning in the 1990s by younger feminists (sometimes referred to as third-wave feminists*) who wanted to emphasize how women's position had improved since the 1960s.*

A related philosophical shift, sometimes referred to as postfeminism, *has occurred among many young women who do not necessarily think of themselves as feminists. The term* postfeminism *is often used to refer to a somewhat vague belief in gender equality, coupled with a belief that women already have won equality and so should now focus on enjoying their freedoms—especially sexual freedom. The young Goth women described in this article by Amy C. Wilkins exemplify this philosophy, its strengths, and its weaknesses. As Wilkins shows,*

Amy C. Wilkins, "So Full of Myself as a Chick," *Gender & Society* 18: 328–349, © 2004 by Sociologists for Women in Society. Reprinted by permission of Sage Publications.

Goth culture allows these women to resist many of the social pressures placed on other women and to celebrate their resistance. At the same time, the particular structure of Goth sexual norms, coupled with Goth women's belief that the battles of feminism have been won within Goth culture, makes it difficult for these women to recognize the ways in which Goth culture reinforces gender and sexual inequality or to recognize the need for broader social change.

At the Haven, a Goth dance club, Goths adorned in black fetish wear, leather and PVC, and dog collars and leashes gather weekly. While some men "gender blend," wearing makeup and skirts, the women are dressed in sexy feminine outfits. The sidelines of the dance floor are populated by pairs and groups of people kissing, caressing, sucking on each other's necks. This environment, Siobhan tells me, is "liberating."

Drawing on interviews, participant observation, and Internet postings, this article analyzes gender in a local Goth scene. These Goths use the confines of the subcultural scene, where they are relatively safe from outsider views, and the scene's celebration of active sexuality as resources to resist mainstream notions of passive femininity. Sexually active femininity is not, of course, unique to the Goth scene: Contemporary young women in a variety of arenas use active sexuality to stake out gender independence. This emphasis on women's emancipated sexuality reflects the substantive turn of postfeminism—what Anna Quindlen has labeled "babe feminism" (1996, 4)—a focus on women's right to active sexuality rather than on broader issues of gender equality. In this article, I probe this Goth scene's (sub)cultural contradictions to critically examine the possibilities and the limitations of strategies of active feminine sexuality in gaining gender egalitarianism....

Young Women's Sexuality: "Walk[ing] a Narrow Line"

The erosion of the old gender bargain, in which women exchanged sex and emotion work for financial support, has propelled young women to experiment with new rules about gender and sexuality (Sidel 1990; Thompson 1995). But while the rules of the sex game are changing, women are still held to a sexual double standard predicated on deep-rooted cultural understandings about differences between men and women. This double standard continues to impede women's sexual agency, but without the economic payoff promised (for many women) by the old gender bargain. Within this disadvantageous framework, young women struggle to exercise sexual agency on their own terms.

Young women's attempts to stretch their sexual wings are greeted with alarm by adults. The media frequently portray young women's sexual behavior to be converging with young men's, as more and more girls and young women engage in sexual relations outside of the context of marriage, engagement, or love. Moreover, changes in expectations for young women (i.e., college, career, and the consequent later marriage) have created a longer period of nonmarital sexuality for women. This alarm is crystallized in outcries about the "epidemic" of teen pregnancy. As Luker (1996) pointed out, the "epidemic" is actually an increase in nonmarital births, indicating that many young women are opting out of the marital prerogative that has been traditionally imposed on pregnant, unmarried, white, middle-class women.

While some feminists applaud women's increasing sexual agency, others argue that changes in sexual expectations have only increased the pressure for young women to engage in sexual behaviors they might not otherwise choose (Jacobs Brumberg 1997; Pipher 1994). A discourse of victimization thus pervades discussions of adolescent girls' sexuality. This discourse, which positions young women as passive recipients of unwanted sexual attention or as pressured into early or more frequent sexual behavior acknowledges girls' relative disempowerment in heterosexual interactions but precludes any discussion of sexual desire on the part of young women. In an article aptly subtitled "The Missing Discourse of Desire," Michelle Fine (1988) noted that girls' voices of desire, submerged under this discourse of victimization, are glimpsed only fleetingly.

By positioning girls as victimized rather than desiring subjects, this argument reproduces the cultural construction of girls as naturally less interested in sex than in emotions and less interested in sex than are men. Girls who violate this construction of proper femininity are heavily stigmatized. As Lees (1993) argued, fear of being labeled a "slag" (slut, ho, or hootchie in the United States) constrains young women's behavior in a number of ways—by keeping them from going to a variety of public places, from walking alone, from dressing too provocatively, from talking to too many boys. The power of the label is that it can be applied at any time for reasons that seldom have anything to do with sexual behavior. To avoid the potentially ruinous label, young women must constantly manage their self-presentations, shelving their own freedom and desires. The label thus results in very real gender differences in behavior, strengthening young men's power over and distinction from young women. Moreover, the label divides young women, pitting good girls against sluts, categories that are often overlaid with race and class codings (see Tolman 1996).

Caught in the cultural trap of increasing expectations for sexual competency, the mandate to appear heterosexually attractive (see Wolf 1991), and the powerful persistence of the "slut" stigma, "girls walk a narrow line: they must not be seen as too tight, nor as too loose" (Lees 1993, 29). The sexual balancing act in which most girls and young women engage has a number of consequences. First, the desire to appear as "good girls" impedes the use of sexual protection, since carrying condoms suggests that the girl anticipated having sex (rather than being "swept away" by the moment) (Thompson 1995). Second, the pressure to fulfill men's sexual needs combined with the absence of a "discourse of [female] desire" reduces young women's ability to make sexual decisions that are rooted in their own desires, putting them in a passive position in sexual negotiations. The result, too frequently, is heterosexual experiences that do not meet the criteria for rape but are also not actively chosen by young women, reinforcing the normativity of female passivity in heterosexual relations (Phillips 2000)....

In her study of adolescent girls' sexuality, Sharon Thompson concluded, "the greatest danger girls narrated was love. Once in love or set on trying to get in love, even cautious girls said they closed their eyes to sexual and psychological danger" (1995, 285). It is the ideology of romance, rather than sexuality, that encourages girls and women to sacrifice for the sake of the relationship or in desperate attempts to hang onto a relationship. Indoctrinated in the intertwined ideologies that "love conquers all" and that "hetero-relationships are the key to women's happiness," girls and women read romantic relationships as signs of their self-worth and of their identities, and thus risk losing both when they lose a relationship. The idea, moreover, that women are responsible for the maintenance of relationships adds to the pressure women feel to make their romantic alliances endure (Phillips 2000). Thus, because romance continues to be ideologically privileged for women, the emancipatory potential of their sexual agency is limited. Furthermore, women's sexual liberation itself is often hard to unpin from romance, as Radway (1984, 16) argued in her study of romance novels, in which she found that the radical validation of women's sexual passion was based on "the natural and inevitable expression of a prior *emotional* attachment, itself dependent on a natural, biologically based sexual difference."

In this article, I explore young women's use of active sexuality as a strategy for gaining gender egalitarianism in one Goth subculture. This Goth scene is a space in which women are actively struggling to reject conventional standards of feminine sexual comportment. They do this both by embracing their sexual agency and by rejecting the restrictions of monogamy and heterosexuality. In many ways, these women are ideally situated to enact this struggle: Race/class and generational privilege enable these women's experiments. They are moderately secure economically, do not have to contend with "welfare queen" demonization, and have clearly benefited from second-wave feminism. Furthermore, the Goth scene allows them to draw boundaries around themselves that mitigate the consequences of their sexual experiments. The "freak" label provides insularity, and the club that is the scene hub is repeatedly described as safe from outside judgment. Moreover, their scene is centered in a Northeastern college town that prides itself on its progressive gender politics and tolerance of sexual diversity. But while these women conduct their sexual negotiations in an unusually advantageous context, some women outside the Goth scene employ similar strategies. The Goth women's efforts provide an exceptional vantage on the limits and the potentialities of young women's struggles both to gain sexual freedom and to use sexuality to enact gender equality....

The Local Goth Scene

Most accounts of Goth locate its roots in an early 1980s melding of the punk scene with glam rock. Goth is thus considered a music-based scene. But to be Goth implies much more than shared musical tastes; it is, as I was repeatedly informed, an "aesthetic," a particular way of seeing and of being seen.

My study is concerned with the local Goth scene rather than the Goth subculture writ large. The participants in my study consider the local scene to be atypical, mostly, I think, because of its location in a less urban area than, say, Boston or New York (the immediate geographic comparisons). The local scene seems to be less rigidly bounded than the scene in other localities and hosts a large number of "Tuesday Goths" (people who dress Goth only for the club on Tuesday nights). While internal debates about authenticity proliferate, tolerance for people who downplay their "freakiness" for work seems to be the norm.

The scene prides itself on its inclusivity. Many in the scene claim overlapping memberships in the queer, polyamorous, bondage-discipline/sadomasochism, and pagan communities. Yet it is demographically homogeneous: With a few exceptions, local Goths are youth or young adults, white, middle-class, college educated, liberal but not radical, unmarried, and childless. They are technologically adept; if they are not employed in tech support, they spend an enormous amount of time online. They are known for their brooding solitude, yet they call each other to task for perceived apathy toward the Goth community. Indeed, they are surprisingly social, coming together regularly at their local club night (called the Haven), at parties, for coffee, and on PVGoth, their online community.

The data for this article combine formal interviews, participant observation, and Web listserver data. I conducted in-depth, open-ended interviews with 17 self-identified Goths (10 women and 7 men). This scene is small enough that groups of friends are highly interconnected. Every person I interviewed knows, to a greater or lesser degree, everyone else in my sample. In addition, I engaged in numerous casual conversations with the interviewees as well as with other Goths. . . .

Goth Women's Sexual Agency: "So Full of Myself as a Chick"

The Goth women in this study present themselves as agentic, independent women in control of their personal lives and their social spaces. PVGoth is replete with such assertions: "I'm so full of myself as a chick in general that I don't want people talking to me whose sole purpose is to stick their dick in my cooter"; "I'm not interested in making someone's life more exciting when they haven't done anything on their own. I'm not a novelty item"; and "Treat me like a person first, and then I might start flirting with you."

Interviews with women root their interpersonal independence in the sexual norms of the local Goth scene. Siobhan describes the "open sexuality" of the Goth scene as "liberating," while for Rory, the scene is a space in which she can be "predatory and female." And for Lily, it engenders the "ability to insist on safer sex." Consistent across these accounts is a notion both of Goth women as strong and independent and of the Goth scene as supportive of women's sexual power. Honeyblossom, one of the most consciously political women in my sample, claims, "From what I've seen, most Goth women are feminists—tends to strongly inform their relationships." In her generalized attribution of feminism to Goth women, she, like those quoted on PVGoth and my other interviewees, locates feminism clearly within the realm of the interpersonal.

These claims are further developed in discussions of two aspects of the Goth scene: The rule to respect spatial boundaries and the freedom "for women to dress sexy." These discussions, elaborated below, elucidate the contradictions in these women's claims to independence and thus point to some of the possibilities and limits of sexual agency as a platform for women's emancipation.

Spatial Boundaries: "I Really, Really Liked It that Nobody Grabbed My Butt"

In a formulation that appears contradictory, Goths present rules as the basis for women's sexual freedom. Rules, in these explanations, serve to rein in predatory men and thus create conditions of greater sexual freedom for women. Perhaps the preeminent Goth social rule is the mandate to respect individual spatial boundaries. People who violate this rule are, by all accounts, shunned: "The rules are that strong that if you break them, you're ostracized" (Honeyblossom). While this phenomenon is in many ways gender neutral, the Goth women and men I interviewed frequently invoked it as a particular benefit to women. Goths presented the rule about spatial boundaries as a fundamental departure from outside norms about heterosexual interactions, one that provides women with the freedom to dress more provocatively and to exercise more control over their sexuality. Alyssa connects these ideas: "If a guy dances closely to you, people will come down on him with a vengeance. They don't say, 'Oh, you wore a corset, what did you expect?'"

The spatial rules at the Haven are a big attraction to women. Many of the women I spoke with told me that the absence of unsolicited physical contact pulled them back to the Haven even if they did not immediately feel at home. For example, Honeyblossom comments, "I really, really liked it that nobody tried to grab my butt." Similarly, a woman on PVGoth writes, "At a regular club, it's fairly common for a guy to come up and grind with random girls.... In fact that's one of the reasons I prefer goth clubs to regular clubs."

Goths repeatedly use "regular" clubs as a foil against which they articulate the cultural and moral superiority of the Haven's social norms. Importantly, they portray their club behavior as superior not because it protects women's sexual purity but because it allows women more control over heterosexual interactions. A woman on PVGoth posts, "I'm perfectly capable of letting people know I'm interested in them, and I don't need to be pursued persistently. If I like you, I'll let you know. I wonder if most women in our scene are like that?" Honeyblossom, who responded affirmatively to the previous woman's query, later told me that "[Goth] women are more comfortable initiating relationships.... I think there is a definite idea within Gothic culture that to be a powerful woman who is able to say yes and no to things is sexy."

Although some Goth men comment that the spatial rules add to their sense of personal comfort, they also construct them as a particular benefit to women. This suggestion, while not necessarily invalid, glosses over the specific benefits Goth men accrue from the combination of spatial boundaries and women's sexual agency. The norms of heterosexual interaction in the Haven do not desex the club but rather change the game rules, distributing the labor of the chase between men and women and reducing the risk of sexual rejection for men. Goth men can count on getting sex, but without the pressures (often lamented by mainstream men) of a unilateral chase.

Dressing Sexy: "An Empowering Statement of Female Choice"

The clubbing outfits worn by most Goth women in this scene are highly sexualized. The typical Goth woman's club ensemble fetishizes the whore, combining corsets with short skirts and fishnet stockings. Goth women use the heterosexual etiquette of the Goth scene to frame their clothing choices in ways that sidestep conventional interpretations of such dress. For example, Beth insists that the rules in the Goth scene allow her "to dress in a way that's sexy without people assuming that [she is] there to get laid." A Goth man echoes this sentiment on PVGoth: "I think people unfamiliar with this scene assume that just because some woman is wearing a short vinyl dress and fish nets that she wants to get some from you."

Goth women, then, use the Haven rule about spatial boundaries to look and feel sexy without the risks that come with overtly sexualized self-presentations in other arenas. Most obviously, the Goth community spatial norms reduce the incidences of unsolicited physical contact, making sexy self-presentations a physically safer option for women than in mainstream clubs or other contexts.[1] But in a questionable conceptual move, Goth women interpret the absence (or invisibility) of sexual assault as the absence of sexual objectification. This interpretation allows them to position themselves as the ones in control of their own sexuality. In Dallas's words, the Goth woman is not "objectified unless that's what [she] wants." At the same time, however, this construction plays off of the culturally hegemonic Madonna-whore dichotomy by allowing Goth women to see themselves as sexually appealing but not easy.

The Goth women's strategy negotiates the feminist dilemma of pleasure and oppression. The ability to participate in sexy self-presentations is pleasurable. For many Goth women, the Haven is an unusual arena in that it validates their particular expressions of sexiness. Many of these women may not be able to access sexual attractiveness in conventional contexts where sexy femininity is defined according to narrow beauty standards that emphasize thin, disciplined bodies. At the Haven, even women with larger bodies wear revealing ensembles involving, for example, the aforementioned corsets and short skirts. This freedom was pointed out to me repeatedly and was quickly confirmed by a cursory appraisal of the Haven crowd. Zoe says, "It's also true that anyone can go and feel sexy," presenting the Haven as a space in which women of all shapes and sizes are sexually validated. . . .

Goths value the Haven because it allows them to play with self-presentations, validates sexual experimentation, and provides an arena for sexual interactions. Goths, especially Goth women, present these possibilities as liberating and enjoyable. But underlying these freedoms and choices is the unspoken (and perhaps unseen) absence of choice. While Goth women may enjoy sexual dress and sexual play, their claim to Goth membership depends on their participation. In Zoe's words, "as long as you dress sexy [you'll fit in]." And in Rory's, "if there is such a thing as a Goth is supposed to be, a Goth is supposed to be sexually open."

Moreover, sporadic evidence that the Goth gaze is not always so friendly peeks through. For example, during my visits to the Haven, I was occasionally advised by women to avoid certain guys with "sketchy" reputations. Likewise, when Beth arranged an interview with a Goth man for me, she warned me not to "hook up with him." The man apparently was willing to participate in the interview only if I were "cute and available." The "loser dance" (described to me independently by Beth, Zoe, and Chad), in which women use a series of gestures to signal their discomfort with an overly aggressive male dance partner to their friends, who then intervene, also indicates an awareness among Goth women that Goth men may not always respect their sexual space.

In addition, the Goth gaze may not always be supportive of the appropriation of sexy self-presentations by all women. One woman self-disparagingly confesses on PVGoth,

> I've been known to be sitting on a cozy little chair at haven and think to myself (or even whisper to a nearby friend) about a passerby "omigod even if I were half her size I would NEVER try to squeeze my ass into something like that, how embarrassing!"

And Zoe admits, "Some women wear very little—large women. I feel two ways. I think it's good that they can feel sexy but think they'd look so much more attractive if they wore something else." Moreover, a number of women (and one man, Hunter) mentioned a few women who made a habit of traversing the Haven naked. While Hunter suggested that this behavior was not appropriate outside of a strip club, the women told me that many of the men complained because the naked women were not attractive. Thus, despite contentions that women are not objectified or limited by mainstream beauty standards, Goth women are objects of the critical gazes of both men and women.. . .

Sexuality and Romance: "It's Not about Sex, It's about Love"

This Goth community's construction of itself as proactively sexual is complicated by the continued reliance on, and even the reproduction of, an ideology of romance. These Goths present free sexuality as an avenue to achieving emotional sophistication. In their attempts to legitimize their sexual experimentation, they reinvest romance with moral and emotional importance without questioning women's special responsibility for emotional intimacy. By positioning romantic relations as a preeminent personal goal, this strategy undermines the benefits of women's sexual agency.

For many Goth women, gender discrepancies increase when they enter romantic relationships. The predominantly heterosexual relationships within the Goth community [typically reflect a commitment to polyamory and] often restrict women's sexual freedoms but not men's.. . .

"Polyamory," which means more than one love, embraces romantic intimacy but rejects sexual exclusivity. According to the polyamory Web site (alt.poly) that many Goths visit regularly, polyamorous relationships can take on a number of forms. For example, each member of a couple may engage in subsidiary sexual and/or emotional relationships with other people or with the same person. Or a polyamorous person may engage in several equally privileged sexual/emotional relationships. Or three or more people may be simultaneously involved.

While the permutations seem endless, they are held together by central relationship ideals of emotional and physical responsibility, honesty, communication, and trustworthiness, which in turn structure a moral differentiation between polyamory and sleeping around. These Goths, polyamorous or not, emphasize the moral dimensions of "real" polyamory, describing it as a lifestyle based in love. "In its purest form, it's not about sex, it's about love," Jeff explains. And Lily says, "I don't think it's impossible to be in love with more than one person at a time romantically." These descriptions routinely level contempt at people who, in Beth's words, "use [the label] as an excuse to sleep around." She adds, drawing a boundary around her own practice of polyamory, "I don't want to be associated with people who I think are irresponsible—whether it be emotionally irresponsible or not using protection." In these claims, Goths suggest that sexuality is a tool they use to rebuild genuine emotional commitment.

Polyamorous discourse thus reinvigorates the importance of emotional intimacy to relationships. For the Goth woman, these relationship values and their assumed moral superiority mitigate her presentation of herself as sexually free, allowing her to play both sides of the Madonna-whore card. At once, she is sexually experimental and emotionally responsible. She is thus able to expand her sexual options without jeopardizing her position as a good woman. Rory raises these issues in her self-described (un)"popular" critique of the use of the "poly" label:

> My experience is it [the poly label] is used to imply that everyone you sleep with you're having a relationship with. People use it who can't handle the label of promiscuity. No matter how open minded or free people say they are, there still needs to be an emotional justification behind the sex.

The values attributed to polyamory may be desirable to many Goth women for other reasons as well. By emphasizing trust and communication, proponents of polyamory privilege relationship styles commonly seen as more important to women. "There truly needs to be openness and respect between all people," Crow comments. Similarly, both Lily and Greg attribute the success of their (separate) polyamorous relationships to "honest[y]" and "communication." Especially in the context of polyamorous relationships, honesty and trust necessitate ongoing negotiations between partners as well as "self-knowledge" (alt.poly) and "emotional literacy" (Beth's phrase). Thus, even if individual relationships do not actually live up to these ideals, the predominance of this discourse may be useful to some women who are seeking to make men more emotionally accountable in relationships. In addition, as Goths themselves claim, the ideal of honesty about other sexual partners combined with strong pressure within the Goth community to practice safe sex may protect women physically from some of the risks associated with sexual behavior (e.g., HIV)....

But while they may benefit women in some ways, these values are not inherently gender egalitarian.... When Goths talk about the dynamics of specific intimate relationships, the contention that relationship negotiations are gender neutral breaks apart. For example, both Beth and Zoe describe a polyamorous couple (Siobhan and Bill) in which (in Zoe's words) "he's dated lots of women but she's only dated one guy. She says it's never worked out but I think he's always protested it." Siobhan, no longer in the relationship, bitterly recalls, "[Bill] was jealous and insecure and didn't want me to date any other men. Women were fine as long as he got a piece of ass too."

While Siobhan condemns Bill as an individual, her situation adheres to a common pattern in the Goth community in which straight men are involved with bisexual women. In these relationships, as Zoe complains, "there seems to be a double standard—girls in heterosexual relationships can date other women but not other men."...

Goth women's relationships with other women are frequently subsidiary to heterosexual relationships. While some Goth women do get involved in enduring relationships with other women, short-lived relationships are normative. Zoe comments,

> I know a lot of bisexual girls who just date other girls for a week at a time.... Even for my own self, I tend to be in these really long relationships with men and barely ever date women.

And Beth notes that "permanent relationships are more likely to be heterosexual—bi girls with boyfriends go looking for girls."

The predominance of this arrangement has both benefits and drawbacks for women. The prevalence of women's bisexuality creates an atmosphere in which women who might otherwise practice strict heterosexuality are able to experiment sexually with other women. Moreover, some women (both in and out of the Goth scene) are able to use bisexuality to traverse the boundaries of monogamy, as Zoe points out:

> I've been in relationships with men who didn't care if I saw other women but I felt like he didn't perceive women as a threat.... I can still fall in love with a woman...felt like he didn't take it seriously but I took advantage of it.

Women like Zoe are able to maintain the advantages of a central heterosexual relationship while also engaging in sexual play outside the relationship....

But, as Zoe's earlier quote makes clear, while individual women may be able to use bisexuality to push against the constraints of feminine sexuality, this strategy is fragile precisely because it uses the terms of gender hierarchy to garner some sexual space. The predominant construction of bisexuality "that doesn't perceive other women as a threat" is predicated on a sexual double standard that defines sex between women as less real. This construction is then turned into reality by the structures that support heterosexual relationships. Furthermore, the eroticization of women's bisexuality (at least between "properly" feminine women) heterosexualizes it by turning it into a performance or a fantasy for men and thereby devaluing the women's own sexual pleasure. Not unique to the Goth scene, this dual use of bisexuality demonstrates the ways in which seeming gender progress can be harnessed to serve traditional sex/gender hierarchies.

Moreover, in polyamorous relationships, women's bisexuality may be used to circumscribe women's sexuality, as in Lily and Sean's case. While Sean's participation in a central committed relationship does not require him to delimit his chosen field of sexual eligibles, Lily's participation requires her to cut hers in half. Her bisexuality is used as the justification for this imbalance. Her ability to sexually engage other women makes it seem like she is gaining something and thus obfuscates the inequity of the arrangement by suggesting that her sexual freedom is equivalent to Sean's.

But it is not sexuality that underpins Lily's relative disempowerment; it is her romantic commitment to Sean. Because of her belief in the enduring love of that relationship, Lily does the emotion work necessary to allow her to stay in it. The pervasiveness of conventional relationship ideals is further evidenced by their on-again/off-again discussions of marriage and by Lily's confession that she engages in fewer and fewer outside relationships at all. Further indicating that monogamous sexuality and love have not been so successfully unpinned after all, Rory, Zoe, and Siobhan, all previously polyamorous, told me that they were currently monogamous because they did not want to hurt their boyfriends. And the woman and man with whom Beth once had a triangular relationship (all three participants were romantically and sexually involved with each other) have recently sealed their monogamy with marriage. In all of these examples, the promise of love triumphs over the freedom and choice of Goth sexual experimentation. . . .

Conclusion

The local Goth subculture at the heart of this study, and its members' sexual negotiations, provide a case study of the relationships between sexual attitudes, sexual behavior, and gender egalitarianism. The victories and limitations of the Goth women's struggle provide insight into the role of sexuality in the quest to create gender egalitarian spaces. The active negotiation of sexual roles by the Goths in this study show that it is possible for women to create a space in which they are able to access sexuality on more gender-egalitarian terms even while they encounter stumbling blocks to full sexual autonomy. Goth women's attempts to balance gender equality on a platform of sexual agency are not successful, however. Intervention in the arena of sexuality does not propel a reconfiguration of other gendered negotiations.

Perceived as freaks by outsiders, Goths create an insulated space for their community in which they can experiment with behaviors that are stigmatized in the mainstream culture. The sexual haven created by the Goths in my study allows Goth women to engage in proactive sexual behavior without the "slut" label. Goth women experience their sexuality as personally empowering: It provides them with a sense of control over their bodies, with the right to feel and act on desire and with external validation of their expressions of sexiness. For women struggling to walk the narrow sexual line mandated by the mainstream culture, these gains should not be understated. They are mitigated, however, by the persistence of sociocultural ideas that position men as sexual consumers/owners. As feminists have argued about the sexual revolution, simply increasing women's right to enjoy sex does not undo the basic heterosexual relationship that confers men with sociocultural power. Indeed, in the absence of other changes, women's sexual freedom benefits men more than it does women by providing men with greater sexual access to women without altering heterosexual power arrangements.

Goth women hope that by transforming the terms of sexuality, they can also transform sexism. But even though they do enact significant transformations in the internal sexual culture of their scene, they do not significantly alter gendered power. First, centering gender change on sexuality only partially challenges interpersonal inequalities between men and women. The relative escape from sexual double standards does not necessitate an accompanying escape from heterosexual, monogamous romance. Even when sexuality and romance are sometimes uncoupled, the meanings attached to relationships within this Goth scene privilege successful romantic ties as symbols of moral and emotional development, maintaining women's sociocultural reliance (for personal meaning, for self-esteem, and even for justification of their sexual behaviors) on the sexual relationships they establish. This reliance, in turn, reproduces their disempowerment within those relationships by undercutting their ability to demand men's accountability for sexism in intimate relationships. As Stombler and Padavic (1997) found in their study of women in fraternity little sister organizations, a central focus on "getting a man" impedes women's ability to enact forms of resistance. Thus, when sexuality is the central emancipatory tool, its continued entanglement with heterosexual romance may even be counterproductive—centering, rather than decentering, sexuality and romance in women's lives.

Second, the focus on sexuality leaves systemic inequality unchallenged. Focusing on sexuality as the arena of change deflects conversations from other areas where gendered power is being enacted. But even more than simply leaving other aspects of sexism undiscussed, the focus on sexuality may also undermine the possibility of enacting systemic change. The psychological investment in the equation of sexual emancipation with feminism too easily allows for the idea that substantial change is already occurring. Interpreting transformed sexuality as inherently feminist allows participants to feel morally and politically superior to people who have not transformed their sexuality and allows participants to justify their own lifestyles on political and moral grounds. The psychological benefit of identifying individually and collectively as gender progressive is often as seductive as the sexual gains themselves and can thus be used to stifle internal or external challenges to sexism. In effect, participants can use their involvement in transformed sexual relations as evidence of their de facto feminism, shielding themselves and their community from further challenges to the configuration of gendered power.

Note

AUTHOR'S NOTE: I would like to thank Robert Zussman, Naomi Gerstel, Janice Irvine, Jill McCorkel, and the anonymous reviewers at *Gender & Society* for their insightful comments and thoughtful reading of multiple drafts of this article. I would also like to thank Shawn McGuffey, Alice Julier, and Meg Yardley for enduring endless conversations about these issues, for plying me with coffee, and especially for dropping their own work to nourish this project.

1. This discussion is not meant to imply that women's dress is responsible for sexual assault in other arenas.

References

Fine, Michelle. 1988. Sexuality, schooling and adolescent females: The missing discourse of desire. *Harvard Educational Review* 58:29–53.

Jacobs Brumberg, Joan. 1997. *The Body Project: An Intimate History of American Girls.* New York: Random House.

Lees, Sue. 1993. *Sugar and Spice: Sexuality and Adolescent Girls.* London: Penguin.

Luker, Kristin. 1996. *Dubious Conceptions: The Politics of Teenage Pregnancy.* Cambridge, MA: Harvard University Press.

Phillips, Lynn M. 2000. *Flirting with Danger: Young Women's Reflections on Sexuality and Domination.* New York: New York University Press.

Pipher, Mary B. 1994. *Reviving Ophelia: Saving the Selves of Adolescent Girls.* New York: Putnam.

Quindlen, Anna. 1996. And now, babe feminism. In *Bad Girls/Good Girls: Women, Sex, and Power in the Nineties*, edited by Nan Bauer Maglin and Donna Perry. New Brunswick, NJ: Rutgers University Press.

Radway, Janice A. 1984. *Reading the Romance: Women, Patriarchy, and Popular Literature.* Chapel Hill: University of North Carolina Press.

Sidel, Ruth. 1990. *On Her Own: Growing Up in the Shadow of the American Dream.* New York: Penguin.

Stombler, Mindy, and Irene Padavic. 1997. Sister acts: Resisting men's domination in black and white fraternity little sister programs. *Social Problems* 44(2): 257–75.

Thompson, Sharon. 1995. *Going All the Way: Teenage Girls' Tales of Sex, Romance, and Pregnancy.* New York: Hill and Wang.

Tolman, Deborah. 1996. Adolescent girls' sexuality: Debunking the myth of the urban girl. In *Urban Girls: Resisting Stereotypes, Creating Identities*, edited by Bonnie J. Ross Leadbeater and Niobe Way. New York: New York University Press.

Wolf, Naomi. 1991. *The Beauty Myth: How Images of Beauty Are Used against Women.* New York: W. Morrow.

III

THE POLITICS OF APPEARANCE

In a society still largely controlled by men, women's appearance dramatically affects women's lives. Attractiveness serves as an indirect form of power by increasing women's odds of obtaining resources from powerful men, whether jobs, promotions, marriage proposals, social approval, or simple courtesies. The articles in this section explore the social norms (i.e., unwritten rules regarding how members of a society should behave) for female appearance, the impact of these norms on women's lives, and the ways women respond to these norms.

The first three articles in this section describe how women grapple with social expectations regarding their hair and breasts. In "Breasted Experience: The Look and the Feeling," Iris Young explores the ways in which women's embodied experiences of their breasts both are, and are not, defined by men's ideas about breasts. In "Designing Women: Cultural Hegemony and the Exercise of Power Among Women who Have Undergone Elective Mammoplasty," Patricia Gagné and Deanna McGaughey continue the discussion of women's embodied experience of their breasts, focusing on women who have breast implants as a means of increasing their power. Similarly, in "Women and Their Hair: Seeking Power Through Resistance and Accommodation," Rose Weitz uses women's narratives about their hair to analyze the advantages and limitations of using one's hair as a source of power and to dissect the meaning and effectiveness of embodied resistance.

The next three articles in this section describe the struggles of women whose bodies make it difficult for them to meet appearance norms. Vivyan Adair writes about the experiences of poor women in her article "Branded with Infamy: Inscriptions of Poverty and Class in the United States." Cecilia Hartley focuses on fat women in "Letting Ourselves Go: Making Room for the Fat Body in Feminist Scholarship," and Andrea Avery describes her own experiences in "Rip Tide: Swimming Through Life with Rheumatoid Arthritis."

In contrast, the final article, by Victoria Pitts, explores the decisions of those women who *choose* to place themselves outside of mainstream appearance norms through tattoos and other forms of body modification.

12

Breasted Experience

The Look and the Feeling

IRIS MARION YOUNG

From Maxim to films to religious iconography, we receive a constant stream of messages regarding men's view of the female breast. Only rarely, however, do we get a glimpse of women's relationships with their breasts. This is the topic Iris Young explores in this article.

A key distinction addressed by Young is the distinction between body as object and body as subject. Men may view women's bodies as objects, evaluating them as they might any other tool or toy, with little or no attention to the person who inhabits that body. Women, too, may internalize or merely accommodate to this perspective and view their bodies as tools to be used or judged by men or by women themselves. At the same time, as Young points out, women's lives and women's bodies are inseparable, and so women must also experience the body as subject (that is, as part of their essential self, not simply as an almost-external resource to be used). Thus in this article she also focuses on how women experience physical sensations of pleasure and pain through their breasts.

A second key distinction Young explores is that between the "Madonna" and the "whore." An underlying thread in Western culture is the assumption that women are either sexually and morally pure or impure—Madonnas or whores. This dichotomy is threatened whenever (as is sometimes the case) women experience breast-feeding as a sensual and even sexual experience, rather than experiencing motherhood and breast-feeding as selfless sacrifice. This, Young argues, is why nipples are considered so much more scandalous than are the rest of women's breasts.

Originally published as Iris Young (1992), "Bresasted Experience," pp. 215–230 in Drew Leder (ed.) *The Body in Medical Thought and Practice*, Boston: Kluwer. Reprinted with kind permission from Springer Science and Business Media.

Young's article is based in part on a neo-Freudian perspective. According to Sigmund Freud (1856–1939), a Viennese doctor, to become a mentally healthy adult one had to respond successfully to a series of biological events and experiences, each invested with sexual meaning. One of these was breast-feeding, which Freud believed gave sexual pleasure to both girls and boys. Freud believed that to become psychologically healthy, girls needed to shift their sexual desires from their mothers' breasts to males, while boys needed to shift from their mothers' breasts to the bodies and breasts of other females. Although Freud's theories were highly conservative and unsupported by empirical evidence, many feminists have found useful ideas within them. Young uses this theory to help explain our cultural discomfort with viewing mothers in sexual terms. She also uses it to argue in favor of highlighting women's and mothers' sexuality, and against the tendency (seen in some feminists) to celebrate women as selfless nurturers.

... For many women, if not all, breasts are an important component of body self-image; a woman may love them or dislike them, but she is rarely neutral.

In this patriarchal culture, focused to the extreme on breasts, a woman, especially in those adolescent years but also through the rest of her life, often feels herself judged and evaluated according to the size and contours of her breasts, and indeed she often is. For her and for others, her breasts are the daily visible and tangible signifier of her womanliness, and her experience is as variable as the size and the shape of breasts themselves. A woman's chest, much more than a man's, is *in question* in this society, up for judgment, and whatever the verdict, she has not escaped the condition of being problematic.

In this essay I explore some aspects of the cultural construction of breasts in our male-dominated society and seek a positive women's voice for breasted experience....

I. Breasts as Objects

I used to stand before the mirror with two Spalding balls under my shirt, longing to be a grown woman with the big tits of Marilyn Monroe and Elizabeth Taylor. They are called boobs, knockers, knobs; they are toys to be grabbed, squeezed, handled. In the total scheme of the objectification of women, breasts are the primary things.

A fetish is an object that stands in for the phallus—the phallus as the one and only measure and symbol of desire, the representation of sexuality. This culture fetishizes breasts. Breasts are the symbol of feminine sexuality, so the "best" breasts are like the phallus: high, hard, and pointy. Thirty years ago it was de rigueur to encase them in wire, rubber, and elastic armor that lifted them and pointed them straight out. Today fashion has loosened up a bit, but the foundational contours remain; some figures are better than others, and the ideal breasts look like a Barbie's.

We experience our objectification as a function of the look of the other, the male gaze that judges and dominates from afar (Bartky 1979; Kaplan

1983, 23–35). We experience our position as established and fixed by a subject who stands afar, who has looked and made his judgment before he ever makes me aware of his admiration or disgust. When a girl blossoms into adolescence and sallies forth, chest out boldly to the world, she experiences herself as being looked at in a different way than before. People, especially boys, notice her breasts or her lack of them; they may stare at her chest and remark on her. If her energy radiates from her chest, she too often finds the rays deflected by the gaze that positions her from outside, evaluating her according to standards that she had no part in establishing and that remain outside her control. She may enjoy the attention and learn to draw the gaze to her bosom with a sense of sexual power. She may loathe and fear the gaze that fixes her in shock or mockery, and she may take pains to hide her chest behind baggy clothes and bowed shoulders. She may for the most part ignore the objectifying gaze, retaining nevertheless edges of ambiguity and uncertainty about her body. The way women respond to the evaluating gaze on their chests is surely as variable as the size and character of the breasts themselves, but few women in our society escape having to take some attitude toward the potentially objectifying regard of the other on her breasts....

Breasts are the most visible sign of a woman's femininity, the signal of her sexuality. In phallocentric culture sexuality is oriented to the man and modeled on male desire. Capitalist, patriarchal American media-dominated culture objectifies breasts before a distancing gaze that freezes and masters. The fetishized breasts are valued as objects, things; they must be solid, easy to handle. Subject to the logic of phallocentric domination of nature, their value, her value as a sexual being, appears in their measurement. Is she a B-cup or a C-cup? Even when sleek athletic fashions were current, breasts were often still prominent. And today the news is that the big bosom is back (Anderson 1988; *Wall Street Journal* 1988).

What matters is the look of them, how they measure up before the normalizing gaze. There is one perfect shape and proportion for breasts: round, sitting high on the chest, large but not bulbous, with the look of firmness. The norm is contradictory, of course. If breasts are large, their weight will tend to pull them down; if they are large and round, they will tend to be floppy rather than firm. In its image of the solid object this norm suppresses the fleshy materiality of breasts, this least muscular, softest body part.[1] Magazines construct and parade these perfect breasts. They present tricks for how to acquire and maintain our own—through rigorous exercise or $50 creams (neither of which generally produces the desired effect), or tricks of what to wear and how to stand so as to appear to have them.

Like most norms of femininity, the normalized breast hardly describes an "average" around which real women's breasts cluster. It is an ideal that only a very few women's bodies even approximate; given the power of the dominant media, however, the norm is ubiquitous, and most of us internalize it to some degree, making our self-abnegation almost inevitable (Bartky 1988). Even those women whose breasts do approximate the ideal can do so only for a short period in their lives. It is a pubescent norm from which most women deviate increasingly with each passing year. Whatever her age, if she has given birth her breasts sag away from the ideal; perhaps they have lost some of their prepartum fullness and roundness, and her nipples protrude. Whether a woman is a mother or not, gravity does its work, quickly defining a woman's body as old because it is no longer adolescent. The truly old woman's body thereby moves beyond the pale. Flat, wrinkled, greatly sagging, the old woman's breasts signify for the ageist dominant culture a woman no longer useful for sex or reproduction, a woman used up. Yet there is nothing natural about such a decline in value. Some other cultures venerate the woman with wrinkled, sagging breasts; they are signs of much mothering and the wisdom of experience. From their point of view an obsession with firm, high breasts would be considered to express a desire to be immature (Ayalah and Weinstock 1979, 136).

II. Woman-centered Meaning

However alienated male-dominated culture makes us from our bodies, however much it gives us instruments of self-hatred and oppression, still our bodies are ourselves. We move and act in this flesh and these sinews, and live our pleasures and pains in our bodies. If we love ourselves at all, we love our bodies. And many women identify their breasts as themselves, living their embodied experience at some distance from the hard norms of the magazine gaze. However much the patriarchy may wish us to, we do not live our breasts only as the objects of male desire, but as our own, the sproutings of a specifically female desire.

But phallocentric culture tends not to think of a woman's breasts as hers. Woman is a natural territory; her breasts belong to others—her husband, her lover, her baby. It's hard to imagine a woman's breasts as her own, from her own point of view, to imagine their *value* apart from measurement and exchange. I do not pretend to discover a woman-centered breast experience. My conceptualization of a woman-centered experience of breasts is a construction, an imagining. . . .

From the position of the female subject, what matters most about her breasts is their feeling and sensitivity rather than how they look. The size or age of her breasts does not matter for the sensitivity of her nipples, which often seem to have a will of their own, popping out at the smallest touch, change of temperature, or embarrassment. For many women breasts are a multiple and fluid zone of deep pleasure quite independent of intercourse, though sometimes not independent of orgasm. For a phallic sexuality this is a scandal. A woman does not always experience the feeling of her breasts positively; if they are large she often feels them pulling uncomfortably on her neck and back. Her breasts are also a feeling of bodily change. She often experiences literal growing pains as her body moves from girl to woman. When she becomes pregnant, she often knows this first through changes in the feeling of her breasts, and many women have breast sensitivity associated with menstruation. When she is lactating, she feels the pull of milk letting down, which may be activated by a touch, or a cry, or even a thought.

Breasts stand as a primary badge of sexual specificity, the irreducibility of sexual difference to a common measure. Yet phallocentric sexuality tries to orient the sexual around its one and only sexual object. Active sexuality is the erect penis, which rises in its potency and penetrates the passive female receptacle. Intercourse is the true sex act, and nonphallic pleasures are either deviant or preparatory. Touching and kissing the breasts is "foreplay," a pleasant prelude after which the couple goes on to "the real thing." But in her own experience of sexuality there is a scandal: she can derive the deepest pleasure from these dark points on her chest, a pleasure maybe greater than he can provide in intercourse. Phallocentric heterosexist norms try to construct female sexuality as simply a complement to male sexuality, its mirror, or the hole—lack that he fills. But her pleasure is different, a pleasure he can only imagine. To the degree that he can experience anything like it, it's only a faint copy of female potency. Imagine constructing the model of sexual power in breasts rather than penises. Men's nipples would have to be constructed as puny copies, just as men have constructed women's clitorides as puny copies of the penis. Of course this all presumes constructing sexuality by a common measure. Phallocentric construction of sexuality denies and represses the sensitivity of breasts.

> For what male "organ" will be set forth in derision like the clitoris?—that penis too tiny for comparison to entail anything but total devaluation, complete decathexization. Of course, there are the breasts. But they are to be classed among the secondary, or so-called secondary, characteristics. Which no doubt justifies the fact that there is so little questioning of the effects of breast atrophy in the male. Wrongly, of course. (Irigaray 1985, 22–23)

Both gay men and lesbians often defy this niggardly attitude toward nipple sexuality. Gay men often explore the erotic possibilities of one another's breasts, and lesbians often derive a particular pleasure from the mutual touching of breasts.

The breasts, for many women, are places of independent pleasure. Deconstructing the hierarchical privilege of heterosexual complementarity, giving equal value to feelings of the breast diffuses the identity of sex. Our sex is not one but, as Irigaray says, plural and heterogeneous; we have sex organs all over our bodies, in many places, and perhaps none is privileged. We experience eroticism as flowing, multiple, unlocatable, not identical or in the same place (Irigaray 1985, 23–33).

The brassiere functions partly as a barrier to touch. Without it, every movement can produce a stroking of cloth across her nipples, which she may find pleasurable or distracting, as the case may be. But if the chest is a center of a person's being-in-the-world, her mode of being surely differs depending on whether her chest is open to touch, moving in the world, or confined and bordered.

Without a bra, a woman's breasts are also deobjectified, desubstantialized. Without a bra, most women's breasts do not have the high, hard, pointy look that phallic culture posits as the norm. They droop and sag and gather their bulk at the bottom. Without a bra, the fluid being of breasts is more apparent. They are not objects with one definite shape, but radically change their shape with body position and movements. Hand over the head, lying on one's back or side, bending over in front—all produce very different breast shapes. Many women's breasts are much more like a fluid than a solid; in movement, they sway, jiggle, bounce, ripple even when the movement is small.

Women never gathered in a ritual bra burning, but the image stuck. We did, though, shed the bra—hundreds of thousands, millions of us. I was no feminist when, young and impetuous, I shoved the bras back in the drawer and dared to step outside with nothing on my chest but a shirt. It was an ambiguous time in 1969. I had a wondrous sense of freedom and a little bit of defiance. I never threw the bras away; they were there to be worn on occasions when propriety and delicacy required them. Why is burning the bra the ultimate image of the radical subversion of the male-dominated order?[2] Because unbound breasts show their fluid and changing shape; they do not remain the firm and stable objects that phallocentric fetishism desires. Because unbound breasts make a mockery of the ideal of a "perfect" breast. The bra normalizes the breasts, lifting and curving the breasts to approximate the one and only breast ideal.

But most scandalous of all, without a bra, the nipples show. Nipples are indecent. Cleavage is good—the more, the better—and we can wear bikinis that barely cover the breasts, but the nipples must be carefully obscured. Even go-go dancers wear pasties. Nipples are no-nos, for they show the breasts to be active and independent zones of sensitivity and eroticism.

What would a positive experience of ourselves as breasted be in the absence of the male gaze? There are times and places where women in American society can experience hints of such an experience. In lesbian-dominated women's spaces where women can be confident that the male gaze will not invade, I have found a unique experience of women's bodies. In such women's spaces women frequently walk around, do their chores, sit around and chat naked from the waist up. Such a context deobjectifies the breasts. A woman not used to such a womanspace might at first stare, treating the breasts as objects. But the everydayness, the constant engagement of this bare-breasted body in activity dereifies them. But they do not thereby recede, as they might when clothed. On the contrary, women's breasts are *interesting*. In a womanspace with many women walking around bare-breasted, the variability and individuality of breasts becomes salient. I would like to say that in a womanspace, without the male gaze, a woman's breasts become almost like part of her face. Like her nose or her mouth, a woman's breasts are distinctive, one sign by which one might recognize her. Like her mouth or her eyes, their aspect changes with her movement and her mood; the movement of her breasts is part of the expressiveness of her body.

III. Motherhood and Sexuality

The woman is young and timeless, clothed in blue, a scarf over her head, which is bowed over the child at her breast, discreetly exposed by her hand that draws aside her covering, and the baby's hand rests on the round flesh. This is the Christian image of peace and wholeness, the perfect circle of generation (Miles 1985). With hundreds of variations, from Florentine frescoes to the cover of dozens of books at B. Dalton's, this is a primary image of power, female power. To be purity and goodness itself, the origin of life, the source to which the living man owes his substance—this is an awesome power. For centuries identification with that power has bonded women to the patriarchal order, and while today its seductive hold on us is loosening, it still provides women a unique position with which to identify (Kristeva 1985; Suleiman 1985).

But it is bought at the cost of sexuality. The Madonna must be a virgin mother. The logic of identity that constructs beings as objects also constructs categories whose borders are clear and exclusive: essence/accident, mind/body, good/bad. The logic of such oppositions includes everything, and they exclude one another by defining the other as excluded by their oneness or essence. In Western logic woman is the seat of such oppositional categorization, for patriarchal logic defines an exclusive border between motherhood and sexuality. The virgin or the whore, the pure or the impure, the nurturer or the seducer is either asexual mother or sexualized beauty, but one precludes the other.

Thus psychoanalysis, for example, regards motherhood as a substitute for sexuality. The woman desires a child as her stand-in for the penis, as her way of appropriating the forbidden father. Happily, her desires are passive, and she devotes herself completely to giving. Helene Deutsch (1985), for example, identifies normal motherhood with feminine masochism; the true woman is one who gets pleasure from self-sacrifice, the abnegation of pleasure.

Barbara Sichtermann (1986, 57) discusses this separation of motherhood and sexuality:

> Basically, women were only admitted to the realm of sexuality as guests to be dispatched off towards their "true" vocation as agents of reproduction. And reproduction was something which happened outside the realm of pleasure, it was God's curse on Eve. Women have to cover the longest part of the road to reproduction with their bodies and yet in this way they became beings existing outside sexuality, outside the delights of orgiastic release, they became asexual mothers, the bearers of unborn children and the bearers of suffering. Breastfeeding too was of course part of this tamed, pleasureless, domesticated world of "maternal duties."

Patriarchy depends on this border between motherhood and sexuality. In our lives and desires it keeps women divided from ourselves, in having to identify with one or another image of womanly power—the nurturing, competent, selfless mother, always sacrificing, the soul of goodness; or the fiery, voluptuous vamp with the power of attraction, leading victims down the road of pleasure, sin, and danger. Why does patriarchy need this division between motherhood and sexuality? This is perhaps one of the most overdetermined dichotomies in our culture; accordingly, I have several answers to this question.

In the terms in which Kristeva (1980) puts it, for both sexes entrance into the symbolic requires repressing the original jouissance of attachment to the mother's body. A baby's body is saturated with feeling, which it experiences as undifferentiated from the caretaking body it touches; repeated pains break the connection, but its pleasure is global and multiple. Eroticism must be made compatible with civilization, submission to the law, and thus adult experience of sexuality must repress memory of this infantile jouissance. Adult meanings of eroticism thus must be divorced from mothers. Even though for both genders, sexual desire and pleasure are informed by presymbolic jouissance, this must be repressed in the particular cultural configuration that emphasizes rationality as unity, identity, thematic reference.

The dichotomy of motherhood and sexuality, I said, maps onto a dichotomy of good/bad, pure/impure. These dichotomies play in with the repression of the body itself. One kind of attachment, love, is "good" because it is entirely defleshed, spiritual. Mother love and the love of the child for the mother represent the perfection of love—eroticism entirely sublimated. Fleshy eroticism, on the other hand, goes on the other side of the border, where lies the despised body, bad, impure. The separation of motherhood and sexuality thus instantiates the culture's denial of the body and the consignment of fleshy desires to fearful temptation.

The incest taboo also accounts for the separation, as even classical Freudianism suggests. Such patriarchal propriety in women's bodies may be unconsciously motivated by a desire to gain control over himself by mastering the mother. But sexual desire for the mother must be repressed in order to prepare the man for separation from femininity and entrance into the male bond through which women are exchanged. As Dinnerstein (1977) suggests, repression of desire for the mother is also necessary to defend his masculinity against the vulnerability and mortality of the human condition.

Now to some explanations more directly related to the interests of patriarchy. By separating motherhood and sexuality men/husbands do not have to perceive themselves as sharing female sexuality with their children. The oedipal triangle has three nodes, and there are issues for the father as well as the child. The Law of the Father establishes ownership of female sexuality. The satisfactions of masculinity are in having her to minister to his ego, the complement to his desire; he has private ownership of her affections

(Pateman 1988). Her function either as the phallic object or the mirror to his desire cannot be maintained if her mother love is the same as her sex love. They need to be projected onto different people or thought of as different kinds of relationships.

The separation between motherhood and sexuality within a woman's own existence seems to ensure her dependence on the man for pleasure. If motherhood is sexual, the mother and child can be a circuit of pleasure for the mother, then the man may lose her allegiance and attachment. So she must repress her eroticism with her child, and with it her own particular return to her repressed experience of jouissance, and maintain a specific connection with the man. If she experiences motherhood as sexual, she may find him dispensable. This shows another reason for repressing a connection between motherhood and sexuality in women. A woman's infantile eroticism in relation to her mother must be broken in order to awaken her heterosexual desire. Lesbian mothering may be the ultimate affront to patriarchy, for it involves a double displacement of an erotic relation of a woman to a man.

Without the separation of motherhood and sexuality, finally, there can be no image of a love that is all give and no take. I take this as perhaps the most important point. The ideal mother defines herself as giver and feeder, takes her existence and sense of purpose entirely from giving. Such a mother-giver establishes a foundation for the self-absorbed ego, the subject of modern philosophy, which many feminists have uncovered as being happily male (Schemen 1983; Flax 1983). Thus motherhood must be separated from her sexuality, her desire. She cannot have sexual desire in her mothering because this is a need, a want, and she cannot be perfectly giving if she is wanting or selfish.

In all these ways, then, patriarchy is founded on the border between motherhood and sexuality. Woman is both, essentially—the repository of the body, the flesh that he desires, owns and masters, tames and controls; and the nurturing source of his life and ego. Both are necessary functions, bolstering male ego, which cannot be served if they are together, hence the border, their reification into the hierarchical opposition of good/bad, pure/impure. The separation often splits mothers; it is in our bodies that the sacrifice that creates and sustains patriarchy is reenacted repeatedly (Ferguson 1983). Freedom for women involves dissolving this separation.

The border between motherhood and sexuality is lived out in the way women experience their breasts and in the cultural marking of breasts. To be understood as sexual, the feeding function of the breasts must be suppressed, and when the breasts are nursing they are desexualized. A great many women in this culture that fetishizes breasts are reluctant to breastfeed because they perceive that they will lose their sexuality. They believe that nursing will alter their breasts and make them ugly and undesirable. They fear that their men will find their milky breasts unattractive or will be jealous of the babies who take their bodies. Some women who decide to breast-feed report that they themselves are uninterested in sex during that period or that they cease to think of their breasts as sexual and to take sexual pleasure in their breasts while they are nursing.[3]

Breasts are a scandal because they shatter the border between motherhood and sexuality. Nipples are taboo because they are quite literally, physically and functionally *undecidable* in the split between motherhood and sexuality. One of the most subversive things feminism can do is affirm this undecidability of motherhood and sexuality.

When I began nursing I sat stiff in a chair, holding the baby in the crook of my arm, discreetly lifting my shirt and draping it over my breast. This was mother work, and I was efficient and gentle, and watched the time. After some weeks, drowsy during the morning feeding, I went to bed with my baby. I felt that I had crossed a forbidden river as I moved toward the bed, stretched her legs out alongside my reclining torso, me lying on my side like a cat or a mare while my baby suckled. This was pleasure, not work. I lay there as she made love to me, snuggling her legs up to my stomach, her hand stroking my breast, my chest. She lay between me and my lover, and she and I were a couple. From then on I looked forward with happy pleasure to our early-morning intercourse, she sucking at my hard fullness, relieving and warming me, while her father slept.

I do not mean to romanticize motherhood, to suggest by means of a perverted feminist reversal that through motherhood, women achieve their access to the divine or the moral. Nor would I deny that there are dangers in the eroticization of mothering—dangers to children, in particular, that derive from the facts of power more than sexuality. Mothers must not abuse their power, but this has always been so. Certainly I do not wish to suggest that all women should be mothers; there is much that would be trying about mothering even under ideal circumstances, and certainly there is much about it in our society that is oppressive. But in the experience of many women we may find some means for challenging patriarchal divisions that seek to repress and silence those experiences.

Some feminist discourse criticizes the sexual objectification of women and proposes that feminists dissociate women from the fetishized female body and promote instead an image of women as representing caring, nurturing, soothing values. American cultural feminism exhibits this move: women will retreat from, reject patriarchal definitions of sexuality and project motherly images of strength, wisdom, and nurturance as feminist virtues, or even redefine the erotic as like mother love.[4] Much French feminism is also in danger of a mere revaluation that retains this dichotomy between motherhood and sexuality, rather than exploding patriarchal definitions of motherhood (Stanton 1989).

A more radical move would be to shatter the border between motherhood and sexuality. What can this mean? Most concretely, it means pointing to and celebrating breast-feeding as a sexual interaction for both the mother and the infant (Sichtermann 1986). It means letting women speak in public about the pleasure that many report they derive from their babies and about the fact that weaning is often a loss for them (Myers and Siegel 1985). But there is a more general meaning to shattering the border, which applies even to mothers. Crashing the border means affirming that women, all women can "have it all." It means creating and affirming a kind of love in which a woman does not have to choose between pursuing her own selfish, insatiable desire and giving pleasure and sustenance to another close to her, a nurturance that gives and also takes for itself. Whether they are mothers or not, women today are still too often cast in the nurturant role, whatever their occupation or location. This nurturant position is that of the self-sacrificing listener and stroker, the one who turns toward the wounded, needful ego that uses her as mirror and enclosing womb, giving nothing to her, and she of course is polite enough not to ask. As feminists we should affirm the value of nurturing; an ethic of caring does indeed hold promise for a more human justice, and political values guided by such an ethic would change the character of the public for the better. But we must also insist that nurturers need, that love is partly selfish, and that a woman deserves her own irreducible pleasures.

Notes

I am grateful to Sandra Bartky, Lucy Candib, Drew Leder, and Francine Rainone for helpful comments on an earlier version of this paper. Thanks to Nancy Irons for research help.

Considering the vast explosion of women's-studies literature in the past two decades, there is an amazing absence of writing about women's experience of breasts, and some of what little there is does not arise from feminist sensibility. One wants to explain why it is that feminists have not written about breasts, even when there is a great deal of writing about sexuality, mothering, the body, and medical interactions with women's bodies. Why this silence about breasts, especially when if you tell women you are writing about women's breasted experience, they begin to pour out stories of their feelings about their breasts? Women are interested in talking about their breasted bodies and interested in listening to one another. But we almost never do it conversation, let alone in writing.

In the darkness of my despair about women's own breast censorship, I uncovered a gold mine: Daphna Ayalah and Isaac Weinstock (1979), *Breasts: Women Speak About Their Breasts and Their Lives.* This is a collection of photographs of the breasts, with accompanying experiential accounts, of fifty women. Ayalah and Weinstock asked all the women the same set of questions about growing up, sexuality, aging, birthing and nursing, and so on. Thus while each woman's stories are her own and in her own words, they can be compared. The authors were careful to interview different kinds of women: old, young, and middle-aged; women of color as well as white women; women who have and have not had children; lesbians as well as straight women; models; call girls; etc. This is an extraordinary book, and many of the generalizations I make about women's experience in this paper are derived from my reading of it.

1. Susan Bordo (1989) suggests that achievement society takes Western culture's denial of the body and fleshiness to extremes, projecting norms of tightness and hardness for all bodies. This is the particular contemporary cultural meaning of the

demand for slenderness in both men and women, but especially women. Bordo does not mention breasts specifically in this discussion, but clearly this analysis helps us understand why media norms of breasts make this impossible demand for a "firm" breast.

2. Susan Brownmiller (1984, 45) suggests that women going braless evoke shock and anger because men implicitly think that they own breasts and that only they should remove bras.

3. Women's attitudes toward breast-feeding and its relation or lack of it to sexuality are, of course, extremely variable. Teenage mothers, for example, have a great deal more difficulty than do older mothers with the idea of breast-feeding, probably because they are more insecure about their sexuality (Yoos 1985). Ayalah and Weinstock (1979) interview many mothers specifically about their attitudes toward and experiences in breast-feeding. The reactions are quite variable, from women who report the experience of breast-feeding as being nearly religious to women who say they could not consider doing it because they thought it was too disgusting.

4. In the feminist sexuality debate, some sexual libertarians accuse those whom they debate of holding a kind of desexualized, spiritualized, or nurturant eroticism. [See Ann Ferguson (1989) for an important discussion of the way out of this debate.] I do not here wish to take sides in this debate, which I hope is more or less over. The debate certainly reveals, however, the strength of a good/bad opposition around eroticism as it plays out in our culture. Ferguson suggests that the debate sets up an opposition between pleasure and love, which is an unhelpful polarity.

References

Anderson, Jeremy Weir. 1988. Breast frenzy. *Self* December:83–89.

Ayalah, Daphna, and Isaac Weinstock. 1979. *Breasts: Women Speak About Their Breasts and Their Lives.* New York: Simon and Schuster.

Bartky, Sandra. 1979. On psychological oppression. In *Philosophy and Women*, edited by Sharon Bishop and Marjorie Weinzweig. Belmont, CA: Wadsworth.

———. 1988. Foucault, femininity and the modernization of patriarchal power. In *Feminism and Foucault: Reflections on Resistance*, edited by Irene Diamond and Lee Quimby. Boston: Northeastern University Press.

Bordo, Susan. 1989. Reading the slender body. In *Body/Politics: Women and the Discourses of Science*, edited by Mary Jacobus, Evelyn Fox Keller, and Sally Shuttleworth. New York: Routledge, Chapman and Hall.

Brownmiller, Susan. 1984. *Femininity.* New York: Simon and Schuster.

Deutsch, Helene. 1985. *The Psychology of Women: A Psychoanalytic Interpretation.* Vol. II. New York: Grune & Stratton.

Dinnerstein, Dorothy. 1977. *The Mermaid and the Minotaur.* New York: Harper and Row.

Ferguson, Ann. 1983. On conceiving motherhood and sexuality: A feminist materialist approach. In *Mothering: Essays in Feminist Theory*, edited by Joyce Trebilcot. Totowa, NJ: Rowman and Allenheld.

———. 1989. *Blood at the Root.* London: Pandora Press.

Flax, Jane. 1983. Political philosophy and the patriarchal unconscious: A psychoanalytic perspective on epistemology and metaphysics. In *Discovering Reality:*

Feminist Perspectives on Epistemology, Metaphysics, Methodology and Philosophy of Science, edited by Sandra Harding and Merrill B. Hintikka. Dordrecht, the Netherlands: D. Reidel Publishing.

Irigaray, Luce. 1985. *Speculum of the Other Woman*. Ithaca, NY: Cornell University Press.

Kaplan, E. Ann. 1983. *Women and Film: Both Sides of the Camera*. New York: Methuen.

Kristeva, Julia. 1980. The father, love, and banishment. In *Desire in Language*, edited by Leon S. Roudiez. New York: Columbia University Press.

———. 1985. Sabat Mater. In *The Female Body in Western Culture*, edited by Susan Rubin Suleiman. Cambridge, MA: Harvard University Press.

Miles, Margaret R. 1985. The virgin's one bare breast: Female nudity and religious meaning in Tuscan early Renaissance culture. In *The Female Body in Western Culture*, edited by Susan Rubin Suleiman. Cambridge, MA: Harvard University Press.

Myers, Harriet H., and Paul S. Siegel. 1985. Motivation to breastfeed: A fit to the opponent-process theory? *Journal of Personality and Social Psychology* 49: 188–93.

Pateman, Carole. 1988. *The Sexual Contract*. Stanford, CA: Stanford University Press.

Schemen, Naomi. 1983. Individualism and the objects of psychology. In *Discovering Reality: Feminist Perspectives on Epistemology, Metaphysics, Methodology and Philosophy of Science*, edited by Sandra Harding and Merrill B. Hintikka. Dordrecht, the Netherlands: D. Reidel Publishing.

Sichtermann, Barbara. 1986. The lost eroticism of the breasts. In *Femininity: The Politics of the Personal*. Minneapolis: University of Minnesota Press.

Stanton, Donna. 1989. Difference on trial: A critique of the maternal metaphor in Cixous, Irigaray, and Kristeva. In *The Thinking Muse: Feminism and Modern French Philosophy*, edited by Jeffner Allen and Iris Marion Young. Bloomington: Indiana University Press.

Suleiman, Susan Rubin. 1985. Writing and motherhood. In *The (M)other Tongue: Essays in Feminist Psychoanalytical Interpretation*, edited by Shirley Nelson Garner, Claire Kahane, and Madelon Sprengnether. Ithaca, NY: Cornell University Press.

Wall Street Journal. 1988. Forget hemlines: The bosomy look is big fashion news, 2 December, 1.

Yoos, Lorie. 1985. Developmental issues and the choice of feeding method of adolescent mothers. *Journal of Obstetrical and Gynecological Nursing* 28:68–72.

13

Designing Women

Cultural Hegemony and the Exercise of Power among Women Who Have Undergone Elective Mammoplasty

PATRICIA GAGNÉ AND DEANNA MCGAUGHEY

Earlier in this volume we discussed the shift among both feminists and the general public toward emphasizing women's sexual pleasure and deemphasizing the sexual dangers women face. This shift was part of a broader shift toward emphasizing women's agency (that is, their ability to freely choose their actions), rather than emphasizing how women's lives are controlled by others and by powerful social forces.

Beginning in the 1960s, second-wave feminists typically had focused on the overlapping issues of constraint (how women's lives are restricted by men's power and by cultural norms that reflect men's desires); subordination (how women are kept under men's control and below men in the social hierarchy); and "false consciousness" (how women internalize men's desires as their own, often seeing themselves through men's eyes, a process sometimes referred to as the "male gaze" or the "internalized male connoisseur"). Each of these forces lead to the "docile bodies" described by Sandra Bartky.

This emphasis made great sense for those writing in the 1960s and 1970s. At the time, the legal, social, cultural, and economic constraints faced by women were far greater than they are today. Moreover, the extreme pressures placed on women by violence (whether rape, incest, battering, or some other form) were typically either blamed on the women or ignored altogether, and so many feminists considered it especially crucial to highlight these pressures.

Patricia Gagné and Deanna McGaughey, "Designing Women: Cultural Hegemony and the Exercise of Power Among Women who Have Undergone Elective Mammoplasty," *Gender & Society* 16(6): 814–838. Copyright © 2002 by Sociologists for Women in Society. Reprinted by permission of Sage Publications.

As women's position in society improved, however, a "third wave" of feminists arose. Compared to second-wave feminists, third-wave feminists (and other writers who might not necessarily accept that label) often downplay constraint and false consciousness and instead emphasize women's agency.

In the following article, authors Patricia Gagné and Deanna McGaughey argue that we can best understand women's bodily experiences by synthesizing these two approaches. Using the example of cosmetic breast surgery, they show how women actively choose to have surgery to improve their lives (exercising free will), but do so in the context of hegemonic (i.e., dominant and dominating) cultural norms that make it difficult for them to even consider other choices (suggesting false consciousness). As Gagné and McGaughey suggest, for women to feel comfortable with their "embodied self"—the part of their self-identity that reflects their sense of their physical body—they must find ways to change their physical self to better match their internalized sense of what an appropriate female body should look like.

Elective cosmetic surgery, like other practices designed to help women achieve hegemonic standards of feminine beauty, is problematic for feminist scholars because it involves agency as well as subordination. On one hand, women choose what procedures to have done. On the other, the choices women make are determined by hegemonic cultural norms.

The academic debate regarding women and beauty has included examinations and theoretical discussions of fashion, makeup, diet and exercise, eating disorders, and elective cosmetic surgery (Bartky 1997; Bordo 1993, 1997; Morgan 1991; Wolf 1991). A salient debate within this literature is based on assumptions about whether women are socially coerced into striving to achieve cultural standards of beauty or whether they freely choose to do so. As Padmore (1998) argued, a dualistic approach to social issues is overly simplified and wrong. What is needed is a theoretical model that incorporates social pressures and agency.

In this article, we draw on in-depth interviews with a nonrandom sample of women who have undergone elective cosmetic mammoplasty [breast surgery] to expand our understandings of women's experiences and motives for trying to achieve hegemonic ideals of beauty, as well as the social forces that compel them to do so. Our goal is to move beyond dualistic conceptualizations of agency and power by demonstrating how power is exercised on women's bodies even as they exercise it themselves.

Unlike most current literature on women and beauty, we do not assume that women are either victims of false consciousness or free agents in their quest to achieve cultural standards of beauty. Rather, our analysis reveals some of the ways that women are caught up in a hegemonic culture of beauty in which they often experience cosmetic surgery as liberating and empowering. In this article, we argue that dualistic conceptualizations of agency and power are inappropriate and inadequate. Our work contributes to the feminist literature by offering a theoretical model that synthesizes the strengths of both perspectives on women and beauty.

Feminist Perspectives on Cosmetic Surgery

In general, there have been two feminist approaches to understanding why women elect to undergo cosmetic surgery and the relationship between plastic surgery and women's subordination in society (Padmore 1998; Wijsbek 2000). The first can be characterized as the false consciousness perspective in which women are assumed to be objectified by men's standards of beauty. The second can be thought of as the free will perspective in which women are assumed to freely exercise agency in electing to undergo cosmetic surgery.

False Consciousness and the Male Gaze

The false consciousness perspective posits that although women freely choose cosmetic surgery, the standards they seek to achieve have been constructed by men and serve men's interests (Morgan 1991). Therefore, women are culturally coerced into seeking cosmetic surgery to meet the standards of beauty constructed by and for men. As Morgan (1991) explained, these are both actual men and abstract, symbolic male figures who may even exercise power over women through women's interactions with one another. Women perceive these hypothetical men as judging them and encouraging them to meet men's standards of beauty. The notion that men exercise power over women through socially constructed standards is known as the "male gaze," a concept developed by Mulvey (1989) to explain how feminine subjectivity is constructed as women judge and create themselves on the basis of their perceptions of men's desires. Mulvey argued that feminine subjectivity is constructed through spectatorship as the viewer identifies with the male and objectifies the female. While women may appear to be active in the social construction of self, they are actually the passive recipients of men's desires and standards (Culbertson 1999).

The male gaze has been criticized for suggesting that women are devoid of agency (Chandler 2000; Saco 1994) and for its lack of specificity (Pratt 1992). The theory presumes that all men have the same control over all women. But relations of power tend to intersect with one another. Therefore, not all men are equally powerful (Bhaba 1995). Men of color, for example, do not have as much social power as do white men (Pratt 1992), and working-class and poor men have less power than more affluent men. Finally, there are no empirical data to support the assumption that women's perceptions of men's desires are accurate reflections of what men want in women (Chandler 2000). Without supporting empirical data, the theory of the male gaze comes into question because it is based on the premise that what men desire in women must change before women can be empowered.

One of the strengths of the male gaze is how the concept highlights the centrality of looking and being seen in the social construction of gender and maintenance of social relations (Chandler 2000). In this way, looking and being looked at are fundamental steps in the process of establishing, perpetuating, or challenging social order. Looking is central to the social construction of the self and has been demonstrated to play an important role in culture by regulating social interaction (Argyle 1983). Specifically, it is through looking that we are constituted as subjects and objects. The problem with the male gaze is not the notion that looking is important but the patriarchal and heterosexist premise that actual and hypothetical men are the sole agents and beneficiaries of the gaze. The extent to which actual and hypothetical women are agents and beneficiaries of a hegemonic cultural gaze has received little academic attention (but see Chapkis 1986). Furthermore, outside of film, few if any scholars have focused on the processes through which women exercise agency by gazing and presenting themselves as objects of the looks of others.

Free Choice

In contrast to the notion of false consciousness is the view that women are rational decision makers and that they seek cosmetic surgery through free choice. Davis (1995) argued for such a perspective in her research on decision-making processes among women who have undergone elective cosmetic surgery. Davis acknowledged that the decision to undergo elective cosmetic surgery can be problematic but concluded that it can be an instrument used by women to control their bodies and lives. In this formulation, the benefits of exercising free choice—feeling and being perceived as normal—outweigh the consequences of embodying hegemonic gender norms.

One of the problems with Davis's (1995) approach is her uncritical adoption of hegemonic ideas of what is normal or natural. The discourse of free choice is predicated on the idea that it is natural for women to want to look better. In addition, looking better or being satisfied with the results of cosmetic surgery is based on judgments of how natural one looks (Adams 1997). This premise is problematic because it presumes that "natural" is outside of culture and hence outside of power relations (Brush 1998). By arguing that the goal of elective cosmetic surgery is to look normal or natural, the relations among cosmetic surgery, the objectification of women, and social relations of power, including race and class, are foreclosed from critique.

In sum, the false consciousness and free will perspectives differ in their understanding of the motivations for, and consequences of, seeking cosmetic surgery. The false consciousness approach assumes that women are duped by a beauty system that is defined by men. Therefore, women are objects of men's desires and standards. The free will perspective argues that although the practices of femininity may be problematic, women are nevertheless active in choosing cosmetic surgery. Therefore, cosmetic surgery is an expression of women's agency.

Although these two perspectives appear to be diametrically opposed, there are two theoretical threads running through them that are more similar than different. First, both draw on a conventional understanding of power that is conceived as a zero-sum phenomenon, which Foucault (1978) argued is incomplete. For the false consciousness approach, power is held by men and exercised over women. For the free will perspective, the power to choose is held by women and is outside existing gendered power relations. The only difference between these two explanations is with respect to who is holding power over whom. Both overlook the sites at which power is exercised, such as through self-perception, social interaction, the fashion industry, the media, and medicine, making both perspectives incomplete.

Second, both approaches perpetuate the idea that an individual is composed of two discrete and opposed qualities: a mind and a body (Cheng 1996; Ender 1999; Grosz 1994; Weiss 1999). The false consciousness and free will perspectives both treat the body as a passive object that is either inscribed by hegemonic norms constructed by men or used by women as a tool in their social construction of a gendered self. In treating the body as an object, both approaches perpetuate dualistic thinking by ignoring the constitutive role the body plays in forming thoughts, feelings, and actions, as well as the interaction between body and mind in the formation and experience of self (Grosz 1994; Weiss 1999).

A Synthesized Approach: Cosmetic Surgery as a Technology of the Embodied Self

We propose a synthesized theoretical perspective that simultaneously accounts for women's agency and subordination within the practice of cosmetic surgery (Padmore 1998). Our approach incorporates aspects from both the false consciousness and the free will perspectives by embracing women's agency in the construction of self while acknowledging and criticizing hegemonic gender norms through which the apparent possibilities of self are created (Padmore 1998). Specifically, we draw on Gramsci's (1971) concept of hegemony to examine the ways in which the dominant culture and major institutions coerce women into having their bodies surgically altered. And we examine women's internalization of a narrow range of acceptable embodiments, which serves as the foundation of their consent to be governed and their desire to have their bodies surgically altered. With this perspective, we transcend the dualism inherent in both perspectives by drawing on the concepts of disciplinary power and the embodied self.

Disciplinary Power and the Embodied Self

The conceptualization of power in the false consciousness and free will perspectives is not so much wrong as it is incomplete (Foucault 1979). Although power may be unequally distributed, it cannot be divided neatly into haves and have nots. Identifying who has power simply masks how it is dispersed throughout social networks. For example, concentrating on the male gaze blinds us to how the gaze emerges through other sites, including women's gazes at one another (Winkler 1994); the clinical gaze (Foucault 1973), in which women's bodies are constructed through the lens of medicine; self-gazing, in which women look at themselves (Brush 1998); and racialized and sexualized gazes, through which white supremacy and heterosexism are constituted. A more comprehensive approach to understanding power seeks to identify not who has power but how it operates and the consequences of those operations (Dreyfus and Rabinow 1982; Foucault 1980; Ransom 1997; Sawicki 1991). The benefit of such an approach is that it allows for critical intervention into multiple sites of power.

Cosmetic surgery does not simply repress or hold women down; it is a tool among many used literally to create the female body and feminine subjectivity. As such, cosmetic surgery can both contest and reify hegemonic culture,[1] although it is more often a tool for creating and maintaining cultural hegemony. Most plastic surgery is completed to meet cultural standards that are informed implicitly by race and class (Gilman 1999). For example, white women tend to have their breasts augmented, African American women tend to have their noses made narrower, and Asian American women tend to have their eyes Westernized (Kaw 1998; Padmore 1998). Class polarization is also reified through cosmetic surgery practices. For example, thinness is currently the norm and is more easily accomplished by affluent women who have access to better foods and a certain amount of expendable income they can use for lyposuction (Fallon 1990). Although women willingly elect to create their embodied selves through plastic surgery and other means, one of the unintended consequences of their actions is the perpetuation and proliferation of sexism, heterosexism, racism, and classism. Hence, it is not the surgery itself that is oppressive but the ends it serves, particularly when those ends reify cultural hegemony.

Understanding self-formation from a disciplinary perspective of power requires examining how people are pressured to become "normal." From a Foucauldian perspective, society constructs a norm and then encourages people literally to embody that standard (Foucault 1979). Individuals are not coerced to do so but instead are guided in their willing obedience (Ransom 1997). Specifically, women are not forced to undergo cosmetic surgery or most of the other practices in their beauty regimens. Rather, they internalize as natural and normal the standards of beauty that are pervasive in the hegemonic culture. As Gramsci (1971) argued, hegemony is insidious because it is internalized. Cosmetic surgery is a technique of feminization located at the intersection between agency and subordination, in which women actively and passively create themselves—through a literal construction of the body—as desirable women.

For the purpose of this article, we assume cosmetic surgery to be a technology drawn on by women in their construction of an embodied self. Therefore, we highlight women's agency in constructing an embodied self, along with the role of hegemonic gender norms that guide women to meet, and literally embody, those norms. We assume women are both subjects and objects of the designing process. "Designing women" refers to women's agency in the process of body/self formation, as well as the ways in which society designs women through hegemonic discourse.

Method

Between 1997 and 1998, we recruited a volunteer sample of women who had undergone elective mammoplasty that was not related to cancer or other medical conditions. We specifically sought women who had undergone breast augmentation, but because of difficulties in recruiting an adequate sample, we included everyone who volunteered whose surgery was elective. We offered a $20 honorarium to encourage participation. Our sample includes 15 women, of whom 12 had breast augmentation, 2 breast reductions, and 1 corrective surgery (augmentation on one breast and reduction of the other). Our sample consisted of 14 white women and 1 African American woman who had breast surgery. The approximate annual family incomes of these women ranged from $10,000 to $105,000 with a mean of $61,181. All but 2 women had some college education, and 2 were pursuing master's degrees. Because our recruitment included posting flyers on the campus of a midsized, Midwestern commuter university, 10 of the women we interviewed were students, 9 of whom held part-time jobs. Three nonstudents worked full-time, 1 worked part-time, and 1 was a homemaker. Their occupations included postal worker, bartender, salesperson, dietician, cosmetologist, secretary, waitress, health care administrator, and teaching assistant....

To enhance the reliability of the data, the first author conducted all of the interviews. They were in-depth and semistructured and lasted approximately two hours. With the written consent of the women in our sample, we tape-recorded all the interviews and then had them transcribed verbatim. We analyzed the data using established principles of analytic induction for the discovery of grounded theory (Charmaz 1983; Miles and Huberman 1984; Strauss and Corbin 1994)....

Findings

In the following sections, we first explain the motives the women in our sample expressed for seeking and undergoing elective cosmetic breast surgery. In those sections, women discuss cosmetic surgery as a solution to a problem, one that opens new opportunities and has a liberating effect on them. Later, we examine the impact that hegemony had on the decisions these women made, as well as some of the sites through which power was exercised over their bodies, even as they believed they were exercising free will. We conclude with a discussion of the ramifications of approaching this issue with the synthetic perspective we advance.

Agents of Beauty: The Motives of Designing Women

The women in our sample all wanted to achieve a level of normalcy, based on their perceptions of who they were as well as what others expected from women in general. Their perceptions came from a variety of sources, including ideals generated by the media and fashion, their own observations of other women, and their own perceptions of men's observations of themselves and other women.

REPRESENTING ONE'S SELF ACCURATELY. In social interactions, individuals are often judged by their appearance, and one's body is an integral component of such assessments. In every social interaction, individuals are looked on, judged, and interacted with on the basis of whether their bodies are young or old; overweight or thin; tall or short; brown, tan, or beige; female or male. The reactions that one receives from others, which are inherently affected by one's embodiment, are crucial factors in the formation of the self. Yet we found that the women in our sample frequently thought of themselves in different terms than those their bodies conveyed to the world. The body and mind are intertwined. When the body does not accurately convey who one believes oneself to be, one option is to readjust one's self-concept to reflect physical reality, giving in to the judgments of others. Another is to exercise power by altering one's body.

As might be expected, each of the women in our sample identified something about her breasts with which she was dissatisfied. But the perception that their breasts belied the self within the body was a primary motive for women's desire to undergo cosmetic surgery. This motive affected women who perceived their breasts as too large, too small, or not appropriately firm and youthful.

Our sample included women who had been pregnant and had breast-fed their babies. Pregnancy and breast-feeding gave temporary satisfaction to women who thought their breasts were too small. This satisfaction was later followed by a realization that the biological changes caused by these aspects of motherhood had taken what women perceived to be a negative toll on their breasts. Even those women who were happy with their breasts and their bodies before childbirth found that after giving birth or breast-feeding their children, they were unhappy with the shape, size, or firmness of their breasts. For example, Ann, a 32-year-old white married woman with three children, who had breast augmentation surgery, explained,

> After I had my third son...my body was destroyed. I had three C-sections, and I breast-fed all my children. So prior to any of my pregnancies, I was a full 34C. I really loved my body, had no problems with my body ever. After the children, I was very saggy.

Like this woman, most of the women we interviewed talked about their breasts (before surgery) in terms of their being too small, too large, or too saggy. Some were very distressed about their appearance. For example, Beth, a 44-year-old white married mother of four, said, "I was always a flat-chested, redheaded, freckle-faced kid and was teased a lot about being flat.... After my children were born and I nursed them, my breasts were saggy nothings and very unappealing to me." Perceptions of physical deformity, combined with a self-concept that did not include physical abnormalities, motivated the women in our sample to seek elective mammoplasty. The reasons they gave for having their bodies surgically altered reflect both agency and an internalization of hegemonic cultural ideals of beauty. Although one's body might not be all one might desire, the post-childbirth body was inevitably described as worse.

The incongruence between body and self-concept was not limited to women who had given birth or breast-fed their children. Age was also a factor. Every woman in our sample had a self-concept or an idealized self that was not represented by her body. Some women thought that because their breasts were too small, they were not treated with the respect normatively accorded adult women. Instead, they were treated like children. For example, Jane, a 21-year-old white woman, explained, "I hated it because I felt like I was getting older mentally and everything else, but I still looked like I was 12 years old." And indeed, that is how she perceived that people treated her. She turned to breast augmentation surgery as a tool that helped her correct the incongruence she felt between who she was and how people treated her. Similarly, women with larger breasts said that people perceived them as older or overweight. For example, Sue, a white mother of three, said that before her surgery, "I had several people say to me, 'Well you're not fat. You just have big boobs. They make you look matronly.'" At 32 years of age, matronly was not the way she thought of herself.

Cosmetic breast surgery was a means of establishing congruency between the body and mind, or developing an embodied self that was comfortable to the women we interviewed. Moreover, by making such bodily changes, the women in our sample perceived that people interacted with them the way they wanted to be treated. Sue, for example, explained that before her surgery, people would stare at or "talk to" her breasts. She said that since her surgery,

> People are paying attention to [me] and not a part of [my] body. They see me for who I am now. I've always been very outgoing. I've always been bubbly. But now, I can relax and be myself and not worry that people don't see that anymore. They see me for who I am, and people do react differently to me.

Women explained that undergoing mammoplasty was important because it prompted people to treat them in the way they perceived themselves. Moreover, they explained that this change alone brought with it greater social opportunities. With more positive reactions from others, their self-confidence was increased, and many said they felt liberated.

INCREASING SOCIAL OPPORTUNITIES. The women we interviewed identified several ways that they thought surgically altering their bodies enhanced their social interactions with others and increased their social opportunities. Because the self is formed in interaction with others (Blumer 1986; Cooley 1902; Mead 1934) and because one's body affects the reactions one receives from others (Grosz 1994; Weiss 1999), it seems logical that changing one's body to fit hegemonic ideals of attractiveness would improve one's social opportunities.

Some women recognized early in their lives that they were ignored by men while their friends received more attention. Interestingly, the women we talked with did not have mammoplasty because they wanted to date or become romantically or sexually involved with more men. Instead, they wanted their bodies to represent them as attractive women. . . .

Taking control of the way one is seen is a way of exercising power in a heterosexist and ageist society. Mammoplasty made it possible for women to project a desired image, achieve greater comfort in sexual situations, command greater respect, and compete in a job market that favors youth. Having others interact with them as the people they believed themselves to be was a motivator for most of the women we interviewed. Jane emphasized, "I feel more confident in my job so I'm able to present what I'm selling better."

By accepting the hegemonic culture, the women we interviewed believed they had learned the rules of the game and thus how to compete and achieve the social opportunities and rewards they desired. Moreover, they looked on cosmetic surgery as a logical technology implemented to achieve rewards that every woman wants. All of the women we interviewed talked about cosmetic surgery as a normal procedure that nearly all women would choose if they had the means to do so. Every one of them explained that all women are dissatisfied with their bodies and that given the opportunity, almost all would change something. For example, Tara, a 27-year-old, white mother of one, said,

> No woman is totally happy with her body. You know, they'll say, oh, "I'm in great shape," but then you'll see them and they're, you know, "Look at this," or "Look at this." Nobody is happy with their body. Or if they are, they're a jerk . . . . So it's just, I think if a guy was like, "Here, I'll give you the money, go get your boobs done," you know, no strings or anything like that, just, "If I give it to you, would you do it?" I think most women would do it.

For the women we interviewed, cosmetic surgery was just another part of the technologies of beauty available to women, on a continuum with makeup, hair color, diet, exercise, or the use of special bras. The main difference between mammoplasty and using clothing or bras to disguise or enhance breasts was that breast surgery was a more permanent choice in the exercise of power. This relative permanence gave women more fashion options and greater control over their choices of clothing. In short, cosmetic surgery was a way of exercising power, controlling their bodies, and normalizing the embodied self within a disciplining beauty regime that is based on compulsory heterosexuality. Although their beauty regimens were more extreme than those of women who have the means yet do not opt for cosmetic surgery, the point here is that the women in our sample experienced breast surgery as liberating rather than oppressive. We believe that this is likely due to a greater level of internalization of standards of hegemonic beauty, which permitted them to overlook the potential risks.

I'M WORTH IT. Despite the distress that many women expressed about their breasts, all of them emphasized that they did not feel coerced or as if they had to have surgery. Instead, most talked about how having mammoplasty was something nice they could do for themselves. For example, Ann said,

> I find that these [types of surgery] are things that suburban mothers are having done after their children. Kind of a treat to themselves. I figure I went through all that to have these kids, I could put myself back together.

Her view reflected that of the other women—that cosmetic surgery is a beauty secret employed by women with the means to pay for it. Like a day at the spa or the beauty parlor, women seek cosmetic surgery not because someone pressures them to do so but because they are worth it.

In all but one interview, participants repeatedly emphasized that no one coerced, cajoled, or otherwise forced them to have cosmetic surgery. Indeed, in most cases, women's family members and partners tried to convince them not to have surgery. In this way, women asserted that they owned and controlled their bodies. They often expressed their desire to have surgery in terms of self-improvement. For example, Sue said, "I did it for me, because I wanted to feel better about myself." And Jane explained, "I wanted to do it because I wanted the self-confidence. I wanted to be able to walk into a room and feel like I didn't have to hide myself."

The women we interviewed framed cosmetic surgery in the feminist discourse of choice. They expressed strong beliefs that no one had the right to judge them for having altered their bodies, just as no one had the right to pressure them into having surgery. For example, Kelly, a 22-year-old, white, single, childless woman who had augmentation surgery said, "[This is] my body, and wanting to get it done has nothing to do with anyone else. ... This is for me, to feel better about myself."

The women we interviewed thought of cosmetic surgery as a normal part of the culture and technology of beauty in the United States. All but one woman were pleased with the results of their mammoplasties, and all of them said they felt more confident and better about themselves as a result.

All but one said they made their decision to have surgery without pressure from any other person or source. The primary motivation for seeking breast augmentation was their prior sense of disembodying femininity. That is, they perceived that before having surgery, they did not present a desirable feminine self, nor did they experience themselves as desirable women. Cosmetic surgery, then, was a tool for creating the self by altering the body in an effort to enhance existing social opportunities or create new ones. What the women in our sample failed to recognize, however, was the way that their personal exercise of power reified the hegemonic culture, including compulsory heterosexuality as well as inequalities based on race, social class, and age.

Within a hegemonic culture in which heterosexuality is compulsory, women's breasts are interpreted as signifiers of who they are as people. Accordingly, pregnancy, childbirth, and breast-feeding are cultural indicators of the achievement of womanhood. Yet, as women pass these mileposts in life, or as they simply age, their bodies may lose the ability to convey youthful femininity, as signified by firm breasts. Thus, as women achieve adulthood, they lose an important aspect of self within a heterosexist society. In this way, society puts reproductive women in a no-win situation in which they can be perceived as perpetually youthful and sexual or in which they can achieve womanhood but risk no longer being perceived as young, sexual, or vital. For many of the women we interviewed, mammoplasty allowed them to regain a sexually vital image after achieving motherhood and mature womanhood or after reaching middle age. For women who thought their breasts were too small, breast augmentation surgery was used as a tool to help them achieve adulthood, just as women who thought their breasts were too large used breast reduction surgery so that their breasts would convey a more youthful image.

Clearly, women exercised agency in deciding to undergo surgery, particularly in the face of opposition from others. The decision, however, to undergo the surgery reified existing hegemonic norms regarding beauty and femininity and has unintended consequences for all women. First, the embodied self these women chose to construct was based on a norm that is inherently ageist. Although some women chose reduction and some chose augmentation, all were seeking a look that signified youthful sexual vitality. The women in our sample sought to distance themselves from a post-reproductive look as is suggested by having saggy breasts or an overall matronly look. Second, by literally constructing the feminine self through the body, they contributed to the process of judging women on the basis of their bodies and appearance rather than on performance. And finally, in claiming that they were worth it, they abstracted themselves from the cultural context in which femininity is constructed. In doing so, they reified existing inequalities among women.

The practice of cosmetic surgery perpetuates racism and classism because only a minority—generally white, economically privileged women—have the means to have surgery and because the hegemonic heterosexist ideal of feminine beauty is essentially a white standard. That surgery is a treat for suburban mothers unintentionally implies that all women should look like (or want to look like) white suburbanites and that their urban and rural counterparts are not worth it. Still, several questions remain: Where did these women get their ideas of what their breasts should look like? What factors influenced them in their desire for cosmetic surgery? Where did they get the idea to have mammoplasty to achieve the bodies they desired? And what factors influenced them as they made their decisions to have the surgery done?

Beauty Objects: The Hegemony of Beauty and the Decision to Undergo Elective Mammoplasty

Listening to the motives women gave for undergoing elective mammoplasty, it appears that surgery had the potential to ease distress they felt about their bodies, to help them overcome insecurities, make them feel more attractive and confident, and give them greater social opportunities. Yet it is important to recall that anyone who makes any bodily alteration—whether wearing makeup, coloring hair, dieting, exercising, getting pierced, getting a tattoo, or having cosmetic surgery—is invariably influenced by the wider society in which one lives. In this section, we identify the social factors that the women we interviewed discussed as having had an influence on their ideas about beauty and their decision to have surgery.

THE MEDIA. Women in the United States are bombarded by images of what it means to be beautiful and desirable. Perhaps the most egregious of the messages women receive about the inadequacy of their own bodies are those portrayed in women's magazines, which are filled with waifishly thin models and buxom babes who know exactly what "your man" wants. Capitalism and the modern media are predicated on the idea that sex sells, but the underlying current is an effort to create anxiety and insecurity among women who otherwise might not realize they have something to worry about (Wolf 1991). The influence of the media was apparent in the narratives of the women we interviewed. For example, Abbey, a 32-year-old, white woman who had breast augmentation surgery, explained how women's magazines had affected her consciousness about her body. She said,

> I do remember when I had made the decision to have the implants, I didn't want them real big and I wanted them to look like they were mine. Like this is what I grew. I remember seeing a model in *Cosmopolitan*, and her breasts weren't very big, but she had some. And I thought, "That's what I want mine to look like."

Referring back to *Cosmopolitan* magazine, she later added, "I'm sure even subconsciously, even if I didn't realize it, yea, it had a big influence on my decision to have bigger breasts."

By appealing to media-induced anxieties, magazines sell themselves while vendors hawk their products through advertisements and articles geared toward teaching women how to improve their looks, their skills as lovers, and ultimately how to save their sexual desirability. Without toning, shaping, working out, dieting, making up, and ultimately going under the knife, women are led to believe that they will end up ugly, undesirable, asexual, and alone. It is for this reason that designing women use all the resources they can summon to fashion and embody what they perceive to be the ultimate expression of feminine beauty.

The print media are only one source of women's anxieties. Perhaps more encompassing is the impact that movies and television programs have on women's ideas of the social adequacy of their bodies and ultimately of their selves. Although the print media often say quite directly that women must do something (e.g., exercise) or purchase a certain product (e.g., perfume or diet aids) to avoid something terrible happening to them (e.g., ending up alone and unloved), the messages of movies and television are more subtle. Those messages take their effect when women consciously or unconsciously compare their own bodies to those of movie and television stars and then seek ways to approximate those bodies (see Mulvey 1989).

As part of our interview, we asked women to describe what they thought to be the body of the ideal woman. Interestingly, almost all began with an abstract physical description, such as "tall, thin, not big chested" or, invoking a reproductive norm, "curvy, vivacious, [the] fertile look." But before they finished the abstract description, almost every woman gave a specific example from the media of the ideal woman's body. Lisa said, "She [the ideal woman] has big breasts, tiny waist, and fairly thin hips. A Barbie Doll or a Pam Anderson." And Abbey began with a concrete example and moved to an abstract description based on that ideal. She said, "What I tend to think of is what everyone else does: Christie Brinkley. You know, the blonde, the tanned skin, the perfect white teeth." Ideals included Helen Hunt, Meryl Streep, and Tyra Banks, who are tall and thin with smaller breasts, and Sophia Loren, Ann Margaret, and Marilyn Monroe, who have larger breasts and portray a curvy and vivacious image. Among our sample, heavier women tended to think the curvy, voluptuous Marilyn Monroe look approximated the ideal, while thinner women preferred the Helen Hunt look. Each idealized an image she thought she could approximate by drawing on medical technology....

FASHION. With apparel, humans cover their bodies, protect themselves from the environment, and communicate important information about status and self. But the fashion industry, like the media, is geared toward making profits. To do so, it is oriented toward what it perceives as normal-sized humans so that the mass production of clothing will result in the maximum number of sales. For women, the norm of fashion is thin and proportionate. Rather than the industry increasing the availability of larger sizes or clothing where the top is smaller or larger than the bottom, women struggle to meet the ideal to enhance the choices available to them even when they recognize the tyranny of fashion. Chris expressed the issue succinctly when she said, "The average size of a model is like a 2 or a 4. The average size of a regular woman is like a 14. What's up with that?"

Fashions are used to create a certain look or image. Some fashions are oriented toward emphasizing the abdomen, breasts, and buttocks for a sensual feminine look. Others streamline the body into an hourglass shape, for a professional, businesslike appearance. Whatever the look women seek, clothing is mass-produced to fit the idealized thin and proportionate body. Women who are overweight, tall, big boned, or whose hips are wider or narrower than their bust sizes often find it difficult to dress fashionably or even to find clothing that fits properly. It is impossible for certain women to conform to the fashion industry's standards of feminine beauty unless they have the resources to have their clothing personally tailored for them. And in not being able to fit, many women blame themselves for not being able to discipline their bodies. The fashion industry dictates available clothing, and when women fail to meet the ideal, it exercises the power to (re)create women's bodies.

Most of the women we interviewed talked about how their too small or too large breasts made it impossible to wear certain styles. For example, Kelly said,

> I was a B before, and a lot of dresses didn't fit. Tank tops were always too low, and I had to get real small sizes, and they didn't fit the proportions of my body. So I wanted more [breast size] for dressing.... [Before surgery] it was just finding a bra that was padded. Always trying not to get low low cut shirts because, you know, when you bend over you could see my belly button.

Sue, whose skirts and slacks were size 7 and who had breast reduction surgery said, "[Before surgery] I couldn't buy dresses. I would have to get a [size] 12 dress just to get it to button." Chris recognized the power of the fashion industry when she said, "They select that few 5 percent of the population that are anorexic [whom] they're going to attend to." Still, she said she felt better being able to buy clothing off the rack since having her breast reduction surgery....

OTHER WOMEN: THE FEMALE GAZE AND REGIME OF BEAUTY. Our respondents believed that women in general have a shared beauty culture, or a sense of a generalized gaze. Speaking about themselves, they said that they constantly compared their own bodies and appearance to that of other women. This comparison was evident in the influence the media had on them and carried over into their everyday lives. For example, Tara said,

> When you think about when you go to the grocery store, if you see a woman walking down the aisle, a voluptuous figure, you notice it. And it's just, you know, there was always a kind of envy. It was like, gosh, I mean, to have a

build like that.... Of course, you envy, I mean every time you see somebody that you think is prettier than you or having a better body or anything, of course you're envious.... I always look at other women.

In addition to constant comparison to other women, the participants in our study explained that an important part of feminine culture is the sharing of beauty tips, including information about makeup, diet, exercise, weight loss products, undergarments, and—more recently—cosmetic surgery. For them, part of being a woman and belonging to feminine culture was knowing and being willing to share the techniques of beauty.

For the women we interviewed, beauty was an element of feminine power. By sharing beauty tips, women believed they empowered one another. Although this practice may empower individual women, it also standardizes ideals of beauty while constantly raising the bar of beauty. In this way, the practice of beauty power is similar to that exercised by the media and fashion industry. Women must become ever thinner; become more muscular; have longer, fuller lashes; permanently avoid becoming gray; have less and less body hair; and now have breasts that meet an increasingly unrealistic ideal. The power regime (Foucault 1979) through which beauty is constructed and deployed is internalized by women. Those who achieve it feel more confident—more powerful. At the same time, they are the women most subjugated by the regime of beauty, which is, ironically, enforced by the totalizing, disciplining gaze of other women less than that of the men in their lives.

With one exception, all of the women we interviewed insisted that they were not influenced by husbands or boyfriends to have surgery on their breasts. In most instances, boyfriends and husbands opposed their partners' decisions....

Men's attitudes stood in stark comparison to the interactions the participants in our study had with other women in their lives. Although many had thought about having breast surgery before actually seeking it, knowing someone who actually had surgery, or was about to do so, made mammoplasty seem less radical and more like a reasonable solution to a problem over which they had only temporary control (e.g., with padded bras and Wonderbras). For example, Kelly said,

> Probably about a year [ago], we all went out... and we had started talking about it [getting implants] then. And she [a friend who had surgery before I did] was more serious on actually doing it than I was. I had been interested in it but just felt it was more out of my reach, I guess.... I really didn't know anything about it. So then a couple of months later... she had a consultation... and started to proceed with what she was going to do. So that's when I started getting books at the library... checking out doctors... I saw her the day that she had it done and... when she came back to work, and I was like, you know, "Oh, how did it go?"... So I knew every detail from her and that really influenced me.... Because she did it, that made me realize that, hey... it's in reach.

Every one of the women in our sample knew at least one other woman who had undergone some form of elective cosmetic surgery, most often mammoplasty. Although they had thought about doing something to correct their breasts, all of them identified their immersion in a culture of beauty and involvement in a network of women whose beauty practices included cosmetic surgery as the most significant influence on their decision to go forward with surgery. Once their minds were made up, the next step was to find a surgeon and decide what their breasts would look like.

MEDICINE AS RESOURCE AND OPPRESSOR. Most of the women we talked with made their decisions to have surgery and found their surgeons over time periods ranging from a few days to more than a year. Those who took longer to decide on a doctor tended to consult with more surgeons and to do more research, including library work and checking on the medical backgrounds, certifications, and work of the physicians they were considering. Those who took the least time acted almost impulsively, choosing a doctor who offered a good deal or credit or whom a friend had used.

Just as there were differences in the amount of information women sought before selecting a surgeon, there were differences in the agency women exercised in their choice of breasts. Some women, such as those previously described, cut out photographs and gave specific instructions to their doctors about how they wanted to look after surgery. Others depended on their surgeons to instruct them on the type and size breasts that would suit them best. Most often, breasts were decided on in consultation between physician and patient. Doctors employed a variety of techniques to help their patients choose breasts, including computer simulation and having women bring in larger size bras and clothing to be worn with prostheses. Although the women we interviewed knew of doctors who would do whatever women wanted, they said that their own doctors placed limits on what they were willing to do. Kelly summarized the use of technology and the exercise of power between patient and doctor. She said,

> You went in and the nurse took a picture of you and then put it in the computer and said that for your weight and the width of your shoulders... this is what I would recommend. And he draws it up on the computer... and says, "What do you think about that? What are your expectations?"... So I said, "I want to be a C... no possibility of being a D... I didn't want to be that big. I wanted to look right." He said, "OK," went into details medically, and that was... basically it with the size.... He will do bigger... [but] he won't do anything that looks outrageous, just because of his name.

As this woman's narrative indicates, medicine can be a resource in constructing the body and self, at the same time that its practitioners dictate the limits of possibility. Therefore, in the commodification of women's bodies, postsurgical breasts are a marketing tool for surgeons.

THE MALE GAZE AND THE GENERALIZED GAZE. The women in our sample appeared to have an internalized idea of what men want or expect in terms of beauty. Even when their ideas were not reflected in the desires of the actual men in their own lives—that is, their own boyfriends or husbands thought they looked fine without surgery or opposed the surgery altogether—they still sought mammoplasty so that they could meet a generalized, perceived male gaze.

Just as women look at and compare themselves to one another, the women we interviewed were aware of men watching other women. They perceived this male gaze as what men desire in women. Perhaps because of the subject matter of our interview, none of the women in our sample talked about what men wanted in women in terms of personality traits or other attributes. Instead, they observed men gazing on other women, noted that men were not looking at them, and deduced—based on media portrayals and common cultural knowledge—what men want. For example, Abbey talked about how men ignored her before she had breast augmentation surgery. She said,

> I think down at the beach, the men...spent most of their day...looking at the girls...looking at the actual breasts....[I remember] being at the beach and...talking to a guy one time and he was talking about his ex-girlfriend....[He said,] "She thought she looked so good. She didn't have any tits." And I thought, "I didn't either."

Rather than seeking to please a particular man, however, the women we talked with generalized from specific interactions, such as those described here, to perceptions of what all men want. Based on a sense of a generalized other (Mead 1934), women attempted to meet a generalized gaze that may be established by men but that is internalized by all women and exercised by women on themselves and other women. Thus, the hegemony of beauty is exercised less in one-on-one interactions wherein a significant other expresses dissatisfaction with a specific woman's beauty than with women's internalization of the generalized other, communicated through the hegemonic gaze.

The hegemonic gaze is an accepted standard of beauty—a sense that individual women have that everyone is looking at them—and the discomfort women feel if they fail to meet this standard of beauty. Having an unruly body is similar to breaking a social norm, with the social sanctions that normally apply to other forms of deviance. Among the women we interviewed, there was a sense that a beautiful body was a proportionate body and that successful breast surgery would look natural or normal. In choosing to have surgery, the women in our sample exercised power over their own bodies. In meeting the ideals of the hegemonic gaze, they could finally relax about their unruly breasts and feel good about themselves. In short, they were liberated from the gaze because they conformed to it, just as deviants are liberated from the sanctions of deviance when they conform to societal expectations. In this way, cosmetic surgery is an expression of the totalization of power rather than a means of liberation. Yet ironically, it is at this point that women feel liberated.

Conclusion

This study has contributed to existing research that examines how women are both objectified by and complicitous in the construction and proliferation of hegemonic gender. Our findings suggest that neither the false consciousness nor free will approach is wrong but that both are incomplete (Foucault 1979). Specifically, our research suggests that it is essential for gender scholars to consider both the agency of those being studied and the ways the larger society compels individuals to meet a social standard and then rewards them for doing so.

Women electing cosmetic mammoplasty exercise agency, but they do so within the confines of hegemonic gender norms. Heterosexual standards of feminine beauty may be created by men, and within a heterosexist, ageist, and racist society, it is primarily socially privileged men who exercise the power to mete out interpersonal and institutional rewards for conformity, including social and economic benefits. Nonetheless, women are complicitous in disciplining themselves and one another. It appears that men exercise power interpersonally, by virtue of the visual attentions they devote to women deemed physically attractive. Interpersonal interactions are one site among many where the power of the male gaze is exercised. Furthermore, men exercise power institutionally, through medicine, the fashion industry, the media, and the workplace. And because the standards of the male gaze are recognized and internalized by many women, men are capable of exercising an insidious form of power over heterosexual women, whether they seek to conform to or resist hegemonic standards of beauty.

Despite the pervasiveness of men's power, women also exercise power. Individual women may choose to resist or rebel against hegemonic standards of feminine beauty, but they are likely to risk discrimination in institutional settings, in large part because they do not fit with the dominant culture. We believe that this is because women's power is primarily limited to personal agency and interpersonal interactions. Specifically, in our study, women exercised considerable power in disciplining one another's embodiment. We find it significant, despite the limitations of our sample, that every one of the women we interviewed knew at least one other woman who had undergone cosmetic breast surgery. It appears that among middle-class, heterosexual women, cosmetic surgery has become an increasingly accepted and expected beauty technique. In this way, women are "token torturers" (Daly 1978) who play a pivotal, though often unrecognized, role in disciplining one another. To the extent that these women seek one another's approval, as well as the attentions of men, they internalize the standard and are led to willing compliance. And it is at the point of this compliance that the torture stops and rewards are achieved, leaving women feeling liberated and empowered at the same time that they embody and thus reify the hegemonic standards.

Ultimately, what our research shows is that the subject-object dualism that characterizes the free will (subject) and false consciousness (object) approaches is limited in conceptualizing the multifarious nature of the beauty regime. This is an issue of language. We know that the language we currently have is limited—women are neither simply subjects nor simply objects in the beauty regime but are both/neither. Nevertheless, the language still does not exist to allow us to transcend the dualism. But by investigating the exercise of power, rather than assuming it to be a zero-sum game, and by investigating the interpersonal, cultural, and institutional sites where it is exercised, researchers and theorists are likely to come to a more complete and dynamic understanding of the social world.

Notes

AUTHORS' NOTE: We are equal coauthors. An earlier version of this article was presented at the annual meetings of the Women's Studies Network (UK) Association International Conference, hosted by the Leisure and Sport Research Unit, Cheltenham and Gloucester College of Higher Education, Cheltenham, England, 12–14 July 2001. Research for this article was funded, in part, by a Research Initiative Grant and a Research on Women Grant from the Office of the Vice President for Research and Development at the University of Louisville. The authors wish to thank Dr. James K. Beggan, Department of Psychology, University of Louisville, for his assistance with this project and are grateful for the insightful comments of three anonymous reviewers.

1. For example, French feminist performance artist Orlan contests hegemonic constructions of femininity by going through a series of cosmetic surgeries in which she literally inscribes her body with European icons of beauty. Through this performance, Orlan demonstrates the ugliness of gender hegemony.

References

Adams, A. 1997. Molding women's bodies: The surgeon as sculptor. In *Bodily Discursions: Genders, Representations, and Technologies*, edited by D. Wilson and C. Laennec. Albany: State University of New York Press.

Argyle, M. 1983. *The Psychology of Interpersonal Behavior*. 4th ed. Harmondsworth, London: Penguin.

Bartky, S. 1997. Foucault, femininity, and the modernization of patriarchal power. In *Writing on the Body: Female Embodiment and Feminist Theory*, edited by K. Conboy, N. Medina, and S. Stanbury. New York: Columbia University Press.

Bhaba, H. 1995. Are you a man or a mouse? In *Constructing Masculinity*, edited by M. Berger, B. Wells, and S. Watson. New York: Routledge.

Blumer, H. 1986. *Symbolic Interactionism: Perspective and Method*. Berkeley, CA: University of California Press.

Bordo, S. 1993. *Unbearable Weight: Feminism, Western Culture, and the Body.* Los Angeles: University of California Press.

———. 1997. The body and the reproduction of femininity. In *Writing on the Body: Female Embodiment and Feminist Theory*, edited by K. Conboy, N. Medina, and S. Stanbury. New York: Columbia University Press.

Brush, P. 1998. Metaphors of inscription: Discipline, plasticity, and the rhetoric of choice. *Feminist Review* 58:22–44.

Chandler, D. 2000. Notes on "the gaze." Retrieved from http://www.aber.ac.uk/media/Documents/gaze/gaze09.html

Chapkis, W. 1986. *Beauty Secrets: Women and the Politics of Appearance.* Boston: South End.

Charmaz, K. 1983. The grounded theory method: An explication and interpretation. In *Contemporary Field Research: A Collection of Readings*, edited by R. Emerson. Prospect Heights, IL: Waveland.

Cheng, P. 1996. Mattering. *Diacritics* 26(1):108–39.

Cooley, C. 1902. *Human Nature and Social Order.* New York: Scribner.

Culbertson, P. 1999. Designing men: Reading the male body as text. *Textual Reasoning.* Retrieved from http://www.bu/mzank/Textual_Reasoning/tr-arthive/tr7.html/Culbertson1.html.

Daly, M. 1978. *Gyn/ecology: The Metaethics of Radical Feminism.* Boston: Beacon.

Davis, K. 1995. *Reshaping the Female Body: The Dilemma of Cosmetic Surgery.* New York: Routledge.

Dreyfus, H., and P. Rabinow. 1982. *Michel Foucault: Beyond Structuralism and Hermeneutics.* Chicago: Chicago University Press.

Ender, E. 1999. Speculating carnally or, some reflections on the modernist body. *Yale Journal of Criticism* 12(1):113–30.

Fallon, A. 1990. Culture in the mirror: Sociocultural determinants of body image. In *Body Images: Development, Deviance, and Change*, edited by T. Cash and T. Pruzinsky. New York: Guilford.

Foucault, M. 1973. *The Birth of the Clinic.* New York: Pantheon.

———. 1978. *History of Sexuality: An Introduction.* Vol. 1. New York: Pantheon.

———. 1979. *Discipline and Punish: The Birth of the Prison.* New York: Vintage.

———. 1980. Body/power. In *Power/knowledge*, edited by C. Gordon. New York: Pantheon.

Gilman, S. 1999. *Making the Body Beautiful: A Cultural History of Aesthetic Surgery.* Princeton, NJ: Princeton University Press.

Gramsci, A. 1971. *Prison Notebooks.* New York: International.

Grosz, E. 1994. *Volatile Bodies: Toward a Corporeal Feminism.* Bloomington: Indiana University Press.

Kaw, E. 1998. Medicalization of racial features: Asian-American women and cosmetic surgery. In *The Politics of Women's Bodies: Sexuality, Appearance, and Behavior*, edited by R. Weitz. New York: Oxford University Press.

Mead, G. H. 1934. *Mind, Self, and Society*, Vol. 1, edited by C. W. Morris. Chicago: University of Chicago Press.

Miles, M., and M. Huberman. 1984. *Qualitative Data Analysis: A Sourcebook of New Methods.* Beverly Hills, CA: Sage.

Morgan, K. 1991. Women and the knife: Cosmetic surgery and the colonization of women's bodies. *Hypatia* 6(3):25–33.

Mulvey, L. 1989. *Visual Pleasures and Narrative Cinema*. Bloomington: Indianapolis University Press.

Padmore, C. 1998. Significant flesh: Cosmetic surgery, physiognomy, and the erasure of visual difference(s). *Lateral: A Journal of Textual and Cultural Studies*. Retrieved from http://www.latrobe.edu.au/www/english/lateral/simple_cp1.htm:1–22

Pratt, M. 1992. *Imperial Eyes: Travel Writing and Transculturation*. New York: Routledge.

Ransom, J. 1997. *Foucault's Discipline: The Politics of Subjectivity*. Durham, NC: Duke University Press.

Saco, D. 1994. Feminist film criticism: "The piano" and the female gaze. Retrieved from http://www.gate.net/'dsaco/Female_Gaze.htm

Sawicki, J. 1991. *Disciplining Foucault: Feminism, Power, and the Body*. New York: Routledge.

Strauss, A., and J. Corbin. 1994. Grounded theory methodology: An overview. In *Handbook of Qualitative Research*, edited by N. Denzin and Y. Lincoln. Thousand Oaks, CA: Sage.

Weiss, G. 1999. *Body Images: Embodiment as Intercorporeality*. New York: Routledge.

Wijsbek, H. 2000. The pursuit of beauty: The enforcement of aesthetics or a freely adopted lifestyle? *Journal of Medical Ethics* 26(6): 454–58.

Winkler, M. 1994. Model women. In *The Good Body: Ascentism in Contemporary Culture*, edited by M. Winkler and L. Cole. New Haven, CT: Yale University Press.

Wolf, N. 1991. *The Beauty Myth: How Images of Beauty Are Used Against Women*. New York: Anchor Books Doubleday.

14

Women and Their Hair

Seeking Power Through Resistance and Accommodation

ROSE WEITZ

Like the preceding two articles, this article addresses the interplay between constraint and agency in women's decisions about and experiences with their bodies. As with breasts, hair plays an especially important role in contemporary Americans' assessments of women's attractiveness. In this article, Rose Weitz shows how women can consciously seek power (exercising agency) by conforming to social norms regarding women's hair (an example of constraint). For example, women who work as waitresses will often dye their hair blonde to get bigger tips. Conversely, Weitz shows how women can also seek power by resisting those same norms, as, for example, when women trial lawyers cut their hair shorter to be taken more seriously by jurors.

Weitz uses her research not only to explore women's relationship to their hair but also to explore larger issues of resistance and accommodation. Building on the work of previous scholars (including Janet Lee, in this volume), Weitz offers a more explicit (and stringent) definition of resistance. She also explores how resistance and accommodation are interwoven in women's everyday bodily experiences. Finally, she analyzes the price women pay for conforming as well as resisting, the different kinds of power women gain through these two different strategies, and the limits embedded in the types of power these strategies offer.

Hairstyles serve as important cultural artifacts, because they are simultaneously public (visible to everyone), personal (biologically linked to the body), and highly malleable to suit cultural and personal preferences (Firth 1973; Synott 1987). In this article, I argue that women's hair is central to their

Originally published as Rose Weitz, "Women and Their Hair: Seeking Power Through Resistance and Accommodation," *Gender & Society* 15(5): 667–686. Copyright 2001 by Sage Publications. Reprinted by permission of Sage Publications.

social position.[1] I explore how women use their hair to try to gain some power and analyze the benefits and limitations of their strategies. More broadly, I use these data to explore how accommodation and resistance lie buried in everyday activities, how they are often interwoven, and why resistance strategies based on the body have limited utility (Dellinger and Williams 1997; Elowe MacLeod 1991). Finally, I use these data to suggest the importance of defining resistance as actions that reject subordination by challenging the ideologies that support subordination.

Introduction

Power refers to the ability to obtain desired goals through controlling or influencing others.... The body is [an important] site for struggles over power.... As Michel Foucault (1979, 1980) describes, to carry out the tasks of modern economic and social life, societies require "docile bodies," such as regimented soldiers, factory workers who perform their tasks mechanically, and students who sit quietly. To create such bodies, "disciplinary practices" have evolved through which individuals both internalize and act on the ideologies that underlie their own subordination. In turn, these disciplinary practices have made the body a site for power struggles and, potentially, for resistance, as individual choices about the body become laden with political meanings.... [In this article, I] study hair as a means of exploring the ordinary ways in which women struggle daily with cultural ideas about the female body.... By describing the strategies women develop to seek power using their hair, I will show that women are neither "docile bodies" nor free agents, but rather combine accommodation and resistance as they actively grapple with cultural expectations and social structures....

Defining Resistance and Accommodation

To date, the term *resistance* remains loosely defined, allowing some scholars to see it almost everywhere and others, almost nowhere. One way that the latter group limits their vision of resistance is by defining actions as resistance only if they are effective. Such a definition seems far too narrow, however, for even failed revolutions would not qualify. Moreover, as Stombler and Padavic (1997) suggest, even small acts with no obvious effects on the broader system may affect individuals and pave the way for later social change....

Another possibility is to define an action as resistance if its intent is to reject subordination, regardless of either its effectiveness or the extent to which it also supports subordination (Stombler and Padavic 1997).... Yet individuals' stated intentions often bear little relationship to the nature of their actions, because individuals often either cannot or will not articulate their motives; Black slaves, for example, routinely denied (for obvious reasons) that their spirituals asking God for freedom reflected anything other than religious longings.... At any rate, intent alone seems a weak measure of resistance: By this measure, for example, women who wear "sexy" clothing to gain power in relationships with men are engaging in resistance against male domination, even though their actions reinforce sexist ideologies and foment competition between women.

The problems with using either effectiveness or intent as definitions of resistance leave us no choice but to try to assess the nature of the act itself. Scott (1990) suggests defining resistance simply as actions that "reject subordination" (with subordination defined as any ideas, practices, and systems that devalue one social group relative to another and place the first group under the domination of the second). For example, low-paid workers who pilfer goods from their factories to sell on the black market fit this definition of resistance because they reject a system that considers their work worthy of only minimal financial compensation and that denies them control over the products of their labor.

When factory workers pilfer, however, their actions and motives remain largely invisible both to their fellow workers and to factory management. As a result, while pilfering benefits individual workers, it neither challenges the ideological basis of the system of subordination nor offers the potential to unite workers as a group in a movement for social change. Moreover, because factory owners recognize that pilfering goes on, interpret it as an indication of workers' low moral values, and use it as an argument for keeping wages low (to counterbalance financial losses caused by employee theft), pilfering unintentionally bolsters the system that keeps workers undervalued and underpaid.

This example suggests the dangers of defining resistance too broadly. In this article, I use examples from women's hair management strategies to suggest that we need to more narrowly define resistance as actions that not only reject subordination but do so *by challenging the ideologies that support that subordination*. For example, factory workers' collective efforts to raise wages through union activity challenge the ideological basis of class subordination by arguing that factory workers have as much right as factory managers and owners to a decent wage. Similarly, and as I will show, some women consciously adopt hairstyles (such as short "butch" cuts or dreadlocks) in part to challenge the ideology that women's worth depends on their attractiveness to men and that women's attractiveness depends on looking as Euro-American as possible. Like slaves' rebellious songs, women's rebellious hairstyles can allow them to distance themselves from the system that would subordinate them, to express their dissatisfaction, to identify like-minded others, and to challenge others to think about their own actions and beliefs. Thus these everyday, apparently trivial, individual acts of resistance offer the potential to spark social change and, in the long run, to shift the balance of power between social groups.... By extension, *accommodation* refers to actions that accept subordination, by either adopting or simply not challenging the ideologies that support subordination. . . .

Methods

This paper is based on interviews collected between 1998 and 2001 with 44 women, all but five of whom live in Arizona. Respondents were obtained primarily through word of mouth. To avoid biasing the sample toward women who were unusually invested in their hair, I asked for referrals to women who "like to talk in general and are willing to talk about their hair." In addition, in three cases, I obtained respondents by approaching women in public places who had specific, unusual characteristics: a store clerk whose hair had the same simple style but a different color each time I saw her, a middle aged woman with a wild mass of shoulder-length graying curls, and a woman with an American accent wearing full Moslem garb including face veil. Because the sample is nonrandom, it is appropriate for exploring the range of attitudes among American women but not for calculating the proportion who hold such attitudes.

Although nonrandom, the sample is highly diverse. Respondents ranged in age from 22 to 83. Twenty-nine were Anglo, eight Mexican-American, four African-American, two Asian, and one half-Chicana and half-Anglo. Twenty-two were raised Protestant, 17 Catholic, one Jewish, and one Moslem; the remaining three were not raised in a religion. Twenty-one of the women are single, 14 are married, 7 are divorced, and 2 are widowed. Four of the 37 describe themselves as lesbian, the rest as heterosexual. As is true nationally (U.S. Department of Commerce 1998), the employed women in the sample are almost equally divided between those who hold professional/managerial jobs (n = 10) and those who do not (n = 11). Five women are retired, four are housewives, and fourteen are students (almost all of whom work part-time). The women in the sample disproportionately are middle class: 46 percent of those over age 25 hold college degrees, compared to 21 percent of similar-age U.S. women (Costello et al. 1998). However, 57 percent of the women come from working-class backgrounds (i.e., their mothers did not attend college and their fathers held nonprofessional jobs). . . .

Findings

In this section, I will describe the ways women use their hair to seek power in both their personal and professional lives. Analysis of the data revealed two strategies women used to accomplish this task: traditional strategies that emphasize accommodation to mainstream norms for female attractiveness and nontraditional strategies that emphasize resistance to those norms. I begin this discussion with traditional strategies (since they create the context that gives meaning to nontraditional strategies), and end the section with a brief discussion of why some women do not link their hair to power.

Seeking Power Through Traditional Strategies

The most common way women use their hair to seek power is through strategies that de-emphasize resistance and instead emphasize accommodation to mainstream ideas about attractiveness.... For purposes of convenience, I will refer to those who meet these norms as "conventionally attractive."

There is widespread agreement that conventionally attractive hair gives women power, or at least makes them feel powerful—a point made by many women in this study.[2] ... Results from numerous research studies (summarized in Jackson 1992 and Sullivan 2001) suggest that conventional attractiveness is in fact a realistic route to power for women, in both intimate relationships and careers. Attractive women are less lonely, more popular, and more sexually experienced, both more likely to marry and more likely to marry men of higher socioeconomic status. Compared to similarly qualified unattractive women, conventionally attractive women are more often hired, more often promoted, and paid higher salaries.

The following story, told by Cecilia, a twenty-something student, demonstrates the conscious and rational decision-making process women may use to get power through conventional attractiveness:

> I can think of an occasion where I changed my hair while I was dating this guy. I had this feeling that he was losing attraction for me and I'd just been feeling the need to do something to my appearance. And my hair is always the easiest way to go. It's too expensive to buy a new wardrobe. There's nothing you can do about your face. So your hair, you can go and have something radically done to it and you'll look like a different person. At least that's the way I see it.
>
> So I remember I was dating this guy, and I was away at school when I was dating him, and I went home for the weekend, and he was going to come down that weekend.... So I went home and I got my hair cut off. I cut off about seven or eight inches, and it was kind of a radical haircut, you know shaved, kind of asymmetrical again, and I put a red tint on it.... And when he saw me, when he walked into my house, it was like, "Whoa!" You know? And he said, "Oh, my God, look at it!" And he just couldn't stop talking about it. He made a comment saying that he felt differently about me. He said, "I don't know, there's just something about you. I don't know. I really want to be with you." (Cecilia)

When I asked Cecilia how she felt about his rekindled interest in her, she replied: "I was pretty pleased with myself."

Although this may seem like a limited form of power compared to, say, winning election to a government office, this power embedded in doing femininity well (Bordo 1989) is power nonetheless: With a minimum investment of money and time, this woman obtained a desired goal and influenced the behavior and emotions of another person.

Once a woman adopts this strategy, she can use her understanding of cultural ideologies surrounding women's hair to increase its effectiveness. Certainly women who dye their hair blonde are well aware of American cultural ideas that link blondeness to sexuality and beauty. For example, Roxanne, a divorced woman in her 40s with dyed blonde hair vowed she would "dye until she dies." When asked why, she responded singing the 1960s advertising ditty "Is it true blondes have more fun?" Other respondents similarly mentioned that they dye their hair blonde because they believe men find blondes more attractive. (Interestingly, none mentioned any concerns that, as blondes, they might be subject to the common stereotype of blondes as unintelligent [Kyle and Mahler 1996].) I did not ask why these women were unconcerned, but would hypothesize that they believed that these stereotypes were not widely held, that their intelligence would be obvious regardless of their hair color, or that looking attractive would benefit them more than would looking intelligent.)

Even women who are uninterested in male attention may find that meeting norms for conventional attractiveness works to their benefit: For example, Erica, a young lesbian, explained that her long hair allows her to pass as heterosexual and thus has helped her get and keep jobs (in the same way that using makeup benefited the lesbians interviewed by Dellinger and Williams [1997]). Similarly, and regardless of sexual orientation, female athletes often wear their hair long, curled, and dyed blonde as part of a "feminine apologetic" that enhances their attractiveness to men and protects them from being stigmatized as lesbian (Hilliard 1984; Lowe 1998).

Dyeing hair red can be an equally effective, if somewhat different, strategy, drawing on traditional stereotypes of redheads as wild and passionate. This was explained to me by Brenda, a quiet, petite young woman who began dyeing her hair red in her early twenties:

> I thought the red hair will let people know I'm a competent person, independent, maybe a little hotheaded—or maybe a lot hotheaded. So it was just conveying, fiery always comes to mind, although that's kind of romance novelish. (Brenda)

When asked if dyeing her hair succeeded in making people see her differently, Brenda replied:

> Yeah. Actually it *made* people see me.... Before I dyed my hair, my sister [who has blonde hair] and I, we would go out and all these guys would ask her to dance and talk to her and ask for her number and I would just be standing there. And after I started dyeing my hair, I started getting noticed a little bit more, but I also stopped waiting to be asked.... And around the

time I started dyeing my hair I decided I was going to quit being what I thought other people wanted me to be, and I was going to just be who I was. And it gave me power because, I don't know, I guess just being myself made me feel more powerful. (Brenda)

Brenda, then, used traditional ideas about women, hair, and attractiveness to change not only how others saw her but also how she saw herself. This in turn opened up possibilities for action and affected the responses she received from others, giving her greater control over her life. Again, like the women who dyed their hair blonde, none of those who dyed their hair red expressed concern that they might be handicapped by stereotypes of redheads as over-sexed, easily angered, or clownish (Clayson and Maughan 1986; Heckert and Best 1997; Kyle and Mahler 1996.)

In sum, the women described in this section are neither blindly seeking male approval nor unconsciously making decisions based on an internalized ideology of femininity. Instead, like women who use cosmetic surgery (Davis 1995) or makeup (Dellinger and Williams 1997), they are actively and rationally making choices based on a realistic assessment of how they can best obtain their goals, given both their personal resources and the cultural and social constraints they face. Yet can these strategies be considered resistance? On the one hand, each of these strategies is an intentional course of action designed to resist subordination by helping members of a subordinate group increase their power—or at least sense of power—relative to the dominant group. On the other hand, most of these strategies pose little if any challenge to cultural ideas about women or to the broader distribution of power by gender, for they implicitly support the ideology that defines a woman's body as her most important attribute and that therefore conflates changes in a woman's appearance with changes to her identity. Because these strategies do not challenge the cultural ideologies supporting subordination, at best they can improve the position of an individual woman, but not of women as a group. If anything, these strategies both reflect and sustain competition between women for men's attention, thus diminishing the potential for alliances among women.

The only traditional strategy that challenged cultural ideas about women was that described by Brenda, the woman who dyed her hair red. Although that strategy supported the ideology that appearance defines a woman, it rejected the assumption that Brenda herself either was or should be meek, submissive, or the passive object of a man's desires. Thus only this strategy fits the definition of resistance proposed earlier. At the same time, however, this strategy does nothing to improve the situation of other women. Rather, by using her hair color to denote her personality and views, Brenda implies that women with other hair colors lack her independence. As a result, she simultaneously resists and accommodates, resembling those Arlene Elowe MacLeod (1991) describes as "accommodating protest" because they simultaneously express dissatisfaction with and acquiescence to current power relations.

The Limits of Power Obtained Through Traditional Strategies

Not surprisingly, given the accommodations embedded in traditional strategies, women often find that power obtained through these strategies is circumscribed, fragile, bittersweet, and limiting. The power to attract a man, after all, is not the same as the power to earn a living independently—although a man can provide economic support, at least for a while. Similarly, women who attract men and increase their power through appearance can at best experience only a modest sense of accomplishment, since they receive attention only for physical characteristics at least partly outside their control. Moreover, women may find that attracting men through appearance is a hollow achievement if the men they attract have little interest in them as persons and, consequently, lose interest in the relationship over the long run.

Power based on conventional attractiveness is also fragile, achieved one day at a time through concentrated effort and expenditures of time and money. Linda, a 40 year old Asian-American woman, pays to have her hair permed every few months because she thinks otherwise it looks "too Asian." Because her hair straightens out when it gets wet, she always carries an umbrella, never swims with friends, and dries her hair after showering before letting anyone see her. Her concern proved justified the one time a lover (of four years) saw her with wet straight hair, and told her never to wear her hair straight.

Even those who look attractive on most days still face the occasional "bad hair day"—a true catastrophe for those who consider their hair a significant source of power. Felicia, a Chicana in her twenties, remarked, "If I'm having a bad hair day, I'm having a bad day in general.... My day is just shot." Moreover, conventional attractiveness must decline with age (although it can be fought with face lifts, hair dyeing, and the like.)

This power is bittersweet, too, for it is only partly under the individual's control: A woman who seeks attention and power through her appearance cannot control who will respond, when, or how. As explained to me by LaDonna, a young African-American woman whose long and wavy hair attracts considerable male attention: "It's kind of funny because I know [my hair] will get me attention, and I do things to make it look nice that I know will get me attention, but sometimes I don't wear my hair down because I *don't* want the attention." Nor can she control which men will be attracted to her (will it be her handsome neighbor or her married boss?) or for what reasons (will he think she is pretty because he simply likes long hair or because he thinks anything that looks "white" is superior?).

Transforming oneself into someone considered conventionally attractive is also bittersweet if it requires a woman to abandon what she considers her true self, which by definition is alienating. The bittersweet nature of this process comes through clearly in Cecilia's story:

> [My friends] would talk about my hair because there wasn't much else they could do with me. I wore glasses, and I had braces, [and] there wasn't much else you could do about that. But they were trying to turn me into a sexy thing, like, you know, they aspired to be. And you want to make all your friends [sexy] like that because you want to go out together to the skating rink or to the mall. I was willing to go along with it, so I let them fix me up. (Cecilia)

When asked if she liked the process, she replied:

> Not especially. Because I felt like I was being transformed into something I just wasn't. [But I still did it] because I felt that perhaps there was a need to be transformed, because obviously what I was was not getting me where I wanted to be. I had no boyfriend, and I didn't have that many friends. I wanted to be who I was and have what I wanted. But I didn't feel I could have what I wanted unless I changed. (Cecilia)

Finally, power obtained through traditional strategies is not only circumscribed, fragile, and bittersweet, but also limiting, since increasing one's power in these ways may *reduce* one's power in traditionally male realms. Most basically, the same hairstyles that identify a woman as conventionally attractive and increase her power in intimate relationships highlight femininity. Yet our culture links femininity with incompetence (Valian 1998; Wiley and Crittenden 1992). Thus, although men can only benefit from attractiveness, women can also be harmed by attractiveness if it leads others to regard them as less competent. For example, Laura, now in her thirties, described how from a very young age she hated it when her mother would curl her hair or put barrettes or bows in it because she realized that, in her

> very male-dominated family, if I looked like a girl, I lost power. . . . I recall feeling that I had a different experience as a person depending on how I was dressed. . . . It was hard to be perceived, I felt, as competent [if I looked girlish]. . . . If you wanted to have power, you needed to be like a boy, because when you acted like a girl, you didn't get—, well, I didn't get what I wanted, I'll say that. (Laura)

Seeking Power Through Nontraditional Strategies

The problems inherent in traditional strategies lead some women, either additionally or instead, to seek power through nontraditional strategies in which elements of resistance to mainstream ideas of attractiveness outweigh any elements of accommodation.

The meanings and implications of the strategies described in this section vary considerably depending on women's ethnicity. Reflecting the broader tendency for individuals to change hairstyles as a way of marking status transitions (McAlexander and Schouten 1989), white women often choose new hairstyles that highlight professionalism and downplay femininity as a first step toward entering professional training or work. For example, Tina, a young graduate student described how, after college, she cut her hair as

> sort of like the completion of transition to adulthood.... I felt like I needed to make some sort of definitive statement about if I was going to get through life... this was the way I was going to do it.... I'm not going to get through life by being girly. I don't want to live that way... relying on the attention, specifically of men, but also relying on people's responses to your appearance. And, particularly, [on] an appearance that is feminine by stereotypical social convention. (Tina)

She now has a short, spiky haircut which, she said, "makes me feel more powerful because it's like I've beat the system, you know?... The system's trying to take [my power] away and I've succeeded in not letting them."

Somewhat similarly, Darla, who had married at age 15 and had four children in quick succession, talked about the first time she cut her hair short, when she was in her 30s:

> That change in my hairstyle was indicative of that resolve [to change] from... sort of dependent and actually thinking there was no way out of that. And... I did not know how I was going to do it, [to change] from someone who had been raising children all her life, and still had a little girl [at home], someone who really felt kind of trapped, and used physical attractiveness as a sense of security, to a person who was going to become different.... And I think the hair was a symbol of that. I never did let my hair grow long again. (Darla)

Once in the world of work, other haircuts often follow, as white women learn to believe—or learn that others believe—that femininity and professional competence are antithetical. In such situations, women may consciously use their hair to defeminize themselves. Stacy, a bi-cultural (Anglo/Chicana) graduate assistant who typically pulls her long hair back into a ponytail when she teaches explained:

> If you have really long hair people tend to see you as more womanly.... Particularly when I teach, I don't want people to look at me as more womanly. That's why I wear my hair back: to be taken more seriously, to look more professional, to just be seen as a person as opposed to like a woman. (Stacy)

Even more than my white respondents, the college-educated Chicanas I interviewed underscored the necessity of "professional" haircuts for success in the work world. Coming from communities that valued long hair styled into large curls and heavily sprayed to meet distinctively Chicana images of femininity, they realized that, as Paloma explained, "Having lots of long hair intensifies the fact that you are a woman and that you are Chicana too, [both of which] make it more difficult to get jobs." As a result, she adopted a shorter hairstyle to meet mainstream ideas of professionalism. Others found themselves unable to take what seemed to them a drastic step, although some of these did take the intermediate step of binding their hair back or eliminating large curls while still leaving their hair long.

African-American women, on the other hand, are far less likely to adopt any strategy that might downplay their femininity. Faced with a dominant culture that already defines them as less attractive and feminine than other women (Hill Collins 1991, 67–90; Weitz and Gordon 1993), they are more likely to seek out a style that looks "professional" but still meets mainstream norms of femininity. They thus typically rely on wigs or on expensive formulations for changing the natural texture of their hair, and avoid both hairstyles that others might associate with radical political stances (such as dreadlocks or Afros) and the elaborate hairstyles often favored by working class African-American women (Fernandez Kelly 1995).

In addition to emphasizing professionalism, women can attempt to increase their power in nontraditional ways by avoiding or rejecting male attention. For example, Wendy, a traditionally pretty white woman described how she had worn her hair long, straight, and dyed blonde throughout high school but cut it drastically short in college when she came out as a lesbian. In her words, "Definitely, my hair cut was a way of protecting myself. It was shielding me, I felt, from men looking at me, from men being interested in me. It made me feel stronger to not be viewed in a traditional feminine way."

Most dramatically, Susan, a conventionally attractive, outgoing, young Anglo-American woman who had married an Arab immigrant and converted to Islam described how she began covering her hair in traditional Arabic fashion while visiting her husband's relatives in the Mideast. Even though her husband regarded hair-coverings as ugly and "backward" and none of his relatives wore them, Susan nevertheless chose to cover her hair to convince others that she was a chaste Moslem (cf. Elowe MacLeod 1991) and thus to protect herself from dangerous sexual harassment when her husband was absent. In this way, she both limited others' power over her (they no longer felt free to harass or touch her) and added to her own power by convincing others to take her more seriously. Against her husband's strenuously expressed wishes, Susan continued wearing the head-covering after returning from the Middle East not only as protection against unwanted male attention but also because it made her "feel empowered" by reminding her of her religion and the presence of God. Tellingly, she noted that in the United States, women "use their body and their beauty as their power. Now my power comes from within and I don't have to use my body."

Other women remain interested in attracting men, but not based on the traditional norms of submissive femininity that underlie mainstream attractiveness norms. Stacy provided a dramatic example:

My boyfriend...used to say that...what made me attractive was my hair was so pretty. So I deliberately kind of cut it off, a little bit spitefully, but kind of just to say I'm more than my hair. I felt powerful when I cut my hair off. Like maybe in the sense that I feel that [men] prefer long hair, that I wasn't ruled by that and I could like set my own standards. And sort of like, it's being in control of your hair gives you somewhat of a power. (Stacy)

Still other women find a sense of power not through rejecting attractiveness *per se* but through broadening the definition of attractiveness to include appearances that occur more naturally within their own ethnic group (Banks 1997; Craig 1995). These new definitions explicitly challenge the ideology that defines minority women's appearances as inferior and that encourages minority women to engage in time-consuming and painful disciplines to conform to dominant appearance norms. Thus three of the four African-American women I interviewed described their past decisions to wear an Afro, braids, or dreadlocks as explicitly political statements about their identities. (The fourth woman, LaDonna, came of age after the Afro went out of the style and had relatively straight hair naturally.) Jenny, an African-American professional, who now wears dreadlocks, explained that her hairstyle

expresses my individuality as well as my value of my heritage and my pride in what is distinctly me, distinctly mine.... I consider myself in a constant state of protest about the realities of cultural alienation, cultural marginalization, cultural invisibility, discrimination, injustice, all of that. And I feel that my hairstyle has always allowed me, since I started wearing it in a natural, to voice that nonverbally. And that has been a desire of mine, to do that. (Jenny)

In sum, like the traditional strategies described previously, the strategies described in this section are intentional actions designed to resist subordination and increase the power of members of a subordinate group. Unlike most of the traditional strategies, however, each of these strategies challenges the ideology that underlies subordination, even though only some of the women frame their actions in ideological terms. Thus all these strategies contain elements of resistance.

At the same time, however, these strategies contain elements of accommodation. Because it is difficult to analyze everyday actions taken for granted within one's own culture, most Americans can probably most easily identify the elements of accommodation embedded in the actions of the Muslim convert, who had to cover herself in a physically constraining, hot, and uncomfortable garment to ward off unwanted male attention and convince others to take her seriously. Although more difficult for most Americans to recognize, there are also elements of accommodation embedded in the other strategies described in this section. Most importantly, using the body as a political tool continues to place women's bodies at the center of women's identities. Moreover, like the woman who dyed her hair red, the women who cut their hair short to declare their competence or independence imply by extension that women who do not do so lack those qualities. Thus only those strategies that promote a hairstyle as a group aesthetic or political statement (such as Afros and hairstyles that are meant to be recognized as "dyke" haircuts) have at least the potential to unite rather than divide women and to help women as a group rather than simply helping some individuals.

The Limits of Obtaining Power Through Nontraditional Strategies

Given these problems, it is not surprising that, like traditional strategies, non-traditional strategies also offer only limited effectiveness. Whereas those who emphasize conventional attractiveness and femininity risk unwanted male sexual attention, those who defeminize their appearance and/or adopt more professional hairstyles risk desexualization (Bartky 1988) and the loss of desired male attention. After all, just because a woman wants a professional job doesn't mean she doesn't want a boyfriend or husband. Although some women enjoy no longer being seen by men in sexual terms, others find this a steep price to pay. This issue seemed especially salient for Chicanas: The eight Chicanas I interviewed all believed they had to have long, waved hair both to attract Chicano men and to maintain their identity as Chicanas, but the six who had attended college also believed they needed shorter, more sub-dued hair to succeed as professionals. None had fully resolved this dilemma. (Although these numbers are small, this sentiment was shared by numerous other college-educated Chicanas who have commented on versions of this article.)

Moreover, if a woman adopts a look that others consider not only less feminine but frankly unattractive, she may find that professional success also eludes her, for, as described earlier, conventionally attractive women receive more job offers, higher salaries, and more promotions than unattractive women. And regardless of a woman's sexual orientation, she risks discrimination if her hairstyle leads others to label her a lesbian—experiences shared by several short-haired respondents.

The stories told by African-American women, meanwhile, emphasize the very real consequences paid by those who reject mainstream ideas about attractiveness—even if they still strive to look attractive by their own definitions (Banks 1997). As Norma described:

> I remember I went to interview for a job and the guy wouldn't hire me because I had an Afro. A white guy. He said, "It's your hair. I don't like your hair style. You've got to do something about your hair." I didn't change my hair style of course, I just walked out. I figured I didn't need that job that much. (Norma)

She went on to explain:

> I think that both white and Black employers, especially men, expect African-American women to have straight hairstyles as opposed to their own natural hairstyles. That one guy rejected me right off the bat. But I see people treated differently depending on their hair style. Especially women who wear dreads, I see they have to fight for respect, demand it. It's almost a constant struggle. As opposed to women who wear their hair straight [and] are perceived to be more intelligent and professional. (Norma)

These comments were seconded by the other African-American women I interviewed. Similar remarks were made by a woman with wildly curling "Jewish" hair and by an immigrant who viewed long braided hair as a valued sign of her Pakistani identity but incompatible with American professional norms. For all these women, any aspect of their appearance that called attention to their minority status reduced their perceived competence and their social acceptability in the workplace. . . .

Conclusions

Findings from this study suggest that, far from being "docile bodies," women are often acutely aware of cultural expectations regarding their hair. Yet rather than simply acquiescing to those expectations, women can consciously seek power by accommodating to those expectations, resisting them, or combining these two strategies. Nevertheless, we must not overstate women's agency in this matter, for their options are significantly constrained by both cultural expectations and social structure. Consequently, the hair management strategies women adopt to increase their power in some realms often decrease it in others. As a result, women do not so much choose between the available strategies as balance and alternate them, using whichever seems most useful at a given time.

The inherent limitations on the power available to women through their hairstyles raise the question of why women continue to seek power in this way (or, more generally, through their appearance). As we have seen, women consciously use culturally-mandated appearance norms to achieve their personal ends. To say that women consciously use these norms, however, does not mean that they are free to ignore them. No matter what a woman does or doesn't do with her hair—dyeing or not dyeing, curling or not curling, covering with a bandana or leaving uncovered—her hair will affect how others respond to her, and her power will increase or decrease accordingly. Consequently, women use their hair to improve their position because they recognize that not doing so can imperil their position. Of course, the power and any other gains achieved through hair or other aspects of appearance are circumscribed, fragile, bittersweet, and limiting. Yet the power achieved in this way is no less real. Moreover, for many women, appearance remains a more accessible route to power than does career success, financial independence, political achievement, and so on.

The same constraints on women's options and agency that make seeking power through appearance a reasonable choice also explain why, although some of the strategies women use to gain power through their hair contain elements of resistance, *all* contain elements of accommodation (cf. Elowe MacLeod 1991). Compared to resistance, accommodation offers women (and any other subordinate group) a far more reliable and safer route to power, even if that power is limited. As a result, the strategies women typically use can help individual women gain power, or at least a sense of power, in some arenas, but do little to improve the situation of women as a group. Rather, these strategies unintentionally lend support to those who equate women's bodies with their identities, consider women's bodies more important than their minds, assume that women use their bodies to manipulate men, or assume that femininity and competence are antithetical (thus handicapping visibly "feminine" women professionally and visibly "professional" women socially). Moreover, all these strategies inescapably foment competition between women. Finally, even the most explicitly radical actions described in this article—the adoption of Afros, dreadlocks, or visibly "lesbian" haircuts—have only temporary utility as tools for social change because of the inherent instability of fashions. Such styles can certainly help to spread a new and radical idea, help members of an incipient social movement identify each other, and spark social change. In the long run, though, even if a style is initially intended to challenge existing power relationships, the more people adopt it, the more likely it will lose its original meaning and become simply another fashion (Craig 1995). As the style goes out of fashion—as all styles do—those who continue to wear it look merely dated and unfashionable, as their hairstyles lose their political meanings. Thus both Afros and the spiky, asymmetrical haircuts once found only on radical lesbians and punks are now merely styles that occasionally appear on fashion runways. (By extension, it is even less likely that the transgressive gender performances of lesbian femmes, male drag queens, and transgendered persons can lead to meaningful social change, as Butler [1990], Bornstein [1994] and others have claimed, for most observers undoubtedly view these actions as personal aberrations devoid of any political meaning.)

As this discussion suggests, it is difficult to identify factors that facilitate resistance because the possibilities for resistance are so constrained and because resistance and accommodation are so intertwined, both in any given action and in each individual's life. Certainly resistance is easier if supported by others, such as husbands or friends who place little emphasis on meeting appearance norms. Resistance to appearance norms is also easier when an alternative ideology exists that can provide a basis for challenging dominant ideologies, especially if that alternative ideology is supported by a broad social movement (as was the Afro during the late 1960s). Finally, resistance is most feasible when individuals can count on other sources of power and status unrelated to appearance (such as a career, education, or inherited wealth) and thus need not worry as much about any loss in power or status that might come from a non-normative appearance. Similarly, resistance against norms for women's hair may be easiest for those who are naturally tall, thin, and blonde and thus otherwise meet appearance norms.

In sum, this research helps us understand both the meaning of resistance and the pitfalls of defining the term over-broadly. It also sheds light on how resistance can be embedded in women's daily lives, and highlights the limitations of resistance strategies based on the body. Despite these limitations, however, these strategies are not useless. For example, whenever women abandon time-intensive, difficult to maintain hairstyles, they gain both time and physical freedom and thereby contribute to changing ideas about and opportunities for women, regardless of their intentions and of how their intentions are interpreted by others. Future research should pay close attention to the interwoven dangers and benefits, opportunities and limitations, of resistance centered on the body.

Notes

Acknowledgments: I would especially like to thank Myra Dinnerstein for her help and support throughout this project. Also thanks to Kathy Davis, Kirsten Dellinger, Dan Hilliard, Judith Lorber, PJ McGann, Cecilia Menjívar, Karen Miller-Loessi, Irene Padavic, Mindy Stombler, George Thomas, and Christine Williams for their comments on this research project. In addition, I would like to thank Jennifer Mata, Sophia Hinojosa, Dana Gray, and Jami Wilenchik for assistance in data collection. Finally, I would like to express my appreciation to Arizona State University for granting me a sabbatical leave to pursue this project and to the Western Alliance to Expand Minority Opportunities and the ASU Women's Studies Program, both of which provided needed research funding.

1. Hair and appearance also affect men's social position, but to a much lesser extent (Jackson 1992; Sullivan 2001). In addition, because the parameters for acceptable male appearance are both narrower (allowing less experimentation and less pressure to adapt to fashion) and broader (allowing much more natural variation), most men can obtain a socially acceptable haircut with little time, energy, or cost. The exceptions are, truly, exceptional: actors and models, gay men whose communities emphasize appearance, middle-aged middle managers whose companies are downsizing, the recently divorced, and so on.

2. I do not distinguish in this paper between actual power and a sense of power because all the data are based on women's perceptions, and the distinction between a woman feeling that she has power or feeling a sense of power is slight at best.

References

Banks, Ingrid. 1997. *Social and Personal Constructions of Hair: Cultural Practices and Belief Systems among African American Women.* Ph.D. diss., University of California, Berkeley.

Bartky, Sandra Lee. 1988. Foucault, femininity, and the modernization of patriarchal power. In *Feminism and Foucault: Reflections on Resistance*, edited by Irene Diamond and Lee Quinby. Boston: Northeastern University Press.

Bordo, Susan R. 1989. The body and the reproduction of femininity: A feminist appropriation of Foucault. In *Gender/Body/Knowledge*, edited by Alison M. Jaggar and Susan R. Bordo. New Brunswick, NJ: Rutgers University Press.

Bornstein, Kate. 1994. *Gender Outlaws: On Men, Women, and the Rest of Us*. New York: Routledge.

Butler, Judith. 1990. *Gender Trouble: Feminism and the Subversion of Identity*. New York: Routledge.

Clayson, Dennis E., and Micol R. C. Maughan. 1986. Redheads and blonds: Stereotypic images. *Psychological Reports* 59:811–16.

Costello, Cynthia B., Shari E. Miles, and Anne J. Stone. 1998. *The American Woman 1999–2000: A Century of Change—What's Next?* New York: Norton.

Craig, Maxine. 1995. *Black Is Beautiful: Personal Transformation and Political Change*. Ph.D. diss., University of California, Berkeley.

Davis, Kathy. 1991. Remaking the she-devil: A critical look at feminist approaches to beauty. *Hypatia* 6(2):21–42.

———. 1995. *Reshaping the Female Body: The Dilemma of Cosmetic Surgery*. New York: Routledge.

Dellinger, Kirsten, and Christine L. Williams. 1997. Makeup at work: Negotiating appearance rules in the workplace. *Gender & Society* 11:151–77.

Elowe MacLeod, Arlene. 1991. *Accommodating Protest: Working Women, the New Veiling, and Change in Cairo*. New York: Columbia University Press.

Fernandez Kelly, M. Patricia. 1995. Social and cultural capital in the urban ghetto. In *The Economic Sociology of Immigration: Essays on Networks, Ethnicity, and Entrepreneurship*, edited by Alejandro Portes. New York: Russell Sage.

Firth, Raymond. 1973. *Symbols: Public and Private*. Ithaca, NY: Cornell University Press.

Foucault, Michel. 1979. *Discipline and Punish: The Birth of the Prison*. New York: Vintage.

———. 1980. *History of Sexuality*. New York: Pantheon.

Heckert, Druann Maria, and Amy Best. 1997. Ugly duckling to swan: Labeling theory and the stigmatization of red hair. *Symbolic Interaction* 20:365–84.

Hill Collins, Patricia. 1991. *Black Feminist Thought: Knowledge, Consciousness, and the Politics of Empowerment*. London: Routledge.

Hilliard, Dan C. 1984. Media images of male and female professional athletes: An interpretive analysis of magazine articles. *Sociology of Sport Journal* 1:251–62.

Jackson, Linda. 1992. *Physical Appearance and Gender: Sociobiological and Sociocultural Perspectives*. Albany: State University of New York Press.

Kyle, Diana J., and Heike I.M. Mahler. 1996. The effects of hair color and cosmetic use on perceptions of a female's ability. *Psychology of Women Quarterly* 20:447–55.

Lowe, Maria R. 1998. *Women of Steel: Female Body Builders and the Struggle for Self-definition*. New Brunswick, NJ: Rutgers University Press.

McAlexander, James H., and John W. Schouten. 1989. Hair style changes as transition markers. *Sociology and Social Research* 74:58–62.

Scott, James C. 1990. *Domination and the Arts of Resistance: Hidden Transcripts*. New Haven, CT: Yale University Press.

Stombler, Mindy, and Irene Padavic. 1997. Sister acts: Resisting men's domination in black and white fraternity little sister programs. *Social Problems* 44:257–75.

Sullivan, Deborah A. 2001. *Cosmetic Surgery: The Cutting Edge of Commercial Medicine in America*. New Brunswick, NJ: Rutgers University Press.

Synott, Anthony. 1987. Shame and glory: A sociology of hair. *British Journal of Sociology* 38:381–413.

U.S. Department of Commerce. 1998. *Statistical Abstract of the United States 1997*. Washington, DC: U.S. Government Printing Office.

Valian, Virginia. 1998. *Why So Slow?: The Advancement of Women*. Cambridge, MA: MIT Press.

Weitz, Rose, and Leonard Gordon. 1993. Images of black women among Anglo college students. *Sex Roles* 28:19–45.

Wiley, Mary Glenn, and Kathleen S. Crittenden. 1992. By your attributions you shall be known: Consequences of attributional accounts for professional and gender identities. *Sex Roles* 27:259–76.

15

Branded with Infamy

Inscriptions of Poverty and Class in the United States

VIVYAN C. ADAIR

According to philosopher Michel Foucault, premodern societies convinced their members to obey the laws of state and church by branding, cutting, burning, or otherwise gruesomely and publicly marking the bodies of any who broke those laws. These marked bodies thus became "texts" that could be read as one would read a book. In contrast, Foucault argued, modern societies instead instill obedience through socializing their members to internalize society's rules and to discipline themselves, making harsh punishments unnecessary. Several articles in this volume, beginning with Sandra Bartky's, have similarly highlighted how contemporary society teaches women to internalize social norms regarding proper feminine appearance.

In this article, Vivyan Adair analyzes how poor women's lives and bodies are controlled through both modern and premodern strategies. The effects of poverty (and resultant lack of health care) physically mark the bodies of poor women and their children, in a very "premodern" way. Simultaneously, however, public portrayals of poor women, combined with assumptions about poor women embedded in public policy, socialize all of us to assume that poverty among women—especially if they are nonwhite—results from their own moral and physical failings. As a result, poor women may internalize a sense of shame and so accept their fate and discipline their bodies—a very "modern" type of social control. Meanwhile, those of us who are not poor may "read" poor women's bodies as markers of their failings. Nevertheless, Adair argues, poor women still find ways to engage in resistance.

Vivyan Adair. 2001. "Branded with Infamy," *Signs* 27: 451–481. Permission of University of Chicago Press.

My kids and I been chopped up and spit out just like when I
was a kid. My rotten teeth, my kids' twisted feet. My son's dull
skin and blank stare. My oldest girl's stooped posture and the
way she can't look no one in the eye no more. This all says we
got nothing and we deserve what we got. On the street good
families look at us and see right away what they'd be if they
don't follow the rules. They're scared too, real scared.

Welfare Recipient and Activist, Olympia, WA, 1998

I begin with the words of a poor, white, single mother of three. Although
officially she has only a tenth-grade education, she expertly reads and artic-
ulates a complex theory of power, bodily inscription, and socialization that
arose directly from the material conditions of her own life. She sees what
many far more "educated" scholars and citizens fail to recognize: that the
bodies of poor women and children are produced and positioned as texts
that facilitate the mandates of a didactic, profoundly brutal and mean-spirited
political regime. The clarity and power of this woman's vision challenges feminists to consider and critique our commitment both to textualizing displays
of heavy-handed social inscription and to detextualizing them, working to
put an end to these bodily experiences of pain, humiliation, and suffering. . . .

Over the past decade or so, a host of inspired feminist welfare scholars and activists has addressed and examined the relationship between state
power and the lives of poor women and children. As important and insightful
as these exposés are, with few exceptions, they do not get at the closed circuit
that fuses together systems of power, the material conditions of poverty, and
the bodily experiences that allow for the perpetuation—and indeed for the
justification—of these systems. They fail to consider what the speaker of my
opening passage recognized so astutely: that systems of power produce and
patrol poverty through the reproduction of both social and bodily markers.

What is inadequate, then, even in many feminist theories of class production, is an analysis of this nexus of the textual and the corporeal. Here
Michel Foucault's ([1977] 1984) argument about the inscriptions of bodies
is a powerful mechanism for understanding the material and physical conditions and bodily costs of poverty across racial difference and for interrogating
the connection between power's expression as text, as body, and as site of
resistance. . . . Particularly useful for feminists has been Foucault's theory that
the body is written on and through discourse as the product of historically
specific power relations. . . .

In *Discipline and Punish*, Foucault sets out to depict the genealogy of
torture and discipline as it reflects a public display of power on the body
of subjects in the seventeenth and eighteenth centuries. In graphic detail
Foucault begins his book with the description of a criminal being tortured
and then drawn and quartered in a public square. The crowds of good parents and their growing children watch and learn. The public spectacle works

as a patrolling image, socializing and controlling bodies within the body politic. Eighteenth-century torture "must mark the victim: it is intended, either by the scar it leaves on the body or by the spectacle that accompanies it, to brand the victim with infamy. It traces around or rather on the very body of the condemned man signs that can not be effaced" ([1977] 1984, 179). For Foucault, public exhibitions of punishment served as a socializing process, writing culture's codes and values on the minds and bodies of its subjects. In the process punishment discursively deconstructed and rearranged bodies.

But Foucault's point in *Discipline and Punish* is precisely that public exhibition and inscription have been replaced in contemporary society by a much more effective process of socialization and self-inscription. According to Foucault, today discipline has replaced torture as the privileged punishment, but the body continues to be written on. Discipline produces "subjected and practiced bodies, 'docile bodies'" (1984, 182). We become subjects not of the sovereign but of ideology, disciplining and inscribing our own bodies/minds in the process of becoming stable and singular subjects. Power's hold on bodies is in both cases maintained through language systems. The body continues to be the site and operation of ideology, as subject and representation, body and text.

Indeed, while we are all marked discursively by ideology in Foucault's paradigm, in the United States today poor women and children of all races are multiply marked with signs of both discipline and punishment that cannot be erased or effaced. They are systematically produced through both twentieth-century forces of socialization and discipline and eighteenth-century exhibitions of public mutilation. In addition to coming into being as disciplined and docile bodies, poor single welfare mothers and their children are physically inscribed, punished, and displayed as the dangerous and pathological other. It is important to note, when considering the contemporary inscription of poverty as moral pathology etched onto the bodies of profoundly poor women and children, that these are more than metaphoric and self-patrolling marks of discipline. Rather, on myriad levels—sexual, social, material, and physical—poor women and their children, like the "deviants" publicly punished in Foucault's scenes of torture, are marked, mutilated, and made to bear and transmit signs in a public spectacle that brands the victim with infamy.

Text of the Body, Body of the Text: The (Not So) Hidden Injuries of Class

Recycled images of poor, welfare women permeate and shape our national consciousness.[1] Yet—as is so often the case—these images and narratives tell us more about the culture that spawned and embraced them than they do about the object of the culture's obsession. Simple, stable, and often widely skewed cover stories tell us what is "wrong" with some people, what is normative, and what is pathological; by telling us who "bad" poor women are, we reaffirm and reevaluate who we, as a nation and as a people—of allegedly good, middle-class, white, able-bodied, independent, male citizens—are. At their foundations, stories of the welfare mother intersect with, draw from, reify, and reproduce myriad mythic American narratives associated with a constellation of beliefs about capitalism, male authority, the "nature" of humans, and the sphere of individual freedom, opportunity, and responsibility. These narratives purport to write the story of poor women in an arena in which only their bodies have been positioned to "speak." They promise to tell the story of who poor women are in ways that allow Americans to maintain a belief in both an economic system based on exploitation and an ideology that claims that we are all beyond exploitation.

These productions orchestrate the story of poverty as one of moral and intellectual lack and of chaos, pathology, promiscuity, illogic, and sloth, juxtaposed always against the order, progress, and decency of "deserving" citizens. Trying to stabilize and make sense of unpalatably complex issues of poverty and oppression and attempting to obscure hegemonic stakes in representation, these narratives reduce and collapse the lives and experiences of poor women to deceptively simplistic dramas, which are then offered for public consumption. The terms of these dramas are palatable because they are presented as simple oppositions of good and bad, right and wrong, independent and dependent, deserving and undeserving. Yet as a generationally poor woman I know that poverty is neither this simple nor this singular. Poverty is rather the product of complex systems of power that at many levels are indelibly written on poor women and children in feedback loops that compound and complicate politically expedient readings and writings of our bodies.

I am, and will probably always be, marked as a poor woman. I was raised by a poor, single, white mother who had to struggle to keep her four children fed, sheltered, and clothed by working at what seemed like an endless stream of minimum-wage, exhausting, and demeaning jobs. As a child poverty was written onto and into my being at the level of private and public thought and body. At an early age my body bore witness to and emitted signs of the painful devaluation carved into my flesh; that same devaluation became integral to my being in the world. I came into being as a disciplined body/mind while at the same time I was taught to read my abject body as the site of my own punishment and erasure. In this excess of meaning the space between private body and public sign was collapsed. . . .

Indeed, poor children are often marked with bodily signs that cannot be forgotten or erased. Their bodies are physically inscribed as "other" and then read as pathological, dangerous, and undeserving. What I recall most vividly about being a child in a profoundly poor family was that we were constantly hurt and ill, and, because we could not afford medical care, small illnesses and accidents spiraled into more dangerous illnesses and complications that became both a part of who we were and written proof that we were of no value in the world.

In spite of my mother's heroic efforts, at an early age my brothers and sister and I were stooped, bore scars that never healed properly, and limped with feet mangled by ill-fitting, used Salvation Army shoes. When my sister's forehead was split open by a door slammed in frustration, my mother "pasted" the angry wound together on her own, leaving a mark of our inability to afford medical attention, of our lack, on her very forehead. When I suffered from a concussion, my mother simply put borrowed ice on my head and tried to keep me awake for a night. And when throughout elementary school we were sent to the office for mandatory and very public yearly checkups, the school nurse sucked air through her teeth as she donned surgical gloves to check only the hair of poor children for lice.

We were read as unworthy, laughable, and often dangerous. Our schoolmates laughed at our "ugly shoes," our crooked and ill-serviced teeth, and the way we "stank," as teachers excoriated us for our inability to concentrate in school, our "refusal" to come to class prepared with proper school supplies, and our unethical behavior when we tried to take more than our allocated share of "free lunch." Whenever backpacks or library books came up missing, we were publicly interrogated and sent home to "think about" our offenses, often accompanied by notes that reminded my mother that as a poor single parent she should be working twice as hard to make up for the discipline that allegedly walked out the door with my father. When we sat glued to our seats, afraid to stand in front of the class in ragged and ill-fitting hand-me-downs, we were held up as examples of unprepared and uncooperative children. And when our grades reflected our otherness, they were used to justify even more elaborate punishment that exacerbated the effects of our growing anomie.

Friends who were poor as children, and respondents to a survey I conducted in 1998, tell similar stories of the branding they received at the hands of teachers, administrators, and peers. An African-American woman raised in Yesler Terrace, a public housing complex in Seattle, Washington, writes:

> Poor was all over our faces. My glasses were taped and too weak. My big brother had missing teeth. My mom was dull and ashy. It was like a story of how poor we were that anyone could see. My sister Evie's lip was bit by a dog and we just had dime store stuff to put on it. Her lip was a big scar. Then she never smiled and no one smiled at her cause she never smiled. Kids call[ed] her "Scarface." Teachers never smiled at her. The principal put her in detention all the time because she was mean and bad (they said).

And a white woman in the Utica, New York, area remembers:

> We lived in dilapidated and unsafe housing that had fleas no matter how clean my mom tried to be. We had bites all over us. Living in our car between evictions was even worse—then we didn't have a bathroom so I got kidney

problems that I never had doctor's help for. When my teachers wouldn't let me go to the bathroom every hour or so I would wet my pants in class. You can imagine what the kids did to me about that. And the teachers would refuse to let me go to the bathroom because they said I was willful.[2]

Material deprivation is publicly written on the bodies of poor children in the world. In the United States poor families experience violent crime, hunger, lack of medical and dental care, utility shut-offs, the effects of living in unsafe housing and/or of being homeless, chronic illness, and insufficient winter clothing (Edin and Lein 1997, 224–31). According to Jody Raphael of the Taylor Institute, poor women and their children are also at five times the risk of experiencing domestic violence (2000).

As children, our disheveled and broken bodies were produced and read as signs of our inferiority and undeservedness. As adults our mutilated bodies are read as signs of inner chaos, immaturity, and indecency as we are punished and then read as proof of the need for further discipline and punishment. When my already bad teeth started to rot and I was out of my head with pain, my choices as an adult welfare recipient were either to let my teeth fall out or to have them pulled out. In either case the culture would then read me as a "toothless illiterate," as a fearful joke. In order to pay my rent and to put shoes on my daughter's feet I sold blood at two or three different clinics on a monthly basis until I became so anemic that they refused to buy it from me. A neighbor of mine went back to the man who continued to beat her and her scarred children after being denied welfare benefits when she realized that she could not adequately feed, clothe, and house her family on her own minimum-wage income. My good friend sold her ovum to a fertility clinic in a painful and potentially damaging process. Other friends exposed themselves to all manner of danger and disease by selling their bodies for sex in order to feed and clothe their babies.

Poverty becomes a vicious cycle that is written on our bodies and intimately connected with our value in the world. Our children need healthy food so that we can continue working; yet working at minimum-wage jobs, we have no money for wholesome food and very little time to care for our families. So our children get sick, we lose our jobs to take care of them, we fall deeper and deeper into debt before our next unbearable job, and then we really cannot afford medical care. Starting that next minimum-wage job with unpaid bills and ill children puts us further and further behind so that we are even less able to afford good food, adequate child care, health care, or emotional healing. The food banks we gratefully drag our exhausted children to on the weekends hand out bags of rancid candy bars, hot dogs that have passed their expiration dates, stale broken pasta, and occasionally a bag of wrinkled apples. We are either fat or skinny, and we seem always irreparably ill. Our emaciated or bloated bodies are then read as a sign of lack of discipline and as proof that we have failed to care as we should.[3]

Exhaustion also marks the bodies of poor women in indelible script. Rest becomes a privilege we simply cannot afford. After working full shifts each day, poor mothers trying to support themselves at minimum-wage jobs continue to work to a point of exhaustion that is inscribed on their faces, their bodies, their posture, and their diminishing sense of self and value in the world. My former neighbor recently recalled:

> I had to take connecting buses to bring and pick up my daughters at child-care after working on my feet all day. As soon as we arrived at home, we would head out again by bus to do laundry. Pick up groceries. Try to get to the food bank. Beg the electric company to not turn off our lights and heat again. Find free winter clothing. Sell my blood. I would be home at nine or ten o'clock at night. I was loaded down with one baby asleep and one crying. Carrying lots of heavy bags and ready to drop on my feet. I had bags under my eyes and no shampoo to wash my hair so I used soap. Anyway I had to stay up to wash diapers in the sink. Otherwise they wouldn't be dry when I left the house in the dark with my girls. In the morning I start all over again.[4]

This bruised and lifeless body, hauling sniffling babies and bags of dirty laundry on the bus, was then read as a sign that she was a bad mother and a threat that needed to be disciplined and made to work even harder for her own good. Those who need the respite less go away for weekends, take drives in the woods, take their kids to the beach. Poor women without education are pushed into minimum-wage jobs and have no money, no car, no time, no energy, and little support, as their bodies are made to display marks of their material deprivation as a socializing and patrolling force.

Ultimately, we come to recognize that our bodies are not our own, that they are rather public property. State-mandated blood tests, interrogation of the most private aspects of our lives, the public humiliation of having to beg officials for food and medicine, and the loss of all right to privacy, teach us that our bodies are only useful as lessons, warnings, and signs of degradation that everyone loves to hate. In "From Welfare to Academe: Welfare Reform as College-Educated Welfare Mothers Know It," Sandy Smith-Madsen describes the erosion of her privacy as a poor welfare mother:

> I was investigated. I was spied upon. A welfare investigator c[a]me into my home and after thoughtful deliberation granted me permission to keep my belongings. Like the witch hunts of old, if a neighbor reports you as a welfare queen, the guardians of the state's compelling interest come into your home and interrogate you. While they do not have the right to set your body ablaze on the public square, they can forever devastate heart and soul by snatching away children. Just like a police officer, they may use whatever they happen to see against you, including sexual orientation. Full-fledged citizens have the right to deny an officer entry into their home unless they possess a search warrant; welfare mothers fork over citizenship rights for the

price of a welfare check. In Tennessee, constitutional rights go for a cash value of $185 per month for a family of three. (2003, 185)

Welfare reform policy is designed to publicly expose, humiliate, punish, and display "deviant" welfare mothers. "Workfare" and "Learnfare"—two alleged successes of welfare reform—require that landlords, teachers, and employers be made explicitly aware of the second-class status of these very public bodies. In Ohio, the Department of Human Services uses tax dollars to pay for advertisements on the side of Cleveland's RTA buses that show a "Welfare Queen" behind bars with a logo that proclaims "Crime does not pay. Welfare fraud is a crime" (Robinson 1999). In Michigan a pilot program mandating drug tests for all welfare recipients began on October 1, 1999. Recipients who refuse the test lose their benefits immediately (Simon 1999). In Buffalo, New York, a county executive proudly announced that his county would begin intensive investigation of all parents who refuse minimum-wage jobs that are offered to them by the state. He warned: "We have many ways of investigating and exposing these errant parents who choose to exploit their children in this way" (Anderson 1999). In Eugene, recipients who cannot afford to feed their children adequately on their food stamp allocations are advised through fliers issued by a contractor for Oregon's welfare agency to "check the dump and the residential and business dumpsters" in order to save money (Women's Enews, 2001b). In April 2001, Jason Turner, New York City's welfare commissioner, told a congressional subcommittee that "workplace safety and the Fair Labor Standards Act should not apply to welfare recipients who, in fact, should face tougher sanctions in order to make them work" (Women's Enews, 2001a). And welfare reform legislation enacted in 1996 as the Personal Responsibility and Work Opportunities Reconciliation Act (PRWORA) requires that poor mothers work full-time, earning minimum-wage salaries with which they cannot support their children. Since these women are often denied medical, dental, and child-care benefits and are unable to provide their families with adequate food, heat, or clothing, through this legislation the state mandates child neglect and abuse. The crowds of good parents and their growing children watch and learn.

Reading and Rewriting the Body of the Text

The bodies of poor women and children, scarred and mutilated by state-mandated material deprivation and public exhibition, work as spectacles, as patrolling images socializing and controlling bodies within the body politic....

Spectacular cover stories of the "Welfare Queen" play and replay in the national mind's eye, becoming a prescriptive lens through which the American public as a whole reads the individual dramas of the bodies of poor women and their place and value in the world. These dramas produce "normative" citizens as independent, stable, rational, ordered, and free. In this dichotomous, hierarchical frame the poor welfare mother is juxtaposed against a logic of "normative" subjectivity as the embodiment of dependency, disorder, disarray, and otherness. Her broken and scarred body becomes proof of her inner pathology and chaos, suggesting the need for further punishment and discipline.

In contemporary narratives welfare women are imagined to be dangerous because they refuse to sacrifice their desires and fail to participate in legally sanctioned heterosexual relationships; theirs is read, as a result, as a selfish, "unnatural," and immature sexuality. In this script, the bodies of poor women are viewed as being dangerously beyond the control of men and are as a result construed as the bearers of perverse desire.... They are understood and punished as a danger to a culture resting on a foundation of inviolate male authority and absolute privilege in both public and private spheres.

William Raspberry frames poor women as selfish and immature, when in "Ms. Smith Goes after Washington," he claims, "Unfortunately AFDC [Aid to Families with Dependent Children] is paid to an unaccountable, accidental and unprepared parent who has chosen her head of household status as a personal form of satisfaction, while lacking the simple life skills and maturity to achieve love and job fulfillment from any other source. I submit that all of our other social ills—crime, drugs, violence, failing schools are a direct result of the degradation of parenthood by emotionally immature recipients" (1995, A19). Raspberry goes on to assert that, like poor children, poor mothers must be made visible reminders to the rest of the culture of the "poor choices" they have made. He claims that rather than "coddling" her, we have a responsibility to "shame her" and to use her failure to teach other young women that it is "morally wrong for unmarried women to bear children," as we "cast single motherhood as a selfish and immature act" (1995, A19)....

Poor women and children's bodies, publicly scarred and mutilated by material deprivation, are read as expressions of an essential lack of discipline and order. In response to this perception, journalist Ronald Brownstein of the *Los Angeles Times* proposed that the "*Republican Contract with America*" will "*restore* America to its path, *enforcing* social *order* and common *standards* of behavior, and replacing *stagnation* and *decay* with *movement* and *forward* thinking *energy*" (1995, A1; emphasis added). In these rhetorical fields poverty is metonymically linked to a lack of progress that would allegedly otherwise order, stabilize, and restore the culture. What emerges from these diatribes is the positioning of patriarchal, racist, capitalist, hierarchical, and heterosexist "order" and movement against the alleged stagnation and decay of the body of the "Welfare Queen."

Race is clearly written on the body of the poor single mother. The welfare mother, imagined as young, never married, and black (contrary to statistical evidence) is positioned as dangerous and in need of punishment because she "naturally" emasculates her own men, refuses to service white men, and passes on—rather than appropriate codes of subservience and submission—a disruptive culture of resistance, survival, and "misplaced" pride to her children (Collins 2000).[5] In stark contrast, widowed women with social security and divorced women with child support and alimony are imagined as white, legal and propertied mothers whose value rests on their abilities to stay in their homes, care for their own children, and impart traditional cultural mores to their offspring, all for the betterment of the dominant culture. In this narrative welfare mothers have only an "outlaw" culture to impart. Here the welfare mother is read as both the product and the producer of a culture of disease and disorder. These narratives imagine poor women as a powerful contagion capable of infecting, perhaps even lying in wait to infect, their own children as raced, gendered, and classed agents of their "diseased" nature. In contemporary discourses of poverty, racial tropes position poor women's bodies as dangerous sites of "naturalized chaos" and as potentially valuable economic commodities who refuse their "proper" roles. . . .

These representations position welfare mothers' bodies as sites of destruction and as catalysts for a culture of depravity and disobedience; in the process they produce a reading of the writing on the body of the poor woman that calls for further punishment and discipline. In New York City, "Workfare" programs force *lazy* poor women to take a job—"any job"—including working for the city wearing orange surplus prison uniforms picking up garbage on the highway and in parks for about $1.10 per hour (Dreier 1999). "Bridefare" programs in Wisconsin give added benefits to *licentious* welfare women who marry a man—"any man"—and publish a celebration of their "reform" in local newspapers (Dresang 1996). "Tidyfare" programs across the nation allow state workers to enter and inspect the homes of poor *slovenly* women so that they can monetarily sanction families whose homes are not deemed to be appropriately tidied. "Learnfare" programs in many states publicly expose and fine *undisciplined* mothers who for any reason have children who do not (or cannot) attend school on a regular basis (Muir 1993). All of these welfare reform programs are designed to expose and publicly punish the *misfits* whose bodies are read as proof of their refusal or inability to capitulate to androcentric, capitalist, racist, and heterosexist values and mores.

Resisting the Text: On the Limits of Discursive Critique and the Power of Poor Women's Communal Resistance

Despite the rhetoric and policy that mark and mutilate our bodies, poor women survive. Hundreds of thousands of us are somehow good parents despite the systems that are designed to prohibit us from being so. We live on the unlivable and teach our children love, strength, and grace. We network, solve irresolvable dilemmas, and support each other and our families. If we somehow manage to find a decent pair of shoes, or save our food stamps to buy our children a birthday cake, we are accused of being cheats or living too high. If our children suffer, it is read as proof of our inferiority and bad mothering; if they succeed, we are suspect for being too pushy, for taking more than our share of free services, or for having too much free time to devote to them. Yet, as former welfare recipient Janet Diamond says in the introduction to *For Crying Out Loud*: "In spite of public censure, welfare mothers graduate from school, get decent jobs, watch their children achieve, make good lives for themselves. Welfare mothers continue to be my inspiration, not because they survive, but because they dare to dream. Because when you are a welfare recipient, laughter is an act of rebellion" (Dujon and Withorn 1996, 1).

Foucault's later work acknowledges this potential for rebellion inherent in the operation of power....As Lois McNay points out, [Foucault shows us how] "repression produces its own resistance: 'there are no relations of power without resistance; the latter are all the more real and effective because they are formed right at the point where relations of power are exercised' " (1993, 39)....

Yet here we also recognize what McNay refers to as the "critical limitations" of Foucault and of post-structuralism in general. For although bodily inscriptions of poverty are clearly textual, they are also quite physical, immediate, and pressing, devastating the lives of poor women and children in the United States today. Discursive critique is at its most powerful only when it allows us to understand and challenges us to fight together to change the material conditions and bodily humiliations that scar poor women and children in order to keep us all in check.

Poor women rebel by organizing for physical and emotional respite and eventually for political power. My own resistance was born in the space between self-loathing and my love of and respect for poor women who were fighting together against oppression. In the throes of political activism (at first I was dragged blindly into such actions, ironically, in a protest that required, according to the organizer, just so many poor women's bodies) I became caught up in the contradiction between my body's meaning as a despised public sign and our shared sense of communal power, knowledge, authority, and beauty. Learning about labor movements, fighting for rent control, demanding fair treatment at the welfare office, sharing the costs, burdens, and joys of raising children, forming food cooperatives, working with other poor women to go to college, and organizing for political change became addictive and life-affirming acts of resistance. Through shared activism we became increasingly aware of our individual bodies as sites of contestation and of our collective body as a site of resistance and as a source of power....

In struggling together we contest the marks of our bodily inscription, disrupt the use of our bodies as public sign, change the conditions of our lives, and survive. In the process we come to understand that the shaping of our bodies is not coterminous with our beings or abilities as a whole. Contestation and the deployment of new truths cannot erase the marks of our poverty, but the process does transform the ways in which we are able to interrogate and critique our bodies and the systems that have branded them with infamy. As a result these signs are rendered fragile, unstable, and ultimately malleable.

Notes

This essay is dedicated to poor women around the world who struggle together against oppression and injustice. With thanks to Margaret Gentry, Nancy Sorkin Rabinowitz, Sandra Dahlberg, and the reviewers and editors at *Signs*. And as always, for my mother and my daughter.

1. Throughout this essay I use the terms *welfare recipient* and *poor working women* interchangeably because as the recent Urban Institute study made clear, today these populations are, in fact, one and the same (Loprest 1999).

2. Unpublished survey, December 1998, Utica, New York.

3. Adolescent psychologist Maria Root claims that a beautiful or "fit" body becomes equated with "purity, discipline—basically with goodness" (DeClaire 1993, 36).

4. Unpublished survey, June 1998, Seattle, Washington.

5. In the two years directly preceding the passage of the PRWORA, as a part of sweeping welfare reform, in the United States the largest percentage of people on welfare were white (39 percent), and fewer than 10 percent were teen mothers (U.S. Department of Health and Human Services 1994).

References

Anderson, Dale. 1999. County to investigate some welfare recipients. *Buffalo News*, 18 August, B5.

Brownstein, Ronald. 1995. Latest welfare reform plan reflects liberals' priorities. *Los Angeles Times*, 24 January, A6.

Collins, Patricia Hill. 2000. *Black Feminist Thought: Knowledge, Consciousness, and the Politics of Empowerment*. New York: Routledge.

DeClaire, Joan. 1993. Body by Barbie. *View*, October, 36–43.

Dreier, Peter. 1999. Treat welfare recipients like workers. *Los Angeles Times*, 29 August, M6.

Dresang, Joel. 1996. Bridefare designer, reform beneficiary have role in governor's address. *Milwaukee Journal Sentinel*, 14 August, 9.

Dujon, Diane, and Ann Withorn. 1996. *For Crying Out Loud: Women's Poverty in the United States*. Boston: South End.

Edin, Kathryn, and Laura Lein. 1997. *Making Ends Meet: How Single Mothers Survive Welfare and Low-Wage Work*. New York: Russell Sage.

Foucault, Michel. (1977) 1984. Discipline and punish. In *The Foucault Reader*, edited by Paul Rabinow, 170–256. New York: Pantheon.

Loprest, Pamela. 1999. Families who left welfare: Who are they and how are they doing? Urban Institute, Washington, DC, August, B1.

McNay, Lois. 1993. *Foucault and Feminism: Power, Gender, and the Self*. Boston: Northeastern University Press.

Muir, Kate. 1993. Runaway fathers at welfare's final frontier. *New York Times*, 19 July, A2.

Raphael, Jody. 2000. Saving Bernice: Women, welfare and domestic violence. Presentation at Hamilton College, May 23, Clinton, New York.

Raspberry, William. 1995. Ms. Smith goes after Washington. *Washington Post*, 1 February, A19.

Robinson, Valerie. 1999. State's ad attacks the poor. *Plain Dealer*, 2 November, B8.

Simon, Stephanie. 1999. Unlikely support for drug tests on welfare applicants. *Los Angeles Times*, 18 December, A1.

Smith-Madsen, Sandy. 2003. From welfare to academe: Welfare reform as college-educated welfare mothers know it. In *Reclaiming Class: Women, Poverty and the Promise of Education in America*, edited by Vivyan Adair and Sandra Dahlberg, 160–86. Philadelphia: Temple University Press.

U.S. Department of Health and Human Services. 1994. An overview of entitlement programs. Washington, DC: U.S. Government Printing Office.

Women's Enews. 2001a. Civil rights bad for welfare moms. Mailing list, available on-line at http://www.womensenews.org, May 4.

———. 2001b. Oregon to women on welfare: Dumpster dive. Mailing list, available on-line at http://www.womensenews.org, May 5.

16

Letting Ourselves Go

Making Room for the Fat Body in Feminist Scholarship

CECILIA HARTLEY

Before the twentieth century, men were far more often drawn to fat women than to thin women.[1] Fatness meant that a woman was well fed, which in turn signaled that she was strong, healthy, from a well-off family, and likely to bear healthy children. Thus, one of the most famous beauties of the late nineteenth century, actress Lillian Russell, continued to charm audiences even as her weight passed 200 pounds.

Today, however, few groups experience as much social stigma as do fat women. In this article, Cecilia Hartley dissects the cultural norms that stigmatize fatness among women. As she shows, the stigma against fatness serves to limit the lives not only of fat women, but also of all women. Moreover, she argues, fatness results at least partly from women's struggles with cultural norms that require them to place others' needs before their own, to discipline their body to match men's desires, and to take up as little space as possible. Thus, Hartley concludes, fat women should be recognized by feminists as engaging in resistance against sexist norms for female bodies.

The body—what we eat, how we dress, the daily rituals through which we attend to the body—is a medium of culture. The body... is a powerful symbolic form, a surface on which the

central rules, hierarchies, and even metaphysical commitments of
a culture are inscribed and thus reinforced through the concrete
language of the body.

SUSAN BORDO, *Unbearable Weight* (1993)

There is something wrong with the female body. Women learn early—
increasingly, as early as five or six years old—that their bodies are fundamentally flawed. The restructuring process begins often as soon as a child is able
to understand that there is a difference between the sexes. When that awareness reveals a female body, the realization soon follows that that body must
be changed, molded, reconfigured into an ideal that will never be reached by
"letting nature take its course."

Not surprisingly, self-hatred often becomes a part of a woman's body
image. By the onset of puberty, a sense of body deficiency is very firmly
in place, and that sense of deficiency is exacerbated as the body matures.
According to one study, 53 percent of thirteen-year-old girls are dissatisfied
with their bodies, and that number increases to 78 percent when the girls
reach eighteen. Seventy-five percent of those over eighteen believe they are
overweight, including 45 percent who are technically *underweight*.[2]

This "tyranny of slenderness" has created a culture in which as many
as 60 percent of women experience some type of difficulty in eating and
one in five teenage girls will develop an eating disorder such as anorexia or
bulimia. Feminist scholars such as Sandra Bartky, Susan Bordo, Naomi Wolf,
and others have rightly identified this epidemic as a feminist issue and have
sought theoretical explanations for women's desire to starve themselves. The
fact remains, however, that pacing the exponential rise in eating disorders in
the last two decades has been the increase in the numbers of women who are,
by modern standards, fat. . . . Despite the prevalence of women who resist (or
fail to resist) the tyranny of slenderness, the fat body has largely been ignored
in feminist studies that attempt to theorize the female body.

How should these women be theorized? Are there similarities between
what drives the starvation impulse and the feeding impulse? Is there a place
in feminist scholarship for the fat body? I examine these questions in terms
of the culture's production of docile female bodies, through which the ideal
female form is constructed in some cases and rejected in others. I scrutinize
the culture's embrace of those who achieve the ideal form (even when those
bodies are literally starving) and its brutal rejection of those who do not,
or cannot, meet that ideal. Finally, I identify the sexism inherent in sizism
(which produces both the slender and the fat body) and look at the ways in
which rejecting fat oppression can lead to a heightened feminist awareness.

The Feminine Ideal and the Production of "Docile Bodies"

Modern American standards require that the ideal feminine body be small.
A woman is taught early to contain herself, to keep arms and legs close to her

body and take up as little space as possible. This model of femininity suggests that real women are thin, nearly invisible. The women idealized as perfect are these days little more than waifs. The average fashion model today weighs 23 percent less than the average woman; a generation ago the gap was only 8 percent.[3] Not surprisingly, those women who claim more than their share of territory are regarded with suspicion. Brown notes that "Fat oppression carries the less-than-subtle message that women are forbidden to take up space (by being large of body) or resources (by eating food ad libitum)."[4] In recent years, of course, there has been an increasing move toward fitness and bodybuilding for women, and some hope that a different ideal female body may be developing. There is reason to regard such a shift with suspicion, however. This new ideal still requires a complete restructuring of the female body, a removal of softness, and a rejection of any indication of fat tissue. It is still based on the notion that the large female body is inherently wrong. In addition, the most successful female bodybuilders, those who become large through muscle mass, are often seen as taking on masculine characteristics. A quick flip through *Vogue* demonstrates that the waif model still persists as feminine.

Men are under no such size restrictions and are allowed—often encouraged—to take up as much space as they can get away with. But when a woman's stature or girth approaches or exceeds that of a man's, she becomes something freakish. By becoming large, whether with fat tissue or muscle mass, she implicitly violates the sexual roles that place her in physical subordination to the man. As Naomi Wolf points out in *The Beauty Myth*, the focus on the smallness of the woman's body has increased in the United States at the same time that women have begun to gain a real measure of power. The male need to establish superiority, undermined by the relative success of the feminist movement, has reasserted itself by inscribing inferiority onto the female body. She declares, "A cultural fixation on female thinness is not an obsession about female beauty but an obsession about female obedience."[5]

Bartky agrees that cultural expectations have progressively shifted away from what a woman is allowed to *do* onto what a woman is allowed to *look like:* "Normative femininity is coming more and more to be centered on woman's body—not its duties and obligations or even its capacity to bear children, but its sexuality, more precisely, its presumed heterosexuality and appearance."[6] As women have claimed intellectual and economic power for themselves, culture has simply found new ways for them to be inferior. Brown calls the ideal feminine body a "manifestation of misogynist norms flowing from a culture where women are devalued and disempowered."[7] That is, because women themselves are seen as somehow less than men, their bodies must demonstrate that inferiority.

These "misogynist norms" are not simply inflicted on women from the outside. Such overt oppression would be relatively easy for women to identify and resist. As Michel Foucault notes, however, the success of a society's imposition of discipline upon bodies depends on those bodies learning to *regulate themselves.*[8] That is, women feel the need to construct female bodies that are demonstrably smaller and weaker than men's bodies in part because they have, in Brown's words, "internalized fat oppressive notions."[9] Because the male gaze is always present, even when it is physically absent, women must continually produce bodies that are acceptable to that gaze. Thus a woman's own gaze becomes a substitute for a man's gaze, and she evaluates her own body as ruthlessly as she expects it to be evaluated by him....

[At the same time,] women who do not maintain rigid control over the boundaries of their bodies, allowing them to grow, to become large and "unfeminine," are treated with derision in our society, and that derision is tied inextricably to the personal freedom of women. Women who are fat are said to have "let themselves go." The very phrase connotes a loosening of restraints. Women in our society are bound. In generations past, the constriction was accomplished by corsets and girdles that cut into the skin and left welts, marks of discipline. The girdles are now, for the most part, gone, but they have been replaced by bindings even more rigid. Women today are bound by fears, by oppression, and by stereotypes that depict large women as ungainly, unfeminine, and unworthy of appreciation. Large chunks of time and energy that could be channeled into making real, substantive changes in society are being spent pursuing the ideal body image: weighing, measuring, preparing and portioning food, weighing and measuring the body, jogging, stair-stepping, crunching away any softness of belly, taking pills, seeing specialists, finding clothes that hide figure flaws. Women in particular are literally terrified of getting fat. In survey after survey, being fat is listed as a primary fear.[10]...

Fat Oppression and American Culture

In modern American culture, women are expected to be beautiful, and beautiful equals thin. Whether we are given waifs or athletes to view, we are constantly bombarded by media images of women with little or no breast tissue and slim, boyish hips. The almost impossible ideal is set before women as the mold in which to construct their bodies, molds which the vast majority of bodies simply will not fit. Virtually every woman learns to hate her body, regardless of her size, and so she learns to participate in her own oppression. As Brown notes, "data suggests that North American women of most cultures, and all body sizes and eating styles tend to have fat-oppressive and fat-negative attitudes towards their own bodies and, by inference, those of other women."[11]

The fat woman, Millman observes, is "stereotypically viewed as unfeminine, in flight from sexuality, antisocial, out of control, hostile, aggressive."[12] Because they do not construct bodies that conform to the feminine ideal, fat women are perceived as violating socially prescribed sexual roles, and that violation is a threat to existing power structures. Women may have made gains in intellectual and economic power, but there is a price to be paid. At all costs, a woman must not be allowed to maintain (or win) physical power as well. If she does, she is in rebellion, not only against male power structures but against all that is feminine.

It is no wonder that such fat-oppressive attitudes have been internalized. Fat women in American society are perpetually victimized by public ridicule. They are "weighed down...by the force of hatred, contempt and pity, amusement and revulsion. Fat bodies are invaded by comments, measured with hatred, pathologized by fear and diagnosed by ignorance."[13] Fat-phobia is one of the few acceptable forms of prejudice left in a society that at times goes to extremes to prove itself politically correct. One study indicates that fat girls have only one-third the chance of being admitted to prestigious colleges as slim girls with similar school records.[14] Fat jokes still abound. Women who get fat publicly (Elizabeth Taylor, Oprah Winfrey, Sarah Ferguson) are openly censured and scorned as if their bodies were public property. And when they lose weight, as all three of these women have, they are met with an approval that again marks their bodies as public property.

Of course, a woman does not have to be a public figure for her body to receive similar treatment. Fat has become a moral issue unlike any other type of deviation from what society considers normal. The fat woman is often dismissed as sloppy, careless, lazy, and self-indulgent. Large women know all too well that strangers often feel no compunction about stepping forward to criticize a woman's size with statements such as "Should you really be eating that?"; "I know a good doctor who could help you"; "You have such a pretty face, if you'd just lose some weight...."

Why does American society have such a visceral reaction to fat? Some, like Brown, agree that "a fat woman by her presence violates primal norms of misogynist society that deny nurturance, space, power and visibility to women."[15] But Wolf and others have drawn an analogy between the view of fat in modern culture and the view of sex in Victorian times: "What hysteria was to the nineteenth-century fetish of the asexual woman locked in the home, anorexia is to the late-twentieth-century fetish of the hungry woman."[16] For the Victorian woman, sex was forbidden, dirty, and shameful, and her repression of her desires led to hysteria. For the modern woman, "fat" is forbidden, dirty, and shameful, and her strict control over and repression of her bodily needs are manifested once again in the body, not in hysteria but in eating disorders. Although many studies refute a simple correlation between weight gain and overeating, Susan Bordo notes that American culture still sees fat only in terms of self-indulgence: "Anorexia could thus be seen as an extreme development of the capacity for self-denial and repression of desire...; obesity, as an extreme capacity to capitulate to desire."[17]...

The same society that valorizes the female body, making it a cultural icon for beauty, subtly undermines any sense of self-love a woman might have for her body—even those bodies that meet the ideal. The body is suspect, needy, always in danger of erupting into something that will grasp more than is allowed. The end result is that women, fat or thin, often develop an antagonistic relationship with their bodies. The size and shape those bodies take on become directly connected to a woman's self-esteem. As Bartky notes, "Overtly, the fashion-beauty complex seeks to glorify the female body and to provide opportunities for narcissistic indulgence. More important than this is its *covert* aim, which is to depreciate woman's body and deal a blow to her narcissism."[18] The fat body, then, comes to represent all that must be avoided and all that is denied to women in American society. Because it must be avoided so strenuously, those who do not, or cannot, avoid fatness are a source of public discomfort, outrage, or both. The fat body, Brown tells us, is a reminder of all that a woman cannot and should not be:

> Fat women are ugly, bad, and not valuable because they are in violation of so many of the rules. A fat woman is visible, and takes up space. A fat woman stands out. She occupies personal territory in ways that violate the rules for the sexual politics of body movement.
>   ...A fat woman has strong muscles from moving her weight around in the world. She clearly has fed herself.... Thus, for women to not break the rules, and for women to not be ugly, bad, and valueless, women must fear fat, and hate it in themselves.[19]

...The link to patriarchy here might well be questioned. My study has focused on the fat *female* body even though a large percentage of the fat population is male. As has been noted, however, it is only the female body that has been rigidly inscribed as *necessarily* thin, that thinness rendering a woman visibly smaller and weaker than the average male. The male gaze, characterized by Brown as a "patriarchal psychic tapeworm,"[20] serves as a continual reminder that the female body must be smaller than man's to be acceptable. Bartky notes that "insofar as the disciplinary practices of femininity produce 'subjected and practiced,' an inferiorized body, they must be understood as aspects of a far larger discipline, an oppressive and inegalitarian system of sexual subordination."[21] I would suggest that the emaciated female body stands as a symbol of woman's sexual subordination.

The Male Gaze and the Sexism of Sizism

Biologically, women have more fat than men, 10 to 15 percent more body fat until the onset of puberty. At puberty, as evidence of maturity and fertility, women's fat-to-muscle ratio increases as the male's decreases, widening the gap even more.[22] Ironically, however, it is that fat, crucial to a woman's reproductive health, that renders her undesirable in a heterosexual relationship. Culturally, women face far stricter limits than men on what amount of body fat is acceptable. The intensity of public scorn of the fat female body drives many women to take extreme measures in order to meet those guidelines. There is evidence, however, that the male sexual gaze indicates the attitude toward corpulence more accurately than does the sex of the body being constructed. It is not only women who must conform to the male ideal of beauty.

Recent research has shown that internalized fat-oppressive attitudes are more often present in persons of *either sex* who want to be found attractive by men and that they are less common in persons of either sex who wish to be found attractive by women.[23] Still, while men are at much higher risk from illness due to obesity, 80 to 90 percent of all weight loss surgery is performed on women, despite the grave risks and complications that have been linked to the procedures.[24] Between 90 to 95 percent of anorectics and bulimics are women.[25]

As Wolf reminds us, "the demonic characterizations of a simple body substance do not arise from its physical properties but from old-fashioned misogyny, for above all, fat is female."[26] That which distinguishes women outwardly from men—the curves of breast and hip—are primarily accumulations of adipose tissue, the same adipose tissue that is attacked with such ferocity and treated as the enemy of women. Brown adds, "Most of the ways in which women feel physically 'wrong' e.g., having womanly hips, bellies, breasts, and thighs, are manifestations of how their body is not that of a man."[27]

It is here that the construction of the sexual female body takes a curious turn. The states of anorexia and obesity, both extreme reactions to the sexism/sizism of American culture,[28] situate women as simultaneously asexual and hypersexual. In the anorexic state, the body is stripped of all excess fat tissue, feminine curves disappear, and the female body is rendered nearly prepubescent in form. The anorexic body changes internally as well. When body fat drops below a certain percentage, ovulation and menstruation cease. "Infertility and hormone imbalance are common among women whose fat-to-lean ratio falls below 22 percent," Wolf points out.[29] In essence, femaleness is rejected in favor of a state of asexuality. One woman refers to her bout with anorexia as "killing off the woman in me."[30]

While anorexia is in very physical and chemical ways an "absolute negation of the female state,"[31] it is the anorexic and nearly anorexic body that is glamorized on runways, on magazine covers, and in television shows and movies. In its asexuality, the thin female body becomes, ironically, hypersexualized, culturally "feminine" and admired, accepted in its very rejection of excess flesh. Anorexia in many ways reflects an ambivalence about femininity, a rebellion against feminization that manifests itself by means of the disease as both a rejection and an exaggeration of the feminine ideal.

The fat body also exists in a state of simultaneous asexuality and hypersexuality. Increased stores of fat exaggerate the outward sexuality of the female body; breasts and hips become fuller and more prominent. A fat woman's body is unmistakably, maturely female. Internally, the body experiences heightened sexuality as well. Fat cells store estrogen, and increases in fat increase levels of that hormone in the body. In addition, some studies suggest that fat women desire sex more often than do thin.[32] Yet even as the thin female body is perceived as hypersexual by culture, the fat female body is perceived as asexual. "In our society," Millman points out, "fat women are viewed as unfeminine, unattractive, masculine, out of the running. In a word, they are desexualized."[33]

In many ways, both of these groups of women are attempting to remove themselves from their bodies, to live from the neck up. Anorexia can be read as an attempt to deny physiology, to make the body itself disappear. While obesity may be characterized as the reverse, as celebrating or reveling in the body, the issue is more complex. Certainly many fat women have made a conscious decision to allow their bodies free rein. Many other women, however, perhaps the majority, become fat because they are disconnected from their bodies and have trouble learning to use and move them in productive ways. Millman links this inability to use the body in physical ways to the male gaze and cultural expectations of femininity: "Women are prone to disembodiment not only because they are constantly exposed to intrusive judgments about their bodies but also because they are taught to regard their bodies as passive objects others should admire. Unlike men who are raised to *express themselves* unself-consciously through physical activity and sports, women's bodies are employed to be looked at."[34] Either extreme, being fat or being anorexic, can therefore be seen as a rejection of the body as object of the male gaze. Thus a first step in reclaiming the female body might well be a loosening of the cultural restraints on it—an acknowledgment that the female body naturally contains more fat cells than a man's and a commitment to living *inside* the body. But such a step on the part of women is sure to be perceived as a threat as great as the suffrage movement of the nineteenth century or the women's liberation movement of the twentieth. . . .

Notes

1. Roberta Pollack Seid. *Never Too Thin.* (New York: Prentice Hall, 1989).

2. Susan Bordo, *Unbearable Weight: Feminism, Western Culture, and the Body* (Berkeley: University of California Press, 1993), 185.

3. Naomi Wolf, *The Beauty Myth: How Images of Beauty Are Used Against Women* (New York: Anchor Books/Doubleday, 1992), 183.

4. Laura S. Brown, "Women, Weight, and Power: Feminist Theoretical and Therapeutic Issues," *Women and Therapy* 4, no. 1 (1985): 61–71.

5. Wolf, *The Beauty Myth*, 187.

6. Sandra Lee Bartky, *Femininity and Domination: Studies in the Phenomenology of Oppression* (New York: Routledge, 1990), 80.

7. Brown, "Women, Weight, and Power," 63.

8. Michel Foucault, *Discipline and Punish: The Birth of the Prison* (New York: Vintage, 1979), 135–228.

9. Brown, "Women, Weight, and Power," 68.

10. Marcia Millman, *Such a Pretty Face: Being Fat in America* (New York: Norton, 1980), and Wolf, *The Beauty Myth*.

11. Brown, "Fat-Oppressive Attitudes," 20.

12. Millman, *Such a Pretty Face*, xi.
13. R. Bull, quoted in Susan Tenzer, "Fat Acceptance Therapy (F.A.T.): A Non-Dieting Group Approach to Physical Wellness, Insight, and Acceptance," in Brown and Rothblum, *Fat Oppression and Psychotherapy*, 47.
14. Millman, *Such a Pretty Face*, 90.
15. Brown, "Fat-Oppressive Attitudes," 26.
16. Wolf, *The Beauty Myth*, 198.
17. Bordo, *Unbearable Weight*, 201.
18. Bartky, *Femininity and Domination*, 39–40.
19. Brown, "Women, Weight, and Power," 65.
20. Ibid., 63.
21. Bartky, *Femininity and Domination*, 75.
22. Wolf, *The Beauty Myth*, 192.
23. Brown, "Fat-Oppressive Attitudes," 25; Millman, *Such a Pretty Face*, 245.
24. Jaclyn Packer, "The Role of Stigmatization in Fat People's Avoidance of Physical Exercise," in Brown and Rothblum, *Fat Oppression and Psychotherapy*, 52.
25. Wolf, *The Beauty Myth*, 181.
26. Ibid., 92.
27. Brown, "Women, Weight, and Power," 85.
28. Studies indicate that dieting itself may cause both eating disorders and obesity; see Wolf, *The Beauty Myth*; Brown, "Fat-Oppressive Attitudes"; and Millman, *Such a Pretty Face*.
29. Wolf, *The Beauty Myth*, 192.
30. Millman, *Such a Pretty Face*, 125.
31. Wolf, *The Beauty Myth*, 184.
32. Ibid., 192.
33. Millman, *Such a Pretty Face*, 98.
34. Ibid., 202.

References

Bartky, Sandra Lee. 1990. *Femininity and Domination: Studies in the Phenomenology of Oppression*. New York: Routledge.
Bordo, Susan. 1993. *Unbearable Weight: Feminism, Western Culture, and the Body*. Berkeley: University of California Press.
Brown, Laura S. 1989. Fat-oppressive attitudes and the feminist therapist: Directions for change. In *Fat Oppression and Psychotherapy: A Feminist Perspective*, edited by Laura S. Brown and Esther D. Rothblum, 19–30. New York: Haworth Press.
———. 1985. Women, Weight, and Power: Feminist Theoretical and Therapeutic Issues. *Women and Therapy* 4(1) 61–71.
Butler, Judith. 1993. *Bodies That Matter: On the Discursive Limits of "Sex."* New York: Routledge.

Foucault, Michel. 1979. *Discipline and Punish: The Birth of the Prison.* Translated by Alan Sheridan. New York: Vintage.

Millman, Marcia. 1980. *Such a Pretty Face: Being Fat in America.* New York: Norton.

Packer, Jaclyn. 1989. The role of stigmatization in fat people's avoidance of physical exercise. In *Fat Oppression and Psychotherapy: A Feminist Perspective,* edited by Laura S. Brown and Esther D. Rothblum, 49–63. New York: Haworth Press.

Tenzer, Susan. 1989. Fat acceptance therapy (F.A.T.): A non-dieting group approach to physical wellness, insight and acceptance. In *Fat Oppression and Psychotherapy: A Feminist Perspective,* edited by Laura S. Brown and Esther D. Rothblum, 39–47. New York: Haworth Press.

Wolf, Naomi. 1992. *The Beauty Myth: How Images of Beauty Are Used against Women.* New York: Anchor Books/Doubleday.

17

Rip Tide

Swimming Through Life with Rheumatoid Arthritis

ANDREA AVERY

Since she was 12, Andrea Avery—a writer by trade—has lived with rheumatoid arthritis (RA). As Avery points out, RA is a common, disabling, and sometimes deadly disease that has received surprisingly little attention—quite possibly because 70% of those affected by it are female.

In this essay, Avery sheds light on the ways in which her embodied experiences are both similar to and different from those of other girls and women. Like others, she sometimes struggles with social ideas of appropriate female appearance. And like others, she sometimes judges herself harshly as a result and sometimes finds that others feel free to publicly judge her, even if they are strangers and especially if they are young men. At the same time, because RA has affected her appearance significantly and has made pregnancy particularly risky for her, it has forced her to consciously confront cultural expectations for female bodies that other girls and women can afford to ignore. Her essay illustrates some of the strategies—from humor to tattoos—that she has used to develop a positive embodied self that incorporates both who she was before RA and who she is now, while simultaneously acknowledging her illness and keeping it from defining her.

I. Depths

I'm 13. I'm home sick from school. My dad is downstairs, having taken time off work. He is probably in the kitchen, standing at the sink, eating a piece of toast over his upturned hand. I'm in the upstairs bathroom, trying to get into my bathing suit. I can't do it. The elastic is too restrictive and every contortion, every manipulation, I have to make to wriggle the not-extraordinarily-tight one-piece over my hips causes a riot of pain in my

Andrea Avery, *Rip Tide: Swimming Through Life with Rheumatoid Arthritis.*

arms and elbows and back and neck and hands. Even trying to grip the blue spandex hurts. My hands are too weak to hold on and pull. I want to get into my bathing suit so I can go soak in the hot tub. I want to soak in the hot tub because I want to be surrounded by something hotter than my own skin, because I want to boil off the stiffness and pain that greeted me when I awoke this morning. Water is the kindest atmosphere; in water, less is asked of me. Water buoys my joints. In water I can almost forget the horrible, heavy fact of lugging a body around. I get the bathing suit up to my belly button. My arms are through the arm holes, but the arm holes are down by my waist so my arms are strapped to my side like I'm in a straitjacket. I'm stuck. I can't get the bathing suit up or down. I will be like this forever.

The girl in the mirror has ragamuffin hair stuck to her face, wet with tears, sweat and fever. I see her bare shoulders, her brand-new, inadequate breasts and her hunched form and I am disgusted. I say silently, *No one will ever want you.*

I don't know how I got out of the bathing suit, whether it went up or down, or if I ever got into the hot tub that day. In the 20 years since I received a diagnosis of rheumatoid arthritis at 12, this point—in my disease's infancy—is among my lowest. I have not told anyone about this moment. I have not written about it. I am ashamed of it. Not because of my helplessness—after all, a kid can get stuck in a bathing suit and it can be a funny story—or because of what it reveals about my body or how sick I really was. I am ashamed of what I thought. What I said to a helpless, hurting kid, even if that kid was me.

And so it is crucial now that I recover, that I say that I have not had many moments like this. That I have had many more moments where I have stood up for my body, been its cheerleader and its advocate, its minister and its mother. That I have, in 20 years, accepted my body's flaws and freakishness and stopped defining my worth by how much my body is desired or depended on or approved of by others—boys, men, employers, teachers, students, friends, strangers.

I will tell you all of that but you will know that this moment—this hulking, hungry truth—is a tide pulling at me, just beneath the surface. And you will understand why I must put everything I have into swimming at a diagonal to this tide, why I must get back to shore.

II. A Toe in the Water

I received a diagnosis on May 25, 1989, though the initial diagnosis would be broad, unspecific, and ultimately inadequate. Rheumatoid arthritis is notoriously difficult to diagnose and my case was no different. I am fortunate to be able to trace my disease's debut in my life thanks to an astoundingly comprehensive set of notes taken by my mother, a note-taker by nature and a nurse by training. The late winter and early spring months of 1989, the second half of my sixth-grade year, were marked by sporadic—but escalating—episodes of pain and swelling in various joints, each with a plausible explanation. Right thumb hurts (jammed it playing basketball at recess?). Left shoulder hurts (delayed onset muscular soreness after basketball practice?). A visit to the family pediatrician on April 25, 1989 yielded a probable diagnosis of "growing pains." By late May, the periods of pain and swelling had increased in intensity and the pain-free periods of reprieve between them had shrunk. The diagnosis I got on May 25 of that year was a diagnosis of best fit: arthritis of some kind, for sure. But whether it was reactive arthritis (it would go away in six weeks) or psoriatic arthritis (I'd develop skin rashes to go with the joint pain) or rheumatoid arthritis (they took my blood to test for a marker of rheumatoid arthritis) was unknown. That summer my blood results were back, and my rheumatoid factor was about four times the normal rate. Rheumatoid arthritis it was, and is.

When I was first diagnosed, teachers and doctors and guidance counselors were always hovering, always telling me it was OK to ask "Why me?" But that's a grown-up question, not a kid question. Kids don't have—at least I didn't have—any expectation that life would be fair. It's adults that Kathy Charmaz is writing about in "Body, Identity, Self: Adapting to Impairment" when she writes:

> Ill people often believe they have already suffered beyond tolerable limits. Thus, they see themselves as having filled their quota of human misery and earned their right to a just reprieve.... New, foreboding symptoms shock them. Moreover, these people experience the unpredictability of their bodies afresh as they grapple with new or intensified distress.

I get that now, now that new secondary and tertiary syndromes pack girth onto the snowball of my original disease and add insult, insult, insult to injury, injury, injury. But kids—kids are used to being powerless. Kids take what's thrown at them and they hold on. I didn't question the justice in my getting arthritis any more than I questioned the justice in my getting two brothers and a sister—even if I didn't always like it. "So now's the part of my life where I get arthritis," I thought. "Whatever. I just hope I get boobs."

But now that I know how it's turned out—how it's turning out—I can't help but feel for the kid in those pages, and I allow myself to feel (what? Pity?) only because she is not me. "Don't do handstands," one of my mom's notes reads. Another: "Much jumping today." Oh, to even *feel* like doing handstands. Why her?

I still don't think "why me?" in anything more than a biological sense. (Does it have something to do with my having mumps as a baby? Or not being breastfed? Or both?) Maybe it's not pity after all. Maybe I envy her, or I don't want to lose whatever part of her is still in me. Didn't she see how hopeless it was to keep playing soccer, to try out for cheerleading, to practice piano for four hours a day? *Why her?*

On the day of my initial diagnosis, though, only my right wrist was hurting and, because I was a kid and kids can be resilient almost to the point of being amnesiacs, I thought of it as a visit about my wrist, not about my life.

I'd forgotten about calling my mom in tears, or any of the other symptoms she'd recorded. We went to the doctor: I brought the body with the simmering disease and a bored expression and my mom brought her yellow pad and a concerned expression, and we collected our diagnosis, and then I was deposited back at school. I remember thinking as I stood at the car door in the parking lot at Children's, waiting for my mom to unlock the door, "So my arm will hurt once in a while. Big deal."

And I'm grateful that I didn't say that out loud, because someone (probably not my mom or the exceedingly gentle Dr. White, since at that time we were all, apparently, putting our money on a transient form of arthritis that would clear right up like a case of mild acne) might have corrected me and told me that no, juvenile rheumatoid arthritis would mean that I would be tired and feverish for the foreseeable future; that I would miss half of seventh grade; that my weight would drop to near-scary lows for a period and then, stuffed with prednisone and unable to exercise, I would get fat; that I would quit basketball, then soccer; that for most of high school I would collapse in a hot pile on my bed at 6 p.m. and sleep through the night, still in my clothes; that my joints would start kinking up and eventually become stuck in bent positions; that tendons would be eaten away by the synovium that lines the joints—a slick, protective covering rendered viscous and damaging by inflammation—and then snap, first in the right hand and then the left; that my knees would be cut up and replaced with cobalt-chromium; that one hip would turn to, and then bite, the dust; that my eyes would become dry and irritated, along with every other mucous membrane I have; that pills and shots and IVs would make me sick and a toxic environment for any fetus I might hope to carry; that boys would call me "gimp" in bars. Because I wouldn't have handled all that very well back then.

III. The Young Girl and the Sea

After I was diagnosed, I was sent to school with a letter on Children's Hospital letterhead and I showed it around to teachers so they would let me chew gum to loosen my jaw or get up to walk around the classroom if I was getting stiff or sit out of P.E. class or be a few minutes late to class. And I showed it to the kids at school and one of them scanned it skeptically till he got to the word "chronic" and then said, nodding, "Chronic. That means serious." Matt Bryant, wherever you are, you were right.

The seriousness of rheumatoid arthritis is something that escapes a lot of people. Part of this is because the word "arthritis" is an umbrella term for lots of different diseases, including osteoarthritis. Osteoarthritis (OA) is the degenerative type of arthritis the weekend warrior gets after years of playing pickup basketball games in the park. It's the arthritis your Grandma has. It's the kind of arthritis pretty much everyone gets after hauling his or her body around for a number of years. About 27 million Americans have OA.

Rheumatoid arthritis (RA), on the other hand, is an autoimmune disease, making it more closely related to Crohn's disease or multiple sclerosis than to osteoarthritis. RA, as the Arthritis Foundation points out, is one of the most serious forms of the disease. In autoimmune diseases, your body picks a fight with itself, mistaking healthy tissue for a foreign invader. In RA, that fight is fought in the joints and the tissues lining the joints—but it can also affect your eyes (in the form of iritis or the less-serious episcleritis), your heart (pericarditis and myocarditis, swelling of the lining of the heart and the heart muscle itself, respectively, both of which can lead to congestive heart failure) and, my favorite, your cervical spine (atlantoaxial subluxation, which can cause—and I'm not kidding—*sudden death*).

Also, or maybe as a result, the Arthritis Foundation reports, people with RA are twice as likely as others to experience moderate to severe symptoms of depression. People with RA die, on average, three to seven years earlier "than expected" (10 to 15 if you have a "severe" form, as I do)—though I'd guess that anyone who's lived with this disease for any length of time has learned not to "expect" anything from her body.

Another reason that rheumatoid arthritis might not get the attention it deserves is that approximately 70 percent of the 1.3 million people in America with RA are women. For most of these people, the onset of RA occurs between the ages of 30 and 50. "The disease collides with women in their childbearing years," writes Mary Lowenthal Felstiner—from experience—in *Out of Joint: A Private and Public Story of Arthritis.* "One thing Americans rely on to keep them fed and mended (for less than a living wage) is women who won't say, 'Take care of me. I'm all crippled up.' Who would fill in for these women of childbearing age—lifting babies, mashing potatoes, cleaning cafeterias, grading papers, doing all the jobs where nobody picks up after them?" (274).

What if the proportions were reversed? What if 70 percent of the people waking up every morning wondering how much they'd hurt, in what new ways their bodies would fail them, or if they'd be able to call on their limbs to do everything the day would ask of them were men? Would the world come to a sudden halt until someone put his nose to the grindstone and figured this damn thing out? Arthritis, wait till your father gets home.

So if people have a hard time understanding and appreciating the seriousness of rheumatoid arthritis in adults, you may be able to imagine the resistance encountered by a kid—a girl, a Girl Scout, a sixth-grader, a member of a soccer team, a pianist—with a reasonably normal-looking body when she tells people—P.E. teachers, friends, boys she likes—that she has arthritis.

IV. Sharks (and Minnows)

I've kept a log of Things People Say. Some of them are unusually sweet, like the friend's brother who looked at the limited range of motion in my arms and legs and said, "I feel sorry for you the way I feel sorry for Star Wars action figures." Or the four-year-old babysitting charge who looked at my limp and asked, "Why are you walking so careful?" Some are downright strange, like the woman who approached me at a coffee shop, interrupted my writing, and asked me if I had cerebral palsy like she was asking me for a pen. "No," I said. "Do you?" She turned and walked away.

I've noticed that most—and the most nakedly vicious—comments on The List come from men and boys, but the honor of the first entry goes to Miss Babuska, my seventh-grade P.E. teacher. When I was diagnosed at the end of sixth grade, I was a pretty healthy kid attached to a sore wrist. When school resumed in August, however, I was more affected by my unpredictable disease: For stretches of weeks at a time my ankles and knees were, every day, hot and swollen; my neck wouldn't turn left or right. But then I'd have spells of normal. And so I had been instructed by my mother to tell Miss Babuska, privately, before class began, about my situation and ask for clemency to be excused from participation in P.E. on an as-needed basis. I don't remember what Miss Babuska said in that private conversation, but I do remember how, as we all sat on the gym floor, our backs up against the blue mats that lined the walls, she explained the zero-tolerance policy on sitting out P.E. class. Periods, menstrual cramps and PMS were not excuses, she explained. Only serious medical conditions would be considered. *Like Andrea's*, she said. And then, addressing me: *It's a shame your body is falling apart at such a young age.*

Miss Babuska wasn't my P.E. teacher for much longer. She and I had one more flare-up that year, when I asked to be excused from running the mile and she refused, and I got sassy, and then she ordered me to the principal's office, and I ran away from her and she screamed, "You're a liar! See! You *can* run when you want to!" Which is true—even now, on my worst day, with three metal joints *and* menstrual cramps *and* high heels on, I'm pretty sure I could and would run from Miss Babuska.

After a parent-teacher conference in which Miss Babuska insisted that she prided herself on how she accommodated "handicapped" students—and revealed that she didn't think that I qualified—I was moved into Miss Sapphire's class and allowed to sit out P.E. class and entertain myself, as long as what I was doing was "related" to the activities of the class. No one checked, so I sat alone in a stairwell and wrote stories, grateful for the solitude and indifferent to the miserable job my public middle school was doing accommodating my disability. In high school I was put in the boys' weight-lifting class, where I wrote more stories, until the public school system could be convinced that I deserved to have my P.E. graduation requirement waived.

There are few entries on The List between this period and my later college years. During these years I didn't "show" very much. My disease seemed to plateau, and even though I was frequently in pain, the joint deformity hadn't yet progressed to a point that strangers would stare, and laugh, and comment, and ask—though that time would come. And when that time did come, I would wish for these days when my disease was more invisible, though invisibility had its downsides: Once, as my aunt and uncle were saying goodbye after a visit to our house, my uncle (the "fun" uncle) curled his hand into a fist and pounded the top of my hand flat on the kitchen table, gamely cheering "Hey, let's pound that arthritis right out of there, OK, kiddo?" And I winced and tried not to cry, shocked by the pain in my hand and the silence in my throat.

During these relatively quiet years, the revelation that I had arthritis was met with "bummer" (from boys or potential boyfriends) or some variant of "you should rub banana peels on your knees—that's what cured my aunt!" or "but you're too young to have arthritis!" (from just about everyone else). I developed a bank of cheerful responses: "Could be worse," I'd say. "At least you can't get arthritis in your brain!" (actually, that one I still put faith in), "It's not a limp; it's a strut!" or "I'm too young to have arthritis? Would you like to hold it for me till I grow up?" Paging Dakota Fanning! You're needed to play a precocious, plucky, pale girl with crumbling joints but a heart of gold and a sunny outlook that can't be beat!

But changes were happening in my body during these years; my disease was progressing unchecked and gradually I lost motion in my knees such that they were stuck in a drastically bent position. By the time I started graduate school in August 2000, I stood a full four inches shorter than my height at high school graduation. Walking was difficult. Stairs had to be approached sideways, slowly, or not at all. Standing up long enough to blow-dry my shoulder-length hair was an impossible dream. I was—outwardly, at least—disabled.

Unfortunately for me, I hadn't noticed. Of course I knew I hurt. All the time. Of course I knew that I couldn't sit in low-slung chairs or excessively squishy couches. Of course I knew that I looked different. But I, stupid girl, had gone and refused to realize that I *was* different—freakish, unacceptable, ugly. People—young men in particular—seemed to want to let me know where I stood, to make sure I knew I was different. How dare I go limping through their campus, their bars, looking the way I did? Didn't I know that I would get laughed at, aped, stared at? And how dare I put on lipstick and go out with my friend Caroline? How dare I allow two boys to approach the table where we were sitting (legs safely stuffed under table, sweet camouflage)? Why didn't I tell them as soon as they sat down that my legs were all messed up? Because if I had, I could have avoided inflicting what looked like injury onto one of those boys when I stood up to limp to the bathroom. "Why are you walking like a gimp?" he asked. "*Are* you a gimp?"

And then later, when I was set up on a kind of double dinner-date with a boy with some kind of congenital defect that rendered his left arm shortened, atrophied, flipper-like (gee, I wonder why they thought we'd made a good match), when, after much mooning and covert hand-holding, we escaped for a nighttime walk through the hot August night and he stopped in his tracks, flipper flipping at his chest, and said, "Wait, you really walk like that? I thought you were goofing!"

Women have said some painful things, too. But by far, the most outraged comments have come from men—young men. *Hold on*, they seemed to be saying to me. *I was never told I'd have to deal with this in a woman.* There were, of course, exceptions, men whose kindness or use of simile touched me ("You walk like both of your legs are asleep," one said).

Now, fortunately, I am out of that dark wood. My contact with men between the ages of 14 and 25 is now limited to situations where I am their teacher, and so it is good and right that I be sexually irrelevant to them. And I also care significantly less—though I do still care—what they think of my body.

But during a long stretch of painful years, the reactions to my body from young men whom I saw as potential dates or mates were overwhelmingly pointed, disgusted, shocked and—paired with the body language that usually accompanied such comments (a step back, a retracted hand)—preoccupied with how my imperfect body affected them, or what they figured women were supposed to be. I was once dumped with this line: *Sometimes your arthritis wears on me.*

Sometimes it wears on me, too.

V. Buoys, Girls

In some intrinsic, caveman-like way, though, those men may have been smart to recoil. After all, as mates go, I am not a great bet. I'm a terrible cook. I own a lot of pairs of shoes. The estimated direct medical expense of my disease over my lifetime probably exceeds $300,000.[1] And there is the little matter of my womb, which is at the center of a body that for years has been pumped full of medicines that may not be baby-safe. It's important to point out that no doctor has told me *not* to have a baby. And I've met women with arthritis at least as severe as mine who have borne two and three lovely, healthy, sturdy babies. One even stayed on her medicine through the pregnancy (with close supervision from her rheumatologist).

Though men can and do get rheumatoid arthritis, it—like all autoimmune diseases—seems to have a special relationship with women's hormones. Breastfeeding and regular menstrual cycles seem to have a protective effect, however minimal, on one's risk of developing rheumatoid arthritis. And pregnancy, that crown jewel in the experience of being a woman in a body, is no exception. For most women with RA, their disease seems to go into a nine-month remission. There are drugs for arthritis that are contraindicated for pregnant women, but now, unlike years ago, there are medicines that can be continued during pregnancy and, perhaps more importantly, there are doctors who are willing to work with women with rheumatoid arthritis who want to experience pregnancy.

But pregnancy is an intricate process with a lot of variables. In short, a whole lot can go really wrong. Having lived in this body of mine for the last 31 years—a body that's had mumps (mumps! Who gets mumps?), arthritis, appendicitis, colitis, ovarian cysts, gallstones—I simply don't have any faith in it. I have no reason to trust that my body would do pregnancy right. And despite the temptation of nine months of respite, there is the ever-present admonition that rheumatoid arthritis frequently comes back emboldened after pregnancy ("with a vengeance" is the corny phrase all the articles seem to favor). I can handle RA for as long as I'm meant to have it; I don't hope for remission and I never have. But to have it go away and then come back would be more pain than I could bear. Not to mention the fact that pregnancies produce babies. What if my Die-Hard arthritis comes back, worse than before, when I've got *two* bodies that need feeding, washing, dressing, tending, and soothing?

And so finally it matters a hell of a lot less how the kid gets into the world than what you do with it when it's here. The athletic enthusiasm with which you love your child; the emotional dexterity that allows you to accept the kid you get, no matter what he does or who she is. The sturdiness you provide in the form of complete and unconditional support. The strength you show in creating and enforcing rules; the flexibility you show when you're wrong. I am unarthritic in these ways; in these ways unlike so many others—I know—I am healthy, unafflicted, more than adequate.

So our children, Fred's and mine, will come to us from someone else's womb, through the gracious, bittersweet miracle of adoption. I've opted out of childbirth; my job is to be as healthy as I can be on the day we bring that baby into our house and our family, and every day thereafter. And Fred learned that on our first date, pretty much, because by the time I met Fred, I'd learned that there are men for whom having their own genetic offspring is non-negotiable. And I'd learned that you need to lay it all out on the table on the first date: Here are all the ways I'm broken, a potential failure, a sucker's bet. Fortunately, Fred thought the bet was worth it.

VI. Fact: Drowning People Will Fight Their Rescuers

And yet, even though I've never seriously entertained the possibility of getting pregnant, and Fred is fine with that, more and more these days—partly because I'm starting to understand how hard, expensive and emotionally taxing the adoption process is—a tiny voice in the back of my head is asking if I've gone and, once again, accepted something I should have fought. Coped with something I should have contested. When I got a tattoo of the Arthritis Foundation logo on my back, flanked by an ornate pair of wings, I thought it was a way of saying, "Some of the pain my body endures will be *my* doing. I will have a say in at least *some* of the permanent changes to my form. I will write the story of this disease on the outside—my way—as the arthritis pens its narrative from within." But when I catch sight of it in a mirror, it looks more like a corporate brand, a logo. Proof of ownership.

Ultimately, there's a tango this disease has me doing. How much do I pull toward arthritis, how much do I push it away? Do I claim the title of "disabled" for myself, or do I reject it? If I claim it, is it permanent? Can I give it back? Will I have to explain to more obviously disabled people why I label myself disabled? Should I involve myself with the Arthritis Foundation as a volunteer and fundraiser, thereby doing some real (albeit self-interested) good but inviting people to strengthen the association between me and my disease? Practically speaking, if my elbow flares up, how long do I let it hurt before I go to the doctor?

My relationship to the label of disabled is complicated because my disease is so unpredictable. I don't live my life at a fixed distance from that word, *disabled*. I have always refused to get a hang tag for my car, even when I was recovering from a double knee replacement or a hip replacement. I struggled with owning that word even when I looked gimpy to the outside world. When I awoke from my knee-replacement surgery in 2004, suddenly restored to my full height of 5'8", and a few weeks later when I could once again conquer stairs and chairs of many heights and pants with vertical stripes didn't look weird on my right-angled knees, the outside world rescinded that word—never mind if I'd started to identify with it. Suddenly, rendered close to normal by the miracle of surgical science, I was accused of "passing" for disabled by a quadriplegic with whom I sat on a panel about women and disability.

I can't tell if I'm passing for able-bodied or passing for disabled. It depends on who I'm with. I'm bi-abled, I guess, and so I feel a kinship with bisexuals who don't quite fit with the gays or the straights: I'm too disabled among my able-bodied friends, too able-bodied to fit in with the disabled ones. And I'm not sure it matters at all whether I'm disabled or not when there's a day to get through—papers to grade, dinner to make, cats to go to the vet—and there's a call-it-whatever-you-want body that needs to be plied with some combination of pills and ice and heat and rest to get through it. My body—and my diagnosis, and the labels you or I might hang on it—is a means to an end. It is not the end. And so this is my mantra: *I am the things I make, I am not the shape I take.*

But this insistence that my body is a necessary container to haul my brain and heart around in but not something I stake a claim to is problematic. My body is not who I am, but it has the potential to get in the way of everything I am and mess it all up. So my sick body must come first so that it can recede. I must live and breathe arthritis so that other people don't see me as my disease. If I do it right, they don't even realize I have it. I am scrambling around behind the curtain, painfully mortal, to convince everyone on the outside that I'm the Great and Terrible Oz, infinitely capable, unceasingly energetic and, most crucially, completely normal and undiseased. I must get my Remicade infusions by IV every six weeks, I must take my pills, I must stay on top of bimonthly blood tests, I must rest when my body insists on it. If I am hurting, I must skip the Saturday night party and stay home rather than go for etiquette's sake and then pay for it by losing Sunday and perhaps Monday. If it sounds like a lot of work, it is. It is my part-time job.

Truthfully, I'm not utterly disembodied. In fact, my husband, who knows what I spend on clothes, shoes, and highlights every eight to 12 weeks, can attest to the fact that I find this rickety frame worthy of money and attention. That I can be downright vain. I can be tender to my body, yielding to it when it refuses to cooperate, when it pins me to the couch or bed and screams "ICE!" And I firmly believe in the power of body modification—in my case, it's my four tattoos—as a way to relate to my body. "Aren't you afraid you'll regret that?" people ask. "What if you wake up one day and wish you hadn't done that?"

To which I always reply: What if you wake up and wish you weren't 40, or gray, or a Type 2 diabetic, or inscribed with scars and wrinkles? A lot of stuff is going to happen to our bodies, yours and mine, that we wish wouldn't happen. Our bodies become scribbled over with the evidence of what happens to and within us. Much of it is outside of our control. Every day, every one of us—every one of us who wants to keep living, every one of us who insists on forging ahead, who has a spouse or children or officemates or friends who expect us to get OK with our bodies enough to show up to the bedroom or the soccer game or the big meeting or happy hour because they need our love and our brains and our wit and they'll forgive us for bringing along the old body—must reconcile who we think we are with that aging, crumbling, shapeshifting form we see in front of us. Isn't it OK for some of those permanent changes to be of our own doing? Regret doesn't have a place in my relationship with my body. It simply doesn't get me anywhere. And so I insist on co-writing my history on my body.

VII. Treading Water

My disease makes for a shitty story. I know that. It's all up and down, back and forth, repeating action, redundancy. I can't give you rising action, climax, denouement.

August 6, 1989: "Elbow would straighten completely for 1st time."
August 7, 1989: "Back to not straightening."

VIII. Land Legs

Before. Those 11 years before all this happened, which get smaller and smaller in the rear-view mirror. Once all I'd known, then the better half, now just a blip—but, like matter itself, never to disappear entirely. When I think of that time, I think of a photograph that my third-grade teacher, Miss Kalo, took. It is a dark picture in profile. I am sitting in a window in the classroom. My tangled hair is hanging in my face. I am wearing an obnoxious black sweater dress with purple handprints all over it. I am sitting at a perfect right angle, legs stretched out in front of me, swathed in horrible plaid stirrup pants, culminating in giant feet stuffed into boy's high-tops with fat, bright blue laces. There is a book on my lap. I am at peace. I am reading.

I cannot believe that I am/was/will never again be that girl. Look at her legs, so beautifully straight. Look at her hands, pudgy around the knuckles, painless. How is that me? And yet it must be. I have decided that I cannot live with a rift in my life. I cannot be one person before and another person after. I must know which parts of me have continued, in which ways I'm impervious. I must know—and pursue, and do—that which is essential and intrinsic about me.

Read, write. Arthritis can't get me, not up here on my raft of books.

IX. Rescue

In the summer of 2000, after college graduation, my two best friends and I fled to California for a week's vacation. It was gray and overcast the whole time we were there and my knees were as stuck and bent as they would get. We went to the beach anyway. I love the ocean, but I couldn't get down onto a beach towel on the sand like they could because I wouldn't be able to get up. My two friends—in their bikinis—set to work industriously and unselfconsciously digging a hole in the sand two feet deep. When they were done, I could lie on my towel with them and then, putting my legs into the cool, damp hole I would find myself sitting on a sandy ledge. From there, they stood on the edges of my hole and pulled me up and out by my hands.

We headed into the water—water, where I am finally on equal footing, where my disability is nearly invisible. I am a good swimmer and the ocean is pretty handicap-accessible, with its sloping ramp. Easy in, easy out. We rode the waves together, three heads bobbing happily on the surface. But then a huge wave came and we were all tumbled onto the sandy floor. I was upside-down and flat on the shore, unable to get up without my sand shelf. And there was another wave coming. "Help me," I yelled. They had righted themselves and they came to me. The wave was looming. We three struggled awkwardly, my two friends trying to help me up by my hands because they knew that was the graceful way I preferred. Finally the wave was too close. "Permission to lift you up gimp-style?" one of them hollered. "YES!" And so they lifted me from under my arms, in the way that always made me feel the most like cargo, like an invalid but in this case, in the arms of my friends, made me feel saved. And they did, and I was up with them. And we laughed all the way back to our towels, where we collapsed: sore with laughter, swollen with happiness.

Note

1. I'm expensive: In "Long-term Morbidity, Mortality and Economics of Rheuma-toid Arthritis" [*Arthritis and Rheumatism*, Vol. 44, No. 12, (December, 2001),

2746–2749], John B. Wong et al. cite an estimated lifetime direct medical cost for RA of $93,296. This figure is the result of a study of people in their fifties who had had the illness for about 10 years. When I am 57, which was the mean age of the subjects in this study, I'll have had arthritis for 45 years. So the projected cost over my lifetime can safely be assumed to be likely three times this number, at least.

18

Reclaiming the Female Body

Women Body Modifiers and Feminist Debates

VICTORIA PITTS

A generation ago, women's decisions about shaping and marking their bodies focused on meeting cultural norms through weight control, hairstyling, makeup, and other culturally approved means. These days, however, many women have embarked on "body projects"—conscious and sometimes long-term strategies to alter their bodies—that in some instances reject cultural norms.

As Amy Wilkins described in her article earlier in this volume, second-wave feminists (especially radical feminists) often focused on the social forces that constrained women's lives and that made sexuality dangerous. Similarly, they often stressed the ways in which women were either socialized or coerced into manipulating their bodies to meet physically and emotionally damaging cultural norms.

In contrast, third-wave feminists more often have emphasized female agency and sexual pleasure and so have celebrated various forms of body modification as individual choices and individual sources of pleasure (including sexual pleasure). Similarly, postmodern and post-essentialist feminists (groups that overlap with third-wave feminists) reject the idea that any action (such as tattooing) or category (such as woman) has one essential meaning and instead argue for recognizing the multiple and competing meanings that different individuals find in all aspects of social life. Consequently, they, too, typically argue that even the most extreme forms of body modification, such as facial tattooing and scarification, may serve for some individuals as empowering forms of resistance against gender norms.

In this article, Victoria Pitts explores these competing interpretations of women's embodied experiences through her analysis of extreme body modifica-tion. As she shows, Western culture regards such body modification as abject (that is, as breaking such deep-seated norms regarding the body that those modifications are regarded as degraded and debased). Nevertheless, individu-als choose body modification in part because they recognize it will place them in a liminal position (that is, poised between two positions—the person they were and the person they want to become—in the same way that a girl at puberty is poised between girlhood and adulthood). As Pitts shows in this arti-cle, women who choose body modification often believe that it has helped them take control of their lives and bodies. At the same time, Pitts argues, women's decisions about body modification do not solely indicate individual agency, since these decisions are products of specific social contexts. Similarly, regard-less of why women choose body modification, they cannot control how others interpret and react to it nor use it to create any wider social change. Thus, Pitts's analysis highlights the benefits and the limits of this type of embodied resistance.

...Although feminists have largely agreed that the disciplining and normal-ization of the female body through sexualized, normalized beauty ideals has been damaging to women, we have famously disagreed over how women can assert control over their own bodies. Radical feminists like Dworkin, Cather-ine MacKinnon, and others have depicted body alterations, even deviant ones, as instances of the patriarchal mistreatment of women's bodies. For MacKinnon, the sexualization of the female body, often achieved through adornments and body modifications, is the height of gender inequality. As she puts it,

> So many distinctive features of women's status as second class—the restric-tion and constraint and contortion, the servility and the display, the self-mutilation and requisite presentation of self as a beautiful thing, the enforced passivity, the humiliation—are made into the content of sex for women.[1]

In this view, body modifications represent both patriarchy's willingness to make literal use of the female body as well as women's psychic internaliza-tion of its aims. Women's willingness to happily endure pain to shape the body, she and Dworkin argue, reflects women's self-abnegation in patri-archal cultures.[2] Along with cosmetic surgery, Chinese foot binding, diet regimes, sadomasochism, and other painful or difficult practices, women's tattoos, piercings, scars, and brands have been described by radical femi-nists as representing women's "[self-] hatred of the flesh."[3] Even though the most provocative of new subcultural body mod practices usually have the effect of distancing women from Western beauty norms rather than bringing them closer, critics have likened the practices to mutilation. Informing this depiction of women's body modifications as self-objectifying or mutilative is a view that the female body should be "spared," to use Dworkin's term, interference, alteration, and, most certainly, pain.

The "sex wars" of the 1980s foreshadowed the disagreements over body art a decade later. Debates over sadomasochism (SM) focused on women's agency in relation to sexuality. Radical feminists objected to women's SM and women-made pornography (including women's obscene art). According to Dworkin and MacKinnon, these represented the worst consequences of misogyny—women's internalization and reenactment of patriarchal abuse of the female body. Their rejection of a sexualized, modified female body depended partly on the notion that a pristine, natural, organic body—a body unmolested by culture—would be a primary resource for resisting patriarchy and its use and abuse of female embodiment. Pro-sex and post-modern feminists, on the other hand, celebrated women's sexual deviance, including SM and porn, and argued in essence that women were reclaiming sexuality and desire and rebelling against oppressive prohibitions on female pleasure. . . .

By the 1990s, tattoos on the bodies of young feminists, Riot Grrrls, and others were beginning to be embraced by some postmodern feminists as subversions of "traditional notions of feminine beauty."[4] Other, even less legitimate forms of body modification have also been claimed as prac-tices of female rebellion. Because they violate gender norms, explore taboo aspects of embodiment, and provoke attention, they can be seen as ironic examples of women's "strength and independence," to use Klein's term.[5] Karmen MacKendrick describes the new body art practices as promoting "mischievous" pleasures that appropriate the body from culture. Tattoos, scars, and piercings violate Western body norms. Women who undertake such body modifications are not ignorant of the abjection that they can pro-voke. Neither, according to MacKendrick, are they unaware of the multiple ways body alteration has usually served patriarchy. Rather, she argues, "the postmodern response on display in modified bodies is fully contextualized, ironically playful, and willfully constructed."[6]

The subcultural discourse also celebrates the practices as empowering. In magazines, ezines, underground films, and in body art studios, the sub-culture depicts women's body modification as having the potential to signify body reclamation for women, including those who have experienced victim-ization. In reclaiming discourse, women (and sometimes men) assert that scarification, tattooing, and genital piercing can achieve a transformation of the relationship between self, body, and culture. In contrast to radical feminist criticisms of women's body modification as mutilation, they claim that women's anomalous body projects can provide ritualized opportunities for women's self-transformation and for symbolically recovering the female body. Far from revealing women's self-hatred and lack of self-control, they argue, the practices demonstrate women's assertion of control over their bodies.

Reclaiming the Body

Reclaiming discourse was first articulated in print in the highly popular book *Modern Primitives* in the late 1980s, where women's body piercer Raelyn Gallina suggested that women can alter non-Western, indigenous body modification practices to create meaningful rituals, in particular to symbolically reclaim their bodies from rape, harassment, or abuse.... [In this discourse,] reclaiming the body is presented as a process of highlighting the power relations that surround the body, and undergoing painful, often emotional ritual to transform the self–body relationship....

Many of the women I interviewed made use of and contributed to the reclaiming discourse surrounding women's body modification. I describe in detail the interview-gathered stories of Jane and Karen.... The women's stories situate reclaiming projects in their larger body-biographies, which often reflect on the impact of sexual violence, beauty norms, and gender relations on their body images and sense of self. I make sense of their reclaiming narratives partly by drawing attention to the ritualized, liminal aspects of the practices they describe. Modifications of the body that open the body's envelope are, from the Western perspective, abject and grotesque, but as the women describe, they also place the body in a physical and symbolic state of liminality and transformation. Later, I interpret these stories through the lens of poststructuralist feminism, which can help highlight their political significance while contextualizing them in larger relations of power.

Karen

Karen was raised in a working-class family, one in which she unfortunately suffered abuse as a young child, and became a single mother in her early 20s. Once on welfare and surviving on various low-wage jobs, including reading meters for the water company and driving trucks, she put herself through night school, and, later, through law school. During this time, she used psychotherapy to address her early victimization. At 24, she had also come out as a lesbian, and in her 30s joined a women's SM organization, where she learned about new forms of body modification. Now in her 40s and a breast cancer survivor, she has worn nipple piercings and sports permanent tattoos and scarifications, and uses reclaiming language to describe their meanings: "they were ways," she argues, "of claiming my body for me."

Karen's breast has been marked with a tattoo in the symbol of a dragon. She explains the dragon tattoo as part of a process of recovering from early victimization and gaining a sense of independence.

> I came out of an abusive childhood. I was sexually abused by an uncle. My family sort of disintegrated when I was five years old... my family moved back to Chicago because that's where my mother's family was and we moved in with her parents and I grew up in this extended Italian family. One of my uncles was a child molester. The dragon was really about finding my way to

stand on my own two feet. Finding a way of separating from that extended
family and being in the world on my own as a real person.

Karen's experience of abuse is presented as an important aspect of her
biography. During her interviews, she also repeatedly describes separating
from her parents and extended family as a difficult and important event.
Karen presents her separation from the family, which had failed to protect
her and later resisted her lesbianism, as an assertion of her own authority over her body. The image of the dragon arrived when one of Karen's
girlfriends suggested she visualize a dragon guarding a cave as a process of
overcoming fear.

> *Karen*: The purpose of that visualization was to give one an awareness of
> what they do with fear and how they deal with fear and where their courage
> comes from. The way I dealt with getting into the dragon's cave was I sat in
> the dragon's mouth very peacefully and made myself one with the dragon.
> Some people actually pick up swords and swipe the dragon mightily and
> others figure ways of getting around it. My way of dealing with it was to
> make myself one with the dragon and make the dragon become me.
>
> *VP*: What was the dragon for you?
>
> *Karen*: I came out of an abusive childhood. I was sexually abused by an
> uncle.

This plan to "make the dragon become me," a strategy of confronting
fear imposed on her body by an abusive adult male, was made literal in
Karen's decision, a year after graduating from law school, to have the image
of the dragon tattooed on her breast. The inscription, she asserts, claims her
ownership of her breast, and symbolically dissolves the fear by incorporating it. She also describes her breasts as a focus of unwanted attention and
harassment by men:

> So, the dragon was my way of claiming my body, claiming my breasts.
> Because I [also] grew up having very large breasts and having men ogle
> me. Being 14 or 15 years old to be walking down the street and have guys
> drive by and yell, "hey baby." Really ugly things that guys who are out of
> control do. And it made it really difficult for me to feel comfortable in my
> body. So having a dragon put on my breast was a way of saying, "this is
> mine." It was an evolution of that whole process of keeping myself safe and
> keeping myself whole.

Reclamation of the body, suggests Karen, is effected by self-writing it.
Her ogled and uncomfortable breast, once a site of sexual abuse and later
of anonymous harassment, becomes less alienating, she seems to suggest,
through inscription. Years later, when she is diagnosed with breast cancer, she
is upset by the idea of losing the mark: "my one request to the doctor," she
says, "was to save the tattoo." Karen perceives her body as recovered through

her marking of it. Through the tattoo, the breasts—and by implication the whole body—have been rewritten with new meanings.

Opening the body transgresses Western bodily boundaries. The boundary transgression of body marking is explicit in Karen's description of her scarifications, one of which created a scar in the shape of an orchid. This mark was created by a body mod artist in an event attended by members of her women's SM community, which was sponsoring workshops on body modification. She describes her scarification as modeled after a "Maui form of tattooing...using a sharpened shell to do the cut and rub ash into the open cut to make the scarring." The practice was ritualized and, as she describes it, "spiritual."

> What was going on here...was about the spirituality of claiming myself. Accepting myself. And that state of concentration, that is about spirit. I think it is the same or similar state that Buddhists, when they spend hours and hours and hours of the state of prayer. It's that place of acceptance and floating and honor. It's very, it's absolutely connected to the spiritual center of myself.... I think that people are really afraid of that state of being. It's terrifying to let go of the control that much. It is really about your control over the moment, and simply being in the moment, being one with the moment. Being completely open.

The openness in scarification ritual creates the liminal stage in what Karen, in modern primitivist fashion, considers a rite of passage. In anthropologist Victor Turner's description of indigenous rituals, liminality is the point of transition in ritual, the middle stage between young and old, unsocialized and socialized, pristine and marked. For example, the male undergoing puberty rites is no longer boy, yet neither a man; he is a liminal persona, a transitional person who resides in the margins.[7] Liminality is the temporal and physical space of ambiguity, in which cultural performance or rite is enacted with initiate and audience. The ritual of scarification invites liminality through its opening of the borders of the body.[8] In Karen's marginal, subcultural view of her rite of passage, the female body can be reappropriated through transgressive, self-marking ritual. The opening of the body violates its surface and also, as Karen describes, its former representations. For Karen, ritualized marking symbolically revokes former claims on the body—those of victimization, patriarchy, and control—and so is deeply meaningful.

Nonetheless, Karen's narrative hints at how such meanings cannot be fixed in the culture. In particular, she worries that the recent popularization of body modifications in her West Coast area, especially tattoos and body piercings, dilutes their significance. In her words, "I think it has become a fad and...that's not what it is to me.... I have managed to keep myself apart from that." Yet conversely, people in mainstream culture can also react with horror: Karen imagines that some would "scream obscenities at us for doing what we're doing."...

Jane

Jane describes her body modifications as acts of reclaiming, although unlike Karen, the reclamation is not a response to sexual victimization. But like them, Jane presents her visual modification as an attempt to claim authority over her body and rewrite its identifications. A 39-year-old student of social work who lives alone in a city on the East Coast, Jane has had a large dream-catcher symbol cut across her chest.[9] It reaches up to her neck and down between her breasts. It is about six inches across and about six inches tall. The scar is highly keloided, and it has been injected with blue and purple tattoo ink. The image is startling, and it visually redefines her. Jane describes getting such a radical scar as a way of acknowledging, and rejecting, the pressure of cultural standards of beauty.

> As a child, I was what might be referred to as an ugly ducking. I was freckly, skinny, gawky, flat-chested, you know, all of the things that are not valued in society. I never thought of myself as cute or good-looking and never of course got told I was....I didn't get positive reinforcement for my looks as a youngster, and I've grown up to become relatively attractive. But that's not how I feel about myself, because I have this lifetime of messages that I received from other people that said that I was not attractive....

Jane presents her scar as a resistance against the normative "lifetime of messages" that pressure her to reach the beauty ideal. As well as self-ownership and renegotiated sexuality, beauty is thus a target for reclamation. In similar fashion, Karen had identified beauty as a target for reclaiming. She had picked an orchid as a scar symbol to represent inner beauty:

> The orchid was about beauty. The orchid was about my having felt that I wasn't particularly beautiful...the orchid was about claiming my beauty and about saying, I'm not a spectacular looking person but I am beautiful and beauty comes from inside. So, that's how I came to have the orchid.

Like the body modifications of the other women, Jane's was undertaken in the presence of supportive friends and ritualized. After seeing cuttings and brandings at demonstrations sponsored by the local pro-sex feminist bookstore and later on a trip to the West Coast, Jane decided to organize her cutting event with the things and people that, in her words, "meant something to me." She set up her home as a ritual space:

> I personally went around and smudged my house with sage. For Native Americans, sage is an herb that purifies spiritual energy....I had my own candles and oils that have to do with power and protection. I set up the living room; I set up the atmosphere, to be clear and clean.

In a sense, the ritual was also for her about representing bravery.

> I got a [Native American] dreamcatcher....I can say that it would be a
> real good thing to have dreams. I haven't been able to allow myself to
> have dreams and wants or whatever for anything, anybody. I've been sort
> of plodding along in a very protective shell in my life...before I got this
> cutting....I was acknowledging that I was going to open myself up more
> and did it.

The cutting as she describes it was extremely painful, more so than she
had expected, and she decided to forego any other painful modifications in
the future. However, she claims not to regret the experience, and explains by
comparing her cutting to another painful body project women undertake or
endure:

> *VP*: Do you wish it had hurt less?
>
> *Jane*: That's a real hard one, because it's sort of like having a baby. After the
> baby's born, you don't remember the pain, and you're just euphoric and
> you've got this new life here, and it was the same kind of experience.

As a physical body, Jane has dis- and re-figured herself. The surface of
her upper torso is radically altered. She can feel the new growth: the scar
tissue is sensitive, felt from within the body (a slight itching feel), and tac-
tile. The highly prominent modification of her appearance also removes a
normative ideal of beauty from possibility. In this way, Jane's transformation
of her physical surface body also transforms her communicative body. Even
though most of her descriptions of the experience are positive, she describes
a shocked feeling at seeing the final result:

> I realized I've got this thing on my body for the rest of my life and said,
> what the fuck did I do? It's like not only do I have this thing on my body,
> but I'm going to be a counselor...and I have to wear button down shirts.
> It's really right there and I'm going to have to cover it up.

In subcultural settings, such as at the fetish flea market which attracts other
body modifiers, she can "show it off and get all kinds of compliments and
attention." In other settings, such as at her field-service placement for her
social work training, she perceives showing the mark as inappropriate. She
also has no plans to let her mother see it: "My mother has seen my eyebrow
piercing, but no, I'm not going to tell her that I've got a cut....It's where
I draw the line."...

Modified Bodies and Feminist Politics

Feminist disagreements over body modification reflect divergent assumptions
about subjectivity, consciousness, and the body. Post-essentialist feminists

view female bodies and subjectivity as socially constructed, culturally nego-
tiable, and saturated with power relations. Such perspectives have argued that
the body is always *already* inscribed by culture. It is socially controlled and
regulated, including through gender socialization and violence, and marked
by relations of power. The "normal" body, in this view, is not a biological category but rather an ideological construct that serves economic and familial
functions. The female body is prescribed roles and practices that lend apparent biological evidence for normalized female identity, thereby naturalizing
gender relations.

From this perspective, anomalous body practices may have the potential,
at least theoretically, to radically challenge the gendered roles and practices
of embodiment. The rituals I describe above create anomalous bodies, and
require the acceptance of moments of bodily uncertainty and ambivalence.
In the liminal state of embodiment that they promote, boundaries are erased
and redrawn; heterogeneity and contradiction are embraced. Transformations between states in rites of passage place the individual into a position of
marginality; the body-subject in the liminal zone manipulates and fluctuates
her identity by enacting, to quote Rob Shields in *Places on the Margin*, "a performance supported by social rituals and exchanges which confirm different
personas."[10]

Postmodern feminists have recognized the liminal, heterogeneous body-
subject—the cyborg—as subversive, largely because it resists the unified,
stable, gendered identity enforced in mainstream culture. Liminality might
reflect, at least temporarily, a "liberation from regimes of normative practices
and performance codes of mundane life," in Shields's terms.[11] As such, it can
denaturalize gender categories. The scarred, branded, or tattooed woman
may destabilize, in the words of medical sociologist Kathy Davis, "many of
our preconceived notions about beauty, identity, and the female body," as
well as focus attention on ways in which female bodies are invisibly marked
by power, including by violence.[12] Shields writes that marginal bodies also
"expose the relativity of the entrenched, universalising values of the cen-
tre, and expose the relativism of the cultural identities...they have denied,
rendered anomalous, or excluded."[13]

Karen's body markings expose stories of sexual victimization, but also
symbolically address women's chances to live in bodies as survivors. All the
women have created bodies that rewrite notions of beauty and counter, in
Jane's words, the "lifetime of messages" that prescribe and normalize beauty
regimens. They have marginalized themselves, but questioned the dominant
culture's control over their bodily appearance, behavior, and safety. In marking their bodies, they appear to shift both their private self-identifications
and their public identities, telling new stories to themselves and others about
the meanings of their embodiment. Rather than depicting hopelessness, the
practices imply that their body-stories are in flux, opened to the possibilities
of reinscription and renaming.

Yet, radical feminists would claim that body modifiers are "not in control" of their decisions, and that the practices themselves are harmful.[14] Some radical feminists, who are also critical of women's SM, have argued that the practices violate the body and reproduce oppressive relations of power by echoing patriarchal violence. Anti-body modification arguments generally either link the technologies themselves to mutilation and pathology or equate women's body modifications with more mainstream cosmetic practices that are seen as objectifying. Redical feminist scholar Sheila Jeffreys, for example, equates SM and body modification (piercing and tattooing) with addictive self-cutting and other self-mutilative practices:

> Some of the enthusiasm for piercing in lesbians, gay men, and heterosexual women arises from the experience of child sexual abuse. Self-mutilation in the form of stubbing out cigarettes on the body, arm slashing and even garroting are forms of self-injury that abuse non-survivors do sometimes employ. ... Sadomasochism and the current fashionability of piercing and tattooing provide an apparently acceptable form for such attacks on the abused body. Young women and men are walking around showing us the effects of the abuse that they have tried to turn into a badge of pride, a savage embrace of the most grave attacks they can make on their bodies.[15]

This argument asserts that the marked body is injured and attacked, either literally through pain or symbolically through harming the body's appearance. The fact that some of these bodily inscriptions make reference to experiences of victimization has not escaped their critics. While body modifiers themselves suggest that the violated female body can be rewritten in personally and politically meaningful ways, radical feminists argue in contrast that modifying the body is a straightforward replay of that violence. A large part of what is at issue here is the possibility of women's agency, which radical feminists have long argued is hampered by the psychological effects of patriarchy. Following this view, Jeffreys interprets the practices as "signifiers of false-consciousness," a criticism also reiterated in mainstream press accounts of feminist opposition to women's tattooing, piercing, and scarring.[16] ...

In my view, any critique of women's body practices as inherently deluded and self-hating must reveal and critique its own assumptions of the truth of female embodiment and subjectivity. The arguments radical feminists make against body modification seem to be informed by implicit assumptions about the body as naturally pristine and unmarked. I would argue that these assumptions are difficult to support in the face of our increasing awareness of the ways in which the body is socially constructed and inscribed by gendered relations of power. We have to ask, where is the elusive unmarked female body that represents women's freedom from bodily intervention? It can be found neither in history nor in anthropology; in the lives of contemporary women, it appears not simply as an ideal type but as a myth. One of the powerful messages of radical feminist thinking of the 1970s was that the threat of rape has influenced the lives and bodies of all women. In her reading of these theories of rape, *Rethinking Rape*, Ann Cahill describes how all women's bodies, not just those that have survived sexual assault, can be comported with what she calls a "phenomenology of fear." Women's bodies have been disciplined both to be wary of the possibility of rape or assault in alleys and on dark streets, and also to be weak and vulnerable as a sign of their femininity and beauty. From the perspective of many women who have suffered from victimization or objectification by patriarchal culture, then, the heralding of the unmarked body appears naive and ideological. Should it be pursued for its own sake despite its practical irrelevance? I would argue that women are not choosing whether or not to be modified and marked, but are negotiating how and in what way and by whom and to what effect.

The problems with charges of false consciousness are many, not the least of which is that they presume its counterpart—a proper, "true" consciousness. This now seems unacceptable. Such a notion asserts a singular, universalized, and essentialist version of feminist enlightenment. The extensive deconstruction of such notions in feminist theory in recent years by women of color, "Third World" and transnational feminists, and others whose views and experiences have traditionally been excluded from feminist discourse should give us pause. In these accounts, the wholly knowing feminist consciousness that can manage to achieve the "true" feminist attitude appears as an ideological fiction, much in the way that the wholly natural, pristine body that stands in opposition to culture has been exposed as a myth by post-essentialist feminists. The feminist debates over the universality of rights and feminist consciousness are far from over, but they have brought us at least to an awareness of how diverse are women's understandings of bodily practices, cultural and human rights, agency and radical consciousness. . . .

I would argue, following a post-essentialist, poststructural approach, that there is no universal standard of the body or of feminist subjectivity against which we can measure the actual practices of lived bodies. Rather, we should look to how the practices come to be surrounded and saturated with meaning. This involves examining the discourses deployed by the people who use the practices and those who observe them, as well as critically situating those discourses in socio-political context. Women's subcultural discourses represent marginal ways of knowing and strategizing the meanings of lived female embodiment. Rather than suggesting self-hatred or even indifference to their own victimization, the subcultural discourse of women's body modification, as I have shown here, explicitly identifies empowerment and rebellion against oppression as integral to their body projects.

But subcultural discourses cannot be accepted as transparent, or as the last word on the importance and effects of these practices. We cannot replace a notion of women as wholly unknowing subjects with one of them as all-knowing ones, as Sarah Thorton has pointed out in her discussion of subcultures.[17] Despite what women themselves may want to accomplish with anomalous body projects, I reject an overly liberal interpretation that would overemphasize women's autonomy and freedom in writing their bodies. Women are not individually responsible for situating their practices in all their larger collective and historical contexts, for predicting the political effects of their practices, or even for wholly authoring their meanings. Amelia Jones writes in *Body Art* that "it is often hard to appreciate the patterns of history when one is embedded in them."[18] Thus, body marks cannot be seen as solely ideographic or autobiographical. Marking the body is not a process that involves simply an individual author executing a strategic design that is read in the way she intends by her readers. The process is intersubjective, and, thus, to some extent, out of the hands of women themselves.

The Limits of Women's "Reclaiming"

Following this warning, I want to point out some of the possible risks and limitations of these practices. In my view, even though the practices are in many ways subversive, there are still serious political and strategic limits to women's reclaiming projects as practices of agency. . . .

First, the aim of symbolically recovering the body from victimization is limited by body projects because eventually, the women must stop. Otherwise, the physical effect would be, even by the standards of body modifiers, harmful and not reclaimative. . . .

Second, bodily resistance, as a private practice, may be not only limited, but also limit*ing*. The language of reclaiming, even written on the body, does not imply material reclamation in an objective sense; past body oppression is not reversed, rape culture is not erased. The rebellion offered is symbolic and communicative [but] . . . often hidden from public view. . . .

Finally, even visibility does not necessarily ensure politically radical messages. Despite women's aims to renounce victimization, objectification, and consumerization, the anomalous female body does not escape these pressures. This is evident in some of the appropriations of body modification practices within mainstream culture. These practices, at their most hard-core still highly deviant, undergo changes in meaning as the broader culture adapts to their presence on the cultural landscape. . . .

This problem is also borne out in the commodification of the subcultural female body as an exotic, sexy Other. . . .

The complexity of women's agency in relation to the body exemplified in reclaiming strategies, I think, counters the sense of political certainty that seems to inform some of the radical feminist pronouncements on women's body modification and on the victimization of the female body more generally. It would also resist overly celebratory interpretations that imply that, in postmodern culture, we are all now fully in control of inscribing our bodies, or that view the body as fully unfixed and individually malleable. Women's marked bodies exemplify both the praxis of culturally marginal body projects and the limits of that praxis. As I see it, they highlight the female body as a site of negotiation between power and powerlessness, neither of which are likely to win fully. . . .

Notes

1. Catherine MacKinnon, "Sexuality," in *The Second Wave*, ed. Linda Nicholson (New York: Routledge, 1997), 197.

2. Andrea Dworkin, "Gynocide: Chinese Footbinding," in *Living with Contradictions: Controversy over Feminist Ethics*, ed. Alison M. Jagger (Boulder, CO: Westview Press, 1994).

3. Karmen MacKendrick, "Technoflesh, or Didn't that Hurt?" *Fashion Theory* vol. 2, no. 1 (1998): 81–108.

4. Melanie Klein, "Duality and Redefinition: Young Feminism and the Alternative Music Community," in *Gender Through the Prism of Difference*, ed. Maxine Baca Zinn, Pierrette Hondagneu-Sotelo, and Michael Messner (Boston: Allyn and Bacon, 1999), 452.

5. Ibid., 454.

6. MacKendrick, 1998: 23.

7. Victor Turner, *The Forest of Symbols: Aspects of Ndembu Ritual* (Ithaca, NY: Cornell University Press, 1967), 95.

8. Which places it in "interaction with the world" where it "trangresses its own limits." Bahktin, Mikhail. 1984. *Rabelais and His World*, trans. Helene Iswolsky (Cambridge, MA: Massachusetts Institute of Technology Press).

9. This is a Native American symbol widely recognized in non-native U.S. culture. Jane's choice of the dreamcatcher symbol and her choice of the scarification ritual reflect the neotribal nature of much contemporary body modification.

10. Rob Shields, *Places on the Margin: Alternative Geographies of Modernity* (London: Routledge, 1991), 269. Even in indigenous rites of passage, as Victor Turner describes, marginality is often regarded as polluting or unclean, but the marginal position of the liminal person is necessary for symbolic transformation to become social reality.

11. Ibid., 84.

12. Kathy Davis, "My Body Is My Art: Cosmetic Surgery as Feminist Utopia?" *European Journal of Women's Studies* vol. 4 (1997): 23–38.

13. Shields, 1991: 277.

14. Valeria Eubanks, "Zones of Dither: Writing the Postmodern Body," *Body and Society* vol. 2, no. 3 (1996), 81.

15. Jeffreys 1994: 21, quoted in Nikki Sullivan, "Fleshing Out Pleasure: Canonisation or Crucifixion?" *Australian Feminist Studies* vol. 12, no. 26 (1997): 283–291.

16. Nikki Sullivan, 1997: "Fleshing Out Pleasure: Canonization or Crucifixion" *Australian Feminist Studies* vol.12, no. 26: 3–24.

17. See Sarah Thornton, "The Social Logic of Subcultural Capital," in *The Subcultures Reader*, ed. Ken Gelder and Sarah Thornton (London: Routledge, 1997), 200–211.

18. Amelia Jones, *Body Art: Performing the Subject* (Minneapolis: University of Minnesota Press, 1998), 11.

IV

THE POLITICS OF BEHAVIOR

The final section of this volume looks at a variety of issues linked to women's—and men's—behavior. Each of these issues touches on the question of the social construction of women's bodies, discussed earlier in this volume, and each illustrates how ideas about women's bodies can serve to constrain women's lives and options. The first two articles address the experiences of girls and women who participate in sports, illustrating how social stigma against athletic females (including accusations of lesbianism) has discouraged girls and women from athletic endeavors, and, in turn, how discouraging females from athleticism has reinforced the idea that the athletic female body is deviant. The next two articles look at how boys' and men's ideas about women's bodies and behavior contribute to sexual harassment, rape, and other forms of coercion and violence directed at girls and women. Finally, the last article in this section and this volume examines how cultural attitudes toward women's lives and bodies are embedded in current controversies over reproductive rights and "fetal rights."

19

From the "Muscle Moll" to the "Butch" Ballplayer

Mannishness, Lesbianism, and Homophobia in U.S. Women's Sport

SUSAN K. CAHN

*In every historical era, some women have desired sexual and romantic rela-
tionships with other women. But as the first article in this volume described,
for most of history, Western societies rarely stigmatized these women or identified them as lesbian. Almost no women had the economic resources needed to
survive if unwed, and women's sexuality was rarely taken seriously, and so few
even considered the potential sexual aspects of women's relationships with other
women.*

*By the early twentieth century, however, a growing number of women were
receiving higher educations, entering professions, or finding other paid work that
gave them the ability, should they choose, to live independently of men. From
this point on, prejudice and discrimination against lesbians became a powerful
social force. This is the backdrop for Susan Cahn's article.*

*In this article, Cahn traces the history of women's participation in sports
from the early twentieth century through the 1960s. She uses this history to show
how attitudes toward women's sports both reflected and reinforced social ideas
about proper female sexuality and the proper place of women in American
society. Prior to the 1930s, Cahn shows, critics of women's sports argued that
participating in sports encouraged unrestrained emotional excitement and exuberant physical activity and thus could increase women's* heterosexual *desires
and activity. Conversely, in later years, critics argued that participating in*

Susan Cahn, "From the 'Muscle Moll' to the Butch Ballplayer: Mannishness, Lesbianism, and
Homophobia in U.S. Women's Sports" was originally published in *Feminist Studies* 19(2)
(Summer 1993): 343–368, by permission of the publisher, Feminist Studies, Inc.

sports could lead women to become homosexual *by reducing their attractiveness to men or their interest in heterosexual relationships. In both eras, gendered fears and stereotypes (complicated by racial stereotypes) served to keep women out of sports and to stigmatize those whose interests or appearance did not fit dominant cultural norms.*

In 1934, *Literary Digest* subtitled an article on women's sports, "Will the playing fields one day be ruled by amazons?" The author, Fred Wittner, answered the question affirmatively and concluded that as an "inevitable consequence" of sport's masculinizing effect, "girls trained in physical education today may find it more difficult to attract the most worthy fathers for their children" (1934, 43). The image of women athletes as mannish, failed heterosexuals represents a thinly veiled reference to lesbianism in sport. At times, the homosexual allusion has been indisputable, as in a journalist's description (Murray n.d.) of the great athlete Babe Didrikson as a "Sapphic, Brobdingnagian woman" or in television comedian Arsenio Hall's more recent [1988] witticism, "If we can put a man on the moon, why can't we put one on Martina Navratilova?" More frequently, however, popular commentary on lesbians in sport has taken the form of indirect references, surfacing through denials and refutations rather than open acknowledgment. When in 1955 an *Ebony* magazine article on African American track stars insisted that "off track, the girls are entirely feminine. Most of them like boys, dances, club affairs," the reporter answered the implicit but unspoken charge that athletes, especially Black women in a "manly" sport, were masculine manhaters, or lesbians.

The figure of the mannish lesbian athlete has acted as a powerful but unarticulated "bogey woman" of sport, forming a silent foil for more positive, corrective images that attempt to rehabilitate the image of women athletes and resolve the cultural contradiction between athletic prowess and femininity. As a stereotyped figure in U.S. society, the lesbian athlete forms part of everyday cultural knowledge. Yet historians have paid scant attention to the connection between female sexuality and sport.[1] This essay explores the historical relationship between lesbianism and sport by tracing the development of the stereotyped "mannish lesbian athlete" and examining its relation to the lived experience of mid-twentieth-century lesbian athletes.

I argue that fears of mannish female sexuality in sport initially centered on the prospect of unbridled heterosexual desire. By the 1930s, however, female athletic mannishness began to connote heterosexual failure, usually couched in terms of unattractiveness to men, but also suggesting the possible absence of heterosexual interest. In the years following World War II, the stereotype of the lesbian athlete emerged full blown. The extreme homophobia and the gender conservatism of the postwar era created a context in which longstanding linkages among mannishness, female homosexuality, and athletes cohered around the figure of the mannish lesbian athlete....

Amazons, Muscle Molls, and The Question of Sexual (Im)morality

The athletic woman sparked interest and controversy in the early decades of the twentieth century. In the United States and other Western societies, sport functioned as a male preserve, an all-male domain in which men not only played games together but also demonstrated and affirmed their manhood (Dunning 1986; Kimmel 1987; Mangan and Park 1987; Mrozek 1983). The "maleness" of sport derived from a gender ideology which labeled aggression, physicality, competitive spirit, and athletic skill as masculine attributes necessary for achieving true manliness. This notion found unquestioned support in the dualistic, polarized concepts of gender which prevailed in Victorian America. However, by the turn of the century, women had begun to challenge Victorian gender arrangements, breaking down barriers to female participation in previously male arenas of public work, politics, and urban nightlife. Some of these "New Women" sought entry into the world of athletics as well. On college campuses students enjoyed a wide range of intramural sports through newly formed Women's Athletic Associations. Off-campus women took up games like golf, tennis, basketball, swimming, and occasionally even wrestling, car racing, or boxing. As challengers to one of the defining arenas of manhood, skilled female athletes became symbols of the broader march of womanhood out of the Victorian domestic sphere into once prohibited male realms.

The woman athlete represented both the appealing and the threatening aspects of modern womanhood. In a positive light, she captured the exuberant spirit, physical vigor, and brazenness of the New Woman. The University of Minnesota student newspaper proclaimed in 1904 that the athletic girl was the "truest type of All-American coed" (1904–5 Scrapbooks of Anne Maude Butner, Butner Papers, University of Minnesota Archives, Minneapolis). Several years later, *Harper's Bazaar* labeled the unsportive girl as "not strictly up to date" (Mange 1910, 246), and *Good Housekeeping* noted that the "tomboy" had come to symbolize "a new type of American girl, new not only physically, but mentally and morally" (de Koven 1912, 150).

Yet, women athletes invoked condemnation as often as praise. Critics ranged from physicians and physical educators to sportswriters, male athletic officials, and casual observers. In their view, strenuous athletic pursuits endangered women and threatened the stability of society. They maintained that women athletes would become manlike, adopting masculine dress, talk, and mannerisms. In addition, they contended, too much exercise would damage female reproductive capacity. And worse yet, the excitement of sport would cause women to lose control, conjuring up images of frenzied, distraught co-eds on the verge of moral, physical, and emotional breakdown. These fears collapsed into an all-encompassing concept of "mannishness," a term signifying female masculinity.

The public debate over the merits of women's athletic participation remained lively through the 1910s and 1920s. Implicit in the dispute over "mannishness" was a longstanding disagreement over the effect of women's athletic activities on their sexuality. Controversy centered around two issues—damage to female reproductive capacity and the unleashing of heterosexual passion. Medical experts and exercise specialists disagreed among themselves about the effects of athletic activity on women's reproductive cycles and organs. Some claimed that athletic training interfered with menstruation and caused reproductive organs to harden or atrophy; others insisted that rigorous exercise endowed women with strength and energy which would make them more fit for bearing and rearing children. Similarly, experts vehemently debated whether competition unleashed nonprocreative, erotic desires identified with male sexuality and unrespectable women, or, conversely, whether invigorating sport enhanced a woman's feminine charm and sexual appeal, channeling sexual energy into wholesome activity.

Conflicting opinion on sexual matters followed closely along the lines of a larger dispute which divided the world of women's sport into warring camps. Beginning in the 1910s, female physical educators and male sport promoters squared off in a decades-long struggle over the appropriate nature of female competition and the right to govern women's athletics (Gerber 1975; Himes 1986; Hult 1985). The conflict was a complicated one, involving competing class and gender interests played out in organizational as well as philosophical battles. It was extremely important in shaping women's sports for more than fifty years. Although historians of sport have examined the broad parameters of the conflict, they have paid less attention to the competing sexual perspectives advanced by each side.

Physical educators took a cautious approach on all matters of sexuality, one designed to safeguard vulnerable young athletes and to secure their own professional status as respectable women in the male-dominated worlds of academia and sport. Heeding dire warnings about menstrual dysfunction, sterility, and inferior offspring, educators created policies to curtail strenuous competition and prohibit play during menstruation. They worried equally about the impact of sport on sexual morality. Alleging that competition would induce "powerful impulses" leading girls into a "temptation to excess" and the "pitfall of overindulgence," educators and their allies pressured popular sport promoters to reduce the competitive stimulation, publicity, and physical strain thought to endanger the sexuality of their female charges (Inglis 1910; Paret 1900, 1567; Sargent 1913).

Popular sport organizations like the Amateur Athletic Union [AAU] agreed that unregulated female competition posed psychological and moral dangers. But AAU officials countered protectionist physical education policies with a nationalist, eugenic stance which argued that strenuous activity under proper guidance would actually strengthen reproductive organs, creating a vigorous cadre of mothers to produce a generation of stalwart American sons (e.g., MacFadden 1929; Steers 1932). Although making some concessions to demands for modesty and female supervision, in the long run AAU leaders and commercial sport promoters also rejected educators' emphasis on sexual control. Sponsors of popular sport found that sexual hype, much more than caution, helped to attract customers and mute charges of mannishness. In working-class settings and in more elite sports like swimming, an ideal of the "athlete as beauty queen" emerged. Efforts to present the female athlete as sexually attractive and available mirrored the playful, erotic sensibility present in the broader commercial leisure culture of the early twentieth century (Erenberg 1981; Freedman and D'Emilio 1988; Peiss 1986).

The class and gender lines in this dispute were complicated by overlapping constituencies. Female educators adhered closely to middle-class, even Victorian, notions of respectability and modesty. But their influence spread beyond elite private and middle-class schools into working-class public schools and industrial recreation programs. And male promoters, often themselves of the middle-class, continued to control some school sport and, outside the schools, influenced both working-class and elite sports. Moreover, Black physical educators advanced a third point of view. Although few in number, early-twentieth-century African American physical education instructors generally aligned themselves with popular promoters in favor of competition and interscholastic sports. Yet their strong concern with maintaining respectability created some sympathy for the positions advanced by white leaders of women's physical education (Arnett 1921; Dunham 1924; Ellis 1939; Roberts 1927).

On all sides of the debate, however, the controversy about sport and female sexuality presumed heterosexuality. Neither critics nor supporters suggested that "masculine" athleticism might indicate or induce same-sex love. When experts warned of the amazonian athlete's possible sexual transgressions, they linked the physical release of sport with a loss of heterosexual *control*, not *inclination*. The most frequently used derogatory term for women athletes was "Muscle Moll." In its only other usages, the word "moll" referred to either the female lovers of male gangsters or to prostitutes. Both represented disreputable, heterosexually deviant womanhood.

By contrast, medical studies of sexual "deviance" from the late nineteenth and early twentieth centuries quite clearly linked "mannishness" to lesbianism, and in at least two cases explicitly connected female homosexuality with boyish athleticism (Chauncey 1989, 90–91; Ellis 1915, 250; Wise 1883, 88). It is curious then that in answering charges against the mannish Muscle Moll, educators and sport promoters of this period did not refer to or deny lesbianism. However, the "mannish lesbian" made little sense in the heterosexual milieu of popular sports. Promoters encouraged mixed audiences for women's athletic events, often combining them with men's games, postgame dances and musical entertainment, or even beauty contests. The image of the athlete as beauty queen and the commercial atmosphere that characterized much of working-class sport ensured that the sexual debate surrounding the modern female athlete would focus on her heterosexual charm, daring, or disrepute. The homosocial environment of women's physical education left educators more vulnerable to insinuations that their profession was populated by "mannish" types who preferred the love of women. However, the feminine respectability and decorum cultivated by the profession provided an initial shield from associations with either the mannish lesbian or her more familiar counterpart, the heterosexual Muscle Moll.

The Muscle Moll as Heterosexual Failure: Emerging Lesbian Stereotypes

In the 1930s, however, the heterosexual understanding of the mannish "amazon" began to give way to a new interpretation which educators and promoters could not long ignore. To the familiar charge that female athletes resembled men, critics added the newer accusation that sport-induced mannishness disqualified them as candidates for heterosexual romance. In 1930, an *American Mercury* medical reporter decried the decline of romantic love, pinning the blame on women who entered sport, business, and politics. He claimed that such women "act like men, talk like men, and think like men." The author explained that "women have come closer and closer to men's level," and, consequently, "the purple allure of distance has vamoosed" (Nathan 1930). Four years later, the *Ladies Home Journal* printed a "Manual on the More or Less Subtle Art of Getting a Man" which listed vitality, gaiety, vivacity, and good sportsmanship—qualities typically associated with women athletes and formerly linked to the athletic flapper's heterosexual appeal—as "the very qualities that are likely to make him consider anything but marriage" (Moats 1934). Although the charges didn't exclusively focus on athletes, they implied that female athleticism was contrary to heterosexual appeal, which appeared to rest on women's difference from and deference to men.

The concern with heterosexual appeal reflected broader sexual transformations in U.S. society. Historians of sexuality have examined the multiple forces which reshaped gender and sexual relations in the first few decades of the twentieth century. Victorian sexual codes crumbled under pressure from an assertive, boldly sexual working-class youth culture, a women's movement which defied prohibitions against public female activism, and the growth of a new pleasure-oriented consumer economy. In the wake of these changes, modern ideals of womanhood embraced an overtly erotic heterosexual sensibility. At the same time, medical fascination with sexual "deviance" created a growing awareness of lesbianism, now understood as a form of congenital or psychological pathology. The medicalization of homosexuality in combination with an antifeminist backlash in the 1920s against female autonomy and power contributed to a more fully articulated taboo against lesbianism. The modern heterosexual woman stood in stark opposition to her threatening sexual counterpart, the "mannish" lesbian (Freedman and D'Emilio 1988; Simmons 1989).

By the late 1920s and early 1930s, with a modern lesbian taboo and an eroticized definition of heterosexual femininity in place, the assertive, muscular female competitor roused increasing suspicion. It was at this moment that both subtle and direct references to the lesbian athlete emerged in physical education and popular sport. Uncensored discussions of intimate female companionship and harmless athletic "crushes" disappear from the record, pushed underground by the increasingly hostile tone of public discourse about female sexuality and athleticism. Fueled by the gender antagonisms and anxieties of the Depression, the public began scrutinizing women athletes—known for their appropriation of masculine games and styles—for signs of deviance.

Where earlier references to "amazons" had signaled heterosexual ardor, journalists now used the term to mean unattractive, failed heterosexuals. Occasionally, the media made direct mention of athletes' presumed lesbian tendencies. A 1933 *Redbook* article, for example, casually mentioned that track and golf star Babe Didrikson liked men just to horse around with her and not "make love," adding that Babe's fondness for her best girlfriends far surpassed her affection for any man (Marston 1933, 60). The direct reference was unusual; the lesbian connotation of mannishness was forged primarily through indirect links of association. The preponderance of evidence appears in public exchanges between opponents and advocates of women's sport.

After two decades of celebrating the female collegiate athlete, yearbooks at co-ed colleges began to ridicule physical education majors and Women's Athletic Association (WAA) members, portraying them as hefty, disheveled, and ugly. A 1937 Minnesota *Gopher* yearbook sarcastically titled its presentation on the WAA "Over in No Man's Land." Finding themselves cast as unattractive prudes or mannish misfits, physical educators struggled to revise their image. They declared the muscle-bound, manhating athlete a relic of the past, supplanted by "lovely, feminine charming girls" whose fitness, suppleness, and grace merely made them "more beautiful on the dance floor that evening" (Mooney 1937; Sefton 1937).

Similar exchanges appeared in popular magazines. After *Literary Digest* published Fred Wittner's assertion (1934, 42) that "worthy fathers" would not find trained women athletes attractive mates, AAU official Ada Taylor Sackett issued a rebuttal which reassured readers that because athletic muscles resembled "those of women who dance all night," women in sport could no doubt "still attract a worthy mate" (1934, 43). When critics maligned athletic femininity, they suggested that athletes were literally un-becoming women: unattractive females who abdicated their womanhood and fell under sexual suspicion. When defenders responded with ardent assertions that women athletes did indeed exhibit interest in men, marriage, and motherhood, it suggested that they understood "mannish" to mean "not-heterosexual."

The Butch Ballplayer: Midcentury Stereotypes of the Lesbian Athlete

Tentatively voiced in the 1930s, these accusations became harsher and more explicit under the impact of wartime changes in gender and sexuality and the subsequent panic over the "homosexual menace." In a post-World War II climate markedly hostile to nontraditional women and lesbians, women in physical education and in working-class popular sports became convenient targets of homophobic indictment.

World War II opened up significant economic and social possibilities for gay men and women. Embryonic prewar homosexual subcultures blossomed during the war and spread across the midcentury urban landscape. Bars, nightclubs, public cruising spots, and informal social networks facilitated the development of gay and lesbian enclaves. But the permissive atmosphere did not survive the war's end. Waving the banner of Cold War political and social conservatism, government leaders acted at the federal, state, and local levels to purge gays and lesbians from government and military posts, to initiate legal investigations and prosecutions of gay individuals and institutions, and to encourage local police crackdowns on gay bars and street life. The perceived need to safeguard national security and to reestablish social order in the wake of wartime disruption sparked a "homosexual panic" which promoted the fear, loathing, and persecution of homosexuals (Bérubé 1990; D'Emilio 1983; Freedman and D'Emilio 1988).

Lesbians suffered condemnation for their violation of gender as well as sexual codes. The tremendous emphasis on family, domesticity, and "traditional" femininity in the late 1940s and 1950s reflected postwar anxieties about the reconsolidation of a gender order shaken by two decades of depression and war. As symbols of women's refusal to conform, lesbians endured intense scrutiny by experts who regularly focused on their subjects' presumed masculinity. Sexologists attributed lesbianism to masculine tendencies and freedoms encouraged by the war, linking it to a general collapsing of gender distinctions which, in their view, destabilized marital and family relations (Breines 1986; Penn 1991).

Lesbians remained shadowy figures to most Americans, but women athletes—noted for their masculine bodies, interests, and attributes—were visible representatives of the gender inversion often associated with homosexuality. Physical education majors, formerly accused of being unappealing to men, were increasingly charged with being uninterested in them as well. The 1952 University of Minnesota *Gopher* yearbook snidely reported: "Believe it or not, members of the Women's Athletic Association are normal" and found conclusive evidence in the fact that "at least one...of WAA's 300 members is engaged" (p. 257). And on May 10, 1956, a newspaper account in the *Texan* regarding the University of Texas Sports Association (UTSA) women's sports banquet led off with the headline, "UTSA Gives Awards," followed by a subheading "Gayness Necessary." The second headline referred to a guest speaker's talk on positive attitudes, entitled "The Importance of Being Debonair," but the lesbian allusion was unmistakable and I believe fully intentional.[2]

The lesbian stigma began to plague popular athletes too, especially in working-class sports noted for their masculine toughness. The pall of suspicion did not completely override older associations with heterosexual deviance. When *Collier's* 1947 article (Lagemann) on the Red Heads, a barnstorming women's basketball team, exclaimed "It's basketball—not a striptease!" the author alluded to both the heterosexual appeal and the hint of disrepute long associated with working-class women athletes. But the dominant postwar voice intimated a different type of disrepute. Journalists continued to attack the mannish athlete as ugly and sexually unappealing, implying that this image could only be altered through proof of heterosexual "success."

The career of Babe Didrikson, which spanned the 1920s to the 1950s, illustrates the shift. In the early 1930s the press had ridiculed the tomboyish track star for her "hatchet face," "door-stop jaw," and "button-breasted" chest. After quitting track, Didrikson dropped out of the national limelight, married professional wrestler George Zaharias in 1938, and then staged a spectacular athletic comeback as a golfer in the late 1940s and 1950s. Fascinated by her personal transformation and then, in the 1950s, moved by her battle with cancer, journalists gave Didrikson's comeback extensive coverage and helped make her a much-loved popular figure. In reflecting on her success, however, sportswriters spent at least as much time on Didrikson's love life as her golf stroke. Headlines blared, "Babe is a lady now: The world's most amazing athlete has learned to wear nylons and cook for her huge husband," and reporters gleefully described how "along came a great big he-man wrestler and the Babe forgot all her man-hating chatter" (Andersen 1945; Gallico 1960; Farmer 1947; Martin 1947).

Postwar sport discourse consistently focused on women's sexual as well as their athletic achievements. As late as 1960, a *New York Times Magazine* headline asked, "Do men make passes at athletic lasses?" Columnist William B. Furlong answered no for most activities, concluding that except for a few "yes" sports like swimming, women athletes "surrendered" their sex. The challenge for women athletes was not to conquer new athletic feats, which would only further reduce their sexual appeal, but to regain their womanhood through sexual surrender to men.

Media coverage in national magazines and metropolitan newspapers typically focused on the sexual accomplishments of white female athletes, but postwar observers and promoters of African American women's sport also confronted the issue of sexual normalcy. In earlier decades, neither Black nor white commentary on African American athletes expressed a concern with "mannish" lesbianism. The white media generally ignored Black athletes. Implicitly, however, stereotypes of Black females as highly sexual, promiscuous, and unrestrained in their heterosexual passions discouraged the linkage

between mannishness and lesbianism. Racist gender ideologies further complicated the meaning of mannishness. Historically, European American racial
thought characterized African Americans women as aggressive, coarse, passionate, and physical—the same qualities assigned to manliness in sport
(Carby 1987; Collins 1990; Giddings 1984). Excluded from dominant ideals
of womanhood, Black women's success in sport could be interpreted not
as an unnatural deviation but, rather, as the natural result of their reputed
closeness to nature, animals, and masculinity.[3]

Within Black communities, strong local support for women's sport may
also have weakened the association between sport and lesbianism. Athletes
from Tuskegee Institute's national championship track teams of the late
1930s and 1940s described an atmosphere of campus-wide enthusiastic support. They noted that although a male student might accuse an athlete of
being "funny" if she turned him down for a date, in general lesbianism
was not a subject of concern in Black sport circles (personal interviews,
Alice Coachman Davis, Lula Hymes Glenn, and Leila Perry Glover, 1992).
Similarly, Gloria Wilson (pseudonym, personal interview, 1988) found that
she encountered far less uneasiness about lesbianism on her Black semipro
softball team in the late 1950s and 1960s than she did in the predominantly
white college physical education departments she joined later. She explained
that the expectation of heterosexuality was ingrained in Black women to the
point that "anything outside of that realm is just out of the question." While
recalling that her teammates "had no time or patience for 'funnies,' " Wilson
noted that the issue rarely came up, in large part because most team members
were married and therefore "didn't have to prove it because then, too, their
men were always at those games. They were very supportive."

Although Black athletes may have encountered few lesbian stereotypes at
the local level, circumstances in the broader society eventually pressed African
American sport promoters and journalists to address the issue of mannish
sexuality. The strong association of sports and lesbianism developed at the
same time as Black athletes became a dominant presence in American sport
culture. Midcentury images of sport, Blackness, masculinity, and lesbianism
circulated in the same orbit in various combinations. There was no particular
correlation between Black women and lesbianism; however, the association
of each with mannishness and sexual aggression potentially linked the two.
In the late 1950s, Black sport promoters and journalists joined others in taking up the question of sexual "normalcy." One Black newspaper (*Baltimore
Afro-American*) in 1957 described tennis star Althea Gibson as a childhood
"tomboy" who "later in life ... finds herself victimized by complexes." The
article did not elaborate on the nature of Gibson's "complex," but lesbianism
is inferred in the linkage between "tomboys" and psychological illness. This
connotation becomes clearer by looking at the defense of Black women's
sport. Echoing *Ebony's* avowal (1955, 28, 32) that "entirely feminine"
Black female track stars "like boys, dances, club affairs," in 1962 Tennessee State University track coach Ed Temple asserted in the *Detroit News*,

"None of my girls have any trouble getting boy friends.... We don't want amazons."

Constant attempts to shore up the heterosexual reputation of athletes can be read as evidence that the longstanding reputation of female athletes as mannish women had become a covert reference to lesbianism. By mid-century, a fundamental reorientation of sexual meanings fused notions of femininity, female eroticism, and heterosexual attractiveness into a single ideal. Mannishness, once primarily a sign of gender crossing, assumed a specifically lesbian-sexual connotation. In the wake of this change, the strong cultural association between sport and masculinity made women's athletics ripe for emerging lesbian stereotypes. This meaning of athletic mannishness raises [the] further question what impact did the stereotype have on women's sport?....

Sport and the Heterosexual Imperative

The image of the mannish lesbian athlete had a direct effect on women competitors, on strategies of athletic organizations, and on the overall popularity of women's sport. The lesbian stereotype exerted pressure on athletes to demonstrate their femininity and heterosexuality, viewed as one and the same. Many women adopted an apologetic stance toward their athletic skill. Even as they competed to win, they made sure to display outward signs of femininity in dress and demeanor. They took special care in contact with the media to reveal "feminine" hobbies like cooking and sewing, to mention current boyfriends, and to discuss future marriage plans (Del Rey 1978).

Leaders of women's sport took the same approach at the institutional level. In answer to portrayals of physical education majors and teachers as social rejects and prudes, physical educators revised their philosophy to place heterosexuality at the center of professional objectives. In the late 1930s, they invited psychologists to speak at national professional meetings about problems of sexual adjustment. Such experts described the "types of people who are unadjusted to heterosexual cooperative activity" and warned women in physical education to "develop a prejudice *against* segregation of the sexes" (National Amateur Athletic Federation-Women's Division 1938). Told that exclusively female environments caused failed heterosexual development, physical educators who had long advocated female separatism in sport were pressed to promote mixed-sex groups and heterosexual "adjustment."

Curricular changes implemented between the mid-1930s and mid-1950s institutionalized the new philosophy. In a paper on postwar objectives, Mildred A. Schaeffer (1945) explained that physical education classes should help women "develop an interest in school dances and mixers and a desire to voluntarily attend them." To this end, administrators revised coursework to emphasize beauty and social charm over rigorous exercise and health. They exchanged old rationales of fitness and fun for promises of trimmer waistlines, slimmer hips, and prettier complexions. At Radcliffe, for example, faculty redesigned health classes to include "advice on dress, carriage, hair, skin, voice, and any factor that would tend to improve personal appearance and thus contribute to social and economic success" (Physical Education Director, no date). Intramural programs replaced interclass basketball tournaments and weekend campouts for women with mixed-sex "co-recreational" activities like bowling, volleyball, and "fun nights" of ping-pong and shuffleboard. Some departments also added co-educational classes to foster "broader, keener, more sympathetic understanding of the opposite sex" (Department of Physical Education 1955).[4] Department heads cracked down on "mannish" students and faculty, issuing warnings against "casual styles" which might "lead us back into some dangerous channels" (Ashton 1957). They implemented dress codes which forbade slacks and men's shirts or socks, adding as well a ban on "boyish hair cuts" and unshaven legs. For example, the 1949–50 Physical Training Staff Handbook at the University of Texas stated (p. 16), "Legs should be kept shaved," while restrictions on hair and dress are spelled out in the staff minutes and physical education handbooks for majors at the universities of Wisconsin, Texas, and Minnesota....

Popular sport promoters adopted similar tactics. Martialing sexual data like they were athletic statistics, a 1954 AAU poll sought to sway a skeptical public with numerical proof of heterosexuality—the fact that 91 percent of former female athletes surveyed had married (Andersen 1954). Publicity for the midwestern All-American Girls Baseball League (AAGBL) included statistics on the number of married players in the league. In the same vein, the women's golf tour announced that one-third of the pros were married, and the rest were keeping an eye peeled for prospects who might "lure them from the circuit to the altar" (All-American Girls Baseball League Records, Pennsylvania State University Libraries; *Saturday Evening Post* 1954).

The fear of lesbianism was greatest where a sport had a particularly masculine image and where promoters needed to attract a paying audience. Professional and semipro basketball and softball fit the bill on both accounts. Athletic leaders tried to resolve the problem by "proving" the attractive femininity of athletes. Softball and basketball tournaments continued to feature beauty pageants. Although in earlier times such events celebrated the "sexiness" of the emancipated modern woman, in later decades they seemed to serve a more defensive function. The AAU's magazine, the *Amateur Athlete*, made sure that at least one photograph of the national basketball tournament's beauty "queen and her court" accompanied the photo of each year's championship team. Behind the scenes, teams passed dress and conduct codes. For example, the All-American Girls Baseball League's 1951 Constitution prohibited players from wearing men's clothing or getting "severe" haircuts. That this was an attempt to secure the heterosexual image of athletes was made even clearer when league officials announced that AAGBL policy prohibited the recruitment of "freaks" and "Amazons" (Markey n.d.; Feminine Sluggers 1952).

In the end, the strategic emphasis on heterosexuality and the suppression of "mannishness" did little to alter the image of women in sport. The stereotype of the mannish lesbian athlete grew out of the persistent common sense equation of sport and masculinity. Opponents of women's sport reinforced this belief when they denigrated women's athletic efforts and ridiculed skilled athletes as "grotesque," "mannish," or "unnatural." Leaders of women's sport unwittingly contributed to the same set of ideas when they began to orient their programs around the new feminine heterosexual ideal. As physical education policies and media campaigns worked to suppress lesbianism and marginalize athletes who didn't conform to dominant standards of femininity, sport officials embedded heterosexism into the institutional and ideological framework of sport. The effect extended beyond sport to the wider culture, where the figure of the mannish lesbian athlete announced that competitiveness, strength, independence, aggression, and physical intimacy among women fell outside the bounds of womanhood. As a symbol of female deviance, she served as a powerful reminder to all women to tow the line of heterosexuality and femininity or risk falling into a despised category of mannish (not-women) women....

Notes

I would like to thank Birgitte Soland, Maureen Honish, Kath Weston, George Chauncey, Jr., and Nan Enstad for their criticisms, encouragement, and editorial advice on earlier versions of this essay.

1. Among the works that do consider the issue of homosexuality are Lenskyj (1986), Zipter (1988), and Bennett (1982). On the relationship between male homosexuality and sport, see Pronger (1990).

2. Although the term "gay" as a reference to homosexuals occurred only sporadically in the mass media before the 1960s, it was in use as a slang term among some homosexual men and lesbians as early as the 1920s and quite commonly by the 1940s.

3. Elizabeth Lunbeck (1987) notes a similar pattern in her discussion of medical theories of the "hypersexual" white female. Because psychiatrists assumed that Black women were naturally "oversexed," when defining the medical condition of hypersexuality, they included only young white working-class women whose sexual ardor struck physicians and social workers as unnaturally excessive.

4. For curricular changes, I examined physical education records at the Universities of Wisconsin, Texas, and Minnesota, Radcliffe College, Smith College, Tennessee State University, and Hampton University.

References

Andersen, Roxy. 1945. Fashions in feminine sport. *Amateur Athlete*, March.
———. 1954. Statistical survey of former women athletes. *Amateur Athlete*, September.
Arnett, Ruth. 1921. Girls need physical education. *Chicago Defender*, 10 December.

Ashton, Dudley. 1957. Recruiting future teachers. *Journal of Health, Physical Education, and Recreation* 28 (October):49.

Baltimore Afro-American. 1957. 29 June, Magazine Section, 1.

Bennett, Roberta. 1982. Sexual labeling as social control: Some political effects of being female in the gym. *Perspectives* 4:40–50.

Bérubé, Alan. 1990. *Coming Out Under Fire: The History of Gay Men and Women in World War Two.* New York: Free Press.

Breines, Wini. 1986. The 1950s: Gender and some social science. *Sociological Inquiry* 56 (Winter):69–92.

Carby, Hazel. 1987. *Reconstructing Womanhood: The Emergence of the Afro-American Women Novelist.* New York: Oxford University Press.

Chauncey, George, Jr. 1989. From sexual inversion to homosexuality: Medicine and the changing conceptualization of female deviance. In *Passion and Power: Sexuality in History*, edited by Kathy Peiss and Christina Simmons. Philadelphia: Temple University Press.

Collins, Patricia Hill. 1990. *Black Feminist Thought: Knowledge, Consciousness, and the Politics of Empowerment.* Boston: Unwin Hyman.

D'Emilio, John. 1983. *Sexual Politics, Sexual Communities: The Making of a Homosexual Minority in the United States, 1940–1970.* Chicago: University of Chicago Press.

de Koven, Anna. 1912. The athletic woman. *Good Housekeeping*, August.

Del Rey, Patricia. 1978. The apologetic and women in sport. In *Women and Sport*, edited by Carole Oglesby. Philadelphia: Lea & Febiger.

Department of Physical Education, University of California, Los Angeles. 1955. Coeducational classes. *Journal of Health, Physical Education, and Recreation* 26 (February):18.

Detroit News. 1962. 31 July, sec. 6. p. 1.

Dunham, Elizabeth. 1924. Physical education for women at Hampton Institute. *Southern Workman* 53 (April):167.

Dunning, Eric. 1986. Sport as a male preserve: Notes on the social sources of masculine identity and its transformation. In *Quest for Excitement: Sport and Leisure in the Civilizing Process*, edited by Eric Dunning and Norbert Elias. New York: Basil Blackwell.

Ebony. 1955. Fastest women in the world. June, 28.

Ellis, A. W. 1939. The status of health and physical education for women in Negro colleges and universities. *Journal of Negro Education* 8(January):58–63.

Ellis, Havelock. 1915. *Sexual Inversion*, vol. 2 of *Studies in the Psychology of Sex*. 3rd rev. ed. Philadelphia: F. A. Davis.

Erenberg, Lewis. 1981. *Steppin' Out: New York Nightlife and the Transformation of American Culture, 1890–1930.* Westport, CT: Greenwood Press.

Farmer, Gene. 1947. What a Babe! *Life*, June.

Feminine Sluggers. 1952. *People and Places* 8(12), reproduced in AAGBL Records.

Freedman, Estelle, and John D'Emilio. 1988. *Intimate Matters: A History of Sexuality in America.* New York: Harper & Row.

Furlong, William B. 1960. Venus wasn't a shotputter. *New York Times Magazine*, 28 August.

Gallico, Paul. 1960. *Houston Post*, 22 March.

Gerber, Ellen W. 1975. The controlled development of collegiate sport for women, 1923–36. *Journal of Sport History* 2(Spring):1–28.

Giddings, Paula. 1984. *When and Where I Enter: The Impact of Black Women on Race and Sex in America*. New York: William Morrow & Company.

Himes, Cindy L. 1986. *The Female Athlete in American Society, 1860–1940*. Ph.D. diss., University of Pennsylvania.

Hult, Joan. 1985. The governance of athletics for girls and women. *Research Quarterly for Exercise and Sport*, April:64–77.

Inglis, William. 1910. Exercise for girls. *Harper's Bazaar*, March.

Kimmel, Michael S. 1987. The contemporary "crisis" of masculinity in historical perspective. In *The Making of Masculinities: The New Men's Studies* edited by Harry Brod. Boston: Allen & Unwin.

Lagemann, John Lord. 1947. Red heads you kill me! *Colliers*, 8 February, 64.

Lenskyj, Helen. 1986. *Out of Bounds: Women, Sport, and Sexuality*. Toronto: Women's Press.

Lunbeck, Elizabeth. 1987. "A new generation of women": Progressive psychiatrists and the hypersexual female. *Feminist Studies* 13(Fall):513–43.

MacFadden, Bernard. 1929. Athletics for women will help save the nation. *Amateur Athlete* 4(February–July):7.

Mangan, J. A., and Roberta J. Park, eds. 1987. *From "Fair Sex" to Feminism: Sport and the Socialization of Women in the Industrial and Post-Industrial Eras*. London: Frank Cass.

Mange, Violet W. 1910. Field hockey for women. *Harper's Bazaar*, April.

Markey, Morris. No date. Hey Ma, you're out! 1951 Records of the AAGBL.

Marston, William. 1933. How can a woman do it? *Redbook*, September.

Martin, Pete. 1947. Babe Didrikson takes off her mask. *Saturday Evening Post*, 20 September.

Moats, A. 1934. He hasn't a chance. *Ladies Home Journal*, December.

Mooney, Gertrude. 1937. The benefits and dangers of athletics for the high school girl. Department of Physical Training for Women Records (Health Ed. folder), Box 3R251. Barker Texas History Center, University of Texas, Austin.

Mrozek, Donald J. 1983. *Sport and the American Mentality, 1880–1910*. Knoxville: University of Tennessee Press.

Murray, Jim. No date. 1970s column in *Austin American Statesman*, Zaharias scrapbook, Barker Texas History Center, University of Texas, Austin.

Nathan, George. 1930. Once there was a princess. *American Mercury*, February.

National Amateur Athletic Federation-Women's Division. 1938. Newsletter, no. 79 (1 June 1938), from Department of Women's Physical Education, University of Wisconsin Archives.

Paret, J. Parmley. 1900. Basket-ball for young women. *Harper's Bazaar*, October.

Peiss, Kathy. 1986. *Cheap Amusements: Working Women and Leisure in Turn-of-the-Century New York*. Philadelphia: Temple University Press.

Penn, Donna. 1991. The meanings of lesbianism in post-war America. *Gender and History* 3:190–203.

Physical Education Director. No date. Official Reports, Kristin Powell's collected materials on Radcliffe Athletics, Radcliffe College Archives, acc. no. R87.

Pronger, Brian. 1990. *The Arena of Masculinity: Sport, Homosexuality, and the Meaning of Sex*. New York: St. Martin's Press.

Roberts, Amelia. 1927. Letter to *Chicago Defender*, 12 March, sec. 2, p. 7.

Sargent, Dudley A. 1913. Are athletics making girls masculine? *Ladies Home Journal*, March.

Saturday Evening Post. 1954. Next to marriage, we'll take golf. 23 January.

Schaeffer, Mildred A. 1945. Desirable objectives in post-war physical education. *Journal of Health and Physical Education* 16:446–47.

Sefton, Alice Allene. 1937. Must women in sports look beautiful? *Journal of Health and Physical Education* 8:481.

Simmons, Christina. 1989. Modern sexuality and the myth of Victorian repression. In *Passion and Power: Sexuality in History,* edited by Kathy Peiss and Christina Simmons. Philadelphia: Temple University Press.

Steers, Fred. 1932. Spirit. *Amateur Athlete* October:7.

Wise, P. M. 1883. Case of sexual perversion. *Alienist and Neurologist* 4:88.

Wittner, Fred. 1934. Shall the ladies join us? *Literary Digest,* 19 May.

Zipter, Yvonne. 1988. *Diamonds Are a Dyke's Best Friend.* Ithaca, NY: Firebrand Books.

20

"Holding Back"

Negotiating a Glass Ceiling on Women's Muscular Strength

SHARI L. DWORKIN

In Part I of this volume, we saw how preschools train girls and boys to sit, move, and speak in ways that make gender differences seem natural and innate, and how doctors' decisions to surgically alter the bodies of intersex children reinforce the idea that there are two and only two sex categories. Similarly, in this article, Shari L. Dworkin illustrates how cultural ideas about the inherent physical limitations of women's bodies help to construct bodies that match those assumed limitations.

As Dworkin describes, athletic activities can offer women opportunities for experiencing physical power and agency over their bodies and lives. These opportunities, however, are constrained by women's concern over meeting norms of "emphasized femininity"—sociologist R. W. Connell's term for a style of femininity that provides women with social status when they accommodate to men's desires for female appearance and behavior.

In her observations at gyms, Dworkin found that athletic trainers routinely tell their female clients that women cannot develop bulky muscle even if they lift heavy weights. In fact, however, some women find that their muscles do grow over time. But because they have been told that this cannot—and, by extension, should not—happen, they often respond by restricting their use of free weights. In this way, they maintain a body shape that conforms to norms of emphasized femininity and reinforce the myth that women's bodies naturally cannot add muscle. Thus, they not only "do gender"—present their body and interact with others in ways that fit gender *expectations—but also create bodies that match and reinforce our ideas about* sex *(i.e., biological) differences.*

Current work in gender studies points to how "when examined closely, much of what we take for granted about gender and its causes and effects either does not hold up, or can be explained differently" (Lorber 1994: 5). These arguments become especially contentious when confronting nature/culture debates on gendered *bodies.* After all, "common sense" frequently tells us that flesh and blood bodies are about biology. However, bodies are also shaped and constrained through cumulative social practices, structures of opportunity, wider cultural meanings, and more. Paradoxically, then, when we think that we are "really seeing" naturally sexed bodies, perhaps we are seeing the effect of internalizing gender ideologies—carrying out social practices— and this constructs our vision of "sexed" bodies (Butler 1993; Lorber 1993; Hargreaves 1994).

As fitness memberships boom and the more muscular new millennium is here, we are presented with a timely juncture in which to examine one popularly acquired paradox of gender: muscles. On the one hand, "commonsense" ideologies tell everyday women in fitness not to fear the weight room because natural, biological difference from men prevents them from getting "too big." At the same time, many women *can* and *do* experience gains in muscle mass when lifting weights, particularly women who do so regularly. The tension that results from the difference between common sense and knowledge of one's own bodily experiences is compounded by widespread bodily ideologies around what women's bodies *should* do. How do women actively negotiate these tensions? What do women in fitness *do?* Why do they do it? Immersed in a cultural moment in which it may seem that strong women are more celebrated than ever, are women in fitness in fact bursting into weight rooms, packing on plates, cranking out sets? Or do many women hold back on weights so as to negotiate what might be termed a culturally produced glass ceiling—or upper limit—on their muscular strength (Dworkin and Messner 1999)? Are both occurring, and to what extent?

Fitness, Gender, Bodies

An analysis of women's participation in sport and fitness reveals a highly politicized terrain of gender relations. Contemporary United States culture tends increasingly to applaud and embrace athletic, powerfully strong women. The 1996 "Year of the Women" Olympics, the 1997 premiere season of the WNBA, the 1999 Women's World Cup, and an ever-increasing number of women participating in high school and college athletics are just a few indicators of this trend. Corporate ad campaigns have hopped aboard the athletic empowerment wave to target women as a demographic, offering powerful messages about female fitness fanatics who "just do it." Many view today's fit women as embodying power and agency in a manner that challenges definitions of women as weak, passive, or docile (Guthrie and Castelnuovo 1998; Heywood 1998; Kane 1995).

There is some question, however, about the extent to which this bodily agency poses resistance to the gender order. For instance, some ask if the more muscular bodily ideal is merely the most recent form of docile bodily self-surveillance, that aids patriarchal capitalism through the suggestion that bodies need to be increasingly industrious (Bartky 1988). Furthermore, cheering women on to "Just Do It" ignores the fact that numerous Third World women stitch Nike sneakers for low wages so that American women may more inexpensively "just do" their privileged leisure time (Cole and Hribar 1995). An individualized, fit bodily politics may be criticized as being removed from collective forms of empowerment that can challenge oppressive institutions and practices (Dworkin and Messner 1999).

Despite these limitations, many women have experienced sport and fitness as sites of power and agency where they have rejected narrow constructions of femininity and where they can embrace physical power and independence (Bolin 1992a; Cahn 1994; Hargreaves 1994; Heywood 1998; Kane 1995). Being physically independent is an important feminist theme if one considers the historical relationship between femininity and dependency. Recent work by Heywood (1998) makes a compelling argument that weight lifting is a specifically third wave feminist strategy to physically self-empower, ward off attack, or heal previous bodily victimization and abuse. This moves us beyond previous conceptualizations of women in fitness/sport as wholly oppressed bodily objects under patriarchal control.

However, while men's participation in many sport and fitness activities has historically been consistent with dominant conceptions of masculinity as well as heterosexuality, women's participation has tended to bring their femininity and heterosexuality into question (Blinde and Taub 1992; Cahn 1994; Griffin 1998; Kane 1995; Lenskyj 1987). Thus, not only do women challenge narrow constructs of masculinity and femininity through being active, fit agents, but they are also subject to narrow conceptions of womanhood that often become conflated with heterosexual attractiveness. Connell's (1987) concepts of hegemonic masculinity and emphasized femininity shed light on this discussion. "Hegemonic masculinity" is defined as the dominant form of masculinity in a given historical period—usually based on a white, heterosexual, and middle-class norm. "Emphasized femininity" refers to the most privileged forms of femininity that shift over time in ways that correspond to changes in hegemonic masculinity (Connell 1987; 1995).

Since female bodybuilders have musculature and size that challenge norms of emphasized femininity, women's bodybuilding has been an intriguing realm in which to examine gendered bodily negotiations. Bolin (1992a, 1992b) demonstrates that women's bodybuilding both challenges and reproduces ideals of emphasized femininity because the increasing size of the female bodybuilder is only acceptable once "tamed" by beauty. It is for this reason that judges of bodybuilding contests have been found to institutionally reward female bodybuilders for various "feminine" physical markers (e.g. breast implants, painted nails, dyed hair) even when the goal of the sport is to display muscle mass, size, symmetry, and density. And, of course, commercialization is integrally linked to the kinds of femininity that are displayed and rewarded by and in the media. Women are not presented solely as resistant and powerful athletes but rather are framed ambivalently through sexualizing and trivializing their athletic performances (Duncan and Messner 2000; Duncan and Hasbrook 1988). Whether these trends will continue should surely concern scholars in sociology, sport, gender, and media studies.

In the last decade a growing number of studies have examined women's bodies at the "extremes." That is, there are more works on female bodybuilders, on the one hand (Balsamo 1994; Bolin 1992a, 1992b; Daniels 1992; Fisher 1997; Guthrie and Castelnuovo 1998; Heywood 1998; Klein 1990; Schulze 1997), and anorexics, on the other (Bordo 1993; Heywood 1996). Yet little work explores the everyday women in fitness who fall somewhere in between.[1] Ultimately, it is far too simple to take what "we see" in fitness centers and use it to reinforce societal beliefs about natural, categorical gender difference. Rather, it is vital to understand women's narratives that reveal careful negotiations regarding bodily knowledge, ideologies, and practices, which in turn construct the bodies we see. As women define, contest, and press current definitions of emphasized femininity in the new millennium, they push upward on what I argue is a historically produced and shifting glass ceiling, or upper limit, on women's strength and size. More than simply "doing gender" or doing difference (West and Fenstermaker 1995), this work highlights how (shifting) gender ideologies, once embodied through cumulative fitness practices, construct the "sexed" flesh of the body itself.

The Study

I employed participant observation over the course of two years, four days a week, for two to six hours a day in several local gyms on the West Side of Los Angeles from 1996 to 1998. One site, which I refer to as "Elite Gym," had a membership fee of about $1,300 per year, with an additional $1,300 required up front. In this site, any comfort I had from having years of sport and fitness knowledge was quite separate from the discomfort that came from being among so many individuals who could afford a vigorous and expensive cult of consumption.[2] Members were mostly white, with a scattering of black men and a very small number of black women, Latino/a men and women, and Asian men and women. Participants at Elite Gym often pulled up to the site in their shiny Mercedes, Porsches, BMWs, and other luxury vehicles and had the option of valet parking. Members frequently entered "the club" with impressively toned and buff bodies that reflected dominant ideals. Their bodies were draped in luxurious work clothes, complemented by gleaming accessories, shined shoes, and expensive leather bags and briefcases. Their fitness gear was a sampling of the latest and greatest sneakers, commodified urban wear, and flashy lycra wear, accompanied by expensive high-tech props. The second site, which I refer to as "Mid-Gym" was far less expensive and required only $25 down and an additional $300 a year. Among the stream of fitness participants who walked into and out of the site, few were draped in silky work clothes or crisp pressed pants or carried expensive leather bags or briefcases. Members were dressed in a wide array of workout or work clothing, and many participants wore jeans, gym shorts, workout tights, and T-shirts into the building. There was a much wider range of masculine and feminine styles, classes, and races on site. Several participants stated that they were unemployed, while others owned the late-model luxury cars that were resting in the parking lot. Far fewer members at this site were obviously taut and fit in ways that are consistent with current middle-class styles and ideals. Approximately half of Mid-Gym's members were white and half were people of color.

In addition to participant observation at the two sites, I also carried out thirty-three in-depth interviews with women and hundreds of more informal interviews with women who attended fitness centers during the course of my ethnographic work. Conversations were taped, pseudonyms were assigned to the interviewees to protect confidentiality, and tapes were destroyed after transcription. The women ranged in age from nineteen to forty; 54.5 percent were white, 15.2 percent were African American, 15.2 percent were Asian, and 15.2 percent were Latina. 33.3 percent were heterosexual and currently married, 60.1 percent were heterosexual and single, and 6.1 percent were single lesbians.[3] One widespread observation that I noted across sites concerned the degree to which women lifted weights. From this observation, I grouped women into three categories of weight lifting: non-lifters (25% of women on sites), light to moderate lifters (65% of women on sites), and heavy lifters (10% of women on sites). Because of race and class differences in the membership bases and the fact that working-class women and women of color disproportionately used their bodies to perform heavy physical labor in the paid labor force (e.g., construction, landscaping, fire fighting), there were proportionately more heavy lifters at Mid-Gym than Elite Gym (15% vs. 5%). There were slightly more moderate lifters at Elite Gym than at Mid-Gym (70% vs. 60%). Both sites had similar proportions of non-weight-lifting participants (25%).

The Glass Ceiling on Women's Strength

Numerous factors affect women's and men's choice of fitness activities, some of which are personal preference, time available, access to organized sport or other fitness activities, and ability to pay for membership and training props.

Less obvious reasons for fitness choices included negotiating commonsense ideas about muscle and women's biology, bodily knowledge and experiences, and ideologies about what women's bodies should do.

Researchers have highlighted how women in male-dominated fields and professional occupations such as law, science, the military, and business reach a glass ceiling. Such a ceiling might be defined as a limit on professional success wherein women attempt to venture upward and are stopped. I argue that although the glass ceiling in the workplace is a structurally imposed upper limit on success that has little to do with blaming individual women for not "reaching the top," the concept of a ceiling is also useful for understanding many women in fitness. That is, women in fitness—particularly those who seek muscular strength—may find their bodily agency and empowerment limited not by biology but by an (ideological) ceiling on their muscularity. This ceiling is defined by ideologies of emphasized femininity (Connell 1987) that structure the upper limit on women's bodily strength and musculature. Approximately three-fourths of the women I interviewed at fitness sites expressed awareness of a glass ceiling, which they described as an upper limit on the quest for seeking more muscular strength. This was expressed through a shared explicit fear of and repulsion to female bodybuilders' bodies, a fear of becoming too big or bulky themselves, and narratives that focused on how to structure fitness practices so as to ensure (new definitions of) emphasized femininity. While there was a shared understanding of the limits that women would allow regarding their muscular size, the three groups of women (non-, moderate, and heavy lifters) consciously negotiated a glass ceiling on strength in unique ways. As so much recent work has been carried out regarding heavy weight lifters, I center here on non- and moderate lifters so as to analyze the largest groups of day-to-day women in fitness.[4]

Non-Lifters

It was common for everyday women at fitness sites to express fears that with the "wrong" kind of exercise, their bodies might develop "excessive" bodybuilders' musculature. This was the case despite the fact that professional bodybuilders engage in rigorous training and eating regimes and some also take steroids to gain size. One expression of this fear emerged from non-lifters, who constituted approximately 25 percent of the women at the two fitness sites. Non-lifters focused on weight work and bulk as "masculine" bodily villains and cardiovascular work as a "feminine" bodily savior. An example of this was Alyssa, a thirty-two-year-old white woman at Elite Gym. She explained that she was a former drug addict who felt that she was "fat" at one time but that "changed one day" when her boyfriend told her she was fat. She said, "[His telling me that was] the best thing that ever happened to me. It totally motivated me to work out." Alyssa did a cardiovascular workout five to seven days a week for at least one hour a day, with *no* weight lifting, and explained,

[I do this to] be more toned, and to burn fat, and to not get bigger... of course. I don't want to be buff, but lean.... I don't want to look like a female bodybuilder.... I don't ever want to be nonfeminine. Women should have curves and be soft to some extent, you know?

Alyssa said first that she was once larger because of excess body fat and then expressed fears around increasing in size from weight lifting. For Alyssa and some others, it appears to be *size*—muscle or fat—that is the powerfully feared transgression against femininity (Dworkin 2002; Lamm 2000). Alyssa stated that female bodybuilders and "buff" bodies were "nonfeminine," while "lean and with curves and soft to some extent" were considered feminine. At the same time, Alyssa was not concerned that her intensive cardiovascular activity would burn too much body fat or contribute to a loss of femininity. It is striking that the realm of the cardiovascular somehow retained its "feminine" status even as it threatened to revoke femininity according to the definitions used by some of the participants themselves. Work and occupations literature commonly reveals that job behaviors and tasks are somewhat randomly designated as masculine or feminine even when they are analogous across industries (Leidner 1993). The realms of sport and fitness reveal similar historically arbitrary and shifting definitions.

Other non-lifters agreed that cardiovascular work somehow contributed to the feminine while weights detracted from it. Several non-lifters in fact had lifted weights in the past but stopped because of tension between what they thought their bodies *should* do and knowledge of what their bodies *actually* do. For instance, Joelle, a forty-year-old, white fitness participant from the same site spoke to me as she walked briskly on a treadmill, her arms moving rhythmically. One afternoon she bragged that she can "have any job I want, the body I want, and any man I want." Her comments reminded me of the individualistic power and agency expressed through Nike "Just Do It" ad campaigns. She explained to me that she walked on the treadmill seven days a week for an hour and a half. When I asked her whether she did weights, she replied:

I do legs sometimes, but nope, no weights, all cardio and walking on the treadmill. I gain muscle really fast... [and] don't want to look masculine. They say lift light and with lots of reps and you won't gain mass, but *not me*! I gain mass so fast! I should have been a man!!

Unlike Alyssa, who had never lifted, Joelle had lifted in the past and knew that her muscles responded to weights in a way that defied what she felt women's bodies "should" do. Not only did she describe gaining muscle as a masculinized look that she disliked, but she did not even see gains of muscle mass as appropriate to or in the realm of the fathomable for womanhood: "I should have been a man!!" Last, when Joelle told me that lifting light weights and doing lots of repetitions would prevent her from gaining mass, she reflected a common pattern of discourse I found in gyms. "They say lift light" was a commonsense solution offered by trainers to female clients' concerns about acquiring big muscles. Rather than cheer women on to simply "just do it" women were told to not do "too much of it" and to "just hold back" on weight lifting. The widespread use of avoiding weights or "lifting lightly" on the two sites so as to "ensure" femininity revealed a conscious struggle with what constitutes an acceptable upper limit on women's strength and size.

Consistent with the historical cult of true womanhood where white women define and are defined by notions of "ideal" femininity that can exclude many working-class women and women of color, a similar process may be partially operating in the realm of fitness (Dworkin and Messner 1999). That is, it was most often white women, particularly from Elite Gym in the non-lifting category, who offered narratives that weights caused bodily harm to currently shifting constructs of femininity. At Mid-Gym, numerous women of color and working-class women also offered strands of the same narrative, revealing how bodily ideals can normalize across various social locations such as race and class (Bordo 1993). However, white women, women of color, and working-class women at Mid-Gym in the non-lifting category also frequently emphasized a lack of time to use the gym given family care and paid labor requirements. Women at Elite Gym were far less likely to mention this need to juggle responsibilities and leisure and in fact discussed their ability to buy off the second shift (Hochschild 1989) so as to be able to have time to come to fitness centers. Once on site, several of these women paid personal trainers to help them adhere to what might be termed a "third shift," or adherence to the latest bodily requirements. Thus, popular advertisement claims that any woman can "have it all" obscure power relations and global and domestic inequality within groups of women that can help elite women to more easily meet bodily ideals. For instance, that women of color work for pay as domestics in the homes of middle- and upper-middle-class women (Hondagneu-Sotelo and Avila 1997) may allow more privileged women (such as those found in Elite Gym) the time to attend a fitness center. Hence, while I have noted that three-fourths of women were aware of and negotiated an upper limit on women's strength and size, it is also clear that an analysis of social locations aids an understanding of agency and constraint within women's fitness "choices." Simultaneously, however, bodily ideals can and do normalize across race and class categories.

While numerous non-lifters told me they stayed away from the weight room so as to avoid bulk and to maintain their femininity, a handful of other non-lifters assigned an economy of value to cardiovascular work while stating that weight work wasn't "necessary." During the course of fieldwork, some non-lifters did not express an overt disgust or fear of muscle but used expressions such as "I don't need muscle," "I don't want muscle," or "I don't see the need for it." Looking at the depth of these narratives made more clear the underlying meanings of these frequently offered statements. Cardiovascular work was indeed referred to as the much more valuable activity. For instance, Mimi, a twenty-four-year-old Latina from Mid-Gym, stated that she did not lift weights and instead chose only cardiovascular work because she had "limited time": "The goal is to maximize the amount of calories burned and cardio gives me the greatest bang for the buck."

After hearing from several non-lifters that weight lifting was unnecessary and cardiovascular work was necessary, the next question became "What's the buck?" For non-lifters, the "buck" appeared to be maintaining femininity, avoiding masculine taint, and, in many cases, "maximum calorie expenditure" (assumed to be derived from cardiovascular work), which was discussed as being consistent with goals of body size reduction. Moderate lifters shared this "buck" with non-lifters but departed from it in unique ways.

Moderate Lifters

Moderate lifters, who constituted approximately 65 percent of the women at the two fitness sites, shared complex and contradictory views of the pleasures and dangers of weights. Both non-lifters and moderate lifters strategically structured fitness practices to ensure "femininity"—defined as the maintenance of curves coupled with a desire to not increase body size from fat or muscular bulk. Both frequently saw cardiovascular work as integral to the maintenance of "femininity," while too much weight work was perceived to threaten its construction. However, moderate lifters also described unique tensions about desiring muscular strength while not wanting to increase body size from muscle mass. Women across numerous race, class, and sexuality categories shared these narratives within the moderate lifting category.

Moderate lifters uniquely mediated the perceived pleasures and "evils" of weight lifting *not* by avoiding weights altogether but by seeking strength and pushing upward on a glass ceiling on strength. At the same time, contrary to the widespread belief that women cannot get big from weights, moderate lifters clearly struggled with their own bodily responses to weights. Moderate lifters carefully negotiated this upper limit, watched their bodies for signs of "excess" musculature, and consciously adjusted or stopped their weight workouts accordingly. So as to mediate an expressed fear of bulk with a simultaneous desire to seek strength, several distinct strategies were used that pushed upward on a glass ceiling on strength yet bumped up against it and then "held back." These strategic practices were to "keep the weight the same" across weight sets instead of increasing weights, to "back off" in terms of the number of days or time spent in the weight room, and to "hold back" on the amount of weight lifted.

"KEEP THE WEIGHT THE SAME". Lucia, a thirty-five-year-old African-American woman from Mid-Gym, stated that she did cardiovascular work three or four times a week for forty-five minutes combined with numerous sets of light weights for fifteen to thirty minutes. When asked why, she said: "Well, cardiovascular work helps me to lose weight...and I do many sets of the same weight and don't increase it because I don't want to be like some women who are losing their femininity, you know, their curves. I don't want to be like a female bodybuilder."

Repeatedly, the icon of the female bodybuilder is drawn on to structure women's fitness choices and to make clear where the upper limit on women's size and strength lay. Like many non-lifters, moderate lifters often described a desire to retain their curves and viewed weights as the transgressive activity that could contribute to a "loss" of femininity. Lucia constructed and was constructed by current definitions of emphasized femininity in which slender is no longer adequate, while toned, firm, curvy, and muscled (but not too much) is (Bordo 1993).[5] Despite fears about weights and masculinization and a loss of femininity, she did not resolve this tension by avoiding weights altogether (as did non-lifters). In fact, she routinely did many sets of the same weight, strategically working with knowledge of an upper limit on strength, and soothed fears of masculinization by not *increasing* the weight across several sets.

Another example of this frequently used tactic was Margaret, a twenty-one-year-old white woman from Mid-Gym. She explained how she trekked to the gym five days a week to do thirty to forty-five minutes of cardiovascular work and lifted weights twice a week for twenty to thirty minutes. I asked her how many sets she lifted and what amount of weight across sets. She explained:

> I do three sets of everything. I keep the weight the same across three sets. I would increase it if I had done it for long enough, if like, I've tried it too much on the same weight, but I'm cautious. I don't wanna look like a female bodybuilder. I don't want to look like a jock either, and I want strength, but I don't want to gain weight and sometimes it makes your muscles bigger even if you don't want them to... but I guess its OK because that means you're getting stronger too, but I *really* don't want to get bigger...

Margaret discussed the joys of desiring strength, yet also revealed that she did not want muscle size or weight gain or to look like a female bodybuilder. There was a tension between wanting strength but at the same time fearing an increase in muscle size and having to hold back. I observed that Margaret's practice of keeping the weight the same across sets was widely used by women, while many male fitness participants (and female heavy lifters) increased the weight across three or more sets. Using ethnographic observation alone might lead one to believe that this is due to women's lack of strength or experience with weights, but interviews revealed the self-consciousness of the enacted strategies. Moderate lifters mediated tensions about common sense (women can't get big), bodily knowledge (women do get big), and bodily ideologies (women shouldn't get big) in such a way that pressed up against today's upper limits on strength but then backed away from it for fear of increasing body size.

"BACKING OFF". Annette, a thirty-three-year-old Asian American woman from Elite Gym, moved through the weight room with confidence and athleticism. When we spoke, she explained that she "spun" (took a stationary bike class) six days a week for an hour and lifted weights twice a week for thirty to forty-five minutes. She stressed that she used to lift five days a week, "religiously," for nearly an hour but that she had decided to "back off" to two days a week. When I asked her if she could help me understand why, she said:

> I like strength, and I like maintaining my physical structure with muscles, but I don't like the look of being too buff. I liked it *then*, but *now* I like lean, fit, a little buff, feminine. I don't wanna look like Cory Everson. I want to lean out more.

Annette pointed to historically arbitrary and changeable notions of "feminine" bodies. "The look" she described certainly extended beyond historical definitions of women's bodies as voluptuous (1950s) or very slim (1960s–1970s) to include current ideals defined as "lean, fit, a little buff, feminine." Yet she also highlighted other functional uses for strength. Seeking strength and desiring longevity were part of why she lifted weights, while not wanting to "look too buff" limited her time in the weight room. Cory Everson is a female bodybuilder who is well known for her success at landing product endorsements through her simultaneous adherence to intense muscularity and emphasized femininity. Although Everson is popular in fitness magazines and is considered by many to succeed at displaying emphasized femininity, her muscularity and mass are profound, and as such, she can still be a symbol of what many women hope not to become. "Backing off" on weights or "holding back" were two of the ways in which moderate lifters mediated the numerous tensions surrounding gender and the body.

"HOLDING BACK". Kit, a nineteen-year-old African American woman at Mid-Gym had one of the most muscular frames among moderate lifters, and she frequently dared to venture into free weight spaces that were often largely male dominated. During our interview, she stated that her workout included one hour of cardiovascular work once a week and thirty minutes two days a week and weight lifting three days a week for fifteen minutes across three exercises (bench press, rowing, and squats). She said that she wanted to "touch the rim" when she shot baskets for fun and added, "That's why I do those crazy squats." When I asked her about her sets and repetitions, she informed me that she carried out three sets on each exercise and that she started with a weight that "is comfortable" and increased the weight over two other sets. In this way she departed from several moderate lifters who kept the weight the same across sets and instead shared this practice with nearly all of the heavy lifters. After describing how she increased the weight over three sets, she laughed, shook her head, and added: "My mother says to not lift too much, that I'll get too big...so I'm always worried about that." When I asked her if she ever responded to her mom, she replied: "Yeah, I tell her not to worry, that women don't have to fear getting big because they don't have a lot of testosterone." Acknowledging the tensions between bodily common sense and actual bodily knowledge and experience, I then asked her why she was always worried about her mom's warning. She replied: "Well, I am worried about getting bigger. That's why I keep the reps low and I don't do too many."

Like Annette, Kit described a functional use for weight lifting. She wanted improved sports performance, and "crazy squats" moved her toward that goal. At the same time, despite commonsense beliefs that women can't get big, she was concerned about the cultural dictates that women should not get too big. To solve the ironic tension between what women are told they *can't* do and yet *shouldn't* do, she sought improved sports experience but was careful not to increase her size. In this way functional reasons led women to push upward on an upper limit on size and strength, yet at the same time fears of bulk consistently led many to bump up against a culturally produced upper limit on strength and size.

Similarly, when I first spotted Carla in Elite Gym, she reminded me of Annette and Kit in how freely she ventured into free weight and designated "heavy" spaces to lift. She moved confidently and fluidly, and her mesomorphic form seemed to speak athletics. She lifted moderately, twice a week for thirty to fifty minutes, and was *much* stronger than most of the women (and some of the men) in Elite Gym. I observed that she did weight assisted pullups on what is known as a graviton machine, and she continued these for an unusually extended period—over three minutes straight. She informed me that, "It's an endurance workout...for strength...but not to build." When asked why she does this, she said:

> I know my body type and I know I have a tendency to build mass, and I've had that in fact, to some degree, before being athletic, so my goals now are to lengthen my muscles and to keep fit to do all the sports I love to do.

Father along in the interview, I asked her to talk about how she decided on the specific repetitions and sets in her workout.

> Well...what I did was I found my max—and I could do that ten or fifteen times. And I would do forty percent of my max and sustain it for two minutes, so, for instance, I'll do forty pounds on something, but that's forty percent of how much I *could* do. I used to do three sets of fifteen, but I *never* maxed out—I worried that it'd make me bulk, so I held back.

While it was common to see a number of everyday men on fitness sites "max out" on their weight-lifting sets or take supplements to make sure that fatigue did not set in, I observed less than a dozen women "max out" in the course of my fieldwork. When I asked Carla how she felt about her workouts, she replied: "I really like it. I don't feel bulked up now. Over the years, people tell me that I look so much better now—and that's so nice, that feels so good—I have this more lengthened look. I think it's just prettier."

While Carla's workout, similar to Kit, Annette, and other women in fitness, served a functional purpose—to keep her in shape for all the sports she loved to do—she simultaneously held back given size expectations and current definitions of emphasized femininity. She expressed pleasure in mediating bodily knowledge with bodily ideologies by holding back so as to no longer be bulky and now felt "lengthened" and "prettier." Some scholars might refer to this "nice" look that "feels so good" as part of our current historical moment where a highly specified kind of "looking good" can become conflated with "feeling good" (Duncan 1994). Thus, while moderate lifters indeed sought out a desired level of physical fortitude and strength, blasting past non-lifters, they also bumped up against a glass ceiling on muscular size and "held back."

Discussion and Conclusions

While the body has always been important to second wave feminism through its emphasis on abortion, reproductive rights, and sexual and domestic violence, it seems to have been taboo in gender studies to directly tackle notions of gender, bodies, and biological difference. This may be because bodies are politically symbolic arenas in which fierce ideological debates about natural male physical superiority and female inferiority are played out (Cahn 1994; Hargreaves 1994; Kane 1995; Messner 1988, 1992). In early second wave feminism physical differences were dealt with by stating that gender was fully socially constructed, and discussions about biology were essentially abandoned. Although it was particularly useful to break away from the potentially oppressive implications embedded in the belief that "biology is destiny," flesh and blood bodies tended to drop out of the analysis. More recently, scholars have moved toward the subject of flesh and blood bodies by pointing out how physical differences between men and women are average differences that are erroneously assumed to be absolute and categorical (Fausto-Sterling 2000; Kane 1995; Lorber 1994). While theorizing on this subject is not necessarily recent, few researchers empirically examine the ideologies and practices that might reproduce, negotiate, and challenge notions of categorical difference.

When using the naked eye, it appears that absolute, biological difference between women and men is the sole culprit in explaining the bodies we see. What is left out of this equation is women's conscious negotiation with a historically produced upper limit on strength and size. In opposition to quick commonsense claims that women are biologically different from men and therefore cannot gain much muscle, this ethnographic work revealed that muscle *is* something that women can and do gain. In fact, based on tensions between what bodies *should* do, what bodies *actually* do, and culturally shifting standards of emphasized femininity, approximately three-fourths of the women at the fitness sites expressed an awareness of an upper limit on the quest for muscular size and strength. Non- and moderate lifters in fact used very specific weight-lifting and cardiovascular strategies in fitness settings to mediate these tensions.

Non-lifters made up approximately 25 percent of the women at the two sites. Many non-lifters employed a strategic avoidance of the weight room so as to prevent an increase in body size while embracing cardiovascular work to help decrease size and maintain curves. These women actively defined and were defined by emphasized femininity described as small, lean, toned, and curvy. In this way non-lifters stayed safely below the glass ceiling, did not frequently challenge dominant bodily ideals, and can be described as enacting a bodily agency that reproduces these ideals. While white women at Elite Gym were most likely to express these themes given their ability to buy off the second shift so as to adhere to a third, many women of color and working-class women at Mid-Gym also shared these themes, revealing how bodily ideals can normalize across social location (Bordo 1993). At the same time, intersections of race and class also revealed situations of agency and constraint that did not even allow many working-class women and women of color time at Mid-Gym to regularly attend fitness centers or to be preoccupied with concerns about an upper limit on strength and size.

Moderate lifters, who constituted 65 percent of the women at the sites, agreed with non-lifters on themes of femininity but also departed from non-lifters in significant ways. Unlike non-lifters, moderate lifters rejected ideals of thin, weak bodies and avoidance of the weight room. Moderate lifters juggled ideologies of strength and functional physical performance with a careful monitoring of the body for signs of muscular excess. To mediate a desire for increased strength with new definitions of femininity they stopped weights for a while, backed off on the time and number of days per week spent in the weight room, struggled with whether to increase the amount of weight across sets, and held back on the amount of weight lifted. Moderate lifters indeed inched past non-lifters, nudged upward toward a glass ceiling but then bumped up against it and held back. In this way moderate lifters represent a negotiated bodily agency that actively pressed beyond thinness ideals but also feared masculinization and what might be considered a loss of heterosexual attractiveness (e.g., Doworkin 2002).

The glass ceiling on muscular size is not simply imposed on women. Rather, they actively define it, wrestle with it, nudge it up and down, and shape its current and future placement. Women in fitness sites are immersed in an arena of continual negotiation as to the placement of the ceiling, which is in part influenced by historically shifting definitions of empha-sized femininity. That 65 percent of women at these two popular fitness sites were moderate lifters who bumped up against the glass ceiling while only 10 percent of women were heavy lifters who blasted through it, is an indication that the present state of emphasized femininity might be tipping toward muscularity rather than away from it. That is, although many women "held back," definitions of emphasized femininity in the new millennium indeed include more musculature than the last several decades. This continual push upward on the glass ceiling over time is due to numerous factors, some of which might include relational definitions of hegemonic masculinity that also dictate increases in men's size over time (Connell 1995; Pope et al. 2000), Title IX and women's increased access to organized sport, media coverage of women's success in sport, feminist consciousness of bodily ideals, and more.

Despite the message that women should "just do it," ideals of emphasized femininity lead many women in the weight room to "just hold back." While seemingly consistent with research that emphasizes the "doing" of gender or of difference (West and Fenstermaker 1995), one cannot ignore that studies of embodiment in sport and fitness also highlight the need to place the relationship between sex and gender itself under more intense scrutiny. If men are free to pack on thick layers of muscle while women carefully negotiate the upper limits of their muscle gains, this symbolizes the gendered nuances of everyday power and privilege but also highlights how internalized ideologies impact the construction of sexed materiality itself. Such insights should urge researchers to consider whether and how a continuum of overlapping bodies and performances by gender (Kane 1995) is masked or uncovered within various social contexts. As women increasingly flock to fitness sites, daring to cross into the previously male-only territory of the weight room, we must ask whether a contained and "held back" musculature for women is now the heterosexy standard that simultaneously creates "new" womanhood as it re-creates "true" womanhood.

Notes

1. Lloyd (1996) and Markula (1996) study women in aerobics classes.

2. Clearly, field workers' personal biographies are relevant as they fundamentally shape their feelings and theoretical, interpretive, and analytical frameworks (Lofland and Lofland 1995).

3. I have carried out a separate pilot study on fitness and lesbian and bisexual women. The sample of twelve lesbian and bisexual women is too small and preliminary to make any definitive comments on the relationship between sexuality and fitness choices.

4. However, it should be noted that while heavy lifters might be assumed to "break through" a glass ceiling, they also shared intriguing negotiations in narratives regarding an upper limit on strength and size with non- and moderate lifters. Heavy lifters' narratives and practices are analyzed in another project.

5. African American women and Latinas in the moderate lifting category offered some strands of thought that revealed that ideals of thinness were not embraced. This was particularly evident when transcribing portions of interviews that

included discussions of media images from fitness magazines. However, describing the icon of the female bodybuilder as despised and undesirable was consistent across race for women in the moderate lifting category, as was an expressed cautiousness about musculature and weight-lifting practices.

References

Balsamo, Ann. 1994. Feminist bodybuilding. In *Women, Sport, and Culture*, edited by S. Birrell and C. Cole. Champaign, IL: Human Kinetics Publishers.

Bartky, Sandra L. 1988. Foucault, femininity, and the modernization of patriarchal power. In *Feminism and Foucault: Reflections on Resistance*, edited by I. Diamond and L. Quinby. Boston: Northeastern University Press.

Blinde, Elaine M., and Diane E. Taub. 1992. Women athletes as falsely accused deviants: Managing the lesbian stigma. *The Sociological Quarterly* 4:521–33.

Bolin, Anne. 1992a. Vandalized vanity: Feminine physique betrayed and portrayed. In *Tattoo, Torture, Mutilation, and Adornment: The Denaturalization of the Body in Culture and Text*, edited by F. E. Mascia-Lees and P. Sharpe. Albany: State University of New York Press.

———. 1992b. Flex appeal, food, and fat: Competitive bodybuilding, gender, and diet. *Play and Culture* 5:378–400.

Bordo, Susan. 1993. *Unbearable Weight: Feminism, Western Culture, and the Body*. Los Angeles: University of California Press.

Butler, Judith. 1993. *Bodies That Matter: On the Discursive Limits of "Sex."* New York: Routledge.

Cahn, Susan K. 1994. *Coming On Strong: Gender and Sexuality in Twentieth Century Women's Sport*. New York: The Free Press.

Cole, Cheryl L., and Amy Hribar. 1995. Celebrity feminism: Nike style post-Fordism, transcendence, and consumer power. *Sociology of Sport Journal* 12(4):347–69.

Connell, Robert W. 1987. *Gender and Power*. Stanford, CA: Stanford University Press.

Connell, Robert W. 1995. *Masculinities*. Berkeley: University of California Press.

Daniels, Dayna B. 1992. Gender (body) verification (building). *Play and Culture* 5:378–400.

Duncan, Margaret Carlisle. 1994. The politics of women's body images and practices: Foucault, the panopticon, and *Shape* magazine. *Journal of Sport and Social Issues* 18(1):40–65.

Duncan, Margaret Carlisle, and Cynthia A. Hasbrook. 1988. Denial of power in televised women's sports. *Sociology of Sport Journal* 5:1–21.

Duncan, Margaret Carlisle, and Michael A. Messner. 2000. Gender in televised sports: 1989, 1993, and 1999. Los Angeles: The Amateur Athletic Foundation.

Dworkin, Shari L. 2002. A woman's place is in the... cardiovascular room? Gender relations, the body and the gym. In *Athletic Intruders: Ethnographic Research on Women, Culture, and Exercise*, edited by Anne Bolin and Jane Granskog. New York: State University of New York Press.

Dworkin. Shari, and Michael A. Messner. 1999. Just do... what?: Sport, bodies, gender. In *Revisioning Gender*, edited by Judith Lorber, Beth Hess, and Myra Marx Ferree. Thousand Oaks, CA: Sage.

Fausto-Sterling, Anne. 2000. *Sexing the Body: Gender Politics and the Construction of Sexuality*. New York: Basic Books.

Fisher, Leslie. 1997. Building one's self up: Bodybuilding and the construction of identity among professional female bodybuilders. In *Building Bodies*, edited by P. Moore. New Brunswick, NJ: Rutgers University Press.

Griffin, Pat. 1998. *Strong Women, Deep Closets: Lesbians and Homophobia in Sport.* Champaign, IL: Human Kinetics.

Guthrie, Sharon, and Shirley Castelnuovo. 1998. *Feminism and the Female Body: Liberating the Amazon Within.* Boulder, CO: Lynne Rienner Publishers.

Hargreaves, Jennifer. 1994. *Sporting Females: Critical Issues in the History and Sociology of Women's Sport.* New York: Routledge.

Heywood, Leslie. 1996. *Dedication to Hunger: The Anorexic Aesthetic in Modern Culture.* Berkeley: University of California Press.

———. 1998. *Bodymakers: A Cultural Anatomy of Women's Bodybuilding.* New Brunswick, NJ: Rutgers University Press.

Hochschild, Arlie. 1989. *The Second Shift.* New York: Avon Books.

Hondagneu-Sotelo, Pierrette, and Erni Avila. 1997. "I'm here, but I'm there": The meanings of Latina transnational motherhood. *Gender and Society* 11:548–71.

Kane, Mary Jo. 1995. Resistance/transformation of the oppositional binary: Exposing sport as a continuum. *Journal of Sport and Social Issues* 19(2):191–218.

Klein, Alan. 1990. *Little Big Men: Bodybuilding Subculture and Gender Construction.* Albany: State University of New York Press.

Lamm, Nomy. 2000. It's a big fat revolution. In *Gender Through the Prism of Difference*, edited by M. B. Zinn, P. Hondagneu-Sotelo, and M. A. Messner. Boston: Allyn and Bacon.

Lenskyj, Helen. 1987. Female sexuality and women's sport. *Women's Studies International Forum* 4:381–86.

Leidner, Robin. 1993. *Fast Food, Fast Talk: Service Work and the Routinization of Everyday Life.* Berkeley: University of California Press.

Lloyd, Moya. 1996. Feminism, aerobics, and the politics of the body. *Body and Society* 2:79–98.

Lofland, John, and L. H. Lofland. 1995. *Analyzing Social Settings: A Guide to Qualitative Observation and Analysis.* Detroit: Wadsworth.

Lorber, Judith. 1993. Believing is seeing: Biology as ideology. *Gender and Society.* 4:568–81.

———. 1994. *Paradoxes of Gender.* New Haven, CT: Yale University Press.

Markula, Pirkko. 1996. Firm but shapely, fit but sexy, strong but thin: The postmodern aerobicizing female bodies. *Sociology of Sport Journal* 12(4):424–53.

Messner, Michael A. 1988. Sports and male domination: The female athlete as contested ideological terrain. *Sociology of Sport Journal* 5:197–211.

———. 1992. *Power At Play: Sports and the Problem of Masculinity.* Boston: Beacon Press.

Pope, Harrison G., Katharine Phillips, and Roberto Olivardia. 2000. *The Adonis Complex: The Secret Crisis of Male Body Obsession.* New York: The Free Press.

Schulze, Laurie. 1997. On the muscle. In *Building Bodies*, edited by P. Moore. New Brunswick, NJ: Rutgers University Press.

West, Candace, and Sarah Fenstermaker. 1995. Doing Difference. *Gender and Society* 9(1):8–37.

21

Compulsive Heterosexuality

Masculinity and Dominance

C. J. PASCOE

No analysis of women's bodies would be complete without a discussion of how men think about and treat women's bodies. This is the topic tackled in the following article by sociologist C. J. Pascoe. Earlier in this volume Karin Martin explored how preschools teach young girls and boys to "do gender" or to engage in "gender performativity" (i.e., to present their bodies as "properly" masculine and feminine in their interactions with others). Pascoe shows us one of the long-term consequences of this socialization. As she describes, male high school students repeatedly demonstrate their heterosexuality and dominance over girls' bodies as a means of claiming masculine power and identity for themselves. Pascoe describes these actions as "compulsive heterosexuality" because they seem almost obligatory for most young men in most social circles. Only by repeatedly performing masculinity will others acknowledge them as masculine and will they be confident of their own masculine identity. Any men who fail to do so risk being placed in what Pascoe describes as the abject fag *position (that is, being labeled as incompetent at masculinity and thus experiencing extremely high social stigma).*

As Pascoe shows, the rituals of compulsive heterosexuality require young men to sexualize and dominate young women's bodies through actions that are sometimes violent or near-violent. Yet these actions are almost never punished by the schools. Meanwhile, girls' options for responding to boys' behavior are limited, since the main way that girls can obtain power or status is through gaining male attention. Thus boys' actions reinforce their own status as subjects who actively control their own fate while reinforcing girls' status as objects for boys to enjoy or use.

...The public face of male adolescence is filled with representations of masculinity in which boys brag about sexual exploits by showing off a girl's underwear (as in the 1980s film *Pretty in Pink*), spend the end of their senior year talking about how they plan to lose their virginity (*American Pie*), or make cruel bets about who can bed the ugliest girl in the school (*She's All That*). In many ways, the boys at River High, [a suburban middle-class high school in north central California where I observed and interviewed students for 18 months,] seemed much like their celluloid representatatives.... Heterosexual innuendoes, sexual bravado, and sexual one-upmanship permeated primarily male spaces.... But boys' talk about heterosexuality reveals less about sexual orientation and desire than it does about the centrality of the ability to exercise mastery and dominance literally or figuratively over girls' bodies (Wood 1984).... Engaging in very public practices of heterosexuality, boys affirm much more than just masculinity; they affirm subjecthood and personhood through sexualized interactions in which they indicate to themselves and others that they have the ability to work their will upon the world around them....

Compulsive heterosexuality[1] is the name I give to this constellation of sexualized practices, discourses, and interactions.... Practices of "compulsive heterosexuality" exemplify what Butler (1995) calls "gender performativity," in which gender "is produced as a ritualized repetition of conventions..." (31). Compulsive heterosexuality is not about desire for sexual pleasure *per se*, or just about desire to be "one of the guys"; rather, it is "an excitement felt as sexuality in a male supremacist culture which eroticizes male dominance and female submission" (Jeffreys 1998, 75). Indeed, ensuring positions of power entails boys' constant "recreation of masculinity and femininity" through rituals of eroticized dominance (Jeffreys 1998, 77). Looking at boys' ritualistic sex talk, patterns of touch, and games of "getting girls" indicates how this gender inequality is reinforced through everyday interactions. Taken together, these ritualized interactions continually affirm masculinity as mastery and dominance. By symbolically or physically mastering girls' bodies and sexuality, boys at River High claim masculine identities....

Getting Girls

... Rituals of getting girls allowed boys to find common ground in affirming each other's masculinity and positioned them as subjects who had a right to control what girls did with their bodies. A close examination indicates that rituals of "getting girls" relied on a threat of sexualized violence that reaffirmed a sexualized inequality central to the gender order at River High.

On Halloween, Heath arrived at school dressed as an elf carrying a sprig of mistletoe and engaged in a fairly typical ritual of getting girls. He told anyone who would listen that an elf costume was a brilliant idea for Halloween because "it's the wrong holiday!" We stood by his friends at the "water polo" table who tried to sell greeting cards as a fundraiser for the team. Heath attempted to "help" by yelling at girls who passed by, "Ten dollars for a card and a kiss from the elf! Girls only!" Girls made faces and rolled their eyes as they walked past. Graham walked up and Heath yelled to him, arms outstretched, "Come here, baby!" Graham walked toward him with his hips thrust forward and his arms open, saying, "I'm coming!" and quickly both of them backed away laughing. Graham challenged Heath's kissing strategy, saying that the mistletoe sticking out of his green shorts wouldn't work because it wasn't Christmas. Heath, to prove his point that mistletoe worked at any time of the year, lifted the mistletoe above his head and, moving from behind the table, walked up to a group of girls. They looked at him with a bit of trepidation and tried to ignore his presence. Finally one acquiesced, giving him a peck on the cheek. Her friend followed suit. Heath strutted back to the table and victoriously shook hands with all the boys.

Heath, in this instance, became successfully masculine both through... [emphasizing he was kissing girls only] and through "getting girls" to kiss him. Graham then congratulated Heath on his ability to overcome the girls' resistance to his overtures. This sort of coercion, even when seemingly harmless, embeds a sense of masculinity predicated upon an overcoming of girls' resistance to boys' desire (Hird and Jackson 2001). Indeed, if one of the important parts of being masculine, as stated by the boys earlier, was not just to desire girls, which Heath indicated through his "girls only" admonition, but also to be desired by girls, Heath demonstrated this in a quite public way, thus ensuring a claim, at least for a moment, on heterosexuality.

While the boys laughed and celebrated Heath's triumph of will, the girls may not have had the same reaction to his forced kisses. In a study of teenagers and sexual harassment, Jean Hand and Laura Sanchez (2000) found, not surprisingly, that in high school girls experienced higher levels of sexual harassment than boys did and were affected more seriously by it. The girls in their study described a hierarchy of sexually harassing behaviors in which some behaviors were described as more problematic than others. The girls overwhelmingly indicated that being kissed against their will was the worst form of sexual harassment, rated more seriously than hearing boys' comments about their bodies or receiving other types of unwanted sexual attention.

Of course, it is unlikely that boys, or girls, would recognize these sorts of daily rituals as sexual harassment; they are more likely seen as normal, if perhaps a bit aggressive, instances of heterosexual flirtation and as part of a normal adolescence (Stein 2002). In fact, I never saw a teacher at River recognize these seemingly flirtatious interchanges as harassment. In auto shop, Tammy, the only girl, often faced this sort of harassment, often at the hands of Jay, a stringy-haired white junior with a pimpled face. One afternoon he walked up to Tammy and stood behind her deeply inhaling, his nose not even an inch away from her hair. Clearly uncomfortable with this, she moved to the side. He asked her if she was planning to attend WyoTech (Wyoming

Technical College, a mechanic school), and she responded, "Yes." He said, "I'm going too! You and me. We're gonna be in a room together." He closed his eyes and started thrusting his hips back and forth and softly moaning as if to indicate that he was having sex. Tammy said, "Shut up" and walked away. Used to this sort of harassment, she had developed a way of dealing with such behavior. But no matter how many times she dismissed him, Jay continued to pepper her with sexual innuendoes and suggestive practices.

Both Jay's and Heath's behaviors show how heterosexuality is normalized as a sort of "predatory" social relation in which boys try and try and try to "get" a girl until one finally gives in. Boys, like Jay, who can't "get" a girl often respond with anger or frustration because of their presumed right to girls' bodies. Marc reacted this way when a girl didn't acknowledge his advances. As usual, he sat in the rear of the drama classroom with his pal Jason. A tall, attractive blonde girl walked into the room to speak to Mr. McNally, the drama teacher. As she turned to leave the class, Marc, leaning back with his legs up on the chair in front of him and his arm draped casually over the seat next to him, yelled across the room, "See you later, hot mama!" Jason, quickly echoed him, yelling "See you later, sweet thing." She didn't acknowledge them and looked straight ahead at the door as she left. Marc, frustrated at her lack of response, loudly stated, "She didn't hear me. Whore." Instead of acknowledging that not getting her reflected something about his gender status, he deflected the blame onto her . . . .

Getting, or not getting, girls also reflects and reinforces racialized meanings of sexuality and masculinity. Darnell, [an] African American and white football player, . . . [was] pacing up and down the stairs that line the drama classroom. He yelled across the room to me "there's just one thing I hate! Just one thing I hate!" Shawna, an energetic, bisexual African American sophomore, and I simultaneously asked, "What's that?" Darnell responded, frustrated, "When mixed girls date white guys! Mixed girls are for me!" Shawna attempted to interrupt his rant, saying, "What if the girl doesn't want to date you? Girls have a say too." Darnell responded, not in as much jest as one might hope, "No they don't. White boys can date white girls. There's plenty of 'em. They can even date black girls. But mixed girls are for me." Darnell's frustration reflects a way in which racialized, gendered, and sexual identities intersect. While he felt that he had a claim on "getting girls," as a "mixed" guy he saw his options as somewhat limited. Girls and girls' bodies were constructed as a limited resource for which he had to compete with other (white) guys.

Touching

Just as same-sex touching puts boys at risk for becoming a "fag" [the epithet used constantly by boys to denigrate any "unmasculine" behavior], cross-sex touching affirms heterosexuality and masculinity. "The use of touch (especially between the sexes)" maintains a "social hierarchy" (Henley 1977, 5).

In general, superiors touch subordinates, invade their space, and interrupt them in a way that subordinates do not do to superiors. At River High masculinity was established through gendered rituals of touch involving boys' physical dominance and girls' submission.

Girls and boys regularly touched each other in a way that boys did not touch other boys. While girls touched other girls across social environments, boys usually touched each other in rule-bound environments (such as sports) or as a joke to imitate fags. While boys and girls both participated in cross-sex touching, it had different gender meanings. For girls, touching boys was part of a continuum of cross-sex and same-sex touching. That is, girls touched, hugged, and linked arms with other girls on a regular basis in a way that boys did not. For boys, cross-sex touching often took the form of a ritualistic power play that embedded gender meanings of boys as powerful and girls as submissive, or at least weak in their attempts to resist the touching. Touching, in this sense, becomes a "kinesic gender marker" producing masculinity as dominance and femininity as submission (Henley 1977, 138)....

Touching rituals ranged from playfully flirtatious to assaultlike interactions. Teachers at River never intervened, at least as far as I saw, when these touching interactions turned slightly violent. In her study of sex education practices in high school, Bonnie Trudell (1993) noted that teachers don't or won't differentiate between sexualized horseplay and assault among students. I also never saw administrators intervene to stop what were seemingly clear violations of girls' bodies. While these sorts of touching interactions often began as flirtatious teasing, they usually evolved into a competition that ended with the boy triumphant and the girl yelling out some sort of metaphorical "uncle."

Darnell and Christina, for instance, engaged in a typical touching ritual during a morning drama class. The students had moved into the auditorium, where they were supposed to be rehearsing their scenes. Christina, a strikingly good-looking white junior with long blonde hair, donned Tim's wrestling letterman's jacket. Darnell asked her if she was a wrestler. In response she pretended to be a wrestler and challenged him to a wrestling match. They circled each other in mock-wrestling positions as Darnell, dressed in baggy jeans and a T-shirt, yelled, "I don't need a singlet to beat you, lady!" She advanced toward Darnell, performing karate kicks with her legs and chops with her arms. Darnell yelled, "That's not wrestling!" and grabbed her torso, flipping her flat on her back. She pulled him down and managed to use her legs to flip him over so that he ended up underneath her on his back while she straddled him, sitting on his waist. Graham yelled out, watching in fascination, "What is going on?!" Many of the students had gathered around to watch and laugh at the faux wrestling match. Finally Darnell won the match by picking Christina up and throwing her over his shoulders. He spun her around as she squealed to be put down.

The general pace and sequence of this interaction were mirrored in many boy-girl touching rituals. Boys and girls antagonized each other in a flirtatious way. The flirtatious physical interaction escalated, becoming increasingly violent, until a girl squealed, cried, or just gave up. This sort of daily drama physically engendered meanings of power in which boys were confirmed as powerful and girls as weak.

While the "wrestling incident" between Darnell and Christina expressed seemingly harmless notions of dominance and submission, other "touching" episodes had a more explicitly violent tone. In this type of touching the boy and the girl "hurt" each other by punching or slapping or pulling each other's hair until in the end the girl lost with a squeal or scream. Shane and Cathy spent a large part of each morning in government class beating up on each other in this sequence of domination. While it was certainly not unidirectional, the interactions always ended with Cathy giving up. One of the many instances in which Cathy ended up submitting to Shane's touch began when Shane "punched" Cathy's chin. Cathy, trying to ignore the punch, batted her eyelashes and in a whiny voice pleaded, "Take me to In and Out for lunch." In response Shane grabbed her neck with one hand and forehead with the other, shoving her head backward and forward. Cathy squealed, "You're messing up my hair!" As he continued to yank her head around, Cathy tried to do her work, her pen jerking across the page. While this sort of interaction regularly disrupted Cathy's work and actually looked exceedingly painful, she never seriously tried to stop it. When I asked Cathy why they interacted like that, she answered, "He has always been like that with me. We used to have a class right on the other side of that wall together, and he always beat me in there, too. I don't know. He just beats on me." Her response echoed Karin Martin's (1996) finding that adolescent girls, especially working-class girls, don't have a strong sense that they control their own bodies. While some girls, such as Shawna, were able to assert subjectivity and deny the primacy of boys' desire—as when she confronted Darnell's "Mixed girls are for me!" comment—not all girls felt entitled to or expressed alternative definitions of gender. It may be that Shawna, with her baggy pants, hip-hop style, and "tough girl" demeanor, found it easier to confront Darnell than did a normatively feminine girl like Cathy, whose status depended on her electability to the homecoming court. Cathy's affectively flat response to my question revealed that she simply didn't have access to or couldn't express her own bodily needs, desires, and rights.

Interactions such as the one between Cathy and Shane rarely drew the notice of teachers (except to the extent that the two were disrupting class time), most likely because these encounters were read as harmless flirting. But in the larger context of the school's gender and sexual order they reflected a more serious pattern in which both heterosexuality and masculinity presumed female passivity and male control. River boys often physically constrained girls in a sexual manner under the guise of flirtation. For instance, in the hallway a boy put his arms around a girl as she was walking to lunch and started "freaking" her, rubbing his pelvis against her behind as she walked. She rolled her eyes, broke away, and continued walking. What really undergirded all of these interactions is what some feminists call a "rape paradigm," in which masculinity is predicated on overcoming women's bodily desire and control. A dramatic example of this "rape paradigm" happened between classes during passing period. Walking between government and drama classes, Keith yelled, "GET RAPED! GET RAPED!" as he rhythmically jabbed a girl in the crotch with his drumstick. She yelled at him to stop and tried to kick him in the crotch with her foot. He dodged and started yelling, "CROTCH! CROTCH!" Indeed, the threat of rape was what seemed to underlie many of these interactions where boys repeatedly showed in cross-gender touching that they were more physically powerful than girls . . . .

Girls Respond

Girls frequently colluded in boys' discourses and practices of compulsive heterosexuality. When interacting with boys, many girls emphasized their own sexual availability or physical weakness to gain and maintain boys' attention. Because a girl's status in high school is frequently tied to the status of the boys she dates, this male erotic attention is critical. Of course, gender practices like this are not limited to teenagers. Grown women "bargain with patriarchy" by submitting to sexist social institutions and practices to gain other forms of social power (Kandiyoti 1988).

The day before winter break, I handed out lollipops shaped like Christmas trees and candy canes to thank students for their help with my research. In government class Cathy took a Christmas tree lollipop, tipped her head back, and stuck the long candy down her throat, moaning as if in ecstasy. Jeremy and Shane laughed as Cathy presumably showed off her roomy mouth or throat and her lack of a gag reflex, both highly prized traits by boys when receiving "blow jobs." Cathy responded with a smirk, "I don't think I'm *that* good." The group laughed at her conclusion. It seems that the social power girls gained from going along with this behavior was more than they gained by refusing. A way to gain male attention and thus in-school status was to engage in these boys' discourses and practices about sexuality.

This approach, illustrating sexual prowess, was danger laden for girls at River and is dangerous for teenage girls in general as they tread the shifting and blurry boundary between sexy and slutty (Tanenbaum 1999). To negotiate this boundary, girls invoked a variety of gender strategies. Some, like Cathy, promoted their own sexual prowess or acted as if the boys' comments were compliments; others suffered quietly; and some actually responded angrily, contradicting boys' claims on girls' sexuality. Teresa, like most girls, quietly put up with boys' daily practices of compulsive heterosexuality. She was one of the few girls who had enrolled in the weight-lifting class. While she told me that she signed up for weight lifting because "I like to lift weights," she continued by saying she didn't like exercising in a class with all boys. "It's really annoying because they just stare at you while you lift. They just stare at you." Like many girls, she quietly put up with this treatment. I didn't see her confronting any of the boys who stared at her.

Other girls developed a more defensive response, though not one couched in feminism or in opposition to sexism. In auto shop Jay expressed frustration about his upcoming eighteenth birthday, saying that soon he couldn't "have sex with girls younger than eighteen. Statutory rape." He continued angrily (presumably referring to his rape charge), "Younger girls, they lie, stupid little bitches." He laughed, "God, I hate girls." He saw Jenny, the female student aide in the class, look at him as he said this. So he looked directly at her and said loudly, "They're only good for making sandwiches and cleaning house. They don't even do that up to speed!" She just looked at him and shook her head. Brook, another auto shop student, said to me, "Write that down!" Jay continued to harass Jenny by throwing licorice at her and yelling, "I agree, her sister is a lot hotter!" Jenny looked at him and shook her head again. Jay commanded, sitting back and folding his arms, "Make me a sandwich!" At first she ignored him with a "whatever." Then Jenny carried back the licorice he threw at her and dumped it on him. Jay responded dismissively, shaking his head and muttering, "Fucking crybaby." In this instance Jenny both acquiesced to and resisted Jay's sexist treatment. She sort of ignored him while he made blatantly sexist remarks and tried to get even with him by dumping licorice on him. Like the girl who tried to fight back as she was being jabbed in the crotch with a drumstick, Jenny developed an off-the-cuff response to let the boys know she didn't appreciate their sexism.

Other girls, like Cathy, seemed flattered by boys' behavior, responding with giggles and smiles. In the drama class Emir... "flirted" regularly with two girls, Simone and Valerie, throughout the class period. He made kissing motions with his lips, ran his tongue slowly over his teeth, and lustfully whispered or mouthed comments such as "Come on, baby. Oooh baby. Yeah, I love you." The girls responded with laughs and giggles, occasionally rolling their eyes in mock frustration. Other girls frequently adopted the smile and giggle strategy. While I interviewed Darnell, he yelled at a passing girl that he liked her "astronaut skirt." She laughed and waved. I asked him what "astronaut skirt" meant, and he explained, "Oh, it's just a little joke. That's an astronaut skirt 'cause your butt is outta this world." As Nancy Henley (1977) points out, this giggle and smile response signifies submission and appeasement, usually directed from a lower- to a higher-status person.

Though most girls submitted to this sort of behavior, not all of them did.... The most apparent resisters were the girls in the Gay/Straight Alliance.... But even girls without an espoused political orientation sometimes rejected boys' control of girls' bodies. In the hallway, for instance, Jessica stood behind Reggie as he backed up and rubbed his behind into her crotch. In response, she smacked him hard and he stopped his grinding. Similarly, in the weight room, Teresa sometimes resisted in her own way. Reggie once said to her, "When we gonna go and have sex? When we gonna hit that?" Teresa responded with scorn, "Never!" and walked away. This, unfortunately, happened more rarely than one would hope.

I'm Different from Other Guys

Thus far this chapter has focused on boys who treated girls as resources to be mobilized for their own masculinity projects, but not all boys engaged in practices of compulsive heterosexuality at all times. Most boys engaged in these sorts of practices only when in groups, and some boys avoided them in general.

When not in groups—when in one-on-one interactions with boys or girls—boys were much less likely to engage in gendered and sexed dominance practices....

When alone some boys were more likely to talk about romance and emotions, as opposed to girls' bodies and sexual availability.... [In addition,]...on another occasion I heard a boy, in a group of other boys, refuse to engage in practices of compulsive heterosexuality by claiming that he couldn't talk about his girlfriend [in derogatory, sexualized terms]. A boy probably could not have argued that talking this way about girls was derogatory on principle without claiming he was speaking about a girlfriend.

Other boys who refrained from participating in these sorts of conversations frequently identified as Christian.... Christian boys at River High had institutional claims on masculinity such that they didn't need to engage in the sort of intense interactional work that Kimmel (1987) claims is characteristic of contemporary "compulsive masculinity." As a result, unlike nonreligious boys, they did not need to engage in the continual interactional repudiation of equality with girls. Their respective religions buttressed male power through their teachings such that the interactional accomplishment of masculinity was less central to their identity projects. Thus the Christian boys at River may have been less interactionally sexist, but their investment in gender difference and gender inequality was little different from that of the other boys at River....

Females are the Puppets

At a country square dance a few years ago I saw an offensive game between two men on opposite sides of a square, to see who could swing the women hardest and highest off the ground. What started out pleasantly enough soon degenerated into a brutal competition that left the women of the square staggering dizzily from place to place, completely unable to keep up with what was going on in the dance, and certainly getting no pleasure from it. The message that comes through to women in such physical displays is: you are so physically inferior that you can be played with like a toy. Males are the movers and the powerful in life, females the puppets.

It is heartbreaking, thirty years after Nancy Henley (1977, 150) wrote this passage, to document the continuing centrality of what she called "female puppetry" to adolescent masculinity. Like these square-dancing men, boys at River High repeatedly enforced definitions of masculinity that included male control of female bodies through symbolic or physical violence . . . .

Just as in the square dance that Henley described, girls' bodies at River High provided boys the opportunity to demonstrate mastery and dominance. These practices of compulsive heterosexuality indicate that control over women's bodies and their sexuality is, sadly, still central to definitions of masculinity, or at least adolescent masculinity. By dominating girls' bodies boys defended against the fag position, increased their social status, and forged bonds of solidarity with other boys. However, none of this is to say that these boys were unrepentant sexists. Rather, for the most part, these behaviors were social behaviors. Individually boys were much more likely to talk empathetically and respectfully of girls. Even when they behaved this way in groups, boys probably saw their behavior as joking and in fun (Owens et al. 2005). Maintaining masculinity, though, demands the interactional repudiation of this sort of empathy in order to stave off the abject fag position. It is precisely the joking and sexual quality of these interactions that makes them so hard to see as rituals of dominance . . . .

Note

1. This is not to say that similar enactments of dominance and control don't occur among gay men. But such behavior is out of the scope of this study, since there were not enough self-identified gay boys at this school from which to draw conclusions about the way sexual discussions and practices interacted with masculinity for gay boys.

References

Butler, Judith. 1995. "Melancholy gender/refused identification." In *Constructing Masculinity*, edited by Maurice Berer, Brian Wallis, and Simon Watson, pp. 21–36. New York: Routledge.

Hand, Jeanne Z., and Laura Sanchez. 2000. "Badgering or bantering? Gender differences in experience of, and reactions to, sexual harassment among U.S. high school students." *Gender & Society* 14(6):718–46.

Henley, Nancy. 1977. *Body Politics: Power, Sex, and Nonverbal Communication.* Englewood Cliffs, NJ: Prentice Hall.

Hird, Myra J., and Sue Jackson. 2001. "Where 'angels' and 'wusses' fear to tread: Sexual coercion in adolescent dating relationships." *Journal of Sociology* 37:27–43.

Jeffreys, Sheila. 1998. "Heterosexuality and the desire for gender." In *Theorising Heterosexuality*, edited by Diane Richardson, pp. 75–90. Buckingham, England: Open University Press.

Kandiyoti, Denise. 1988. "Bargaining with patriarchy." *Gender & Society* 2(3):274–90.

Kimmel, Michael S. 1987. "The cult of masculinity: American social character and the legacy of the cowboy." In *Beyond Patriarchy: Essays by Men on Pleasure, Power, and Change*, edited by Michael Kaufman, pp. 235–49. New York: Oxford University Press.

Martin, Karin. 1996. *Puberty, Sexuality and the Self: Girls and Boys at Adolescence.* New York: Routledge.

Owens, Laurence, Rosalyn Shute, and Philip Slee. 2005. " 'In the eye of the beholder...': Girls', boys' and teachers' perceptions of boys' aggression to girls." *International Education Journal* 5:142–51.

Stein, Nan. 2002. "Bullying as sexual harassment." In *The Jossey-Bass Reader on Gender in Education*, edited by S. M. Bailey, pp. 209–28. San Francisco: Jossey-Bass.

Tanenbaum, Leora. 1999. *Slut! Growing up Female with a Bad Reputation.* New York: Seven Stories Press.

Trudell, Bonnie Nelson. 1993. *Doing Sex Education: Gender Politics and Schooling.* New York: Routledge.

Wood, Julian. 1984. "Groping towards sexism: Boy's sex talk." In *Gender and Generation*, edited by Angela McRobbie and Mica Nava, pp. 54–84. London: MacMillan.

22

Till Death Us Do Part

MARGO WILSON AND MARTIN DALY

The first article in this volume described how throughout most of history, women's bodies have been considered men's property in law and culture. In this article, Margo Wilson and Martin Daly examine how this philosophy underpins wife battering and murder. This concept encourages men to respond with violence whenever they believe their "property rights" to their wives' bodies—especially their right to exclusive sexual access—are threatened. As a result, women are especially at risk when they attempt to leave a husband or boyfriend but also may be at risk any time they leave the house, smile at a man on the street, or visit a girlfriend, should any of those activities lead their husbands to suspect their sexual fidelity.

As Wilson and Daly note, this philosophy is common around the world, although rates of violence against women vary substantially. Each year since 2001, almost 1,200 women (compared to a few more than 300 men) were killed in the United States by intimate partners. Similarly, a large-scale, national study concluded that a minimum of 30% of American women who had lived in a heterosexual relationship (whether married or not) had been raped or assaulted by an intimate partner at some point in their lives.[1] (Seven percent of men were also battered in heterosexual relationships, but with far less severe consequences on average.) Thus, although Wilson and Daly do not use the term, their data (like those presented in the previous article) address both the social construction of women's bodies (as property) and the social construction of masculinity (i.e., the process through which both men and women come to consider certain ways of thinking and acting to be appropriate and necessary for males).

The revelation of wifely infidelity is a provocation so extreme that a "reasonable man" is apt to respond with lethal violence. This impulse is so strong and so natural that the homicidal cuckold [a man whose wife has had an affair] cannot be held fully responsible for his dreadful deed. So says the common law.

Other spousal misbehavior—snoring or burning supper or mismanaging the family finances—cannot be invoked as provocation. Reasonable men do not react violently to their wives' profligacy or stupidity or sloth or insults. In fact, the *only* provocations other than a wife's adultery that are invested with the same power to mitigate a killer's criminal responsibility are physical assaults upon himself or a relative (e.g., Dressler 1982).

The law of provocation reflects a folk theory of the male mind, for which the apprehension of female infidelity allegedly constitutes a uniquely powerful impetus to violence. This folk theory is not peculiar to Western societies but is extremely widespread. Does it match reality?

Provocation and the "Reasonable Man"

Despite the contemporary scourges of serial killers, rape-murders, and homicides in the course of robbery, most murdered women are killed by their mates.

A small proportion of the men who kill their wives are found "unfit to stand trial" or "not guilty by reason of insanity." Such men are often deemed to be suffering from a psychiatric condition called "morbid jealousy" (Mowat 1966), diagnosed on the basis of an obsessive concern about suspected infidelity and a tendency to invoke bizarre "evidence" in support of the suspicion. But most men who kill in jealous rage are not considered insane. Not only is jealousy "normal," but so, it seems, is violent jealousy, at least if perpetrated by a man and in the heat of passion.

The English common law relies heavily upon a conception of the way in which a "reasonable man" could be expected to behave. This hypothetical creature embodies the judiciary's assumptions about the natural order of marital relationships and men's passion, assumptions that are laid bare in this legal scholar's summary characterization: "The judges have gone a considerable way toward establishing—so far as the law of provocation is concerned—a standard portrayal of the make-up and reactions of the reasonable man. They say he is not impotent and he is not normally drunk. He does not lose his self-control on hearing a mere confession of adultery, but he becomes unbalanced at the sight of adultery provided, of course, that he is married to the adulteress" (Edwards 1954, 900).

The "reasonable man" may strike the reader as a quaintly English invention, but he is more than that. Solon's law gave the same right to Greek cuckolds, while Roman law excused the homicidal cuckold only if the adultery occurred in his house. Various such provisions remain in effect in continental Europe today.

Until 1974, it was the law in Texas that homicide is justified—not a criminal act, and therefore subject to no penalty whatever—"when committed by the husband upon the person of anyone taken in the act of adultery with the wife, provided the killing takes place before the parties to the act of adultery have separated" (Texas Penal Code 1925, article 1220). Elsewhere, this is the "unwritten law," and cases both in Texas and in other states with analogous practices based on precedent have considered the justification to extend to lethal assaults upon the errant wife, the rival, or both. (The factors that are predictive of the likelihood that a violent cuckold will assault his wife versus his rival have yet to be elucidated.)

Many other legal traditions quite different from our own address this question of the "victimized" husband's legitimate response in similar fashion. More than merely entitling the wronged husband to material compensation, adultery is widely construed to justify his resorting to violence that would in other circumstances be deemed criminal. Among the Melanesian Islanders of Wogeo, for example, the principal subject of law and morality is adultery, and "the rage of the husband who has been wronged" is considered predictable and excusable; the Wogeans say, "he is like a man whose pig has been stolen," only much angrier (Hogbin 1938, 236–37). Among the Nuer of East Africa, "it is commonly recognized that a man caught in adultery runs the risk of serious injury or even death at the hands of the woman's husband" (Howell 1954, 156). Having caught his wife in flagrante delicto [the act of sexual intercourse], the Yapese cuckold "had the right to kill her and the adulterer or to burn them in the house" (Muller 1917, 229). Among the Toba-Batak of Sumatra, "the injured husband had the right to kill the man caught in adultery as he would kill a pig in a rice field" (Vergouwen 1964, 266). In general, the ethnographic record suggests that the violent rages of cuckolds are universally considered predictable and widely considered legitimate.

Male Sexual Proprietariness

Men exhibit a tendency to think of women as sexual and reproductive "property" that they can own and exchange. To call men sexually "proprietary" is conceptually similar to calling them sexually "jealous" but lacks certain constraining implications of the latter term, such as the sometime connotation of jealousy as excessive or socially undesirable. Proprietariness implies a more encompassing mind-set, referring not just to the emotional force of one's own feelings of entitlement but to a more pervasive attitude toward social relationships. Proprietary entitlements in people have been conceived and institutionalized as identical to proprietary entitlements in land, chattels, and other economic resources. Historically and cross-culturally, the owners of slaves, servants, wives, and children have been entitled to enjoy the benefits of ownership without interference, to modify their property, and to buy and sell, while the property had little or no legal or political status in "its" own right (e.g., Dobash and Dobash 1979; Russell 1982; Sachs and Wilson 1978).

That men take a proprietary view of female sexuality and reproductive capacity is manifested in various cultural practices (Wilson 1987; Wilson and Daly 1992). Anglo-American law is replete with examples of men's proprietary entitlement over the sexuality and reproductive capacity of wives and daughters. Since before the time of William the Conqueror there has been a continual elaboration of legal devices enabling men to seek monetary redress for the theft and damage of their women's sexuality and reproductive capacity. These torts, all of which have been sexually asymmetrical until very recently, include "loss of consortium," "enticement," "criminal conversation," "alienation of affection," "seduction," and "abduction" (Attenborough 1963; Backhouse 1986; Brett 1955; Sinclair 1987; Wilson and Daly 1992). In all of these tort actions the person entitled to seek redress was the owner of the woman, whose virtue or chastity was fundamental; those holding proprietary entitlements in prostitutes and other women of dubious reputation had no legal cause. Furthermore, the woman's consent did not mitigate the wrong.

Throughout human history and around the world, powerful men have tended to accumulate as many women of fertile age as they could manage and have invested substantial efforts and resources in attempting to sequester them from other men (Betzig 1986). A wide range of "claustration" practices, including veiling, foot-binding, and incarceration in women's quarters, as well as such mechanical and surgical interventions as chastity belts and infibulation, have been employed by proprietary men in their efforts to retain sexual and reproductive exclusivity (Dickmann 1979, 1981; Hosken 1979). The bride-price paid in many patrilineal societies by the groom and his family to the bride's father (e.g., Comaroff 1980; Borgerhoff Mulder 1988) is really a child-price that may even be due in installments after each birth. Barrenness is often a grounds for male-initiated divorce with refund of the bride-price (Stephens 1963). The acquisition of rights to a woman's reproductive capacity entails rights to the labor and other value of the children she produces and the right to sire those children. Husbands are almost invariably entitled to exercise control over their wives' sex lives, and that almost always means retaining sexual access for themselves. Sexually asymmetrical adultery laws that make sexual intercourse with a married woman an offense against her husband are characteristic of the indigenous legal codes of all the world's civilizations (Daly et al. 1982).

Not only have husbands been entitled to exclusive sexual access to their wives, but they have been entitled to use force to get it. The criminalization of rape within marriage, and hence the wife's legal entitlement to refuse sex, has been established only recently (Edwards 1981; Russell 1982). English husbands have been entitled to place disobedient wives under restraint, and it was not until 1973 that a husband was convicted of kidnaping for restraining a wife intending to leave him for another man (Atkins and Hoggett

1984). The expression "rule of thumb" derives from the judicial ruling that a husband was entitled to use only a stick no thicker than his thumb to control an overly independent wife (Edwards 1985).

Homicide and Sexual Proprietariness

Granting that men wish to control their wives and are prepared to use force to do so, the question remains why they kill them. Paradoxical though it may appear, there is compelling evidence that uxoricide [wife murder] is a manifestation of proprietariness.

Most studies of homicide "motives" have depended upon summary police files and have been limited by the sparse, special-purpose information recorded there. The two leading motive categories in Marvin Wolfgang's (1958) trendsetting study of Philadelphia homicides, for example, were "altercation of relatively trivial origin" and "domestic quarrel." Neither of these category labels tells us much. "Jealousy" ranked third and was thus the leading substantive issue on Wolfgang's list, as it has proved to be in many studies.

In Canada, the investigating police file a report on every homicide with the federal agency Statistics Canada, using a standardized multiple-choice form. The police are offered a choice of 12 motives, one of which is "jealousy." Between 1974 and 1983, Canadian police made an attribution of motive for 1,006 out of 1,060 spousal homicides (Daly and Wilson 1988). Of these, 214 (21.3 percent) were attributed to jealousy: 195 of 812 homicides committed by husbands and 19 of 248 perpetrated by wives. But this is surely a gross under-estimate of the role played by jealousy, since the great majority of cases were not linked to any substantive source of conflict: the police attributed 513 cases simply to "argument or quarrel," and another 106 to "anger or hatred." These motive categories reflect detectives' and prosecutors' concern with the question of premeditation versus impulsive reaction, but they tell us nothing about the substance of marital conflict. Any of these cases might have been provoked by the suspicion or discovery of infidelity.

Our claim that the Statistics Canada motive data underestimate the importance of adultery and jealousy in spousal conflict is more than just a conjecture. Catherine Carlson's (1984) study of the spousal homicides investigated by one Ontario police force provides clear evidence on this point. Carlson examined the police files on 36 spousal homicides for which the motive category reported to Statistics Canada was noted in the file. Only four had been labeled "jealousy" cases by the police, and yet sexual proprietariness was clearly relevant to several others. Here, for example, is a statement made to police by an unemployed 53-year-old man who shot his 42-year-old estranged wife:

> I know she was fuckin' around. I had been waiting for approximately five minutes and seen her pull up in a taxi and I drove over and pulled up behind

her car. I said "Did you enjoy your weekend?" She said "You're fuckin' right I did. I will have a lot more of them too." I said "Oh no you won't. You have been bullshitting me long enough. I can take no more." I kept asking her if she would come back to me. She told me to get out of her life. I said "No way. If I get out of this it's going to be both of us." (Carlson 1984, 7–8)

In reporting to Statistics Canada, the police classified this case under the motive category "mentally ill, retarded."

In another case classified under "anger or hatred" (the most popular category with this police force, accounting for 11 of the 36 spousal homicides), a 31-year-old man stabbed his 20-year-old common-law wife after a six-month temporary separation. In his statement to police, the accused gave this account of the fatal argument:

Then she said that since she came back in April she had fucked this other man about ten times. I told her how can you talk love and marriage and you been fucking with this other man. I was really mad. I went to the kitchen and got the knife. I went back to our room and said were you serious when you told me that. She said yes. We fought on the bed, I was stabbing her and her grandfather came up and tried to take the knife out of my hand. I told him to call the cops for me. I don't know why I killed the woman, I loved her. (Carlson 1984, 9)

Police synopses and government statistics are obviously not ideal sources of information on homicide motives. Fortunately, there have been at least a few intensive studies in which the researchers have interviewed the killers themselves about the sources of the conflicts that culminated in spousal homicide. Such studies are unanimous in confirming that male sexual proprietariness constitutes *the* dangerous issue in marriage regardless of whether it is the husband or the wife who is finally slain.

Accused killers are commonly obliged to undergo a psychiatric examination to determine whether they are "fit to stand trial." In 1955, Manfred Guttmacher, the fitness examiner for the city of Baltimore, published a report summarizing his examinations of 31 people who had killed their spouses, 24 men and 7 women. These represented all such killers among 36 consecutive Baltimore cases of intrafamilial homicide, and Guttmacher tabulated what he called "apparent motivational factors" on the basis of his personal interviews with the perpetrators. While the data are presented a little ambiguously (some cases were tabulated under more than one motive), it appears that as many as 25 (81 percent) of the 31 spousal homicides were motivated by sexual proprietariness. Fourteen cases were provoked by the spouse's deserting for a new partner, five by the spouse's "promiscuity," four by "pathological jealousy," one by the discovery of adultery in flagrante delicto, and one by a delusionary suspicion of adultery between the killer's wife and his son-in-law.

A similar report from the Forensic Psychiatry Clinic of the University of Virginia reveals a preponderance of cases of male sexual proprietariness that is even more dramatic than in the Baltimore sample. Showalter, Bonnie, and Roddy (1980) described 17 cases of "killing or seriously wounding" a legal or common-law spouse. Six cases were attributed to psychiatric disorders, but the authors were so impressed with the essential similarity of the remaining 11 that they called their report "The Spousal Homicide Syndrome." All 11 attackers were men, and all professed that they were deeply in love with their victims. Ten of the 11 attacks were precipitated by "an immediate threat of withdrawal," and 8 of 11 victimized wives had left the offender at least once previously, only to return. Moreover, "in all 11 cases, the victim was engaged in an affair with another man or had led the offender to believe that she was being unfaithful to him. In 10 of the cases, the victim made no attempt to conceal her other relationships" (127). Barnard et al. (1982) reported very similar results in a Florida study.

A Canadian study of convicted spouse killers points again to the over-whelming predominance of male sexual jealousy and proprietariness as motives in spousal homicide. Sociologist Peter Chimbos (1978) interviewed an "availability sample" of 34 spouse killers, 29 men and 5 women. The inter-views were conducted at an average interval of three years after the homicide; 30 interviewees were in prison, 4 had recently been released. Seventeen had been legally married to their victims and 17 had been living in common-law relationships. In a finding reminiscent of the Virginia "syndrome," 22 of the 34 couples had previously separated owing to infidelity and had later been reconciled.

The most striking result of Chimbos's study is the near unanimity of the killers in identifying the main source of conflict in their ill-fated marriages. Twenty-nine of the 34 (85 percent) pointed to "sexual matters (affairs and refusals)," 3 blamed "excessive drinking," and 2 professed that there was no serious conflict. Remarkably, these few issues exhaust the list. Most of the killers were of low educational and occupational status, but not one pointed to financial problems as the primary source of conflict. Although 28 of the 34 couples had children, no one considered them to be the main source of conflict either. The conflicts were over sexual matters, and that mainly meant adultery.

Unfortunately, Chimbos did not break down the infidelity quarrels according to sex. Nevertheless, it is clear that the wives' adulteries were a far greater bone of contention than the husbands', no matter which party ended up dead. Scattered through the monograph are verbatim quotations from the interviewed killers. Thirteen such quotes from the male offenders included allusions to infidelity, and all 13 were complaints about the faithfulness of the wife. By way of comparison, there were 4 quotes from female killers that made reference to infidelity, but these were not mirror images of the male complaints. All 4 of the women's allusions to adultery concerned their husbands' accusations against themselves; in one of the 4, the accusations were mutual.

Chimbos chose 6 cases for detailed narrative description. Four were committed by men, 2 by women. In every one of these 6 cases—selected, according to the author, to represent the full range of conflicts in the entire sample—the husband angrily accused the wife of adultery before the homicide. In 3 cases, the accusations were mutual.

If I Can't Have You, No One Can

Men do not easily let women go. They search out women who have left them, to plead and threaten and sometime to kill. As one Illinois man told his wife six months before she divorced him and seven months before he killed her in her home with a shotgun, "I swear if you ever leave me, I'll follow you to the ends of the earth and kill you." (*People v. Wood*, 391, N.E. 2d 206).

The estranged wife, hunted down and murdered, is a common item in police files. The converse case of a vengeful murder by a jilted wife is an extreme rarity, the popularity of the theme in fiction notwithstanding. In Canada between 1974 and 1983, 117 of 524 women slain by their registered-marriage husbands (22 percent) were separated from them as compared to 11 of 118 men slain by their registered-marriage wives (9 percent). Among these estranged couples the ratio of wife victims to husband victims was 10.6 to 1 (117 versus 11), compared with a ration of 3.8 to 1 (407 versus 107) for co-residing couples (Wilson 1989). And whereas 43 percent of the 117 homicides by estranged husbands were attributed by the police to "jealousy," only 2 of the 11 by estranged wives were so attributed; the rare case of a woman killing her estranged husband is likely to be a case of self-defense against a man who will not let her be. Wallace (1986) found an even stronger association between estrangement and uxoricide in an Australian study: 98 of 217 women slain by their husbands were separated or in the process thereof, compared with just 3 of 79 men slain by their wives.

The homicides that police and criminologists attribute to "jealousy" include a couple of somewhat different sorts of dramas, which might usefully be distinguished. On the one hand we have what some criminologists have referred to as "love triangles": cases in which there is a known or suspected third party. In other killings, it is not clear that any particular third party was involved or even suspected by the jealous individual, who simply could not abide his partner's terminating the relationship. The jealous party is even more often male in such cases than in triangles. In Detroit in 1972, for example, a man was the jealous party in 30 out of 40 "triangle" murders, and in 17 out of 18 cases where the killer simply would not abide being deserted (Daly et al. 1982).

The distinction between a wife's adultery and her departure illustrates two separable but related considerations underlying male jealousy (Daly and Wilson 1988; Wilson and Daly 1992). Only the former places the man at risk of cuckoldry and misdirected parental investment in another man's child, but the risks are partly the same: in either case, the man is at risk of losing control of his wife's reproductive capacity (Wilson 1987). And this reproductive strategic commonality between the two sorts of cases evidently imparts a psychological commonality as well: researchers have tended to lump these together as "jealousy" cases because of the aggressive proprietariness of the husband, who seems to consider adultery and desertion equivalent violations of his rights. The man who hunts down and kills a woman who has left him has surely lapsed into futile spite, acting out his vestigial agenda of dominance to no useful end.

Conjugal Jealousy and Violence Around the World

The phenomena we have been discussing are not peculiar to industrial society. In every society for which we have been able to find a sample of spousal homicides the story is basically the same: most cases arise out of the husband's jealous, proprietary, violent response to his wife's (real or imagined) infidelity or desertion.

Several monographs have been published, for example, on the topic of homicides among various aboriginal peoples in India. These include the Bison-Horn Maria (Elwin 1950), the Munda (Saran 1974), the Oraon (Saran 1974), and the Bhil (Varma 1978). Rates of lethal violence among these tribal horticulturalists are high, and 99 percent of the killings are committed by men. These homicide samples include 20 cases of Bison-Horn Maria wives killed by their husbands, 3 such Munda cases, 3 Oraon, and 8 Bhil. In each of the four societies, the majority of spousal homicides was precipitated either by the man's suspicion or knowledge of wifely infidelity or by the woman's leaving or rejecting her husband. Moreover, in each of these studies, about 20 percent of the much more numerous male-male homicides were expressly due either to rivalry over a woman or to a man's taking offense at sexual advances made to his daughter or another female relative.

Fallers and Fallers (1960) collated information on 98 consecutive homicide cases (that is, 98 victims) between 1947 and 1954 among the Basoga, a patrilineal, polygynous, horticultural tribe in Uganda. Eight of these were apparently accidents, leaving 90 cases. Forty-two were cases in which a man killed a woman, usually his wife, and some sort of motive was imputed in 32 of these: 10 for adultery, 11 for desertion or for refusing sex, and 11 for a diversity of other motives. An additional 5 male-male cases were clear matters of sexual rivalry. Only 2 women were offenders, one taking the life of a man and one a woman; the latter case was the only one evidently arising out of female sexual jealousy or rivalry, as compared with 26 male jealousy cases. (In polygynous societies, co-wives can be fierce rivals, but they still kill one another far less often than do males).

Sohier (1959) reviewed court records on 275 homicides leading to convictions between 1948 and 1957 in what was then the Belgian Congo. Many cases were assigned to no particular motive category, but of those with identified motives, 59 were attributed to male jealousy and only one to female jealousy. Sixteen cuckolded husbands killed their adulterous wives or the male adulterer or both. Ten more killed their wives for desertion or for threatening desertion. Three killed an ex-wife after she had obtained a divorce, and 3 more killed an ex-wife's new husband. Another 13 men killed faithless fiancées or mistresses. And so forth. Only 20 spousal cases were not attributed to male jealousy, and their motives were unspecified. The single female jealousy case was one in which a wife killed her husband's mistress.

Are there no exceptions to this dreary record of connubial coercion and violence? Certainly there are societies within which the homicide rate is exceptionally low. But is there even one exotic land in which the men eschew violence, take no proprietary view of their wives' sexuality, and accept consenting extramarital sex as good, clean fun? The short answer is no, although many have sought such a society, and a few have imagined that they found it.

The most popular place to situate the mythical peaceful kingdom is a South Seas island. Margaret Mead (1931, 46), for example, portrayed Samoa in innumerable writing as an idyllic land of free, innocent sexuality and claimed that sexual jealousy was hardly known there.

> Granting that jealousy is undesirable, a festering spot in every personality so afflicted, an ineffective negativistic attitude which is more likely to lose than gain any goal, what are the possibilities if not of eliminating it, at least of excluding it more and more from human life? Samoa has taken one road, by eliminating strong emotion, high stakes, emphasis upon personality, interest in competition. Such a cultural attitude eliminates many of the attitudes which have afflicted mankind, and perhaps jealousy most importantly of all . . . .

Derek Freeman finally exploded Mead's myth in 1983, showing that violent responses to adultery and sexual rivalry are exceptionally frequent in Samoa and have long been endemic to the society.

The factual evidence that Margaret Mead's Samoa was a fantasy had long been available. But the facts were ignored. Scholars who should have looked at the data critically wanted to believe in a tropical island where jealousy and violence were unknown. The prevalent ideology in the social sciences combines the premise that conflict is an evil and harmony a good—fair enough as a moral stance, although of dubious relevance to the scientific study of society—with a sort of "naturalistic fallacy" that makes goodness natural and evil artificial. The upshot is that conflict must be explained as the product of some modern, artificial nastiness (capitalism, say, or patriarchy), while the romantic ideal of the "noble savage" is retained, with nobility fantastically construed to mean an absence of all conflictual motives, including sexual possessiveness.

Part of the confusion about the alleged existence of exotic people devoid of jealousy derives from a failure to distinguish between societal sanctions and the private use of force. In an influential volume entitled *The Family in Cross-cultural Perspective*, for example, William Stephens (1963, 251) asserted that in 4 societies out of a sample of 39, "there seems to be little if any bar to any sort of non-incestuous adultery." Yet here is one of Stephen's own sources discussing the situation in one of those four societies, namely the Marquesa Islanders: "When a woman undertook to live with a man, she placed herself under his authority. If she cohabited with another man without his permission, she was beaten or, if her husband's jealousy was sufficiently aroused, killed" (Handy 1923, 100). In fact, when one consults Stephens's ethnographic sources, one finds accounts of wife beating as punishment for adultery in every one of the four permissive societies (Daly et al. 1982). What Stephens evidently meant by claiming there was "little if any bar" to adultery was that no criminal sanctions were levied against adulterers by the larger society. Cuckolded husbands took matters into their own hands.

Ford and Beach's classic work *Patterns of Sexual Behavior* (1951) contains an assertion very like Stephens's but even more misleading. These authors claimed to have discovered 7 societies, out of a sample of 139, in which "the customary incest prohibitions appear to be the only major barrier to sexual intercourse outside of mateship. Men and women in these societies are free to engage in sexual liaisons and indeed are expected to do so provided the incest rules are observed" (113). Once again, we can make sense of these assertions only by assuming that Ford and Beach intend "barriers" to refer to legal or quasi-legal sanctions by the larger society. For just as in Stephens's sample, the original ethnographies make it clear that men in every one of the seven societies were apt to respond with extreme violence to their wives' dalliance (Daly et al. 1982). Cuckolded men in these societies sometimes killed their adulterous wives, and they sometimes killed their rivals. If the fear of violent reprisal was not a "major barrier" to "sexual liaisons," it's hard to imagine what would be.

Violence as Coercive Control

In attempting to exert proprietary rights over the sexuality and reproduction of women, men walk a tightrope. The man who actually kills his wife has usually overstepped the bounds of utility, however utility is conceived. Killing provokes retribution by the criminal justice system or the victim's relatives. At the least, murdered wives are costly to replace.

But killing is just the tip of the iceberg. For every murdered wife, hundreds are beaten, coerced and intimidated. Although homicide probably does not often serve the interest of the perpetrator, it is far from clear that the same can be said of sublethal violence. Men, as we noted earlier, strive to control women, albeit with variable success; women struggle to resist coercion and to maintain their choices. There is brinkmanship and risk of disaster in any such contest, and homicides by spouses of either sex may be considered the slips in this dangerous game.

What we are suggesting is that most spousal homicides are the relatively rare and extreme manifestations of the same basic conflicts that inspire sublethal marital violence on a much larger scale. As in homicide, so too in wife-beating: the predominant issues are adultery, jealousy, and male proprietariness. Whitehurst (1971), for example, attended 100 Canadian court cases involving couples in litigation over the husband's use of violence upon the wife. He reported, without quantification, that "at the core of nearly all the cases...the husband responded out of frustration at being unable to control his wife, often accusing her of being a whore or of having an affair" (686). Dobash and Dobash (1984) interviewed 109 battered Scottish wives, and asked them to identify the main source of conflict in a "typical" battering incident. Forty-eight of the women pointed to possessiveness and sexual jealousy on the part of the batterer, making this far and away the leading response; arguments over money ranked second (18 women), and the husband's expectations about domestic work ranked third (17 women). A similar interview study of 31 battered American women in hostels and hospitals obtained similar results: "jealousy was the most frequently mentioned topic that led to violent argument, with 52 percent of the women listing it as the main incitement and 94 percent naming it as a frequent cause" (Rounsaville 1978, 21). Battering husbands seldom make themselves available for interview, but when they do, they tell essentially the same story as their victims. Brisson (1983), for example, asked 122 wife-beaters in Denver to name the "topics around which violence occurred." Jealousy topped the list, with alcohol second and money a distant third.

Although wife beating is often inspired by a suspicion of infidelity, it can be the product of a more generalized proprietariness. Battered women commonly report that their husbands object violently to the continuation of old friendships, even with other women, and indeed to the wives' having any social life whatever. In a study of 60 battered wives who sought help at a clinic in rural North Carolina, Hilberman and Munson (1978, 461) reported that the husbands exhibited "morbid jealousy," such that "leaving the house for any reason invariably resulted in accusations of infidelity which culminated in assault" in an astonishing 57 cases (95 percent). Husbands who refuse to let their wives go to the store unescorted may run the risk, in our society, of being considered psychiatric cases. Yet there are many societies in which such constraints and confinement of women are considered normal and laudable (e.g., Dickemann 1981).

The Epidemiology of Spousal Homicide

The above review suggest that the incidences of wife battering and uxoricide are likely to be exacerbated by anything that makes sexually proprietary husbands perceive their wives as likely to betray or quit the marital relationship.

One such factor is the woman's age. Youth makes a woman more attractive to rival men (Symons 1979)....

One might anticipate that demographic and circumstantial factors associated with an elevated risk of divorce will often be associated with an elevated risk of homicide as well, for two reasons. The first is that we consider homicide a sort of "assay" of interpersonal conflict, and divorce is surely another. Moreover, if men assault and kill in circumstances in which they perceive women as likely to desert them, then female-initiated separation and divorce (as well as men's divorcing of adulterous wives) are likely to be relatively frequent in the same sorts of circumstances as uxoricides.... These facts indicate that patterns of separation risk and homicide risk are often similar. However, insofar as wife killing is the act of proprietary husbands, its eliciting circumstances are more likely to match those of separation desired and enacted by the wife, and to be distinct from the reasons why men discard wives they no longer value.

Though the motives in wife killing exhibit a dreary consistency across cultures and across centuries—and although the epidemiological patterns of elevated risk to younger women, de facto unions, and so forth, are also robust—it is important to note that the actual rates at which women are slain by husbands are enormously variable. Women in the United States today face a statistical risk of being slain by their husbands that is about five to ten times greater than that faced by their European counterparts, and in the most violent American cities, risk is five times higher again. It may be the case that men have proprietary inclinations toward their wives everywhere, but they do not everywhere feel equally entitled to act upon them.

Note

1. Patricia Tjaden and Nancy Thoennes, "Prevalence, Incidence, and Consequences of Violence against Women: Findings from the National Violence against Women Survey," *National Institute of Justice Research in Brief*, November 1998.

References

Atkins, S., and B. Hoggett. 1984. *Women and the Law*. Oxford: Blackwell.

Attenborough, F. L. 1963 [1922]. *The Laws of the Earliest English Kings*. New York: Russell and Russell.

Backhouse, C. 1986. The tort of seduction: Fathers and daughters in nineteenth-century Canada. *Dalhousie Law Journal* 10:45–80.

Barnard, G. W., H. Vera, M. I. Vera, and G. Newman. 1982. Till death do us part: A study of spouse murder. *Bulletin of the American Academy of Psychiatry and Law* 10:271–80.

Betzig, L. L. 1986. *Despotism and Differential Reproduction: A Darwinian View of History*. Hawthorne, NY: Aldine de Gruyter.

Borgerhoff Mulder, M. 1988. Kipsigis bridewealth payments. In *Human Reproductive Behaviors: A Darwinian Perspective*, edited by L. Getzig, M. Borgerhoff Mulder, and P. Turke. Cambridge: Cambridge University Press.

Brett, P. 1955. Consortium and servitium. A history and some proposals. *Australian Law Journal* 29:321–28, 389–97, 428–34.

Brisson, N. J. 1983. Battering husbands: A survey of abusive men. *Victimology* 6:338–44.

Carlson, C. A. 1984. *Intrafamilial Homicide*. Unpublished B.S. thesis, McMaster University.

Chimbos, P. D. 1978. *Marital Violence: A Study of Interspouse Homicide*. San Francisco: R&E Research Associates.

Comaroff. J. L. 1980. *The Meaning of Marriage Payments*. New York: Academic Press.

Daly, Martin, and Margo Wilson. 1988. *Homicide*. Hawthorne, NY: Aldine de Gruter.

———, and S. J. Weghorst. 1982. Male sexual jealousy. *Ethology and Sociobiology* 3:11–27.

Dickemann, M. 1979. The ecology of mating systems in hypergynous dowry societies. *Social Science Information* 18:163–95.

———. 1981. Paternal confidence and dowry competition: A biocultural analysis of purdah. In *Natural Selection and Social Behavior: Recent Research and New Theory*, edited by R. D. Alexander and D. W. Tinkle. New York: Chiron Press.

Dobash, Rebecca E., and Russell P. Dobash. 1979. *Violence against Wives: The Case against the Patriarchy*. New York: Free Press.

———. 1984. The nature and antecedents of violent events. *British Journal of Criminology* 24:269–88.

Dressler, J. 1982. Rethinking heat of passion: A defense in search of a rationale. *Journal of Criminal Law and Criminology* 73:421–70.

Edwards, J. Ll. J. 1954. Provocation and the reasonable man: Another view. *Criminal Law Review*, 1954:898–906.

Edwards, S. S. M. 1981. *Female Sexuality and the Law*. Oxford: Martin Robertson.

———. 1985. Male violence against women: Excusatory and explanatory ideologies in law and society. In *Gender, Sex and the Law*, edited by S. Edwards. London: Croom Helm.

Elwin, V. 1950. *Maria: Murder and Suicide*. 2d ed. Bombay: Oxford University Press.

Fallers, L. A., and M. C. Fallers. 1960. Homicide and suicide in Busoga. In *African Homicide and Suicide*, edited by P. Bohannan. Princeton NJ: Princeton University Press.

Ford, Clelland S., and Frank A. Beach. 1951. *Patterns of Sexual Behavior*. New York: Harper & Row.

Freeman, D. 1983. *Margaret Mead and Samoa*. Cambridge MA.: Harvard University Press.

Handy, M. J. L. 1923. *Blood Feuds and the Payment of Blood Money in the Middle East*. Beirut: Catholic Press.

Hilberman, E. and K. Munson. 1978. Sixty battered women. *Victimology* 2:460–70.

Hogbin, H. I. 1938. Social reaction to crime: Law and morals in the Schouten Islands, New Guinea. *Journal of the Anthropological Institute of Great Britain and Ireland* 68:223–62.

Hosken, Frances P. 1979. *The Hosken Report. Genital and Sexual Mutilation of Females*. Lexington, MA.: Women's International Network News.

Howell, P. P. 1954. *A Manual of Nuer Law*. London: Oxford University Press.

Mead, Margaret. 1931. *Sex and Temperament*. New York: Morrow.

Mowat, R. R. 1996. *Morbid Jealousy and Murder. A Psychiatric Study of Morbidly Jealous Murderers at Broadmoor.* London: Tavistock.

Muller, W. 1917. *Yap,* band 2, halbband 1 (HRAF trans.). Hamburg: Friederichsen.

Rounsaville, B. J. 1978. Theories in marital violence: Evidence from a study of battered women. *Victimology: An International Journal* 3:11–31.

Russell, Diane E. H. 1982. *Rape in Marriage.* New York: Macmillan.

Sachs, A., and J. H. Wilson. 1978. *Sexism and the Law.* Oxford: Martin Robertson.

Saran, A. B. 1974. *Murder and Suicide among the Munda and the Oraon.* Delhi: National Publishing House.

Showalter, C. R., R. J. Bonnie, and V. Roddy. 1980. The spousal-homicide syndrome. *International Journal of Law and Psychiatry* 3:117–41.

Sinclair, M. B. W. 1987. Seduction and the myth of the ideal woman. *Law and Inequality* 3:33–102.

Sohier, J. 1959. *Essai sur la criminalité dans la province de Léopoldville.* Brussels: J. Duculot.

Stephens, W. N. 1963. *The Family in Cross-cultural Perspective.* New York: Holt, Rinehart and Winston.

Symons, D. 1979. *The Evolution of Human Sexuality.* New York: Oxford University Press.

Varma, S. C. 1978. *The Bhil Kills.* Delhi, India: Kunj Publishing House.

Vergouwen, J. C. 1964. *The Social Organization and Customary Law of the Toba-Batak of Northern Sumatra.* The Hague: Martinus Nijhoff.

Wallace, A. 1986. *Homicide: The Social Reality.* Sydney: New South Wales Bureau of Crime Statistics and Research.

Whitehurst, R. N. 1971. Violence potential in extramarital sexual responses. *Journal of Marriage and the Family* 33:683–91.

Wilson, Margo. 1987. Impacts of the uncertainty of paternity on family law. *University of Toronto Faculty of Law Review* 45:216–42.

———. 1989. Marital conflict and homicide in evolutionary perspective. In *Sociobiology and the Social Sciences,* edited by R. W. Bell and N. J. Bell. Lubbock: Texas Tech University Press.

———, and Martin Daly. 1992. The man who mistook his wife for a chattle. In *The Adapted Mind,* edited by J. Barkow, L. Cosmides, and J. Tooby. Oxford: Oxford University Press.

Wolfgang, Marvin E. 1958. *Patterns in Criminal Homicide.* Philadelphia: University of Pennsylvania Press.

23

Backlash and Continuity

The Political Trajectory of Fetal Rights

RACHEL ROTH

Throughout history, the law has typically regarded women's bodies as men's property. As the previous article showed, this legal philosophy has often fostered violence against women. This article, by political scientist Rachel Roth, also looks at how cultural attitudes about women's bodies become inscribed in law and restrict women's lives. Roth provides a useful overview of the history and current status of reproductive rights law and shows how earlier struggles over abortion have led to the increasing acceptance of the idea of "fetal rights." This idea, she argues, has served more to punish women for nontraditional behavior than to protect their children, while reinforcing the idea that women's bodies are and should be public property.

Roth's article also makes it clear that U.S. law and culture consistently have placed the greatest emphasis on restricting reproductive rights among poor and minority women, whether through forced rape under slavery, involuntary birth control for women on welfare, or arrests of pregnant women who use "crack" cocaine but not of those who illegally use powerful prescription sedatives.

Current research suggests that poor and minority women continue to have much less access than do other women to high-quality contraceptives (e.g., pills versus condoms).[1] At the same time, the financial, emotional, and practical dislocations caused by poverty make it more difficult for poor and minority women to use contraception consistently, resulting in higher rates of unwanted pregancies. Consequently, these women have higher rates of abortion than do other women, even though governmental restrictions such as mandated waiting periods before abortion, combined with the dramatic decline in the availability of

Rachel Roth, "Backlash and Continuity: The Political Trajectory of Fetal Rights," from *Making Women Pay: The Hidden Costs of Fetal Rights*. Cornell University Press, 2003.

abortion providers, has made it far more difficult for poor and minority women to obtain abortions.

... In 1973 the *Roe v. Wade* decision legalizing abortion created new conditions for women's autonomy, provided a legal framework for thinking about fetuses, and realigned abortion politics by satisfying many people working for abortion reform while galvanizing the fetal rights movement in opposition. . . .

The creation and promotion of fetal rights [that is, the idea that fetuses have rights separate from those of the pregnant woman] in situations besides abortion has led to a highly demanding set of expectations about how women ought to behave during pregnancy for the sake of their fetuses. Disseminated through popular media, advice books directed at women, and legal scholarship, these expectations politicize pregnancy itself. In other words, it is not just the decision whether to continue a pregnancy but the entire period of pregnancy that has come under political scrutiny.

The Abortion Connection

Roe v. Wade was a tremendous victory for women: The nation's highest court legalized abortion across the country, granting women the authority to decide whether to carry a pregnancy to term. In many parts of the United States women had access to hospital abortions before World War II. After the war hospital abortions fell sharply as the medical establishment narrowed the health indications for abortion and state laws continued to permit abortion only to save women's lives. Many women who were able to obtain abortions had to agree to a "package deal" of simultaneous sterilization (Solinger 1993). Other women lived in communities where skilled illegal abortionists ran thriving practices, operating under a tacit agreement with law enforcement: no death, no intervention. But their availability, too, dropped after the war (Solinger 1994). The Supreme Court's decision in 1973 thus gave women a new power over their reproductive lives, one that ended the need to resort to dangerous back-alley abortions and also the humiliation of trying to secure permission for an abortion from all-male hospital committees in those states that had liberalized their abortion laws (Kaplan 1995). . . .

Roe v. Wade established a three-part framework of "separate and distinct" competing interests and set up a particular formula for balancing those interests. During the first trimester of pregnancy, a woman's fundamental privacy right encompasses her decision to terminate a pregnancy without state interference. Women obtain at least 90 percent of abortions within the first three months. . . . During the second trimester, the state may regulate abortion in ways reasonably related to its compelling interest in protecting women's health. The Court found that a woman's privacy right is not absolute, and so after viability, during the final trimester, the state may regulate and even prohibit abortion to further its compelling interest in "the potentiality of human life," except where abortion is necessary to preserve a woman's life or health.

The Court also ruled that a fetus is not a person within the meaning of the Fourteenth Amendment. This ruling is consistent with the Anglo-American legal tradition of treating a fetus as part of a pregnant woman, not as a separate entity with rights of its own. . . .

In response to *Roe v. Wade*, the anti-abortion movement has sought to establish rights for fetuses in a vast array of contexts. Its fundamental goal is to abolish abortion, something it has sought by resisting the reform efforts of the 1960s and by pursuing a "human life amendment" to the Constitution, the appointment of federal judges who disagree with *Roe*, and policies at the state and federal level that interfere with abortion. Unable to achieve this bedrock goal, the movement has successfully limited women's access to abortion services while also shaping the cultural and political terrain for other fights over fetal rights. Some organizations, such as the Chicago-based Americans United for Life, lobby for both parental consent laws and homicide laws that endow fetuses with independent rights. Although these groups tend to support anything that would enhance the legal status of fetuses, some are concerned that criminalizing behavior during pregnancy will backfire by encouraging women to have abortions. . . .

In 1992 the Supreme Court reconsidered its decision in *Roe v. Wade* and replaced the trimester framework with an "undue burden" standard in *Planned Parenthood v. Casey*. *Casey*'s undue burden standard recasts the state's interests, holding that the state has a profound interest in protecting fetal life throughout pregnancy, not just at the point of viability. The state can therefore enact obstacles to abortion as long as they are not so substantial as to be unduly burdensome. Pennsylvania's mandatory twenty-four-hour waiting period after a state-scripted counseling session designed to discourage abortion passed this test. Although it still requires a significant interpretive leap to read these restrictions on women's ability to terminate a pregnancy as permitting restrictions on their conduct during pregnancy, *Casey* creates a new point of departure for analyzing fetal rights claims, one that is arguably more favorable to those claims. . . .

The Historical Connection

. . . Fetal rights politics is continuous with a long history of reproductive politics in the United States. Reproductive control of women has taken many forms. On plantations, slave owners and overseers wielded tremendous power over female slaves and their families by raping women and deciding whether to sell off their children (Davis 1983; Roberts 1991). In the nineteenth century, all states passed laws making abortion a crime (Petchesky 1984). Around the time criminalization was consolidated, campaigns against "vice" successfully restricted women's access to birth control devices and information that might have reduced the need for abortion (Gordon 1976;

McCann 1994). The eugenics movement succeeded in institutionalizing and sterilizing masses of "unfit" persons, ranging from developmentally disabled individuals to sexually promiscuous women (May 1995; McCann 1994). The legacy of sterilization abuse continued throughout the twentieth century, shifting primarily to African American, Native American, and Puerto Rican women (Davis 1983; Lopex 1993; May 1995). In Puerto Rico, women have been the subjects of contraceptive experimentation as well as of aggressive sterilization policies; more than one-third of all Puerto Rican women have been sterilized (Davis 1983; Lopez 1993). The stigma associated with out-of-wedlock births operated as an effective mandate for white women to relinquish their children in the years following World War II (Solinger 1992).

Ever since abortion was legalized in 1973, Congress and a majority of state legislatures have enacted barriers to access, including spousal consent, parental consent for minors, public funding cuts, and mandatory waiting periods. Courts have upheld many of these measures. The anti-abortion movement has become emboldened in the past decade, with groups such as Operation Rescue staging mass demonstrations outside health clinics to intimidate women seeking abortions. In the climate of accelerating violence, scores of clinics have been bombed, torched, or vandalized, and many people have been injured and even killed escorting women to clinics and working in them. Consequently, it is harder and harder for women in many parts of the country to find anyone willing to provide abortion services where they live. Poor women dependent on government assistance have much higher rates of sterilization than other women (Petchesky 1984, 180). The federal government subsidizes sterilization costs for Medicaid recipients, but not abortion, constraining poor women's reproductive choices (see Petchesky 1984 on the Hyde Amendment).

Women's rights advocates have been actively challenging the social relations of reproduction since at least the 1840s, when white, middle-class women first called for "voluntary motherhood" (Gordon 1982). The demand for voluntary motherhood was part of a larger movement for women's rights that valued motherhood but recognized that women would not be able to exercise their hard-won political rights if they were incessantly burdened by pregnancy and childrearing. The voluntary motherhood movement promoted women's right to decide when to become pregnant, giving women the right to refuse their husbands' sexual advances (Gordon 1982). Early twentieth-century feminists continued the demand for motherhood on women's terms but added a positive sexual dimension. Where their Victorian counterparts had advocated abstinence and refuge from predatory male lust, these activists, including Crystal Eastman, Emma Goldman, and the young Margaret Sanger, demanded birth control, claiming for women a lust of their own (Eastman 1978, 1920).

A contemporary illustration of reproductive politics is the way Norplant, the first major new contraceptive device to hit the U.S. market in more than twenty years, quickly played into class, race, and gender politics. Norplant is a 99-percent-effective hormonal contraceptive that lasts five years when surgically implanted under a woman's skin. Approved by the U.S. Food and Drug Administration in December 1990, Norplant immediately became a proposed means of legal and economic coercion. Within the first month of its availability, an editorial in the *Philadelphia Inquirer* called for implanting all welfare mothers with the device, and a judge in California made Norplant a condition of probation for a woman who pled guilty to child abuse. Legislatures quickly entertained measures to give AFDC [Aid to Families with Dependent Children, commonly known as *welfare*] recipients cash bonuses for using Norplant or to make it a condition of receiving benefits; some considered establishing mandatory Norplant as a condition of probation for women convicted of child abuse or drug possession (Mertus and Heller 1992, 362–67). These proposals raise serious constitutional concerns, including equal protection, because men are nowhere subjected to similar treatment and because African American women rely disproportionately on welfare for support. The health implications of coercing Norplant use are especially troubling for African American women, who are more likely to have high blood pressure, diabetes, and heart disease, all of which contraindicate Norplant (Mullings 1984; Mertus and Heller 1992, 360). Finally, in 1993, the Michigan legislature earmarked $500,000 to distribute Norplant in family-planning clinics. The program's champion, Senator Vern Ehlers, described it as "totally voluntary" but added that the program targets prostitutes, drug addicts, and teenage mothers. Ehlers explained that the Norplant program was "developed strictly on the standpoint of rights— every child has a right to be born normally" (*State Legislatures* 1993). Rather than facilitating women's right to control their fertility, Ehlers sees the Norplant funding as safeguarding fetal rights. [Ed: Because of lawsuits, health concerns, and other problems, Norplant was taken off the market in the United States in 2002; another contraceptive implant, Implanon, is now available.] . . .

Current struggles over fetal rights fit into this political history. Ultimately, it should be clear that the debate about fetal rights is not so much about fetal personhood as it is about women's personhood. Notice the dehumanizing language that fetal rights advocates commonly use to describe pregnant women: Women are called "maternal hosts" and even the "fetal environment" (Raines 1984; Blank 1993). Pregnant women's drug use is referred to as "gestational substance abuse," an expression that reduces women to incubators (Flannery 1992; Lowry 1992). These advocates also describe pregnant women's bodies as inanimate objects: The title of a scholarly article calls the "maternal abdominal wall" a "fortress" against fetal health care (Phelan 1991). In his role as "lawyer for the fetus," the public guardian in Chicago asked the court to order a pregnant woman to submit to a cesarean against her will. He argued in court that the judges had to decide whether the fetus is "a real life form being kept prisoner in a mother's womb" (quoted in Terry 1993, A22). This language makes two things clear: that pregnant women are not considered full-fledged human beings, but merely better or worse vessels for fetuses, and that the pregnant woman's body, once thought of as a nurturing sanctuary, is now often seen as a form of solitary confinement for the fetus.

Politicizing Pregnancy

The experience of pregnancy today, at least among middle- and higher-income women, is governed by doctors' appointments, expert advice books, and classes, as well as cultural norms about the ever-narrowing bounds of appropriate behavior that affect all pregnant women. Pregnant women are told what to eat, how to exercise, when to stay in bed, and whether to work or have sex. Lisa Ikemoto calls this "the code of perfect pregnancy" (1992).

Helena Michie and Naomi Cahn argue that middle-class women internalize the code by consuming advice books that teach them to police their own conduct, while the state polices poor women, disciplining them and sending a symbolic message to all others. They deftly reveal the way the best-selling "yuppie bible" *What to Expect When You're Expecting* constructs an autonomous fetus who monitors and ultimately effaces the pregnant reader, ironically producing a "homeless fetus, a baby without walls," even as it is deeply invested in domesticity (Michie and Cahn 1997, 31). . . .

Moving beyond exhortation to enforcement, a Boston-area health club owner canceled a woman's membership when she became pregnant. The member was a longtime bodybuilder and was consulting with her obstetrician about her training activities. The owner hinted at fears of liability should the bodybuilder injure herself, but she told a reporter that she didn't understand why a "mother" would want to burn calories or "overheat." Renee Solomon interprets these remarks as evidence of the owner's sense of entitlement to replace her client's motivations with her own sense of concern for the fetus (1991, 421). This sense of entitlement to make unilateral decisions for pregnant women politicizes disagreements over fetal health in a way that simply giving unsolicited advice does not. . . .

. . . [Similarly, legal scholar] John Robertson argues that women have both legal and moral duties to protect the fetus. Because his scholarship has been so influential, it is worth considering in some detail. Robertson situates his argument for controlling pregnant women and for punishing those who do not comply within the context of a sweeping defense of procreative freedom. He does this by distinguishing between the right to procreate, which he supports, and women's "right to bodily integrity *in the course of* procreating," which he does not (Robertson 1983, 437; emphasis in original).

In his most famous declaration, Robertson claims that "once she decides to forgo abortion and the state chooses to protect the fetus, the woman loses the liberty to act in ways that would adversely affect the fetus" (437). Put somewhat differently, he says, "Although she is under no obligation to invite the fetus in or to allow it to remain, once she has done these things she assumes obligations to the fetus that limit her freedom over her body" (438).

The loss of freedom that pregnant women experience under Robertson's scheme is almost total. He argues that women can be compelled to take medication or submit to surgery on the fetus as well as to be force-fed in the case of anorexia, to be civilly committed to an institution in the case of mental illness, or to be subjected to any other intervention that poses "reasonable" risks to their health and safety (444–47). Decisions about where to give birth (home or hospital), how to give birth (vaginally or by cesarean), and whether to submit to electronic fetal monitoring, episiotomy, or other procedures should be subordinated to expert opinion about the "child's well-being" (453–58). Robertson also asserts that the state may validly prohibit women's use of alcohol, tobacco, and drugs, as well as their employment in potentially harmful workplaces (442–43). . . .

According to Robertson, if women choose not to exercise their constitutionally protected right to have an abortion, then they become liable for less than perfect outcomes of their pregnancies. The meaningfulness of women's "choices"—in the case of a poor woman, for instance, whose state Medicaid program does not pay for abortions—or the timing of women's decisions to carry to term is ultimately irrelevant, because women are held accountable for their actions from the moment of conception. Robertson retreats from his claim that a woman's "obligations to the fetus arise only after she has already exercised her procreative rights by choosing to bring the child into the world," arguing later that a woman who has not yet made up her mind "should have a duty to avoid the harmful activities in case she decides not to abort. Similarly, she should be penalized for failing to use a fetal therapy before viability, so that the infant will be healthy if she decides to go to term. If she does not want the therapy, her choice will be to abort or to risk the penalty" (442, 447, n129).

Under this regime, women have no room for error or indecision. Robertson's attitude toward women is nothing short of callous and, if implemented as policy, would probably result in women feeling pressured to abort pregnancies they would rather bring to term, for fear of the consequences. Waxing philosophical, Robertson concludes that freedom "provides meaning only through the acceptance of constraint" (464). For some reason, this applies only to women. . . .

. . . [In sum,] as fetuses attain independent legal status, women are finding themselves not only erased as important social beings but also disenfranchised as people entitled to fair, equal treatment. New fetal rights claims get layered on top of older moral claims and increasing cultural demands, all in a context in which pregnancy is highly medicalized, enhancing professional and state authority over women. . . .

Note

1. Susan A. Cohen, 2008. "Abortion and Women of Color: The Bigger Picture." *Guttmacher Policy Review*, vol. 11, no. 3(2008):1–12.

References

Blank, Robert. 1993. *Fetal Protection in the Workplace: Women's Rights, Business Interests, and the Unborn.* New York: Columbia University Press.

Davis, Angela. 1983. The legacy of slavery: Standards for a new womanhood; Rape, racism, and the myth of the black rapist; and Racism in the reproductive rights movement. In *Women, Race, and Class.* New York: Vintage Books.

Eastman, Crystal. 1978. Birth control in the feminist program (1918) and Now we can begin (1920). In *Crystal Eastman on Women and Revolution*, edited by Blanche Wiesen Cook. Oxford: Oxford University Press.

Flannery, Michael. 1992. Court-ordered prenatal intervention: A final means to end gestational substance abuse. *Journal of Family Law* 30:519–604.

Gordon, Linda. 1976. *Woman's Body, Woman's Right: A Social History of Birth Control in America.* New York: Penguin Books.

———. 1982. Why nineteenth-century feminists did not support "Birth control" and twentieth-century feminists do: Feminism, reproduction, and the family. In *Rethinking the Family: Some Feminist Questions*, edited by Barrie Thorne and Marilyn Yalom, 40–53. White Plains, NY: Longman.

Ikemoto, Lisa. 1992. The code of perfect pregnancy: At the intersection of motherhood, the practice of defaulting to science, and the interventionist mindset of law. *Ohio State Law Journal* 53:1205–1306.

Kaplan, Laura. 1995. *The Story of Jane: The Legendary Underground Feminist Abortion Service.* New York: Pantheon Books.

Lopez, Iris. 1993. Agency and constraint: Sterilization and reproductive freedom among Puerto Rican women in New York City. *Urban Anthropology* 22(3–4):299–323.

Lowry, Susan Steinhorn. 1992. The growing trend to criminalize gestational substance abuse. *Journal of Juvenile Law* 13:133–43.

May, Elaine Tyler. 1995. *Barren in the Promised Land: Childless Americans and the Pursuit of Happiness.* Cambridge, MA: Harvard University Press.

McCann, Carole. 1994. *Birth Control Politics in the United States, 1916–1945.* Ithaca, NY: Cornell University Press.

Mertus, Julie, and Simon Heller. 1992. Norplant meets the new eugenicists: The impermissibility of coerced contraception. *Saint Louis University Public Law Review* 11:359–83.

Michie, Helena, and Naomi Cahn. 1997. *Confinements: Fertility and Infertility in Contemporary Culture.* New Brunswick, N.J.: Rutgers University Press.

Mullings, Leith. 1984. Minority Women, Work, and Health. In *Double Exposure: Women's Health Hazards on the Job and at Home*, edited by Wendy Chavkin, chap. 6. New York: Monthly Review Press.

Petchesky, Rosalind. 1984. *Abortion and Women's Choice: The State, Sexuality, and Reproductive Freedom.* Boston: Northeastern University Press.

Phelan, Jeffrey. 1991. The maternal abdominal wall: A fortress against fetal health care?" *Southern California Law Review* 65:461–90.

Raines, Elvoy. 1984. Editorial comment to Ronna Jurow and Richard H. Paul, Cesarean delivery for fetal distress without maternal consent. *Obstetrics & Gynecology* 63(4)(April):598–99.

Roberts, Dorothy. 1991. "Punishing drug addicts who have babies: Women of color, equality, and the right of privacy," 104 *Harvard Law Review*, vol. 104:1419–1482.

Robertson, John. 1983. Procreative liberty and the control of conception, pregnancy, and childbirth. *Virginia Law Review* 69:405–64.

Solinger, Rickie. 1992. *Wake Up Little Susie: Single Pregnancy and Race before "Roe v. Wade."* New York: Routledge.

———. 1993. "A complete disaster": Abortion and the politics of hospital abortion committees, 1950–1970. *Feminist Studies* 19(2):241–68.

———. 1994. *The Abortionist: A Woman against the Law.* New York: The Free Press.

Solomon, Renee. 1991. Future fear: Prenatal duties imposed by private parties. *American Journal of Law and Medicine* 17(4):411–34.

State Legislatures. 1993. Norplant approval in Michigan unmarred by controversy 19(5):7.

Terry, Don. 1993. Illinois is seeking to force woman to have cesarean. *New York Times*, 15 December, A22.